Multiethnic American Literatures

Multiethnic American Literatures

Essays for Teaching Context and Culture

Edited by Helane Adams Androne

McFarland & Company, Inc., Publishers
Jefferson, North Carolina

LIBRARY OF CONGRESS CATALOGUING-IN-PUBLICATION DATA

Multiethnic American literatures : essays for teaching context and culture / edited by Helane Adams Androne.
   p.   cm.
Includes bibliographical references and index.

ISBN 978-0-7864-7691-6 (softcover : acid free paper) ∞
ISBN 978-1-4766-1734-3 (ebook)

1. American literature—Minority authors—Study and teaching.
2. Minorities in literature—Study and teaching—United States.
I. Androne, Helane Adams, 1972– editor.
PS153.M56M83 2015
810.9'920693—dc23   2014039832

BRITISH LIBRARY CATALOGUING DATA ARE AVAILABLE

© 2015 Helane Adams Androne. All rights reserved

No part of this book may be reproduced or transmitted in any form or by any means, electronic or mechanical, including photocopying or recording, or by any information storage and retrieval system, without permission in writing from the publisher.

Cover graphics © iStock/Thinkstock

Printed in the United States of America

McFarland & Company, Inc., Publishers
   Box 611, Jefferson, North Carolina 28640
      www.mcfarlandpub.com

For Becky Benoit,
my first and best teacher

Acknowledgments

This book would in no way be possible without the contributors' commitment to teaching. My many thanks to each of them for participating this way in this ongoing discussion about teaching amazing and complex literatures. In particular, my thanks go to Tawnya Pettiford-Wates, who reminded me that literature ritualized provokes the best kind of drama, and Jeffrey Sommers, who invited me into the work of the scholarship of teaching and learning and introduced me to the National Writing Project model. Likewise, many thanks to the myriad of teachers who have helped me along the way in so many ways: Mrs. Helen West, who changed the course of my life in the third grade in an elementary school in Chula Vista, California. Thanks to Robert Cancel for teaching and demonstrating the intersections of oral and literary culture, but thanks even more for teaching me the impact of knowing your students. Thanks to Johnnella Butler, John Walter, Juan Guerra and Connie So, who taught me important intersections within and around literature, culture and educational practice. Thank you to Michael Dantley, who demonstrated to me the intersections between culture, spirit, and justice in the pulpit and in the classroom. Thank you to John Paul Tassoni for taking the time for our many hallway musings and reminding me of the value of real inquiry for educational transformation. Thank you to Mary Fuller, who mentored me, supported me, and set me to flight and who also taught me the value of optimism, humor and an accepting spirit. Thank you also to the staff of the Ohio Writing Project at Miami University: Monica Fisher, Beth Rimer, Linda Tatman, Jean McLear, and Angela Faulhaber for their energy, commitment, and for all they continue to teach me about K-12 teachers and education. Finally, thank you to the two, without whom I could not have had the time and space to complete this project: Toni Simpson, one of those rare and naturally gifted teachers and the guardian angel to my children, and my husband, Semion E. Androne, who proves to me regularly what a partnership is truly worth.

Table of Contents

Acknowledgments — vi

Introduction: Teaching to the (Con)Text — 1

Section I: Focus on the Margin

Introducing Multiple Readings of Ralph Ellison's *Invisible Man* in the Classroom
- STEFANIE DUNNING — 15

More Than Music and Food: Teaching About Cajun and Creole Cultures and Peoples
- MONIKA GIACOPPE — 29

Neither Crow nor Sparrow: Teaching Intersectionality in Chay Yew's *Porcelain*
- C. WINTER HAN — 55

The Possibilities and Pitfalls in Teaching Sherman Alexie's *The Absolutely True Diary of a Part-Time Indian*
- TEREZA M. SZEGHI — 72

Section II: Focus on the Method

Reflect and Act: Using Applied Learning Projects to Engage Students in Text and Community
- HELANE ADAMS ANDRONE — 101

The Answer Is the Story: Teachers and Students Authoring American Literature to Understand American Literature
- MARY F. DULWORTH GIBSON — 122

Teaching *Spidertown* in the Blended Classroom
- DULCE MARÍA GRAY — 141

Performing Community: Teaching Ethnic American Literature
Through the Short Story Sequence
- DAVID MAGILL -   169

Problem-Based Learning and Landscape Perspective in a
Jewish-American Fiction Course
- JEFF SOMMERS -   184

Section III: Focus on the Philosophy

Using Ethiopian Healing Scrolls as Ethnomedicine to Read Healing
in African American and Contemporary American Literature
by Women
- SHAWNRECE D. CAMPBELL -   205

Engaging Rites of Passage in Performative Text: Using Ritual
Poetic Drama as an Applied Theater Practice
- TAWNYA PETTIFORD-WATES -   224

Finding Connections, Contexts and Ourselves: Strategies for
Moving Beyond Generalizations in the Ethnic Literature
Classroom
- BEN RAILTON -   249

The Power of Visual Pedagogy in Teaching American Ethnic
Literature
- DANETTE DIMARCO -   264

About the Contributors   285

Index   287

Introduction:
Teaching to the (Con)Text

Ask a teacher of literature about what characterizes American literature, and you will likely elicit a number of worthwhile answers. One might hear the familiar explanations about literatures borne of the pursuit of liberties big and small, about familiar tropes that suggest visions of bootstraps and American fortitude. American literature is where postmodern and bildungsroman structures loom large and where the pursuit of individuality articulated against the expectations of communalism emerge as a driving force behind an "American spirit." As teachers of multiethnic American literatures, we often find ourselves facing difficult questions based on our role as the ones who introduce students to these literatures and by default suggest through that introduction what is important, interesting and representative. Even so, we long for students to stumble upon the rhetorical patterns, the deeply astute characterizations and complexities of plot. We want them to discover the ironies and the beauty of the voices that emerge within literature. As teachers of American literatures by people "of color," the imperatives and opportunities are even more complex. As J.D. Isip's sarcasm suggests: "Any syllabus of an American Literature survey course will prove this: the march is chronological, the narrative is constant—it all started with Bradford and Winthrop and ended at the latest 'writer of color,' a demonstration of unity and progress" (Isip 25).

These days, many of us struggle to teach multiethnic American literatures. We may or may not wish to "blow up" the canon, but we at least struggle to make sure that students note that there is a dominant literature that can monopolize the canon, and that both the traditional canonical texts as well as the canon's "others" ought to be of interest because of what they reveal about issues of privilege and attending identity politics that also characterize what it means to be "American." Traditionally these texts can find their way into the last bits of the instructional time within the American literature survey course, or out of the canon altogether with only honorable mention, keenly represented by how much time and energy and emphasis their complexities receive in the larger discourse of the course. As Isip suggests, plenty of teachers, in a basic buck against the limitations of chronology and anthology, sprinkle their classes with literatures from the margins, but grow to understand the difficulty of that when dealing with students who have been long exposed to dominant ideologies that make the classics seem familiar and that make the literatures of minoritized populations seem different, strange, and transgressive. Marci L. Carrasquillo notes that, despite a change of venue from a "very small, private, religiously affiliated liberal arts college in the Midwest where, in 2008–2009, 3.6 percent of a 1479-member student body belonged to an underrepresented group," to a "a mid-sized, public university in a major metropolitan area in the northeast" where the students tend to be less affluent, more diverse, and have had significantly more interaction with texts by writers "of color," she finds that her students were similarly ill-equipped to address more complex questions that often emerged if not characterized such texts (64, 65). Instead, Carrasquillo finds that:

> Unfortunately, when such students find themselves reading literature that not only does not reflect their experiences as American citizens or their understanding of what an American is, can, or should be, but that also requires them to examine the often unequal ethno-racial, class, gender, and linguistic dynamics from which they might benefit, some simply refuse to participate in discussions, while others assume an antagonistic presence in the classroom. Both responses can seriously disrupt the learning environment [71].

It is this reality of which most of us are keenly aware. Teaching these literatures means engaging students in deeply troubling discourses at times, conversations that fly in the face of their present day assumptions and beliefs about race, ethnicity, class, gender, spirituality and sexuality. And so we code these literatures as "ethnic" or "multicultural," often separating them from the American literature survey to free the traditional canon from the opportunity to really engage such "others" or to allow the necessary space to engage the complexities and question traditional assumptions, with the un/fortunate result that we signal to students that these literatures are indeed "different," that there are ideological questions within them that require specific acknowledgment. And that is the conundrum for teachers of American literature who wish to teach in the plural. The authors of these texts are historically non-canonical to the body of work that has been legitimately attached to American literature by virtue of their identities and the attachment of those identities to histories and politics that education systems have and continue to struggle to acknowledge. These literatures remind us of the flaws within the Dream, the boundaries of citizenship, and the underbelly of the idealism, which have as much characterized this nation as any other trait of opportunity has built its reputation. Teaching culture and context in American literatures means we attempt to legitimize and complicate the existential questions that our students struggle to engage typically through texts written by Americans "of color." We teach what is often referred to in the post-secondary environment as "American ethnic literatures," which implies both the foregrounding of ethnicity and the explicit difference of that ethnicity in relationship to what it means to be "American." Many of us seek to adjust the focus toward specificity. Multiethnic American literatures, as it's used in this book interchangeably with American clinic literature, includes literatures by authors "of color" and by those considered "white" who identify in ethno-cultural ways, less because of their actual invisibility than for the passion with which they undermine and reveal the less frequently spoken truths about human experience within the United States. Because these literatures force our serious examination of the assumptions of privilege, equal citizenship and justice, and sometimes call up raw and intense experiences from the liminal spaces that rapidly growing minority and academically marginalized populations occupy, these texts find themselves flying in the face of the idealism of mobility, universality of privilege, and absence of persistently restrictive systems modeled in much of the literature in the canon. Instead, many of the texts that question these limits end up on "banned" lists in many educational systems, available only to the persistent after activism or approval. For our students, this leaves a gap not only in their understanding of the rich and diverse literature of the United States, but also a gap in both a deeper sense of the multiply interpreted contexts that produce American literatures and a greater understanding of the variety of ways that human experience in such a unique nation has been and continues to be expressed and revealed.

In more contemporary arguments, there is the notion that these literatures should be included within the canon and no longer separated out as different from it. In other words, there is no need to fetter out branches of American literature as much as take on a more inclusive perspective for what American really means. The activist work of the 1960s that called attention to the race, class and gender absences within public education's literary and cultural studies, some have argued, was an effort to prove the necessary inclusion of these texts as part of the canon. Others argue that these original efforts recognized that these literatures required and determined to have their own spaces for study precisely because those spaces would allow for the deeper engagement with the contextual realities that affect and produce such works. These spaces would provide a safe space for the conversations that might critique and address the inequalities and inherent revelations about the realities of living in an idealized and unique nation. In either case, the argument presses us to understand that these texts carry with them contexts that intervene in the text, build upon the text, and help us to reveal and learn about the text in ways that are unique, important and useful to balancing our disciplinary knowledge (history, sociology, law, sciences, politics, etc.) because of the ways in which they question accepted modes and tenets of American experience as it has been customarily idealized and universalized. Yes, some of us necessarily teach cultural studies precepts; and, no, others of us would argue that we do not teach cultural studies. What we do is deeply informed by cultural studies, but rarely can we do justice to the breadth and depth of cultural studies when it comes to teaching introductory or survey literature courses; what we can do is deal deeply, in one way or another, with context and with the text itself. In the *University of Chicago Magazine*, Elizabeth Station's article, "Teaching to the Text," looks at the Edgar J. Goodspeed collection of New Testament manuscripts and fragments, discussing the beauty, the personal and tactile encounter with these texts, the portable codex that represented a "media revolution" of the time, and the inevitable damage that comes from deep engagement with these texts. For K-12 teachers, the phrase is a rhythmic revision on the heavily debated and most recently maligned idea that one must focus on the standardized tests when teaching and, therefore, "teach to the test." While I openly and adamantly reject this latter notion for K-12 learning, in this book, I accept the revision of this phrase through the metaphor Station provides by suggesting that there is indeed a dangerous encounter, a specific and forceful purpose in what we do as well: We "teach to the text."

Whatever the stance and whichever way these debates about the positioning of multiethnic literatures resolve institutionally, the assumption of this book is that our experiences have at least revealed that the reading of these literatures requires an intimacy of interaction with texts and their contexts that usually involves difficult conversations about the interplay of history, politics, and religion with regard to race, ethnicity, culture, spirituality, gender, and class. It is this that allows multiethnic text to sharpen our view of canonical texts. We can also agree that these texts, though they intersect so fluidly with contextual realities, they are not only their contexts. They are not only about the memories and questions, they are also about the strategies, stylistics and poetics that we adore as lovers of literature. These literatures are as much about the textual choices as any and these choices can as much point us to unique author styles as they can simultaneously speak to issues of context. Teaching to the text suggests teaching to engage the content and form of that expression Multiethnic American literatures expand our understanding of structure, rhythm, and voice even as they stretch us to cross established boundaries of space, language, nation, and spirit.

The obvious debate emerges from the commentary above: every author is "ethnic" and every text has a context. True. What I find most interesting about what I teach is the way that the texts within the texts, the contexts to which authors openly refer and those which are implicit, present counter-arguments to dominant ideologies that have been perhaps previously unquestioned by our students. And so, the interplay of identity politics that happen in literatures that are written by people who are located on societal margins is part of the interpretation of meaning and craft in these texts. They are speaking back to the canon from within and outside of it and our jobs in the classroom have often meant helping students to hear that conversation and draw meaning from it. Not all American literatures have required the kinds of conversations that teaching these literatures require, nor have traditional literatures always facilitated the approach into deeply ingrained sensitivities within students regarding their core beliefs and values with regard to race, gender, language, religion, citizenship and class. I would argue that many such texts simply didn't intend to move in that direction. In fact, it's not that traditionally canonical works don't comment on these concepts; American literatures have always commented upon these realities by virtue of absence and exclusion, which is at least a comment, if not a specific argument. Those canonized works that begin to articulate scathing truths related to race, gender and class have rocked the canon and society, and have been at times historically situated as propaganda, or in the other extreme, have been held up as the acceptable methods for addressing such issues, though arguably they have been deeply neglected outside specialized circles for their representations of craft and artistic merit. The stretch into sensitive spaces is, however, unavoidable for literatures written by and about American "minorities." Is it possible to address the craft of writing by African Americans without engaging the metaphors of invisibility and privilege that are part of a context of racism, or to appreciate the stylistic language choices of Latino/a writers without necessarily remarking on the politics of linguistic identity and citizenship, or to understand the delicate dialogics of Asian American literatures without a sense of the social politics between generations, or to read metaphors of internalized exile in Arab American literature outside the United States' response to extremist protest, or to imagine that one can sustain a conversation about the rhythm and symbolism of Native American literature without consideration to the cultural tokenism that abounds in the popular culture of the United States? As teachers of American literatures, we cannot dwell only in the contexts of the literatures we teach; however, we can stress that the privilege of not reading such issues abounds within the constructs of much traditionally canonical American literature, which can speak to the issues of life as if they are matters of individual choices held in isolation, by virtue of theme and possibility. It is that privilege that teachers of American literatures necessarily obscure in the classroom simply by suggesting that there is another reality, another body of work that makes different assumptions, operates under different rules, and makes altogether different suggestions about the state of freedom, democracy, spirituality, and the moral obligations of the writer.

I mean to suggest, then, that there is a difference between teaching these literatures in a separated context and teaching them within the context of American Literature as a course. There is work to be done when teaching these literatures that involves the unpacking of privilege and the disclosing of racially dependent stereotypes and assumptions, the recovering of history and politics that worked to immobilize some as it mobilized others, whether we engage these conversations at the center or margins of our teaching practices. Taking on the teaching of American literatures written by authors committed to the relevance of perspectives that scrape and tatter dominant views of what it means to be American in an American context feels for students very much like personal affronts to the values they hold dear, quite often the same values that led them to our classrooms in the first place.

We teach these students, trying to find ways to weave in and out of the texts they read and the texts they've built up in their minds about who they are and how the world works. So we try to find balance between our focus on the creativity and skill of the authored text and what it teaches us about craft even as we need to provide reasonable contextual foundations for our students for whom American history seems a distant and expansive Pandora's box. The premise of this compilation is that we assist students in reading, recognizing, interpreting, positioning, analyzing and imagining American literatures not as different, but differently. We want students to hear the voices, examine the contexts, and even develop their own texts as they develop their relationship to American literatures. Some of us work from the context in, others from the text out. Whatever our methods, we engage deeply with texts and contexts to help our students engage more deeply with meaning. While we well know what engaging these texts and contexts meant in the culture wars of the 1960s when the struggle looked even worse for expanding the canonical spaces to include conversations about the relevance of race, gender and class, what does such a designation mean for a twenty-first century classroom within which students are likely more accustomed to intercultural contexts—at least through popular culture, if not their own personal experiences—and in a time when "information" has in some ways become interchangeable with "knowledge" and students interact in modes that question the very structure of current educational systems?

There are many texts available that address approaches to teaching texts established as classic during the twentieth century, but not even a few actually provide instructors with a variety of opportunities to incorporate contemporary American literatures and both culturally and pedagogically based methods into their classrooms. American literatures present an ongoing dialogue between ethnic individual and mainstream culture, history, class, religion, politics and sexuality. All of these issues are at play for teachers attempting to establish ethnically inclusive literary curriculums. Not since the middle 1990s has a book been published to speak to the questions that we have as teachers of American literatures in the plural. In 1996, John R. Maitino and David R. Peck published the very useful *Teaching American Ethnic Literatures: Nineteen Essays* in which they offer critical essays on teaching longer prose by the four "major" ethnic groups of the United States. Other books on the teaching of American literatures are more specifically focused on one or another group, or are those which have served as important resources for our thinking about the contexts inherent in the texts we teach. Maitino and Peck's book is useful for those who teach survey courses as well as those who are planning their experiences in specialized courses. The book is a wonderful precursor to this one in that it features the most currently canonized of American ethnics, such as N. Scott Momaday, Alice Walker, Amy Tan, Rudolfo Anaya, and Sandra Cisneros among others; however, it is poised in a time when criticism on these works was emergent and only beginning to truly flourish. To this point, the book remains more useful for teachers desiring an initial exploration of these works in their classrooms. The pedagogical strategies associated with each essay is secondary; the critical reading of the texts and their associated discourses are the primary focus. In that respect it opens an important conversation on the pedagogical complexities of teaching such texts, but it also presents an opportunity for an expanded discourse now that criticism, exposure, and technology have changed enough to allow for another conversation to emerge.

When I began teaching American literatures, it was as an English department graduate student working in a diverse, public research university that served over 30,000 students and boasted a separate American ethnic studies department. I assisted instructors with Asian American studies courses and had the great fortune of being assigned as the instructor of my own (recently vacated) Introduction to Black Studies course. So, armed with someone else's syllabus, deep insecurities about my preparedness, and energy sustained by the course content and its relationship to my future interests, I dove right in and waded into the deep waters with my students. As a novice, certain questions would often follow me into my classes: Am I doing justice to these texts? How do I get students to inquire, engage and learn something worthwhile about themselves and their world through their interactions with these texts? As an English graduate student, I was deeply invested in the study and teaching of writing alongside the study and teaching of literature. I sought after opportunities to do both, resolved that engaging texts could also emerge within the processes involved in creating texts. I have since taught as much or more composition as I have taught American ethnic literatures. Now, as a tenured associate professor, I cross programmatic borders between rhetoric and composition and literature regularly, but it is rare that I get to sit in on a colleague's course without the stigma of evaluation, despite in my own mind being deeply interested in sharing with others as well as learning from the classrooms of my dynamic and fruitful senior and junior colleagues. But research, family, service opportunities and such can press us further and further into our own corners of the academy, create and sustain for us imagined distances more often than collaborations and, if we are not careful, we can find ourselves operating in practiced isolation, imagining that we have become "experts."

At multiple moments within my own teaching, I have felt those same questions emerge from when I was a graduate student; armed with the attitude that I can specialize without being an "expert" who is somehow beyond innovation. I thrive on the kind of pedagogical interaction that challenges my interpretations, my philosophies, and my methods for teaching multiethnic American literatures and I pursue learning from multiple sources that do not always seem to communicate on equal terms. There is a clear line others have drawn between educational levels, perhaps even more stringent than that of the line often etched out between rhetoric and composition programs and literature programs, American literatures and American ethnic literatures, that I have actively crossed and I have encouraged others to do so as well. And so this book is for border crossers, those who, like me, still want fresh perspectives on real classroom practices that make a difference in the experience that students can have with American literatures, and still want to imagine the multiple ways of getting students to engage texts and generate texts themselves so that they better understand how and from what American literature emerges. Some have said that one should write the book one desires to read. This book is what I wanted in my hand as a graduate student and on my shelf as a teacher scholar, a book that both challenges me and provides me with an opportunity to look into the classrooms of my peers to learn from them and, well, to adapt their best practices, a sort of appreciative and less covert thievery, into my own courses.

I should note that this is not a handbook; that was not at all what I needed since it would have encouraged my prescriptive enforcement of the "correct" moves to make in the classroom. No book could possibly provide for the "correct" way to teach anything. Seeking that seems akin to looking for random visits from upper administration into one's classes; teaching handbooks provide an unnecessary amount of stress if and when the handbook's carefully constructed and articulated methods fail miserably in one's own class. Inevitably, a handbook would stand as perfect and the teacher using it would be the failure, along with her obstinate and unprepared students. What we learn from each other is what works for certain teachers in certain contexts. Then, we can consider our similarities and differences, adapt and apply as we see fit. Teachers who are deeply invested in their students' learning are usually deeply invested in their own learning. We have to be connected enough to our contexts and to the needs and abilities of our students to understand there is no handbook for what we do because our students are ever changing and evolving in their motivations, their experiences, their commitments. Part of the reason that we do this work is to be always learning and revising and updating our thinking about the world and its texts.

As a teacher open to this sort of pedagogical input, I want to do more than expand my thinking about the classroom and institutional goals. Sometimes I just want to be excited and refreshed. I want to reach out to my colleagues near and far and be renewed by their thinking about pedagogy in the same way that I am renewed by innovative thinking in my research area. Fortunately, we now have multiple teaching journals and online resources that feature the variety of teaching strategies associated with American literatures in varied contexts and using multiple modes. Publishing about teaching practice does much to affect our teaching by providing a space within which we reflect and acknowledge our achievements and challenges with our multiple texts and contexts. Professional journals, like *Pedagogy: Critical Approaches to Teaching Literature, Language, Composition and Culture* and *Teaching American Literature: A Journal of Theory and Practice* provide critical forums for teacher-scholars to share and re-think professional and ideological groundings within realistic circumstances of teaching.

My stance on cross-disciplinary/level/program sharing is inspired by a history of interacting with educators and the experience of my work with the writing project at my university, which is a site of the National Writing Project. If there is a mantra of a writing project site, it is that "the best teacher of a teacher is another teacher" and the testimonies of K-12 teachers in our university writing project reflects that. Because teaching in higher education is a particularly isolated activity (some would say much more sovereign), which can breed unnecessary competition and fear such that exchanging best practices almost always has to come through the invested work of institutes that provide neutral ground for thinking about teaching, the kind of work that writing projects do can provide a worthy model for breaking down barriers and re-focusing those of us in higher education on the greater imperative of student learning. The kind of exchange that happens within a writing project, the kind of best practices and good thinking that happens through a writing project is immeasurable for thinking about and integrating innovative teaching, not only at K-12 levels, but also in the amazing adaptations that can happen through a model that demands collaboration and sharing as that of the National Writing Project does. Some of the most useful practices I have adapted into my classroom come from reflective pedagogical exchange with K-12 educators.

In higher education, we also find within faculty learning communities and special writing center initiatives that draw faculty together to work on particular assignments or projects in their classrooms, a method for refreshing and re-thinking our work as teachers. I have greedily participated in a lion's share of them, sponsored by centers committed to teaching and learning, where the kind of mutual sharing about teaching practice can happen. I also find that dynamic and informative teaching conferences, such as the Lilly Conference on Teaching, which often crosses the kind of educational levels that I value, and others are amazing spaces for learning among teacher scholars. All of these interactions with pedagogical practice are part of the continuum of teaching excellence. They help us to build bridges across the isolated expanses between our classrooms such that we can continue to learn from one another and invest ourselves in the conversation about teaching.

It follows, then, that it was important to me in proposing this book that it is useful across educational levels, for those seeking similar conversations and opportunities, based on the common ground that comes with teaching American literatures. I hope you find, as I did, that the essays included are straightforward and challenging, that they offer unique perspectives for the re-consideration of classic and the new consideration of more contemporary American literatures, and that they offer resources for reflection, organization, and assignment consideration. These essays are not just about the texts that they discuss; they help one think about the principles in use, the resources that are out there, and the formats that are possible for twenty-first century contexts. Teaching American literatures in this new millennium requires that we acknowledge the contemporary contexts and technologies to which students are exposed as we develop pedagogical frameworks for our courses. For teachers in the twenty-first century, this necessarily means the adjustment of certain traditional teaching practices and formats, the application of interdisciplinary pedagogies and literary theories in the teaching of both classic and more contemporary texts, and the recognition of an ever-diversifying, globalized student body. Even as I have suggested this sense of contemporaneity, this book is not focused on the twenty-first century as a metaphor for the "technological." It does not propose that the "new" way of teaching these texts is in online formats, though many of us are exploring the opportunities and pitfalls of that option in our own courses. What this century invites is the recognition that there are classic and contemporary texts that are worth teaching, that a new opportunity to consider the connections between technological platforms, access across ability and class barriers, as well as resource availability for teaching American literatures using multiple texts, is important. This collection of essays acknowledges the changing landscape of teaching multiethnic texts. The twenty-first century means that our student body may be more diverse, not only representing the intersections of race, ethnicity, class and gender, but also in terms of age, experience and professional goals. The accompanying needs and contexts necessitate that instructors are theoretically grounded with practical methodologies for teaching American literatures in secondary, post-secondary, and online education courses. Our relationship to technology varies widely from institution to institution, but our sense of an ever-changing and rapidly evolving context faces all of us daily and in multiple, sometimes surprising ways. I am excited that in this book is gathered the thoughtful sharing of deeply committed colleagues who have offered us an open door into their classrooms to see contextually motivated ways of doing what we love to do.

As the contributors discuss their approaches to teaching particular American literatures, they also provide discussion questions, writing topics, and pedagogical strategies for enhanced experience of these literatures, including reinventing classic pedagogical methods alongside newer strategies such as problem based learning, hybrid course structure and other student centered learning strategies. The essays included in this volume intend to connect the scholarship of teaching and learning with interdisciplinary theories to show, by example, the variety of approaches available for a twenty-first century audience and literary atmosphere. This text provides a much-needed resource for teachers who wish to augment their teaching with contemporary literature, methods, and discussions. You will find that in these essays, your colleagues reflect on their objectives, how they situate themselves and their students to acknowledge theirs and the contexts of others, even as they provide clear examples and resources for innovation and opportunities to transform the formats and structures of the literature classrooms. For many teachers, this book will be invaluable for incorporating newer, challenging and interesting texts into their classrooms to compliment their use of classic texts. For others, this book provides innovative, culturally emergent methods for teaching contemporary texts. Still others will find that there are new and multiple ways of refreshing their assignments and discussions to provide a more engaging experience for their students and themselves.

The contributors grapple with several key questions: What does it take to get students to better understand and synthesize textual and contextual details associated with ethnic American experiences that would assist in their critical thinking and application of knowledge to current contexts? How do students understand their realities in the twenty-first century in relationship to the realities represented in the texts by and about Americans? How do authors of contemporary American literatures address past and present themes and issues and how are these understood as associated with "classic" American texts? These and other questions, alongside multiple pedagogical discussions, workshops and seminars, among colleagues, led me to realize that many of us have new approaches to these questions and issues in the classroom—and that other scholars and teacher-practitioners had a multitude of other answers. Surely, the principles of creativity and careful study of detail that scholar instructors bring to the classroom create an environment conducive to the critical thinking involved in critical reading, cross-cultural connections, and creative student engagement.

The structure of this book reflects all these interests and desires and a number of questions. It is divided into three sections that speak to the different purposes for using this text for teaching. There are a variety of ways to approach teaching, but I have learned that it is important to try one thing at a time. Focus on engaging a particular text and its context differently, on a method for re-thinking classroom space, or on refreshing your philosophy and how it is represented within your course. Take that area of focus and find the change or adaptation to try. Use it, tweak it, make it your own, and then assess it. If you are interested in considering how you might refresh and re-think the complex conversations that can be had in the classroom about race, gender and class, the first section has as its focus the idea of the margin. In it, classic and newer texts are re-thought for their possibilities: What if Ellison's *Invisible Man* was bi-racial? Where and how might we begin to teach Cajun or Creole literatures within the canon of American literatures? How do we teach the intersectionality of race, sexuality and stereotype? How might we re-direct students to the stylistic elements of how a text reveals its comments about race and ethnicity and away from the broader tokenizing of whole groups based on limited exposure to other texts? The second section of this book presents essays that focus on the methods for teaching these literatures: How might we facilitate student translation of what they learn in our courses into their very specific communities of practice? How might generating text help urban youth with deeply challenging contexts to better connect to American literatures? What are the opportunities and challenges for using American literatures to teach writing in a technologically blended classroom? How might the short story sequence reveal a social and political tool that allows students to re-examine the idea of community? How might problem-based learning provide a foundation for facilitating student community, knowledge creation, and a broader view of texts? The third section presents philosophical challenges for what motivates and drives our teaching and how to involve students in transformative processes that get at our ideological grounding for teaching. These essays ask us to consider larger paradigms for teaching American literatures: How might we engage students in how texts reveal larger principles for personal healing? How can a ritualized right of passage method engage students in dramatic text composition, facilitate community and provide room for conversations about the intersectionality of oppressions? What can we do to help students acknowledge structural complexities—literary and visual—of author choices? This book offers many questions to explore, plenty of resources and direct suggestions for processes that could impact your courses and students' experiences within it. Texts about teaching are never one-time pick-ups; my hope is that these essays will serve over and over again, as you focus on your own particular questions, as you tweak, personalize and assess what you do, as I know I will.

Works Cited

Carrasquillo, Marci L. "Facilitating Discussions About White Privilege in the American Literature Survey Classroom." *Teaching American Literature: A Journal of Theory and Practice* Summer 2013 (6:2). Print.

Isip, J. D. "Lose the Chronology, Lose the Anthology: Clearing the Way for Innovation in American Literature Survey Courses." *Teaching American Literature: A Journal of Theory and Practice* Spring 2011 (4:3). Print.

Maitino, John R., and David R. Peck (1996). *Teaching American Ethnic Literatures: Nineteen Essays.* Albuquerque: University of New Mexico Press. Print.

Station, Elizabeth. "Teaching to the Test." *University of Chicago Magazine.* Nov-Dec 2009. http://magazine.uchicago.edu/0912/investigations/original_source.shtml. Web.

Section I: Focus on the Margin

Introducing Multiple Readings of Ralph Ellison's *Invisible Man* in the Classroom

STEFANIE DUNNING

Black Is, Black Ain't

Debates about the value of African American literature surfaced when in 2013, the Randolph County school board of North Carolina banned (and then un-banned) the teaching of Ralph Ellison's *Invisible Man*. One board member opined that he'd read the book and "found no literary value in it." While the literary value of Ellison's novel is firmly established for literary scholars, this recent flap over the book demonstrates the continued importance of articulating precisely why it is important to teach African American literature. Though the banning of *Invisible Man* may seem arbitrary, I'd like to assert that the perception by a group of conservative Southern whites that the book lacks value is directly (if subconsciously) related to the way the novel devalues standard American racial logistics.

The ban on the book, from the perspective of any college teacher, is laughable precisely because *Invisible Man* is understood to be one of the most canonical works of American literature. On almost any list of the top 50 or 100 books of American literature, *Invisible Man* always appears. It has been written about extensively, with at least 830 articles written about it between 1993 and 2013—that is 41 articles published per year, at a rate of 3.4 per month. The amount of scholarship on Ellison's novel suggests that writing about it is like writing about Shakespeare; what new is there to say? I cite the prevalence of writing about Ellison's novel not only to demonstrate its importance, but also to explain why I cannot, and hence do not, provide even a cursory overview of the scholarship here. Yet despite all that has been written about this important novel, there are some perspectives on the text that are rarely articulated. I would like to suggest that despite the voluminous scholarship on *Invisible Man* there remains unexplored territory in relation to its revelations about the black body's ontological relationship to the trope of invisibility. The insights made possible by a reading of *Invisible Man* have never been more important; at a moment when the rhetoric of the post-racial enables the advances made in the Civil Rights movement to be overturned, such as was the case with the 2013 overturning of the Voting Rights Act by the Supreme Court, understanding how the social construction of blackness operates facilitates the growth of consciousness in students which in turn, one hopes, mitigates the racism of American society.

The standard approach teachers and scholars take to *Invisible Man* is that it is a novel about blackness. This may seem ridiculously obvious and even silly to point out, but this simple observation is necessary in order to frame the novel's reception as well as how it has been used pedagogically. Writing brilliantly about the novel in her book *Punctuation: Art, Politics, and Play* (2008), Jennifer DeVere Brody argues that blackness in *Invisible Man* should be understood as formative, that "there is an unnamed 'speaker'; the concept-metaphor of blackness is played out against an idea of illumination; blackness is repeated with a difference; the action is 'circular,' it appears between parentheses—bracketed as if in a black hole, the blackness of blackness is performed viscerally for an audience." (63) Here Brody asserts that the performative ethos of Ellison's novel is one in which blackness is "staged and re-staged" through "various formative moments of 'blackness' in American culture." (64) Brody's subtle and deft reading teases out the formulations of racialized knowledge with which Ellison's novel is initially concerned.

Framing a reading of *Invisible Man* within the seemingly obvious conclusion that it is a novel about blackness, characterizes other teachers' analysis of the novel. Writing about her students' response to *Invisible Man* in the classroom, Mary Ann Navarro situates her relationship to Ellison's text through anecdotes about her first African American instructor in college who emphasized experiences of racism by telling the class about racist events he experienced. Navarro later goes on to offer an exercise for helping students gain "cultural proficiency" vis-a-vis ethnic or racialized knowledge in order to develop the critical thinking skills they need to analyze Ellison's novel. Furthermore, she utilizes musical texts to help students engage the text, such as Miles Davis and Public Enemy. In all, Navarro's pragmatic approach to the teaching of Ralph Ellison's *Invisible Man* emphasizes the "blackness" of the text.

In fact, almost all writing on Ellison's novel iterates a reading that explicates the novel through the framing episteme of blackness. At this point, this may be beginning to sound like a complaint; therefore, let me clarify that I am not suggesting that this is *wrong*. I am, instead, suggesting that it represents *one way* of reading the text. Before *Invisible Man* was published, every single African American text of note, up to that point, featured a story line that was centered on a character of mixed race. And these texts staged the question of black humanity in the context of interraciality; it is an inescapable fact of pre-1950s African American literature. In this way, *Invisible Man* represents a bold new direction for African American literature in one sense—there is not a single theme of overt passing in the novel—and yet also, as I will show, the novel signifies on the questions of racial ambiguity and ambivalence which characterized the African American literary tradition that produced *Invisible Man*. Therefore, I do not assert that *Invisible Man* is *not* about blackness. In one sense, it is about blackness and is a critique of racism and its ocular violation (invisibility), in precisely the way almost all the critical work about it suggests. I do assert, however, that it is also about the racialized subject who is "in-between," invisible to both black and white subjects—the mulatto. And, of course, there is the fact that the distinction between "blackness" and the "mulatto" is not much of a distinction at all.

I do not mean to suggest that the protagonist is mixed race, though he may well be (these details are unknown). The distinction between black and mulatto is a fine one, a vexed one, and this line is one that African American literature, as I indicate above, was deeply concerned with until the mid-twentieth century. I do mean to suggest, however, that the metaphor of race and invisibility invoked in *Invisible Man* is not one that can be reduced to a simple black-white binary. Technically speaking, *all* African Americans are mixed race subjects; but the theorization of race through a racialized dialectic or through a disruptive third space, is the difference between understanding Ellison's novel as being solely about "blackness" or additionally about something else. In other words, what I show here is not a particular body, but a particular ideological position in the American racial matrix. I would like to suggest that Ellison's novel begins within the context of a racialized dialectic and then unravels as it proceeds, so that the protagonist ultimately ends up *outside* of the black-white racial logic of American culture and that it is by occupying this problematic third space that the protagonist is invisible to both black and white people in the novel. It is the articulation of this "third space" that makes Ellison's novel infinitely interesting to scholars and endlessly threatening to conservative racists, whose racial ideology depends upon a stable and unchanging racial polarity of white and black. In his essay "Cosmopolitan Afrocentric Mulatto Intellectual," (to which I will return throughout this essay) Robert Reid-Pharr, in relation to Western (American and German, specifically) intellectualism, argues that "it is imperative, I believe, that we understand that this fear of mixing is in many ways indistinguishable from the fear of racial mixing that has preoccupied Western intellectuals, including Black American intellectuals, for a least the past three centuries.... To put the matter bluntly, the specter who hides just below the surface of much of the discourse of Western intellectualism (German, American or otherwise) is indeed the mulatto" (Reid-Pharr, 48–49).

Part of the problem is that as a society we have never learned how to theorize about the person who, by virtue of culture, first or multi-generation ancestry, or choice identifies as "bi-cultural" or "bi-racial." The inability to do so is quite evident in how President Obama is understood—or not understood. He is popularly understood as black, his white mother notwithstanding. But there is, in recent mixed race scholarship, an attempt to approach the complicated interplay of blackness and mixed race identity, which as Raina L. Joseph argues in *Transcending Blackness: New Millennium Mulatto to the Exceptional Multiracial* (2013), exist in dynamic interplay rather than in opposition. Understanding this particular racial play between the idea of the mulatto and the idea of blackness is essential to understanding my reading of *Invisible Man*, which does not intend to undermine readings of the blackness of that text, but rather to show that there is an invisible aspect of this important text around race, a kind of double invisibility that points us toward a third space that cannot be understood as discretely "white" or "black." Writing about Ralph Ellison's conception of what it means to be black, Robert Reid-Pharr demonstrates that Ellison's conception of blackness was not bound to problematic notions of the biological, but rather he saw black identity as a choice (such that one could even be a white Negro). Reid-Pharr writes, "Thus, the Negro is not born per se but reborn out of the detritus of American racialism. It is not such much a matter of deracination as *re*racination, the production of the Negro as a marker of the universal and the cosmopolitan such that even the "whitest" individual (the mulatto) might proudly proclaim, 'I am a Negro American'" (Reid-Pharr, 52). Reid-Pharr goes on to argue that black intellectuals in the 1920 sought to "erase the prior distinction that had once existed between the black and mulatto.... This process was helped along by whites, blacks, and even persons who once thought of themselves as mulatto in order to produce a stable black community, one that could be better exploited by industrial capital while simultaneously resisting that exploitation." (55) Erasing this distinction, through a linguistic erasure, does not make the figure of the mulatto disappear from the historical and representational imagination. Instead, it haunts the text and becomes the thing that cannot speak its name. It is everywhere alluded to and hinted at, but never rears its head. It is, to use Reid-Pharr's earlier term, a specter—a phantasmagorical aspect of *Invisible Man*.

It is only possible to avoid a realization of the protagonist's shaky racial position by ignoring the fact that not only is he invisible to whites, but he is invisible to blacks. The earliest instance of invisibility the protagonist encounters is the white man on the street, who insults the protagonist, causing a fight. Later, the incident is entirely misunderstood and reported in the *Daily News* as a mugging. We are meant to understand that because the protagonist is not white, the encounter is put down not to a conflict between two men over an insult, but rather to racialized criminality. This misunderstanding, then, is established as the mark of invisibility—one may be perceived in the flesh, but one can never be understood, one's actions cannot be seen. "I am invisible, understand, simply because people refuse to see me" (Ellison, 3). This refusal to see, which is equated with invisibility, not only characterizes the protagonist's relationships to whites, but also to blacks. When the protagonist goes to college, and has his ill-fated encounter with Mr. Norton, the president of the college, Bledsoe, cannot "see" the protagonist either. When Bledsoe questions the protagonist about why he took Mr. Norton to the "Quarter," where he heard the salacious tale of Trueblood's accidental incest, he refuses to believe that it was at Norton's bidding that he drove him there. "Nigger, this isn't the time to lie! I'm not white man. Tell me the truth!" (Ellison, 139). The protagonist is shocked about being called a nigger and then the scene switches suddenly, where his racial allegiance is questioned—where Bledsoe suggests that he thinks "white is right." Cast between blackness and whiteness, the protagonist's experience is invisible. He is victimized by Bledsoe's inability to "see" the truth of who he is in much the same way he is victimized by the blonde man he fights with in the opening paragraphs of the novel.

The problem of invisibility rests not only with the white characters in the book, but with the black characters as well. It is worth pointing out that the protagonist does not find refuge in black spaces and is not only invisible among whites; but even in the most intimate of black spaces—the home of the black matriarch, Mary Rambo—the protagonist feels misunderstood, pressured, unseen. He is irritated by Mary's expectation that he make something of himself, and though she perceives him as someone who will be successful and is simply temporarily down on his luck, he doesn't agree. "I didn't see it that way. I had lost my sense of direction" (Ellison, 258). Again, she doesn't see what he sees, doesn't see him as he sees himself and in this failure of sight, lies invisibility. The trope of invisibility is taken even further through the character of Rhinehart. The lack of recognition in this scene demonstrates the protagonist's invisibility in a complete black cultural context. By putting on dark glasses and a hat, the protagonist is mistaken for an identificatory shape-shifter, Rhinehart—who is recognized as a numbers-runner, a preacher, and a lover. "I trembled with excitement; they hadn't recognized me. It works, I thought. They see the hat, not me. There is a magic in it. It hides me right in front of their eyes" (Ellison, 485). Later he continues to marvel at his invisibility among African Americans, "It's working, I thought, perhaps it's working very well. Certainly something was working on me, profoundly" (Ellison, 486). What is "working" on the protagonist at that moment is the realization that even in the context of his own community, he could disappear—become invisible. Through the character of Rhinehart, Ellison complicates the earlier dialectic of invisibility, where it is a failure of racialized seeing. When Rhinehart appears, it is not as an "other," not as a racialized outsider. And yet he can still not be perceived. This suggests that perhaps no one was ever intimately engaging him at all, regardless of his, or their, racial affiliation.

It is telling that the protagonist gains access to a recognizable identity—Rhinehart's—after putting on glasses. The Rhinehart section is full of references to how the dark lenses of the sunglasses condition his sight. This conditioning of his own sight changes not only how he is perceived but also how he perceives the world. He notes, "I walked, struck by the merging fluidity of forms seen through the lenses. Could this be the way world appears to Rhinehart? All the dark-glass boys? 'For now we see as through a glass darkly but then—but then—' I couldn't remember the rest" (Ellison, 491). This is part of a Bible verse, 1 Corinthians 13:12 and the entire quote is: "For now we see through a glass, darkly; but then face to face: now I know in part; but then shall I know even as also I am known" (ESV). The part of the verse that the protagonist does not remember is the part about knowing and being known. To "see through Rhinehart's eyes," to inhabit the experience of another person is as close as our protagonist gets to experiencing the reality everyone around him seems to partake of. But experiencing a few hours as Rhinehart fails to validate or solidify his identity as it could—I am similar to this other black man—but rather undermines it further. He asks himself, "What on earth was hiding behind the face of things? If dark glasses and a white hat could blot out my identity so quickly, who actually was who?" (Ellison, 493). The overlap between Rhinehart and the protagonist is further problematized when he discovers that Rhinehart is also a preacher who exhorts his followers to "Behold the Invisible." Confronting the truths embodied by Rhinehart leads the protagonist to conclude:

> His world was possibility and he knew it. He was years ahead of me and I was a fool. I must have been crazy and blind. The world in which we lived was without boundaries. A vast seething, hot world of fluidity, and Rine the rascal was at home. Perhaps only Rine the rascal was at home in it. It was unbelievable, but perhaps only the unbelievable could be believed. Perhaps the truth was always a lie [Ellison, 498].

Rinehart is "years ahead" of the protagonist because he refuses one role; rather than choosing to understand himself through boundaries and limits, Rinehart seems to understand himself as limitless. The thing that made the protagonist a "fool" was to embrace a notion of himself that was about limits rather than about the "hot world of fluidity."

As mistaken as it is to assign the symbolism of this language to conceptions of the mulatto—and it is mistaken precisely because, as I demonstrated above, the distinction between the black and mulatto is a strategic racial construction and not a fact—this notion of fluidity gestures towards a space outside of a rigidified black-white binary. This is particularly evident in the section of the novel that deals with the protagonist's work at the Liberty Paint factory. The protagonist, unlike Lucius Brockaway, is unable to produce perfect "Optic White" paint. Instead, he produces white paint with a slightly gray tinge. "I looked at the painted slab. It appeared the same: a gray tinge glowed through the whiteness, and Kimbro had failed to detect it. I stared for about a minute, wondering if I were seeing things, inspected another and another. All were the same, a brilliant white diffused with gray" (Ellison, 205). The white paint is produced by adding 10 black drops to the mix; it is these black drops that the protagonist cannot measure in a way that doesn't produce paint that is slightly gray. Unlike Brockaway, who is a master at producing Optic white, our protagonist can only produce the color between black and white—gray. If this same scene occurred in the novel *Caucasia*, our conclusions would be foregone. This paint scene could easily be read as commentary on intermixture, of blacks and whites—but it undeniably assaults the notion of racialized purity as it relates to color and in doing so, undermines the binary of black and white. On this note, Reid-Pharr points out that "Indeed, the critique of the fetish of biological purity, the emphasis on intermingling and crossings, might be properly understood as Ellison's and Locke's attempts to reinvigorate a racialized (mulatto) cosmopolitanism in relation to the newly achieved nationalist provincialisms of twentieth-century Black America" (Reid-Pharr, 51). This point captures Ellison's complicated negotiation of both the history and figure of the mulatto as well as his articulation of certain black nationalist insights in relation to racism. If we only focus on the latter, however, we fail to see the specter of the mulatto, whose ghost haunts the protagonist throughout *Invisible Man*. It is this implicit critique of the racial dialectic that accounts for *Invisible Man*'s enduring appeal. The last sentence of the novel opens the protagonist to the universal; it moves him into a place of speech for all readers: "Who knows but that, on the lower frequencies, I speak for you?" (Ellison, 581). This "you" is general, not specific and it interpolates every reader regardless of our various racial identifications. This turn to the universal is accomplished by Ellison through the metaphor of race; and *Invisible Man* implicitly demonstrates that to confront "the Negro," is to confront the mulatto.

The protagonist is constantly told, during his time at the paint factory, that he doesn't belong in a paint factory. His inability to fit into the factions at the factory, along with his inability to produce Optic White, all belie his status as "outside" every possible group in society. The story of *Invisible Man*, then, is not about a black man who cannot fit into the white world because of his invisibility; it's a story about a man who cannot fit into the world structured by a blinding racial logic. While racism is a singular characteristic of his experience, it is not the only factor that contributes to his alienation. If it were, he could find comfort enough in the black community, at the very least as a healing haven from a white racist America—but he has no visibility or coherence there either. Staging an intervention into the strictly racialist discourse which structures how we read *Invisible Man*, enables students to see the social construction of race from both within and without. Arguing that perhaps the protagonist is both mulatto and black, that the novel disavows the sloppy notion that invisibility only happens to one from without, undermines the racialist logic of American society.

This perhaps bifurcated approach to the question of racial identity in *Invisible Man* can complicate blackness in a way that enables students to begin to "see" the diversity of what we understand to be "the black community," historically and contemporaneously, in American society. In doing so, we encourage them to understand work by black authors anew, rather than through the lens of tired and well-rehearsed popular tropes of racism. The point of a novel like *Invisible Man* is not simply to say, "here is racism, let us count the ways it manifests itself." The novel itself makes visible an aspect of racialized experience that is not consistent, that doesn't fall back on the predictable tropes or offer the expected answers. As such, it is a text that offers rich possibilities for engaging the age-old question of racial identity in America in fascinating new ways. In the dream sequence where the protagonist hears the preacher's sermon and the preacher asserts that "Black is, and black ain't," Ellison implies the complicated space of the protagonist—he both is and ain't, meaning is at once disclosed and allusive, present and absent, simultaneously ambiguous and certain.

Practicum: Staging Racial Ambiguity in Invisible Man

In order to help students come to terms with this difficult novel, it is important to prime them for these discussions by having some frank and illuminating discussions about this formation that we call "race." Many students are fearful of talking openly about racial issues. Part of this fear comes from never being able to ask questions without fear of ridicule or censor. Another aspect of this trepidation in talking about race is related to the desire to always appear "smart." Therefore, I suggest that the teaching of *Invisible Man* unfold over a period of six weeks. The first week of the unit should be focused on establishing a safe environment for students to talk about race. This does not mean that an instructor permits students to use racial slurs, to attack other students, or to say insulting things. But questions asked from a place of pure ignorance should not be responded to in a harsh way. Establish for students the sense that any question can be asked and any topic raised as long as respect for everyone, present and not present, is maintained.

On the first day of the first week of the unit, teachers can invite students to talk about their own thoughts about race and about phenotypic difference. The role of the teacher here is mostly to listen; of course, teachers must be sure that the discussion does not become offensive—but the function of this session is simply to allow students to become comfortable talking about race in an environment free of judgment. It might help the teacher to realize that all of our students (and even ourselves) hold some problematic and racist views; teachers should *expect* students to say problematic things. Doing so will disable the shock reflex which is so damaging in pedagogical settings where complicated issues, such as race, class, gender, and sexuality, are discussed. I call this open period of free discussion "unwinding." Teachers should feel free to spend several days, or even the entire first week, *unwinding* depending on how evolved the class is in relation to discussing issues of race. This creates the necessary fertile ground upon which the other units can be built.

The "unwinding" period may seem like a gratuitous waste of time, but important work is being done here. The students are learning, during this period, the limits of their own thinking about the matter—it is a time in which they figure out their most unexamined and basic thoughts about race. It is also a time for them to take stock of their classmates—the students who have a more sophisticated grasp of the issues will become known, as will those who do not. The fault lines become clear and this is extremely helpful to the instructor as she proceeds through difficult textual material. Furthermore, this is a valuable opportunity for the teacher to establish trust with the students. By remaining unflappable in the face of undoubtedly problematic ideas, assertions, and beliefs, the teacher shows that even if she does not agree with the position of the students, she does not become angry or upset. This is especially important if the classroom dynamics are such that the instructor is a person of color and the majority of the students are white. Likewise, if the instructor is white and the majority of the students are of color, downshifting into a more attentive listening mode, with light re-direction when necessary, will cultivate a learning community founded on trust and mutual respect. Some of this work should be done in groups, and the instructor may structure each unwinding day with a series of questions to commence and shape discussion. Some of the questions could be:

1. What are the most popular racial stereotypes?
2. What complaints have you heard about various racial groups?
3. What is the view of your community on race issues?
4. What is your experience with people of various racial backgrounds?
5. What role does race play in our contemporary lives?
6. How does talking about race make you feel and why?
7. How did you acquire your knowledge and/or views about race? List the sources of your information and discuss the trustworthiness of those sources.
8. What is "race talk" and how does it affect our thinking about race?

For homework this week, ask students to pay attention to racialized "talk" around them outside of the classroom. Getting students to focus on "race talk" enables them to approach the idea of discourse, which will be valuable as they interrogate race as a social construction in the next unit. What sorts of things are said to them or do they overhear? What major news stories related to race occur in that week? Have them keep a notebook to write down their observations related to "race talk." The purpose of this is to get them to pay attention to the way racialized discourse works, so that the assumptions related to race slowly begin to be un-embedded. After a week of paying attention to race talk, lead the class in a discussion about the effect such talk has on actual people. Use examples from their notebooks as the catalyst for this exercise. So, for example, if a student has written in his or her notebook that they overheard someone say "Mexicans always steal," consider in class how this discursive assertion undoubtedly structures the interlocutor's relationship to Latinos and how it functions pedagogically for whomever is listening. In this way, students can begin to see how "race talk" functions discursively to constitute itself as racist practice and discourse. In the above example, guide the students through a non-racialized iteration of this speech act. Ask the class, "What if the person had said instead, 'I hate it when people steal.'" Or, ask them to consider if they would frame a theft by a white person in racialized terms. "I hate it when white people steal." Then reveal to them that by linking ethnicity with the pathology of stealing, the speaker participates in a repetitive discourse that perpetuates racism. Hence, the goal of the "race talk" exercise is to draw students' attention to the way race functions discursively. In this particular case, it is through the discourse of speech acts. In the next unit, you will show them how visual assumptions about race function discursively to perpetuate the notion of black and white identity as opposites. The second week of the unit should be devoted to helping students understand why race is understood as a social construction. Students are often told that "race is a social construction," but in my experience this has rarely been explained to them in a way that makes sense. Though for educators it may seem like a fairly obvious and simple assertion, for students it defies the logic most of them have been raised to embrace. If how one looks is heredity, i.e., biological differences, how is it possible that race is not biological—that race is simply a "social construction?" There are several ways teachers can begin to help students see that race is not simply a matter of phenotype and to help students explore how race is constructed. First, teachers can assign the American Anthropological Association's statement on race. In the first paragraph, the statement asserts:

> In the United States both scholars and the general public have been conditioned to viewing human races as natural and separate divisions within the human species based on visible physical differences. With the vast expansion of scientific knowledge in this century, however, it has become clear that human populations are not unambiguous, clearly demarcated, biologically distinct groups. Evidence from the analysis of genetics (e.g., DNA) indicates that most physical variation, about 94 percent, lies *within* so-called racial groups. Conventional geographic "racial" groupings differ from one another only in about 6 percent of their genes. This means that there is greater variation within "racial" groups than between them. In neighboring populations there is much overlapping of genes and their phenotypic (physical) expressions. Throughout history whenever different groups have come into contact, they have interbred. The continued sharing of genetic materials has maintained all of humankind as a single species.

A close reading of this will enable students to begin to undo some of their faulty biological assumptions about race. A useful analogy, after students have read and discussed the aforementioned article, is to invite students to understand how two people—one with brown eyes and one with blue—can still be understood as belonging to the same race, despite the slight genetic variation caused by the difference in eye color. Why is it that, in the case of variations in eye color and hair color, we can class some people as one race, but use skin color (which has the same genetic weight in one's DNA as hair color or eye color) to create racial classifications? To further press against the biological and phenotypic notions of race, the teacher should be prepared to show the students pictures of African Americans who appeared and appear to be white. Among these are Walter White (a former president of the NAACP), Wentworth Miller, Jennifer Beals, and Jean Toomer. Images of these people are easily accessible on the internet. This methodology will begin to force students to question their assumptions about appearance and race. Yet even when confronted with these ruptures of racial logic, many students will assume that the white-skinned African Americans are simply those with "negligible" amounts of black blood, and hence maintain their biological view of race.

After spending two or three days on the AMA statement and the related activities, show the students the short performance piece, available on YouTube, by Adrian Piper titled "Cornered." In it, Piper—a white looking African American—cogently explains many of the issues the students are thinking through. Among them is her statement that the average white American is of 5 percent to 20 percent Sub-Saharan African descent. After allowing the students to discuss Piper's performance piece for a day, next introduce them to the 1993 issue of *Colors* magazine, which features prominent figures as different races—including Pope John Paul, Queen Elizabeth, Arnold Schwarzenegger, Spike Lee, and Michael Jackson. In these images, only the hair, skin and/or eye color of the celebrities has been changed—and yet our perception of them is deftly altered—despite the fact that their other features (the shapes of their noses, lips, and so on) have not changed. In this way, you can bring students to an awareness that the very way they see the contours, features, and "looks" of another person has been so heavily conditioned by a societal racist logic that it affects even our ability to see that the phenotypic differences between those we consider "white," and those we consider "black" is not as broad a gulf as our ideas about race make them out to be. It might also be helpful during this discussion to show students that one's cultural position can even affect a seemingly objective sense—the sense of seeing. A good way to demonstrate this to students is to how them the Muller-Lyer illusion, which demonstrates that where one grows up determines even how one sees objects in space.

Though the two lines are exactly the same size, most Americans think that the one on the left is shorter because of the sorts of buildings we spend most of our time in. Our seeing has been so conditioned, that we are unable to see the two lines as the same size. If this is the case with an object as neutral as a line, how much more so might it be with something as over determined as racialized viewing?

In order to further demonstrate to the students the genetic relation between black and white Americans and the fallacy of notions of a separate biology, you can pair Adrian Piper's revelation about white genetic make-up with an introduction of the rule of hypodescent. Hypodescent refers to the juridical logic under slavery and Jim Crow that argued that "one-drop" of black blood was enough to determine one's racial designation as black. Assign students the definition and history of the one-drop rule written by the sociologist F. James Davis for PBS and discuss it with them. It might be instructive to include recent events of relevance as well. For example, in 2013 a white supremacist that was attempting to create a "whites only" town underwent a DNA haplotype test at the behest of a TV talk show host only to discover that he had 14 percent sub–Saharan African ancestry. This can help students begin to understand that the discrete notions of race we have, of an utterly separate white and black, is an illusion designed to maintain racist attitudes and views. By the end of these two weeks in the unit, the students should have a drastically different intellectual and personal relationship to the question of "race." It should be clear to them that race is indeed a social construction that uses broad skin color phenotype as its (faulty) operating logic. As students work through these units, have them continue to write informally in their notebook. They should continue to record whatever "race talk" they come across as well as note down thoughts, feelings, and observations in relation to the material being presented in class. Once the students have grasped this idea on a deep and fundamental level, have them write a short response paper, culled from their informal writing in the notebook, about how their views on the subject have evolved.

Invisible Man is a long and complicated novel; teachers should devote three weeks to reading it. In the process of reading the novel, the students will need a lot of historical background on Historically Black Colleges and Universities, the debates in African American theory between Booker T. Washington and W.E.B. Du Bois, a thorough history of the black writer's relationship to publishers, a lecture on "positive" and "negative" representations in relation to the True Blood incident, historical information about the "Great Migration" of African Americans from the South to the North around 1910, Marcus Garvey and the Garveyites, a history of liberation movements such as the Black Panther Party, and a discussion of the black spiritual rhetorical tradition. Resources for how to discuss and teach these aspects of the text are vast and I provide some references in the works cited page. During the active reading period, I suggest that students continue to write in their notebooks. These should be collected once a week and read by the instructor so that she can see the progress of each student's thinking. Once students have worked through the meat of the text, the considerations of the protagonist's ambiguous racial state, which I explicate above, can be discussed. The unit should culminate in the writing of a longer paper, so that students can deeply explore all of the complicated questions that have been raised by the text and by class discussion. The paper should be accompanied by a visual text—a painting, a collage, a short video—that the student makes as a companion to their essay. In this visual text, they should consider the trope of invisibility and its relationship to race. Given what they have learned, isn't it the case that we are all—to some extent—racially "invisible," with significant parts of our history silenced and hidden? Encourage students to open themselves to a full exploration of these implications in text and visual form. In the past, I have had students write papers about their results from their own haplotype tests. I have never had a (white) student *not* discover some African ancestry. Students have also done short films, collages, and paintings. In this way, students can use multiple modalities to encounter these ideas and use text and visuality to translate those into a personal and intimate experience.

The valuable work performed by *Invisible Man* is that it contests the logic of a totalizing blackness and in doing so it implicitly ruptures the logic of whiteness. This is an intimate intellectual re-imagining for the students who, through this text, have the opportunity to change how they think about themselves and all other Americans as related, interconnected, subjects—as one people, regardless of skin color phenotype. Thus, at the end of the novel when the protagonist suggests, "Who knows but that, on the lower frequencies, I speak for you?" becomes a personal and legitimate hail to the student to see herself as interpolated into the story not exclusively at the site of the oppressed or the oppressor. Race, then, is no longer a thing outside one's self, confined and contained by a racist logic of purity. Instead, it is right here—inside one's own house, rattling in one's own bones. The hope is that this adjustment of how students understand and perceive race will alter their relationship to their fellow citizens in productive ways and that students will cease to see African American literature as marginal to their lives and instead understand that these stories belong to them too.

Works Cited

"American Anthropological Association Statement On Race." May 17, 1998. Web. December 2013.
The Bible. English Standard Edition. Web. December 2013.
Brody, Jennifer DeVere. *Punctuation: Art, Politics, Play*. London and Durham: Duke University Press, 2008.
Colors Magazine. Web. December 2013.
Davis, F. James. "Who is Black? One Nation's Definition." *Frontline. WGBH Educational Foundation*. Web. December 2013.
Ellison, Ralph. *Invisible Man*. Vintage, 2d edition, 2010.
Fox, Frank. "Washington, DuBois, and the Problem of Negro Two-ness," *Markham Review*, 7:21–25, 1978.
Navarro, Mary. "I Find this Very Offensive!: The Unintended Consequences of Teaching Ralph Ellison's *Invisible Man*." *Teaching American Literature: A Journal of Theory and Practice*, 2011 Spring; 4(3): 86–104.
Joseph, Raina L. *Transcending Blackness: New Millennium Mulatto to the Exceptional Multiracial*. London and Durham: Duke University Press, 2013.
Parr, Susan Resnick. *Approaches to Teaching Ralph Ellison's* Invisible Man, MLA Publications, 1989.
Piper, Adrian. "Cornered." Web. December 2013.
Reid-Pharr, Robert. "Cosmopolitan Afrocentric Mulatto Intellectual," in *Black Gay Man*. New York and London: New York University Press, 2001.
Watters, Ethan. "We Aren't The World." *Pacific Standard: Society of Science*. February 25, 2013. Web. December 2013.
"Video of White Supremacist learning he is 14% Black May Be the Best Thing Ever." *Huffington Post*. November 11, 2012. Web. December 2013.

More Than Music and Food
Teaching About Cajun and Creole Cultures and Peoples

Monika Giacoppe

For many people, the words "Cajun" and "Creole" lead to visions of gumbo, red beans and rice, crawfish, and just about anything that's been "blackened, Cajun-style." While these culinary traditions are distinctive and delicious, they have overshadowed the many other unique cultural contributions made by Louisiana's Cajun and Creole communities, and are often considered without reference to the social and historical contexts that produced them. When "Cajun" and "Creole" are reduced to adjectives on menus and food labels, it becomes easy to lose sight of the people those adjectives first described. As poet Sheryl St. Germain writes in "Cajun," she fears "the word's been stolen" by retail commodifiers of a culture emptied of its content and its history, reduced—quite literally—to an object of consumption.

Indeed, the very words "Cajun" and "Creole" are contested, the results of complicated histories and relationships. The controversies surrounding these words warrant (and will receive) more extensive discussion later in this essay. For the moment, however, it may be useful to mention that the people whose descendants are now known as Cajuns arrived in Louisiana soon after being violently uprooted from their homes in Canada in 1755 by a British government eager to re-settle the region with Protestant colonists who would presumably make more obliging subjects. The survivors of this forced exile were refused entry at many ports along the Eastern seaboard, but eventually found refuge in the then Spanish-governed colony of Louisiana, which actively encouraged their resettlement. Often disdained by the more aristocratic, planter class of Creoles who still maintained close ties to France, the Acadians had to adapt to their new environment by re-making their culture from the ground underneath them on up. This they accomplished, while retaining their language and a strong sense of cultural identity—retentions facilitated by long-lasting isolation and poverty. According to historian Shane K. Bernard, "most Cajuns remained culturally isolated from the rest of America for nearly the entire first half of the twentieth century" (xx). What little attention they received from people outside their community was often derisive, dismissing Cajuns with negative stereotypes that responded to their poverty and perceived ethnic (if not racial) difference (Bernard xxi).

While those negative attitudes have faded, Cajun history and culture remain little-known outside of Louisiana and francophone Canada. Aside from a brief time in the 1980s and early '90s, when Cajun music and its Afro-Creole counterpart, zydeco, attracted a popular audience nation-wide, attention to Cajuns has come primarily from specialists in folklore, music, and Louisiana studies. Cajun and Creole literatures are virtually never considered in anthologies, journals, or courses dedicated to studies of "ethnic American" cultural productions. Yet these communities and their traditions are valuable aspects of our national heritage, and their omission from so many conversations about race, ethnicity, identity, and even history distorts those conversations.

The transnational nature of Cajun/Cadien and Creole literatures and cultures, given their close ties to Canada, France and St. Domingue/Haiti, exemplifies the value of the "transnational turn" that the study of American literature has taken, while undermining claims to American exceptionalism. Cajun and Creole literature and culture also raise questions about how we often define who or what is "American." The study of Cajun and Creole literature quickly leads us outside many of the familiar paradigms of American history and literature, as these populations were largely in place before Napoleon sold the vast Louisiana territory to the United States in 1803 to offset his losses in trying to regain the newly emancipated Haiti and return it to a slave-holding colony of France.

It also highlights the often overlooked fact that not all "American" literature is written in English (or Spanish). Furthermore, at a time when so many students (and other citizens) associate Louisiana most immediately with disasters such as Hurricane Katrina (and its aftermath) and the BP oil spill, teaching about Louisiana's distinctive cultural traditions provides a different window onto the state, an opportunity to understand its history—and a way to better understand the rest of U.S. history as we see how the events and attitudes that defined colonial New England and even the rest of the U.S. southeast were by no means universal, but culturally specific.

This essay, then, is designed to facilitate—and inspire—the integration of these cultures into the academic canon of multi-ethnic literatures. It will provide background, resources, and suggestions for instructors interested in including Cajun, Creole, and Afro-Creole literatures and cultures in their courses. These materials would enrich courses in several disciplines, including American Studies, Literature, Women's and Gender Studies, Ethnic Studies, Music, and History. Furthermore, as Creoles, Cajuns, and Chicano/as have all been cast as the racialized, Catholic "Other" by the Anglo-Americans who settled in the regions previously predominated by those three groups, some of the readings suggested here might also be of use to instructors looking to incorporate a comparative perspective in courses in Chicano/a Studies.

"Why Haven't We Heard About This Before?"

"Why haven't we heard about this before?" is the question I have probably heard most often while teaching about Cajuns and Creoles, primarily in American Studies course on Louisiana, and in an interdisciplinary honors seminar about the French empire and the postcolonial Francophone world. In both of those contexts, students responded with enthusiastic surprise. Throughout the semester, they remarked on how exciting it was to be learning something so unfamiliar. (As I teach in northern New Jersey to a mostly local population, few of these students had any experience with Louisiana or the southeastern United States, more broadly speaking.)

One of the favorite texts of students in both courses was Ned Sublette's lively history, *The World That Made New Orleans: From Spanish Silver to Congo Square* (2008), which explains with painstaking and delightful detail why Louisiana is so different from other states. Sublette, also a professional musician, traces the development of musical trends—particular rhythms, instruments, dances, etc.—as they circulate throughout the Atlantic world. His engaging approach illustrates for students how the transnational past lives on in the music and dance of today. Even including just a chapter or two from Sublette can provide a valuable backdrop for individual literary texts, such as the nineteenth-century poems by the *Les Cenelles* authors, and Rodolphe Desdunes' early twentieth-century ode to his community, *Our People and Our History*.

While my courses are typically discussion-based, I have found it beneficial to do a little lecturing at the start of class in these two courses. Accordingly, many days, I prepare a vocabulary list, which I put on the board, and open class by introducing those key terms. For instance, on the day when we discussed Sublette's Chapter 21, "A Most Extraordinary Noise," we started the day by covering "bomba," "wanga," "tumba francesa," and Marie Laveau—all drawn from the chapter, and all (fortuitously) illustrated with material available online through YouTube and other websites. As someone whose involvement with technology and pop culture is admittedly limited, I nevertheless found that I was constantly using the internet and other media to illustrate for my students things that we had read about; similarly, they brought in references from movies and TV shows, comparing the Louisiana they were learning about in class with the Louisiana presented in programs such as *American Horror Story*. I also soon realized that traditional papers were of limited utility in this course: for example, a paper about Cajun music that didn't include music just didn't seem to do its subject justice. So, for the first time in my teaching life, I invited students to produce end-of-semester multimedia presentations, accompanied by short essays, in place of the usual research papers. Nearly half of the students accepted that option, and most of their projects demonstrated well the value of that approach.

Ultimately, learning about Cajuns and Creoles creates opportunities to discuss with students their beliefs and expectations about what is and isn't "American," and how this country has chosen to define itself. When we try to make sense of the exclusion of Cajuns and Creoles from our national history, we must wrestle with questions of race, language, history, religion, and ethnic identity—including questions of prejudice and bias that some students would prefer to avoid. But when they ask that question, "Why haven't we heard about this before?" (and they do), then those conversations arise organically from their curiosity, and clear the air for a very open discussion.

Zachary Richard: Singer/Songwriter, Poet, Activist

Zachary Richard's multi-media presence and his passion for Acadian/Cajun history and culture make his work a natural—and highly accessible—choice for instructors wishing to integrate Cajun material in their literature, history, American Studies, or French classes. The body of his work serves as an archive of the francophone American experience. Richard draws material from Quebec, Acadia, Louisiana, and even Massachusetts to keep memory alive and to educate his listeners. Described as "the Cajun Mick Jagger" in a 1988 profile *Tulanian* article (the magazine of his alma mater), Richard has created a musical style which he characterizes as "a holy trinity mix of Cajun, Zydeco, and New Orleans rhythm and blues cooked in a rock-n-roll pot" (Simon, cited in Mattern 46). This mixture illustrates how Acadian/Cadien culture has survived by evolving and incorporating new influences, even while maintaining ties to tradition. While his innovation and militant stance have sometimes made him controversial, they have also ensured his enduring relevance and probably even (at least in part) his devoted fan base. Since the early 1970s, Richard has recorded over 20 albums (21 original collections, plus two "greatest hits"); aside from a 10-year span of English-language recordings, (1984–94) he has relied upon the French language and francophone cultural references for an enthusiastic francophone audience. While this audience is truly international, it is concentrated primarily in French-speaking Canada, where his 1996 album, *Cap Enragé*, went double platinum, and his 2007 release, *Lumière dans le noir* [*Light in the Darkness*], immediately soared to the top of the charts. Moving beyond the musical, Richard has published three books for children and three collections of poetry: *Voyage de nuit* [*Night Voyage*] (1987); *Faire récolte* [*Harvest*] (1997), and *Feu* [*Fire*] (2001). The film he produced in 2000, *Against the Tide: The Story of the Cajun People of Louisiana* (available in English and French) provides an excellent introduction to the making of the Acadian/Cadien/Cajun diaspora, with footage from historically important locations in Canada and Louisiana.

Richard also communicates with his fans through his bilingual website (www.zacharyrichard.com), a tremendous resource for instructors. Through the site, faculty can access video clips of Richard's live performances, song lyrics in French and English, and monthly essays exploring myriad environmental, historical, political, and cultural topics including, of course, the survival of the French language in North America. For example, the August 2004 posting provides a narrative describing how Richard came to consider himself "Acadian," and how that definition became meaningful to him. His essay engages the complexities of ethnic definition, the diminishing use of French by Acadians/ Cadiens, and whether the Acadian/Cajun cultures can survive without the French language. An April 2013 post explores southwest Louisiana's turbulent era of frequent vigilante activity in the late 1850s, including violence in which Richard's own great-great grandfather was involved. This drive to educate others about Acadian/Cajun history has also led to his publication of *Histoire des Acadiennes et Acadiens de la Louisiane* (2012), designed for use in French immersion classes in Louisiana public schools, a cause to which he has dedicated considerable energy.

Zachary Richard is a founding member of Action Cadienne, an organization dedicated to the promotion and survival of French in Louisiana. "The fundamental premise of Action Cadienne," explained Richard in a 1999 interview, "is that without the language we cannot conceive of the culture; so that if we lose our language, we won't be able to retain our link to the culture" (Allman 1999). Through media of all kinds, mainstream U.S. culture encroaches nearly everywhere, and threatens to leave a homogeneous anglophone culture in its wake. Richard's response to this situation has been to memorialize the past and fight for the future. In addition to contributing through his music, poetry, interviews, and website, Richard has promoted French-language education for Louisiana children through his involvement with Action Cadienne and other venues.

One of the most complex problems Richard grapples with, in his choice of musical forms and in his lyrics, is reaching an appropriate balance for preserving tradition while still embracing the change that keeps cultures evolving, relevant, and alive. The same concern reverberates throughout his poetry, in a tone that often departs markedly from that in the lyrics. In the concluding poem of the "Arrangements pour la catastrophe [Arrangements for the Catastrophe]" series in *Feu*, titled "Aller-retour court-circuit [Round-trip short-circuit]," the poet imagines the Virgin Mary describing a voice she heard over the loudspeaker at a "shopping center," a voice that "called out for help to all the francophones of America, of the world, for the Cadiens of Louisiana" (104). This voice, anxious that the next generation of Cadiens will be the first not to hear their language spoken, nonetheless affirms that "the defense of the French language consists, not of preventing the assimilation of anglo-american words into its vocabulary, but of preventing the abandonment of the language by heretofore francophone communities" (104).

Richard's writing represents just one of his efforts to make sure that French does not disappear from southern Louisiana, and he confesses, in the preface to *Feu*, that it is not easily done. French, he tells his readers, is not his mother tongue, but rather his "grandmother tongue" (9–10). His attempts to keep the language alive are not only intended to preserve a culture embodied by distant disparate persons, heirs to Acadian culture throughout the Americas. Perhaps just as importantly, through his writing, he says, "I try to pay homage to the language of my ancestors, even knowing that this homage is no more than an approximation. I do what I can, playing with the cinders of a burnt language" (10).

Yet with this "burnt language," Richard educates readers and listeners about the francophone experience throughout North America, ignoring national boundaries in order to focus on a transnational sense of cultural unity and solidarity. On *Cap Enragé*, the 1996 album that marked his return to performing in French, he covers "Petit Codiac," a song written by Yves Chiasson of the group Zéro Celcius. In the classroom, this song can be an effective way of initiating conversation about translation and cultural literacy. Largely a list of place names and people such as Beausoleil (who fought back during the Grand Dérangement and then led Acadians to settle in Louisiana), Louis Riel (the Canadian Métis leader who advocated for Métis rights, both peacefully and through rebellion, and was eventually hanged as a traitor in 1885), and Jackie Vautour (an Acadian who refused to leave his New Brunswick home when the federal government claimed it by eminent domain as part of the newly established Kouchibouguac National Park), the song's lyrics remain essentially the same in English as in French. When I play the song (on YouTube) for students, I ask them (especially those who have studied French) to listen for words they understand. Students quickly realize that the song's intelligibility depends more on cultural than linguistic competence, a fact confirmed by showing them the lyrics in French and the "English translation" available on Richard's website. Ironically, rather than providing a translation—which would be impossible—Richard notes that the song needs none. It thus illustrates beautifully how we are all shaped by our cultural contexts, and helps students to imagine how some of the things that are second nature for them might be obscure for listeners from other backgrounds.

Other songs that work well in the classroom include "Pagayez [Paddle]," on *Cœur fidèle*, which offers a tribute to the "coureurs du bois" whose trade was instrumental in the early New French colonies. "Massachusetts," from the same collection, recuperates Beat icon Jack Kerouac as a member of this larger francophone community, isolated in a largely Protestant, anglophone America. Even a cheery dance tune like "Crawfish/Écrevisse" repeats (in French, in both the English and French versions of the song) the Cadien legend that Louisiana's crawfish are really lobsters that followed the Acadians down the coast during the Deportation, shrunk along the way by the rigors of the journey. But while Zachary Richard often evokes the memory of loss, those evocations always aim toward survival, endurance. And, as he assures his listeners in "Ma Louisiane," (*Mardi Gras*), he does expect the legacy of the Acadians in Louisiana to survive. His influence has greatly impacted some younger musicians, including the Lafayette Bande Feufollet, whose cover of Richard's "Belle Louisiane" on their eponymous 2002 album garnered positive critical attention.

Barry Ancelet [Jean Arceneaux], Cris sur le bayou, and Cajun Pride

Zachary Richard is one of several highly visible individuals who have sought to inspire a sense of pride in Acadian/ Cajun heritage. In the 1970s, the upheaval brought on by the Civil Rights movement and resistance to the Vietnam War led to a generalized questioning of "establishment" values. Shane Bernard dubs this era the "Age of Ethnicity," when "[e]thnic groups rebelled against the old melting pot idea, which held that a homogenous national group could be created from an amalgam of minorities, the outcome being distinctly WASP in character" (87). He details how, in "south Louisiana, this trend spawned two parallel ethnic pride movements, one organized, autocratic, elitist and the other nebulous, egalitarian, grassroots. Colliding in the 1970s, the grassroots movement emerged triumphant" (88). Richard was one key participant in this grassroots movement; Barry Ancelet was another. A professor of French and francophone studies at what was then the University of Southwest Louisiana (now the University of Louisiana at Lafayette), in 1980 he facilitated the publication of *Cris sur le bayou* [*Shouts on the Bayou*], billed as "the birth of an Acadian poetry in Louisiana." While Ancelet took credit for his work as editor and for his introductory essay, his own poems in the anthology were attributed to "Jean Arceneaux." Ancelet has continued using that pseudonym for other literary ventures, including a narrative poem, *Je Suis Cadien* [*I am Cadien*], first published in 1994, and then released with facing translation by Sheryl St. Germain in 2002. Unfortunately, few of the poems in *Cris sur le bayou* are available in translation. These are mostly poems by Arceneaux [Ancelet], translated by Clint Bruce, one of the directors of Éditions Tintamarre, which appear in the second issue (2004) of the online journal *Equinoxes*. Ancelet has also dedicated considerable energy to documenting the oral literatures of Cajun and Creole communities, and published multiple books and articles on the musical traditions of south Louisiana. Any of these would be good starting points for instructors looking to add to their courses an essay on language, ethnic identity, music, or other cultural practices.

Jeanne Castille of Louisiana

If Zachary Richard and Barry Ancelet are representative of the "grassroots" aspect of the Cadien/Cajun pride movement, then Jeanne Castille is their foil, representing its more autocratic side. The ascendance of a younger generation, more willing to preserve tradition through innovation, is probably one reason why she is relatively unknown. Another is that her 1983 autobiography, *Moi, Jeanne Castille de Louisiane* [*I, Jeanne Castille of Louisiana*], a work of American literature, has paradoxically never been made available in the United States. First published in France, it was re-issued in 2006 by Éditions Luxe of Montreal. Although no English translation has yet been published, Castille's memoir warrants attention from scholars and teachers interested in Cajun history, foodways and folkways, music, architecture, and in autobiography as a form. *Moi, Jeanne Castille* weaves together menus, wills, Acadian and Cajun history, and excerpts from other francophone Louisiana texts, creating a book that unites social history and personal memoir. Castille, a former teacher, recounts her own efforts to "preserve" the French language in Louisiana, including her participation in the early years of CODOFIL, the Council for the Development of French in Louisiana, an organization that has promoted the use of the French language, including instruction in public schools, since its founding in the late 1960s.

Castille provides fascinating and detailed information on topics such as food preparation, the observance of religious traditions, and children's games. But what may be the most compelling aspect of this memoir arises not from the information it provides but the questions it raises. From the book's very opening, we are introduced to the complexities Castille faces as she negotiates multiple identities—the challenges and contradictions that result from her position as a French-speaking descendent of Acadians in the United States. The first few lines evoke frequent disagreement between Castille and her mother about the possibility of disconnecting language from nationality: "I used to say to my mother, 'Mama, you're not French; you are American!' A bit embarrassed and grumpy, she would reply: 'But no! I speak French!' And I would say, 'Yes, you speak French, but you aren't French; you're American. That's your nationality.' She would say, 'Hmm! Hmm!' She didn't want to understand and I know that, deep within herself, Mama didn't believe me" (1). Castille explains how, during her youth in the early twentieth century, "the Acadians thought that, because they spoke French, they were French. Other people, people who expressed themselves in English, were Americans. And in fact, for the Acadians, not only the Americans were "Americans": for them, anyone who spoke only English and therefore could not pass for French from France or French from Louisiana was American!" (1). Despite initially contradicting her mother and laying claim to an American identity in those opening lines, on the very next page, Castille adopts a different title, including herself in the collective whole of "we Acadians of Louisiana"—a group she has just explicitly described as placing themselves outside of the "American" community (2). And just a few pages later, when advocating for the study of genealogy as a means of preserving a sense of Acadian identity, she names herself as "American," but describes her life as "French": "My love for the past—especially for the past of my people, which is surely the source of my vocation as a historian—makes me passionate about genealogy. If I had the power to do so, I would require that genealogy be studied in school. I see the practice of genealogy as one of the ways to save, in the French Louisiana that is vanishing, the French language that is being lost, depriving Acadians of their essence. I was born American and I will die American, but I often think that mine will have been a French life." (17).

Those readers who can access Castille's autobiography in French will find it useful for her eyewitness account of the infamous 1927 flood, and for many of the details of daily life. She describes community rituals such as the famous Cajun "fais do-do" dances, the "Courir du Mardi Gras," and the practices surrounding All Saints' Day. In many ways a social history, *Moi, Jeanne Castille* also serves as a sourcebook as she incorporates materials from the public domain and from other writers, including Lucille Augustine Gabrielle Landry, who will be discussed below.

"Creole": Deciphering the Term

When asked what the word "creole" means to them, students at my public college in northern New Jersey associate it with people of mixed racial and ethnic heritage, generally French and African American. Their reaction is probably common, but also ironic, given the term's complicated and contested history, and the controversies that still surround it. In a class on Louisiana, it's a term we never finish covering, because the songs, readings, and movies we study tend to employ the term with equal certainty—and often contradictory meanings. For some Creoles, it's insufficient to identify themselves as Creole: they want to exclude others from the group. Meanwhile, others want the Creole identity to subsume all others. (For instance, see musician Cedric Watson's argument for the erasure of "Cajun," posted on his website, www.cedricwatson.com.) Students may therefore feel that, the more they read about the term, they less they understand it. I found it helpful to ask them to consider what is at stake in the definition of this particular word. What is to be gained in laying claim to this identity, and, sometimes, in preventing others from claiming it?

A useful resource in helping students to understand what is (and what has been) at stake is "Creoles and Americans," an essay by Joseph Tregle, Jr., which argues that the history surrounding the term's creation and early usage is "clearer than the later controversy would lead one to expect" (137). He cites the Inca Garcilaso de la Vega as indicating that the word was originally used by blacks to distinguish between slaves born in the New World and those born in Africa. The term was then adopted more widely to distinguish native-born from foreign-grown people, plants, and, occasionally, goods (137). Most notably, in its early usage, the word distinguished a place, not a race, of origin—an anomaly in a "New World" obsessed with classification by skin color.

Tregle recounts that, throughout the French and Spanish colonial regimes, the term was little used (133). This situation changed dramatically after 1803. As Tregle notes, "[i]t was the clash between original Louisianans and migrant Anglo-Americans after the Louisiana Purchase which for the first time made place of birth a critical issue and gave the *creole* label its crucial significance" (133–4). Reconstruction gave rise to the first efforts to define "creole" in racial terms, efforts initiated by white Creoles who feared loss of privilege if the term remained racially neutral. Tregle explains that, earlier, "[n]ativity was all, because its sanction of local birth as a claim upon preferential political power had evolved in a society which knew only white men as political persons. [...] No reason had existed, therefore, to deny any native-born child classification as a creole, whether white or black, free or slave, Latin or Yankee, given the social and political emptiness of the term. Unchallengeable white supremacy, in short, had made it possible to accommodate a pan-racial creolism" (172). As Americans from outside Louisiana increasingly imposed on the state a two-tier racial system, with "white" and "black" as the only categories meaningful before the law, white Creoles grew increasingly attached to a mythology whereby "Creole" had always mean white-only. In the preface to her 1929 *French Literature of Louisiana*, Ruby Van Allen Caulfield makes her feelings clear: "This word [...] was adopted by the French [...] to mean or signify a white human being bred in their colonies of Africa and America—a native of European extraction, whose origin was known and whose superior Caucasian blood was never to be assimilated to the baser liquid that ran in the veins of the Indian and African natives. This explains why one of the privileged class is to this day proud of calling himself a 'creole' and clings to the appellation" (xi-xii). With vigorous advocacy, this usage also gained credence.

While it is appealing to return to the early use of the term, avoiding racial or ethnic distinction, such ambiguity would unfortunately further complicate discussion of various "Creole" texts by authors whose communities and interests were quite dissimilar. For that reason, following James H. Dormon, this essay will use the term "Creole" for individuals who identify themselves as white, and "Creole of Color" for those who claim a mixed ancestry and cultural heritage. Although Joseph Tregle describes the term "creole of color" as "a favorite of more recent times, seized upon to support post–Civil War theories of distinction based on race, the term is essentially foreign to antebellum usage," James H. Dormon offers a different history for the phrase (Tregle 139). Dormon asserts that the use of "Creole" for "native Louisianans" continued "throughout the antebellum period, though by the 1820s one group of such Creoles began to distinguish themselves from all others. The growing community of Afro-European miscegens who were descended from colonial free persons of color and who occupied a special, intermediate place in the racial and social order of antebellum Louisiana and the Gulf port cities began referring to themselves as 'Creoles of Color'" (x). More recent scholarship by Andrew Jolivétte, drawing on a rich supply of interviews with community members, insists on the presence of American Indians in this ethnic and cultural mix. In *Louisiana Creoles: Cultural Recovery and Native American Identity* (2007), Jolivétte argues that "[w]hile Indians are often (but not always) included in definitions of the Creole population, they are often forgotten about in studies dealing with Creoles for a more binary treatment of black-white relations in the making of Creole identities in and around the New Orleans area" (7).

Instructors wishing to explore these issues with their classes will find valuable resources in three films that present differing perspectives on Louisiana Creole history and identity. As indicated in its title, *Faubourg Tremé: The Untold Story of Black New Orleans*, directed by Dawn Logsdon and released in 2008, avoids the term "Creole" altogether, subsuming Creoles into a larger black or African American identity, even while commenting on the specificity of this particular community. With compelling archival photos and contemporary footage of New Orleans, the film documents the participation of Tremé residents in early attempts to win equal rights for all Americans. They left a powerful activist legacy, including the Plessy v. Ferguson case. Although the Supreme Court decision in that case tragically sanctioned racial segregation, it also highlighted the senselessness of segregation laws. Physically able to "pass" as white, Homère Plessy, acting on behalf of the Comité de Citoyens [Citizens' Committee], arranged in advance for the conductor to question his racial identity when he boarded a "whites only" train car, intentionally getting arrested in order to initiate a challenge to legalized segregation. *Faubourg Tremé* shows how members of this community wielded considerable cultural influence, using newspapers and other literary avenues to express themselves in personal and political terms. One of the movie's central figures, Irving Trevigne, is the great-great nephew of Paul Trevigne, the editor of two nineteenth-century African American newspapers and a source of living history in his own right. Stories told by Trevigne while restoring the Tremé home of the film's narrator, Lolis Eric Elie (then a journalist for the *New Orleans Picayne*, now a writer for the HBO series *Tremé*), inspire Elie to learn more about his neighborhood. *Faubourg Tremé* makes explicit the loss of precious historical artifacts and communal memory caused by the aftermath of Hurricane Katrina, including footage from before, during, and after the storm.

Despite its emphasis on Tremé as a multi-racial, multi-cultural neighborhood in its earlier years, *Faubourg Tremé* nevertheless speaks only in terms of "black" or "African American" history. In that respect, it provides a stark contrast to *American Creole: A New Orleans Homecoming*, and *The Spirit of a Culture: Cane River Creoles*, both of which insist on the right of Creoles to claim their own identity. As Lair La Cour says in *Spirit of a Culture*: "I don't want to be a white person. I don't want to be a black person. I want to be who I am." This 2005 documentary, directed by Bill Rodman and produced with guidance from the Louisiana Creole Heritage Center at Northwestern State University in Natchitoches, argues passionately for a model of identity construction that considers cultural practices rather than race, especially the "one-drop" rule of racial identification that retains a certain power in the U.S. even today. This argument is also central to the 2006 *American Creole*, directed by Michelle Benoit and Glen Pitre, which centers on the experiences of Don Vappie, a jazz banjo player from New Orleans, as Vappie tries to reconstruct his family, career, and identity post–Katrina. The film features a conversation in which Vappie is gently taken to task by a friend from his old neighborhood, the trumpeter Wynton Marsalis, for identifying himself as Creole. Marsalis—also an executive producer of *Faubourg Tremé*—chides Vappie for a lack of solidarity in choosing "Creole" over "black" or "African American." Watching moments such as these can help students far removed from Louisiana understand why it is difficult to assert these claims of personal identity without entering into conversations about history and privilege that can quickly become emotionally charged. (When students who express difficulty in understanding why some individuals hold so tightly to these identities and affiliations are asked about their own family backgrounds, they get the analogy pretty quickly.) Whether in New Orleans, the Cane River Valley, or far-flung migration destinations such as California, Creoles have had made significant contributions to their local culture and to our national history. These films bring that history to life.

Armand Lanusse and Les Cenelles *[The Hawthorne-Berries]*

One of the landmark texts created by the New Orleans Creoles of Color was *Les Cenelles* [*The Hawthorne-Berries*], edited by Armand Lanusse, and published in 1845. Rodolphe Desdunes, who dedicates two chapters of his 1911 *Our People and Our History: Fifty Creole Portraits* to the collection *Les Cenelles* and its contributors, describes the anthology as "a sacred heritage."

For Desdunes, "[i]t is a duty of the highest order that we perpetuate the memory of those who bequeathed this volume to us. We wish, therefore, to rescue from oblivion the names of the seventeen Creoles who, at the cost of great sacrifice, left us this treasured book, because our people during this time were forbidden even to complain of their plight, of the civil, political, and social deprivations they were suffering" (11). A short but thorough article by Jerah Jones explicating the book's title substantiates Desdunes' assertions about the difficulties involved in producing the collection. According to Jones, the fruit named in the title are May-haws. These berries, hard to find, and difficult to collect and prepare, were sought out by young men and presented as gifts to women, who then distilled the fruit into a highly prized jelly. As Jones puts it, "The authors and editor of *Les Cenelles*, all free men of color in antebellum New Orleans, in calling their pieces *May haws*, and presenting them to the 'Fair sex of Louisiana,' subtly and poetically evoked the image of small, uniquely flavored, and rare local delicacies that struggled for life in surroundings so hostile as to make the very gathering of them a dangerous travail, but one worth the risk because of the richness of the reward" (410).

The efforts of Régine Latortue and Gleason R. W. Adams have made the entire book available in English, while Norman Shapiro's *Creole Echoes: The Francophone Poetry of Nineteenth Century Louisiana* offers verse translations of some of the *Cenelles* poems alongside others. But translation alone does not resolve all possible challenges for readers. My students were put off by the poems' formality and diction—even in English. In order to break the ice in this conversation, I brought a handful of markers to class, and asked each student to list on the whiteboard their most and least favorite two poems from those we had read. I also asked them to include a line or two exemplifying what most bothered, pleased, or intrigued them about the texts. This lead to a lively discussion, especially as some poems appeared on both the most and least favored lists—a situation that decentered the conversation, as students addressed each other (instead of me), while explaining their preferences and interpretations.

But language and form are only two of the obstacles that impede our reading of *Les Cenelles*. Those who approach the book expecting to find a political consciousness similar to that of the slave narratives written during the same era may find themselves perplexed, if not disappointed, by these poems. Most of the themes that preoccupied African American writers during this period are not readily apparent in this collection. Instead, in many ways, it is more closely related to French Romantic poetry of the era, a fact that highlights the unusual, liminal space inhabited by these authors. However, when reading *Les Cenelles*, dedicated "To the Fair Sex of Louisiana," it is essential to recall that in 1830, state-wide legislation in Louisiana barred "the writing or publishing of any matter tending to breed discontent among the free people of color or insubordination among the slaves, the penalty involved being life imprisonment at hard labor or death" (Roussève, cited in Latortue and Adams xi). Critics attentive to the possible impact of this censorship have offered intriguing interpretations of the poems. For instance, Floyd Cheung (1997) reads them as subtly critiquing the popular quadroon balls, where white men only could select paid companions from among beautiful young women of color. Seen from this perspective, the collection's many poems about love become a covert way for the authors to address the difficulties faced by Creole men facing competition from whites for the affections of Creole women. Alternately, for Thomas Haddox (2001), they emphasize the poets' commitment to a Catholic, franco-centric world as a means of protesting the loss of status faced by Creoles of Color under American governance.

Despite the circumstances constraining the authors of *Les Cenelles*, some of the poems do offer an explicit critique of the deteriorating conditions for all those with African ancestry in New Orleans. Perhaps most striking in tone is Camille Thierry's "Le nautonier [The Sailor]," narrated by a young lover who has been rejected by his sweetheart's father: "That man, that hoary man refused your hand to me/ And vilified my race" (Latortue 141). Although its opening lines propose that the lovers "mingle [their] sighs" and let "[their] sweet words intertwine," the sailor soon threatens that, if the father were to appear, "[m]y face would darken and my dagger, long and keen/ Would play his lullaby" (Latortue 141). Two poems by Armand Lanussse condemn the then-common practice of "plaçage," facilitated by "quadroon balls," where young women were "placed" with wealthy white men. While these relationships were not legally sanctioned, they were typically negotiated by members of the woman's family, and generally required legal recognition of any children produced by the couple, and the provision of a home that the woman would retain even if/ when the relationship ended. For example, in "Epigram," a priest reprimands a mother who "every New Year, brought her sins, outspread/ Before him in a never-ending list" (Shapiro 95). The mother replies that she *does* want to renounce Satan—then asks, "'But before grace sparks my soul, tell me I can/ To rid all need for future sinning....' 'What? ...' / 'Set up my daughter with a rich white man!'" (Shapiro 95) Perhaps even more pointedly, in "To Elora," the speaker addresses a young woman rumored to have broken her engagement to accept an offer of plaçage. "It is whispered," he says, "[t]hat self-interest has opened to another your heart,/ That you are fleeing marriage and its severe laws/ To adopt other laws less sure but more lenient" (Latortue 99). The speaker reminds Elora of her "young, pretty

Noémie/ Whom you once called your very best friend," and whose mother, "without remorse, was an accomplice/ To the corruption of her innocent mind" (Latortue 99). Desertion by her first lover puts Noémie's initial affluence at risk; before long, she "turned to vice, holding low her head/ Fallen prey to passions whose excess will kill her" (Latortue 101). While Lanusse's poems reproach the mothers who "place" their daughters, Michel St. Pierre's "La jeune fille agonisante [The Dying Young Girl]" celebrates the good fortune of a young woman who is dying before her mother might intervene in the marriage plans she has made, if she finds a more advantageous situation. "How lucky you are, how worthy of envy!" the speaker in this poem exclaims (Latortue 129).

Most of the poems in *Les Cenelles* avoid confronting these contentious topics directly, however, and approach love (and heartbreak) in somewhat more stereotypical fashion. One intriguing exception to this generalization is "A mon ami P., Qui me demandait mon opinion sur le mariage [To My Friend P., Who Asked Me for My Opinion on Marriage]," by Auguste Populus. The poem presents something of a puzzle, as is pointed out by both Shapiro and Latortue and Adams. When the lines are all read consecutively, the verses offer the promise of happiness in married life. But reading the first and third, then second and fourth lines of each verse leads to an altogether different conclusion, as this final verse shows:

> Ah! Man is right to think that joy is his
> When, wedded by chaste bonds, the belle is his;
> If evermore the bachelor's life he plies
> Each day moist tears will come and fill his eyes [Shapiro 141].

The formal sophistication and intellectual playfulness of this poem, offered in the guise of friendly advice, provide readers with a glimpse into a circle of highly educated individuals for whom poetry was a vital form of communication. If we read this poem as indicative of the workings of the book overall, though, it becomes even more important. The poets of *Les Cenelles* were clearly practiced at using art to say one thing, while meaning something altogether different. As this poem's conventional praise of matrimonial bliss masks its true purpose, the encouragement of celibacy, it also alerts us that the volume, overall, may not be as conventional (or as transparent) as it seems. Faced with outright censorship, the poets of *Les Cenelles*, like other writers before and since, sometimes chose to cloak their concerns in allegory and ambiguity, rather than remain silent.

Indeed, one example of such ambiguity is M. F. Liotau's "Une impression [An Impression]," which thematizes religion rather than love. Addressed to the famous St. Louis Cathedral, it laments that the "old temple, shrine" is "today empty and deserted!" (Latortue 89). The speaker fears that in this "final resting place/ Of respected men still mourned by the people," the deceased may be "moaning like us from inside their graves" (Latortue 89). Shifting to a different addressee, the speaker then exhorts, "Christians, let us unite," expressing hope that "[g]ranting our prayers, [God] will change our destiny" (Latortue 89). Because the earlier verses mourning the desertion of the cathedral are entirely focused on the church and its waning attendance, the reader is left to wonder what this shift from religious practice to "destiny" means. Here, as elsewhere, ambiguity gives rise to differing interpretations. For Thomas Haddox, it is evidence of concern over the increasing Protestant (that is, anglophone, non-native to Louisiana) influence in New Orleans. Caryn Cossé Bell offers an alternative, proposing that Creoles of Color were migrating away from the Cathedral as "the city's Catholic leaders, like church leaders elsewhere in the South, consolidated their authority over church affairs by identifying their interests with those of the region's slaveholding elite" (Bell 146-7). Bell suggests that, due to frustrations with the Church hierarchy, some "Creoles of color supported the founding of a new church [St. Augustine's] in the Faubourg Tremé," while "[s]ome black Catholics, completely disillusioned by events in the church, turned to an alternative form of religious expression" (146).

While this ambiguity leaves much room for student debate about how to interpret the poems in *Les Cenelles*, one thing is clear: Armand Lanusse hoped that it would not be forgotten. In the closing paragraph of his introduction to the collection, he ventures, "And if, by chance, this volume survives to the generation which must follow ours, the poets of that future time will probably consider it with the same interest with which one regards simple monuments erected by mortals as simple as the monuments themselves" (Latortue xli).

The Desdunes Brothers: Rodolphe and Pierre-Aristide: Nos Hommes et notre histoire *[Our People and Our History] and* Rappelez-vous, Concitoyens! *[Fellow Citizens, Remember!]*

Two people who took very seriously the responsibility to carry forward the memory of the *Les Cenelles* writers were the brothers Rodolphe Lucien and Pierre-Aristide Desdunes. The Desdunes family fought vigorously to preserve the rights, pride, and unique culture of Creoles of Color in New Orleans as the climate they faced grew more hostile over the course of the nineteenth century. Perhaps it was, in part, their family's Haitian roots that helped to fortify this sense of pride and justice. According to Dana Kress, Jeremiah Desdunes, their father, came to Louisiana from Haiti; one of the brothers, Emile, "returned to Haiti for his education and served as an agent there to facilitate immigration from Louisiana to Haiti during the last years of the 1850s" (44). A nephew, Daniel Desdunes, also involved in the Citizens' Committee, "boarded a whites-only car in a train bound for Mobile and was arrested," in an organized challenge to the 1890 "Separate Car Act" that prefigured the Plessy case (Kress 44). Rodolphe Desdunes was an influential member of the Citizens' Committee which plotted Plessy's challenge to legalized segregation.

Rodolphe and Pierre-Aristide Desdunes recognized that the written word could be both a powerful weapon in the battle for justice and a valuable tool for preserving cultural memory. While both men were active in the literary and cultural circles of resistance in nineteenth-century New Orleans, the work of Rodolphe Desdunes is more readily accessible in English, thanks to a translation by Sister Dorothea Olga McCants, published in 1973 by the Louisiana State University Press. First published in 1911 as *Nos Hommes et Notre Histoire*, this collection of "portraits" memorializes Creoles of Color whose contributions to their community Desdunes feared would be forgotten. Much of this collection focuses on educators and writers who played a role in community uplift, including, most prominently, those involved with *Les Cenelles*, but this loving collection pays homage to people who served the social good or provided role models in other ways, as well. Desdunes' entry on Paul Trévigne, editor first of *L'Union* and then of *La Tribune*, two Black newspapers that courageously challenged the status quo, exemplifies the book's general tone. Remarking on the dangers facing Trévigne and others like him, Desdunes bluntly declares, "Nothing fired the indignation of the Democrat so much as the sight of a man of color holding a position of prominence in the intellectual world. All that he could say, do, or write to defend his cause, to emphasize his progress, or to prove his ability, was only another sign of his impertinence; and the hatred for a man like Trévigne was ever intense and ready to burst into flame at the slightest provocation" (67). Desdunes declares that, because of Trévigne's work as a writer and editor, "our people therefore owe him a place among the immortals" (68). He continues, "The grave must not efface the memory of Trévigne's merit, hence we have chosen to memorialize him. [...] The truth of history is the nourishing mother of justice" (68). Desdunes' valuing of memory meshes logically with his belief that community history is the key to community pride—and that both are invaluable sources of resistance in a racist society.

Even Desdunes' shortest vignettes are rich with details of historical interest. For instance, we learn through him of Dr. Alexandre Chaumette, born in New Orleans, but, like many Creoles of Color, educated in France. Desdunes describes him as "the first colored doctor to come to New Orleans as a practicing physician," and notes that "his arrival in our city created quite a stir" (76). He records how "the other doctors, whether because of prejudice or dislike, or perhaps for both reasons, opposed his practice" and "initiated a humiliating examination for him" (76). However, because he held "a recognized diploma from France, he could not be forced to submit to this ordeal" (76). The theme of Creoles of Color leaving the U.S. for better opportunities in Europe and, occasionally, Haiti, recurs throughout the collection. Desdunes recounts, for example, how the sculptor Eugène Warbourg emigrated to Paris, then Florence, and finally Rome, where he could gain recognition for his artistic talents. Meanwhile, his brother, Daniel, also a sculptor, stayed in New Orleans. Desdunes uses his remarks on the brothers to critique the limitations and preoccupations of typical writing about blacks; he notes "in passing," he says, how "certain writers never fail to talk at length about the talents of Negroes as dancers, but the reader will search in vain among the works of these same authors to find a single line about the genius of such men as the Warbourgs" (71).

Privileging writers and educators as he does, it is no surprise that Desdunes reserves his greatest praise for Armand Lanusse, editor of the famous collection *Les Cenelles* [The Hawthorn-berries]. Desdunes' appreciation for Lanusse as a writer and editor is unmistakable, but his most passionate admiration is inspired by Lanusse's status as an educator and as a role model. Intriguingly, in his comments on these points, he dwells on the loss of the "Latin influence among our people," which he fears "disappeared with the death of Armand Lanusse. With his passing away we are bereft of his example, of the stimulating force provided us by the classics. No longer do we occupy ourselves with reading La Fontaine, Boileau, Fénelon, Racine, Corneille. No longer are we ardent students of the master" (15–6). Desdunes asserts that reading these authors had taught "our young people" to "disdain the temptations of self-interest" (16). He insists that Creoles of Color need to study "Latin" authors for appropriate character formation, and warns that "rejecting the influence of the classics has meant condemning ourselves to live without the knowledge of certain principles indispensable to the formation of character" (16). This American's reliance on a list of only French authors—in 1911—hints at "Latin," francophone identification as a form of resistance to the U.S. values—and system of racial stratification—that have taken hold in the city.

Pierre-Aristide's literary production has received far less attention than that of his brother. He left behind two manuscript ledgers; these were donated to Howard University in 1952. They are filled with his own poetry and prose, and with his handwritten copies of most of the poems included in *Les Cenelles*. The Éditions Tintamarre recently (2010) published *Rappelez-vous concitoyens!* [*Fellow Citizens, Remember!*], collecting Aristide's poetry (in French only), alongside an introductory essay by Caryn Cossé Bell, provided in both French and English. Fortunately, a fine essay by Dana Kress (2007) also introduces readers to Pierre-Aristide, and includes both original and translated versions of several of his poems, as well as poems by Victor Ernest Rillieux, preserved only through Desdunes' handwritten copies. Like his brother's testimonies, Pierre-Aristide's poems seek to inspire resistance, pride, and hope. In "Thoughts of a slave soldier," his criticisms of racist society are as explicit as his exhortations to rebellion. "To weep while the world laughs, to weep while the world sings;/ To smother within our heart every great and noble thought," he begins (50). The stanzas shift from lamentation to a call for action. Here, instructors may want to draw attention to Desdunes' sense of continuity and solidarity between Creoles and a larger community of "sons of Africa," even before the restrictions of Plessy vs. Ferguson officially became the law of the land.

"Elegy," far less confrontational than "Thoughts of a slave soldier," emphasizes the unspoken, unknowable aspirations that animate the lives of those who are not empowered to articulate (or achieve) their desires. The speaker's musings close with comments that highlight the value of history and communal continuity, as they describe a nearly mystical power connecting generations.

While this metempsychotic view of an existence that continues after death does not explicitly challenge the injustices of a racist social system, it questions their logic, as the essence of an individual endures after death and may be re-born in another without regard to race, ethnicity, or skin color.

While other poems by Desdunes, including "Heartbreak of a man without a country," would make for valuable additions to classroom discussions, instructors might also consider using those by Rillieux. His "Love and Devotion," dedicated "To Miss Ida B. Wells," compares the anti-lynching crusader, the "brown-skinned virgin in the land of the savage" to the biblical Judith and to Joan of Arc (Kress 49).

Ironically bestowing upon the United States a title so often reserved for the African continent, "the land of the savage," Rillieux simultaneously places Wells in a heroic historical context, and re-writes the history that has deemed "civilized" a nation invested in a brutalizing slave system. Pierre-Aristide

Desdunes' preservation of Rillieux's poems is both fortunate and appropriate to the larger project in which he and Rodolphe participated. In terms that recall Pierre-Aristide's "Elegy," Caryn Cossé Bell compares the brothers to French historian Jules Michelet, declaring that all three men "recognized the power of history in the struggle for freedom and equality. In discussing his passion for recreating the past, Michelet [...] explained that history writing sustained the living as well as the dead: 'I have exhumed them [the dead] for a second life.... Thus a family is formed, a common city between the living and the dead'" (64).

Lucille Augustine Gabrielle Landry ("Tantine") and the Story of Her Life

The autobiography of Lucille Augustine Gabrielle Landry (also known by the nickname "Tantine") is a little-known text that merits more attention, but is available only in French. A short but fascinating piece, it provides an instructive study in contrast with *Moi, Jeanne Castille*, published two years later by a woman who lived just miles away, but in a different world. The contrasts begin with the titles: rather than the bold first-person self-naming we see from Castille, the full title of Tantine's autobiography, *Tantine: l'histoire de Lucille Augustine Gabrielle Landry, racontée par elle-même à 82 ans* [*Tantine: The Story of Lucille Augustine Gabrielle Landry, As Told By Herself at 82 Years of Age*], makes the *subject* of the book the *object* of its title. Written in the third person, the title reveals that Tantine did not *write* her own life story; rather, she narrated it to two researchers who transcribed it. Tantine remains the object of the book's opening sentence, "Everyone calls me Tantine," but shifts to a first-person voice immediately thereafter, explaining how her young nieces and nephews were the ones to begin calling her "Tantine," which they found easier to say than "Tante Augustine [Aunt Augustine]" (1). Explaining what her name communicates (or doesn't) about her identity, she jokes that her last name, Landry, is Acadian, and might lead people who don't know her to assume that she her ancestors were French. "But no," she says. "I am *Creole*," defining "Creole" in terms of race and language (1). Avoiding all mention of possible racial mixing, she observes that her family names, Landry and Gabriel, indicate only the families that bought her ancestors, including her own father, and her husband's ancestors, as well (3). In short, the kind of genealogical research that Castille has done for herself, and recommends for others, would not be possible for Tantine.

Another core element of Castille's text, her own education and her career as a teacher, also stands in stark contrast to the experience described by Tantine, who never mentions schooling at all. Instead, she recounts how she went to work for the Catholic Church in Mauriceville, probably in her early teens, although the text does not specify a date. She describes moving on to a second job, this time with the bishop, Monseigneur Jeanmard, when she was fifteen (9). Tantine pointedly declares that she was driven from Catholicism by an incident of violent racism in her Mauriceville church on the day she was to make her First Communion. She explains that someone disregarded the church's segregated seating arrangements, and that shots were fired within the building—but stops short of explaining who sat where, and why (7–8). Was it intentional protest? A simple error? From her text, we cannot know; these silences are characteristic of the narrative.

Born in 1897 in Lafayette Parish, one of nineteen children, Tantine evokes a far less peaceful racial climate than that described by Castille. Tantine's summary statement about her childhood is telling: "Oh! I have such painful memories of those years. I saw some terrible things happen" (5). Oddly, even as Castille describes how "whites" and "blacks" generally lived in harmony, she cites, in its entirety, Tantine's description of an attack on one of her brothers. "One day," she says, "the Whites came; they took my brother. They put a rope around his neck, then they dragged him behind a buggy on the gravel road. They beat him up badly: he was covered in blood. And when they had finished, they came back and threw him at my mother, saying 'Fix him up so he can work tomorrow!'" (5) In a move that is typical Tantine's approach throughout the narrative, Tantine offers no antecedent to this assault, no conclusion, and no emotional commentary. We don't know what pretext, if any, was given for the attack; nor do we know whether her brother recovered from his wounds. Tantine's story, with its many gaps and silences, inspires readers to ask questions about what she has excluded and why. Those who compare it with Jeanne Castille's autobiography will surely find even more questions to ask.

Victor Séjour, Sidonie de La Houssaye, and Alfred Mercier

Throughout the nineteenth century in particular, Creole writers (and here I mean both Creoles of color and those whose heritage was more specifically European) produced an array of plays, poems, essays, novels, and short stories that has garnered little attention from scholars of American literature. Unfortunately, little of this work has been translated, and space precludes adequate consideration of all of their contributions here. Furthermore, the careers of some of these writers, such as Victor Séjour, challenge our usual expectations of "American" authors, and not just because they wrote in French. Born a "free person of color," as the phrase went, in New Orleans in 1817, Séjour was part of a prosperous family with roots in Haiti. Frustrated by the racism of his home city, Séjour left New Orleans for Paris somewhere between 1834 and 1836 (Weiss xviii–xix). There, he enjoyed tremendous success as a playwright whose first play was produced by the Comédie Française in 1844 (Weiss xx–xxi). That play, *Diégarias* (known as *The Jew of Seville* in English) employs the story of a Jewish man's persecution in fifteenth-century Spain to thematize the destruction wrought by a racialized "otherness" ostensibly passed down through the bloodlines. It would be hard to miss the parallels between the dangers of the idea of an inherited, if invisible, difference that sabotages the play's protagonist, Diégarias, and the obsession with racial classification and biological determinism that characterized Séjour's homeland in the nineteenth century. Fortunately, *The Jew of Seville*, like Séjour's *La Tireuse de cartes* [*The Fortune-Teller*], is available in English translation, thanks to the efforts of Norman Shapiro. Both volumes offer helpful introductions by M. Lynn Weiss that include listings of the few other translations of Séjour's works. Unfortunately, no translation is readily available for Alfred Mercier's *L'Habitation Saint-Ybars*, an 1881 anti-slavery novel that illustrates both the ongoing cultural links between Louisiana and France and the usage of the Louisiana Creole language by people from all racial backgrounds and social classes. A white Creole who deeply valued the linguistic and cultural heritage unique to Louisiana, Mercier produced a *Study of the Creole Language in Louisiana* in 1880, and several other novels. He also helped to found the Athénée louisianais, an organization dedicated to the advancement of the French language in the state. French-language editions of several of his books are easily available from the Éditions Tintamarre, a publishing endeavor supported by Centenary College in Shreveport and by the Louisiana Board of Regents. In fact, the Éditions Tintamarre have reprinted a host of valuable nineteenth-century French-language texts from Louisiana, including several novels by Sidonie de La Houssaye. A prolific author, de La Houssaye is known for a short novel about two Acadian lovers separated during the Grand Dérangement of 1755, and (unlike Evangeline and Gabriel) happily reunited in Louisiana: *Pouponne et Balthazar: conte acadien* [*Pouponne and Balthazar: An Acadian Story*] (1888). She is also famous for a trilogy of novels published under a pseudonym, Louise Raymond: *Les Quarteronnes de la Nouvelle-Orléans* [*The Quadroons of New Orleans*]. These books, which began appearing in serialized form shortly after de La Houssaye's death in 1894, describe in vivid detail the opulent lives of the "quadroons" whose charms apparently overpower the upstanding white men of New Orleans' upper classes, and the havoc these women wreak on the men's unsuspecting, respectable families (Hommel 10–11). While undeniably lurid and exoticising, the novels are nonetheless often sympathetic to the young women who were bargained away by family members seeking financial gains, and whose aspirations were limited by the laws restricting opportunities for anyone whose blood was not purely "white." Interestingly, however, in the eyes of de la Houssaye, the "quadroons" also seem to enjoy greater financial freedom and independence than do the lawful wives, whose property is never truly their own. Christian Hommel's introductory essays in these volumes situate the novels historically, biographically, and culturally, but again, these texts are available only in French.

Conclusion

When the United States purchased Louisiana in 1803, capitalizing on Napoleon's unsuccessful attempt to win back the profitable colony of St. Domingue/ Haiti, the nation found that it needed to assimilate a population that had already developed its own ways of life. Distinctive patterns of settlement and governance during the colonial era, and a population of free people of color unparalleled throughout the nation, made Louisiana a state unlike any other during the era of slavery, and long after that era ended. Continuing links to France and Haiti throughout most of the nineteenth century helped to maintain the unique cultural practices of Creole communities, while the preservation on many Cajun traditions was assisted by the relative isolation of their communities until World War II. Yet interest in the cultural productions of these peoples from beyond the state borders has been sporadic at best. It is time to recognize that these vibrant local cultures are an essential part of our national heritage.

Note: All translations by the author unless otherwise indicated.

Works Cited

Against the Tide: The Story of the Cajun People of Louisiana. Directed by Pat Mire. Louisiana Public Broadcasting, 2000. DVD.

Allmann, Kevin. "C'est Zach! An Interview with Zachary Richard." First published in *Where New Orleans* in 1999. Accessed online at http://zachary.waiting-forthe-sun.net/Pages/Interviews/CestZach.html. August 10, 2013.

American Creole: A New Orleans Reunion. Directed by Michelle Benoit and Glen Pitre. Louisiana Public Broadcasting, 2006. DVD.

Ancelet, Barry. "Dewey Balfa: A Cultural Ambassador." 1981. In *Fiddles, Accordions, Two-Step & Swing: A Cajun Music Reader*. Ed. Ryan A. Brasseaux and Kevin S. Fontenot. Lafayette: University of Louisiana at Lafayette Press, 2006. 453-8.

Baudoin, Richard. "The Cajun Mick Jagger." 1988. In *Fiddles, Accordions, Two-Step & Swing: A Cajun Music Reader*. Eds. Ryan A. Brasseaux and Kevin S. Fontenot. Lafayette: University of Louisiana at Lafayette Press, 2006. 459-66.

Bell, Caryn Cossé. *Revolution, Romanticism, and the Afro-Creole Protest Tradition in Louisiana, 1718-1868*. Baton Rouge and London: Louisiana State University Press, 1997.

Bernard, Shane K. *The Cajuns: Americanization of a People*. Jackson: University Press of Mississippi, 2003.

Bruce, Clint. "Translations of Jean Arceneaux." *Equinoxes: A Graduate Journal of French and Francophone Studies*. Issue 2 (Fall/Winter 2003-4). http://www.brown.edu/Research/Equinoxes/journal/issue2/eqx2_bruce_tr.html. Accessed August 15, 2013.

Castille, Jeanne. *Moi, Jeanne Castille, de Louisiane*. 1982. Montreal: Lux Éditeur, 2006.

Caulfield, Ruby Van Allen. *French Literature of Louisiana*. 1929. Gretna, LA: Pelican, 1998.

Cheung, Floyd. "*Les Cenelles* and Quadroon Balls: 'Hidden Transcripts' of Resistance and Domination in New Orleans, 1803-1845." *Southern Literary Journal* 29.2 (Spring 1997): 5-16.

Desdunes, Rodolphe. *Our People and Our History: Fifty Creole Portraits*. 1911. Trans. Sister Dorothea Olga McCants. Baton Rouge: Louisiana State University Press, 2001.

Dormon, James H. "Preface." *Creoles of Color of the Gulf South*. Ed. James Dormon. Knoxville: University of Tennessee Press, 1996. ix-xv.

Faubourg Tremé: The Untold Story of Black New Orleans. Dir. Dawn Logsdon. California Newsreel, 2008. DVD.

Haddox, Thomas. "The 'Nous' of Southern Catholic Quadroons: Racial, Ethnic, and Religious Identity in *Les Cenelles*. *American Literature: A Journal of Literary History, Criticism, and Bibliography* 73.4 (December 2001): 757-78.

Hommel, Christian. "Introduction." *Les Quarteronnes de la Nouvelle-Orléans, Tome I: Octavia la quarteronne*, suivi de *Violetta la quarteronne*. Sidonie de La Houssaye. Shreveport: *Éditions Tintamarre*, 2006.

J'ai été au bal [I Went to the Dance]. Dir. Les Blank, Chris Strachwitz, and Maureen Gosling. Brazos Films, 1989. DVD.

Jones, Jerah. "*Les Cenelles*: What's in a Name?" *Louisiana History: The Journal of the Louisiana Historical Association* 31.4 (Winter 1990): 407-10.

Landry, Lucille Augustine Gabrielle. *Tantine: l'histoire de Lucille Augustine Gabrielle Landry racontée par elle-même à 82 ans*. Transcribed by Monica Landry and Julien Olivier. Bedford, NH: National Materials Development Center for French and Creole, 1981.

Latortue, Régine, and Gleason R. W. Adams, trans. and introduction. *Les Cenelles: A Collection of Poems by Creole Writers of the Early Nineteenth Century*. Boston: G. K. Hall, 1979.

Laxer, James. *The Acadians: In Search of a Homeland*. Scarborough, Ontario: Doubleday Canada, 2006.

Kress, Dana. "Pierre-Aristide Desdunes, *Les Cenelles*, and the Challenge of Nineteenth-Century Creole Literature." *Southern Quarterly* 44.3 (Spring 2007): 42-67.

Mattern, Mark. "Cajun Music, Cultural Revival: Theorizing Political Action in Popular Music." *Popular Music and Society* 22.2 (Summer 1998): 31-48.

Richard, Zachary. *Faire récolte*. Moncton, N.B.: Les Éditions Perce-Neige. 1997.

———. *Feu*. Montreal: Les Éditions des Intouchables, 2001.

———. www.zacharyrichard.com. Accessed May 10, 2013.

St. Germain, Sheryl. *Let It Be a Dark Roux: New and Selected Poems*. Pittsburgh: Autumn House, 2007.

Shapiro, Norman, trans. *Creole Echoes: The Francophone Poetry of Nineteenth-Century Louisiana*. Introduction and notes by M. Lynn Weiss. Urbana-Champaign: University of Illinois Press, 2004.

The Spirit of a Culture: Cane River Creoles. Dir. Bill Rodman. Louisiana Public Broadcasting, 2005. DVD.

Tregle, Joseph, Jr. "Creoles and Americans." *Creole New Orleans: Race and Americanization*. Ed. Arnold R. Hirsch and Joseph Logsdon. Baton Rouge: Louisiana State University Press, 1992. 131–85.

Watson, Cedric. www.cedricwatson.com. Accessed February 2, 2014.

Weiss, M. Lynn. "Introduction." *The Jew of Seville* [*Diégarias*]. Trans. Norman R. Shapiro. Urbana and Chicago: University of Illinois Press, 2002.

Neither Crow nor Sparrow
Teaching Intersectionality in Chay Yew's Porcelain

C. Winter Han

As bell hooks noted in her now seminal work, *Feminist Theory: From Margin to Center,* feminist of color in the late 1960s and early 1970s began challenging the assumption that gender was "the" primary factor determining the fate of all women. Instead, these scholars and activists realized that the narratives about "women's experiences" based on the lived realities of white, middle-class women, often failed to capture the realities they confronted in their everyday lives, particularly as they related to their experiences as people who are simultaneously gendered and raced. Following this earlier lead, scholars such as Kimberlé Crenshaw, who coined the term "intersectionality theory" in 1989, Angela Davis, and Patricia Hill Collins began calling for examining the ways that various social positions, such as race and sex, intersect in ways to create and maintain subordination that was greater than simply the sum of their parts. Following its early introduction as a way of exploring the lives of black women, intersectional analysis has been broaden to include ways that multiple different social positions and social identities have come to influence and impact the lives of those who occupy these positions, including people who are raced, gendered, and (homo)sexualized. Yet, despite this growing recognition of the importance of examining intersectionality, most undergraduate courses on subaltern groups tend to treat differences as being additive rather than multiplicative. That is, courses on "diversity" focus on race, gender, sexuality, (dis)ability, etc. as independent weekly topics (or chapters in textbooks) as if these were discreet categories that exert independent influences on people's lives, often leading students to mistakenly believe that people who are multiply positioned, such as gay Asian men, experience "racism" in the same ways that straight Asian Americans, both men and women, experience it and homophobia in the same ways that gay white people, again men and women, experience it. Because this approach fails to capture the true impact of the interlocking matrix of oppression based on multiple categories which would help students better understand that there are multiple ways that racism, sexism, homophobia, classism, etc. can be experienced, there is an urgent need for intersectional approaches to teaching race, gender, sexuality, class, (dis)ability, etc. that would better reflect the true experiences of people who possess multiple marginal identities.

Experiences of Gay Asian Men

In the introduction to the now seminal collection, *Asian American Sexualities: Dimensions of the Gay and Lesbian Experiences*, Russell Leong notes that:

> In the United States, the myth of Asian Americans as a homogeneous, heterosexual "model minority" population since the 1960s has worked against exploration into the varied nature of our sexual drives and gendered diversity [3].

According to Leong, the "model minority" myth that constructs all Asian Americans as hard working, studious, and *family oriented*, precludes the idea that Asian Americans can be both gay and Asian. Given these tendencies, gay Asian men and women have been largely absent from the literature by, and about, Asian American communities of the early and mid-twentieth century that attempted to collectively define and construct a "coherent, unified Asian American identity" that centered on migration, family separation, and eventual reunification, and that has largely defined the experiences of early Asian immigrants to the United States (Diehl 150). This unacknowledged centrality of heterosexuality in Asian American literature is evident from even the most rudimentary glance at what has come to be seen as the canons of the genre. This particular canon often places family, and the unspoken heterosexuality that drives narratives about family relations, at the center, thus moving the possibilities of a different type of sexual expression to the margins.

Complicating the matter further has been the tendency to view "gay" as being equated with "white," and to understand "gay America" as being composed largely of middle and upper-class white men and women (Bérubé). In fact, "gay" and "people of color" are often perceived, by the majority of people in both the gay community and the Asian community (as well as other communities of color), as being mutually exclusive.

While more recent scholarship on Asian Americans has promoted the "diversity" found within that category, this "diversity" has largely focused on geographies of origin rather than on more nuanced categories such as sexuality. Thus, gay Asian men and women continue to remain largely invisible (Takagi). Given the invisibility of gay men and women in the larger narrative of "Asian America," Song Cho states:

> The pain of being a gay Asian, however, is not just the pain of direct discrimination but the pain of being negated again and again by a culture that doesn't acknowledge my presence.... Not only did I have to deal with the question of sexual invisibility as a gay man, there was also the issue of racial invisibility [2].

This sentiment, that gay Asian American men and women view themselves as on the margins of both communities, was preluded earlier by Dana Takagi. Caught in the margins of both race and sexuality, gay Asian men have been lost in the shuffle of both the "gay" movement (as have other gays and lesbians of color) and the "Asian" movement. As a step-child to both communities, gay Asian men (as well as women and other gays and lesbians of color), have been told to refrain from muddling the primary goal by interjecting race into sexuality or sexuality into race. Not surprisingly, gay Asian men often feel that they are invisible in both the Asian American community and the mainstream gay community (Chan). For example, in searching for a gay Asian identity, Eric Reyes (85) asks exactly where it is that we should be searching, "the Eurocentric and heterosexual male-dominated America, the white gay male-centered Queer America, the marginalized People of Color (POC) America, or our often-romanticized Asian America?" In fact, for many gay Asian men, "to be gay and Asian is at most times a contradiction" (Lee 13).

Given this very peculiar heteronormative history of Asian American literature as described above, there is a critical need to expand the definition of "Asian America" by exploring and examining more current literary text that work to expand the boundaries of what it means to be a member of this group. More importantly, the contradictions found in what it means to be "Asian American," what it means to belong to this category, and how "being" Asian American influences, and influence, other ways of being is in dire need of exploration. These questions of belonging and not belonging, the contradictions of race and sexuality, of identities and dis-identities, are at the center of Chay Yew's critically acclaimed play *Porcelain*. In addressing these questions, *Porcelain* challenges the very notion of "Asian American" by dismantling the neat and tidy categorization of Asian Americans as the "model minority," deeply rooted in "traditional" family values, restrained sexual desires, and quiet existences.

Background

Written as a movie script as part of Yew's graduate work at Boston University, the film was never produced as few students on campus were willing, or desired, to audition for the movie due to its gay content and the controversial story line. It wasn't until 1992 when Yew re-adapted it as a five chair voice play during his tenure as resident playwright at Mu-Lan Theatre, a London-based Asian theatre company, that Porcelain found an audience.

First staged at the Etcetera Theatre Club on May 12, 1992, the play transferred to the Royal Court Theatre Upstairs on August 4, eventually winning the London Fringe Award for best play in the same year. Since its first production, Porcelain has been produced in regional theaters throughout the United States and has been published in the *Performing Arts Journal* in 1994, reprinted in *Staging Gay Lives*, an anthology of contemporary gay dramas edited by John M. Clum published by Westview Press, and as its own Grove Press edition in 1997 (along with Yew's play *A Language of Their Own* which premiered at the Celebration Theater in Los Angeles on May 6, 1994). As Health Diehl (152) noted, "that Yew has had two of his plays published in their own editions places him among the ranks of such world-renowned Asian American playwrights as Frank Chin and David Henry Hwang."

Porcelain traces the story of John "Lone" Lee, a nineteen-year-old Asian man who meets a self-described "straight" man, William Hope, in a London public toilet and eventually murders him after falling in love with, then being discarded by, the older white man. In summarizing the play for his collection, Clum wrote:

> As a gay man, [John Lee] is alienated from the culture and family into which he was born. As an Asian man in London, he feels ignored, rejected. In the gay bars and clubs, he is invisible. Occasionally, for a moment, sex in the toilet gives him a sense of belonging, even love. For a few weeks, William Hope offers Lee what he has always wanted, but for Hope, the toilets are a place to get sex without having to admit to himself or anyone else that he is gay.... When the relationship starts to become more than physical, to move toward the love John Lee seeks, Hope panics, tries brutally to move the relationship back to a merely physical one, and, when that isn't possible, leaves John and returns to furtive, safe encounters in the toilet. John's anger and desperation at Hope's rejection take him beyond rational behavior into the realm of operatic passion [356].

While Yew has stated that the play is "not about racism. Nor is it about homosexuality and homophobia or about toilet sex. [And that he] didn't expect to delve into all these issues and answer them. It's really about loving and relationship. It's also about being different, which is a universal theme"

(McCulloh n.p.), the play nonetheless exquisitely traces racism in the gay community and homophobia in Asian American communities, using public toilet sex as the medium by which these themes are explored. Yet as Yew has noted, the play is, in fact, mostly about difference. Not simply the difference between Asian and white, or gay and straight, but of differences within these categories. Specifically, while Asian American writers (as well as other writers of color) are "saddled with the added responsibilities of representativeness, authenticity, and universality" of their experiences (Diehl 150), *Porcelain* demonstrates the impossibility of constructing an "authentic" or a "universal" experience where one simply does not exist. Rather, *Porcelain* demonstrates how differences between and within those categories that are sometimes viewed as being constructed out of universal and shared experiences manifest themselves. Doing so, it challenges the very notion of the existence of a "universal" experience based on race, sexuality, or any other "shared" identity and highlights the need to examine racial and sexual experiences within the larger social context and, more importantly, the need to examine these experiences using an intersectional lens.

Contextualizing Porcelain

A starting point to discussing *Porcelain* begins with placing the play within both historic and contemporary context. Of particular note is the way that Asian men, both gay and straight, have been historically constructed in the Western imagination through the orientalizing discourse of domination. As Edward Said noted, "the Orient was almost a European invention and had been since antiquity a place of romance, exotic beings, haunting memories and landscapes, remarkable experiences" (11). These are all images that happen to be female evocations in the Western mind, and indeed the association between the Orient and the feminine can be traced back to ancient times. The West's view of itself as the embodiment of the male principle was further justified by, and undoubtedly served to justify, Europe's subordination of much of Asia starting in the eighteenth century: its "masculine thrust" upon the continent.

Thus, for Asian men, the discourse of domination focused largely on the "feminine" East opposed to the "masculine" West. Historic projects that have hindered Asian American family formations and excluded Asian men from the "masculinized" labor market of the "West," have simultaneously produced an image of Asian men that has both racial and gendered implications. Therefore, Asian American male identity has always been and continues to be, "produced, stabilized, and secured through mechanisms of gendering" (Eng 16). Moreover, popular media portrayals further emasculated Asian and Asian American men until they "[were] at their best, effeminate closet queens like Charlie Chan and, at their worst, [were] homosexual menaces like Fu Manchu" (Chan et al. xiii).

Given this tendency to view Asian men through the prism of femininity, cultural critic David L. Eng notes that the main character, Song Liling, in the critically acclaimed play *M. Butterfly* by David Henry Hwang, is able to explain his ability to fool a French diplomat, Rene Gallimard, into believing that he was a woman for nearly two decades not on his mastery of deception but on the diplomat's inability to see him as anything other than a woman. In fact, in Hwang's play, when Song Liling is asked how it was that he managed to maintain this deception for decades, he responds: "The West thinks of itself as masculine, big guns, big industry, big money, so the East is feminine, weak, delicate, poor ... I am an Oriental. And being an Oriental, I could never be completely a man" (83).

If we consider the way that mainstream media has catapulted the image of effeminate Asian men into the national consciousness, this explanation does not seem far-fetched.

While being portrayed as meek asexual houseboys or as sexual deviants (Hamamoto), Asian men have also been portrayed as being more "traditional" and "conservative" when it comes to sex. While the stereotypes of Asian men being sexual deviants and sexual conservatives may seem contradictory, they both serve the purpose of emasculating Asian men in a process that Eng calls "racial castration." According to Fung, this desexualization of Asian men helps neutralize concerns regarding a rapidly reproducing racial class and thus eases the mainstream's fear of a growing "yellow peril," eager to dominate western locations. If Asian men are not "true" men, capable of sexuality—thus, sexual reproduction—they become less threatening to western minds.

Even when presented as masculine "heroes" by the dominant culture, Asian men continue to be denied sexual prowess. For example, in the blockbuster movie, *Romeo Is Dying*, the main "hero" of the film, played by Jet Li, makes no romantic connection with the female lead. When compared to the other films in the action movie genre using the "damsel in distress" formula, the omission of a sexual relationship (implied or explicit) between the male "hero" and the female lead is striking. On a similar thread, the popularity of Jackie Chan in a string of American main-stream films has yet to land him a girl. Instead, his role seems to be limited to playing the comedic sidekick to a male lead who does get the girl (*Shanghai Noon*) or to a female lead who is not the least bit interested in him romantically (*The Tuxedo*). Also, it is important to note that the roots of their "heroic" acts are based on "ancient" and "mysterious" Eastern ways that continue to shroud Asian men under the veiled cloak of orientalism. As such, "Asian men are not able to fulfill their role as 'real men' because they are 'weak,' 'passive,' and 'eunuch-like'" (Chen 68).

At the root of the process that has constructed Asian men as a gendered body lie various historical processes that have shaped what it means to be an Asian man in the white imagination. Far from a recent phenomenon, the gendering of Asian men has a long history in Western narratives. As Joseph Boone discusses, early European writings about the "orient" were filled with the sexual politics of colonialization that marked "oriental" men as feminine while at the same time constructing European men as masculine. As Boone puts it:

> For many Western men the act of exploring, writing about, and theorizing an eroticized Near and Middle East is coterminous with unlocking a Pandora's box of phantasmic homoerotic desire, desire whose propensity to spread without check threatens to contaminate, indeed to reorient, the heterosexual "essence" of occidental male subjectivity [50].

As such, the gendering of "oriental" men was used to disguise western homoerotic desires within the confines of occidental heterosexuality. As the logic goes, if the desired male "oriental" body was not really a male body, then the homoerotic desires of western travelers were not really homosexual. While Boone's analysis is limited to narratives about the Near and Middle East, the same orientalizing narratives were often used to describe Asian men from both East and South East Asia.

For gay Asian men, these narratives of domination, subordination, and otherness are reflected intimately in their sexual lives. For example, in his essay "China doll," Tony Ayres discusses his sense of being outside the gay mainstream due to his Chinese ethnicity. In addition to discussing the overt forms of racism, such as gay classified ads that specifically state, "no fats, no femmes, no Asians," and being told by other gay men that they are "not into Asians," Ayres describes some of the more subtle forms of racism, such as that of "rice queens" who desire Asian men purely for their exotic eroticism. What rice queens are often attracted to in Asian men is an idealized notion of a passive, docile, submissive, in short, a feminized lover, eager to please his virile white man.

John's personal experiences in the gay community are thus representative of biographical accounts like those of Ayres. For example, John speaks of being marginalized at gay bars where:

> Everyone there looks intimidating, dressed to the nines. Most of them talk among themselves, have a good time, laughing and drinking with their perfect smiles and perfect hair. And I spend the whole night standing alone in

a dark corner.... And waiting for someone to say something to me. Something nice. Say anything to me. Perhaps it's just that I'm Oriental [57].

Clearly, John understands his marginalized status within the gay community. Especially that "white guys aren't into Orientals." In this world, John finds it difficult to "belong." It is this "belonging" that he seeks as he explains that, "sometimes, [he] wishes that [he] was white." It is this desire for belonging that leads John to engage in anonymous sex at public toilets. "I hate the toilets," he explains, but "there's people there who want [him]. Even for a moment." And that feeling of being wanted, even for a moment, lead John to believe that he belongs, and to think that "perhaps all these moments will amount to something, someone who will, like [him], love [him]." Being rejected at mainstream gay outlets, John seeks the underground sphere of anonymous toilet sex seeking love, which he believes will mark him as belonging.

The way that Asian men have been constructed as being feminine and submissive, by default, white men have been constructed as masculine and dominant, set the stage, so to speak, for the relationship between John and William. First, the relationship between John and William must be understood within the contemporary context of gay racialized desires. In his essay, China Dolls, Tony Ayres notes: "The sexually marginalized Asian man who has grown up in the West or is western in his thinking is often invisible in his own fantasies. [Their] sexual daydreams are populated by handsome Caucasian men with lean, hard Caucasian bodies" (91).

In fact, "the unsatisfying script of sexual submission of Asians to whites is particularly central" to gay Asian American writings (Murray 111). For John, William represents all that he desires. Whereas John is a quiet, courteous student headed to Cambridge University, John is an older, white man with a more "masculine" occupation of a builder who likes football, who self-identifies as heterosexual. More importantly, while John himself is Asian, a fact he sometimes wishes were not true, William is white. In this way, William not only represents all that John wants, but also all that John wants to be.

For William, John represents a possibility of engaging in a romantic relationship (rather than simply a sexual relationship) with a man while not fully disrupting his self-conception as a straight man. Early in their relationship, William shares with John that he likes music from Puccini's opera, an allusion to *Madama Butterfly*, his favorite, a production deeply rooted in colonial images of the submissive and feminine "East" and the dominant and masculine "West." First introduced in 1898 in a short story written by John Luther Long published in the *American Century Magazine*, given theatrical life in 1900 through a play produced by Long that premiered in New York

City, brought to prominence in 1904 by Puccini in his now widely recognized opera, *Madama Butterfly*, and given a contemporary twist in the musical production, *Miss Saigon*, the butterfly mythology follows the typical trope of a submissive Asian woman who falls uncontrollably in love with a white man. Not surprisingly, of course, these Asian butterflies always meet a tragic end as they make the ultimate sacrifice for their white lovers.

In his award winning play, *M. Butterfly*, a retelling of the butterfly mythology, David Henry Hwang noted that white men fail to see Asian men as "men" precisely because "oriental" men are not men in their world view. Much like Gallimard, William's initial and uncharacteristic pursuit of John outside of the tea room trade can be attributed to his failure to see John as a "real" man. Much like the way Gallimard failed to see Song Liling as a man, William's perception of John as not "truly" being a man leads him to uncharacteristically pursue a romantic relationship with the younger "oriental" man despite his own self-proclaimed "straight" sexual identity. In John, William finds a way to engage in his homoerotic desires while still being able to maintain a heterosexual identity precisely because John is not "truly" a man. In describing John, William notes that "he looked so, what's the word? Fragile? Yeah, fragile." In William's eyes, John is "not [his] type, generally" but the fragility that he sees in John's face leads him to break his normal routine habit of using the toilets to "just get off" and pursue, in a very limited way, a relationship with him. As their relationship progresses, William becomes more aggressive and descriptions of their sexual escapades takes on a decidedly gendered script as William forces himself on John, and sexual acts become one of domination and subjugation rather than one of mutual pleasure. William takes what he wants without regard to John's needs or desires, and seems almost to relish in his ability to physically and emotionally dominate his Asian lover.

Given the way that the relationship starts, develops, and ends, it provides a significant pedagogical opportunity to discuss a number of different thematic issues, including race, racism, gender, gendered representations, sexuality, and sexual domination along a number of different levels as discussed below.

Teaching Difference and Intersectionality

Given Yew's earlier professional experiences, it's not surprising that representations of difference take a central position in his various works, with *Porcelain* being no exception. For example, his first play, *As If He Hears*, which dealt with issues of AIDS and homosexuality, was banned in his native Singapore after being deemed "not true to Singapore values" (Drukman 58). More importantly, Yew's narratives of difference is not just between the more widely understood categories of race and sexuality, but difference within these categories, speaking to the ways that identities are instersectional. It is the way that these differences are presented in the play that allows for an analysis and discussion surrounding race, racism, gender, gendered representations, sexuality, and sexual domination along a number of different levels as previously noted. In *Porcelain*, difference is presented in multiple ways. While there are the obvious differences between John and William along several dimensions such as age, class, nativity, race, and class, it is the differences within the obvious categories that are truly interesting to note. That is, John and William are different despite sharing the same identity of "men who have sex with men" and John and his father are different despite sharing the same identity of "Asian." More importantly, these differences interact and intersect with each other in a number of interesting, and contradictory, ways. In class, students are asked to discuss how John is different from his father and from William. Students usually answer that John is different from his father because of his sexuality and that he is different from William because of his race. Then students can be asked how he is similar to his father and to William. Predictably, they answer that he is similar to his father in race and similar to William in sexuality. The intersectional approach is highlighted when students are asked who John is "more" similar to, his father or to William. The third question leads to a more robust discussion as students explore the relative importance of race or sexuality on the way John sees himself and his relationship with his father and with William. During this discussion, students come to see that John is both similar and different from his father and William and the more simple answer that he is similar to either his father of William based on the perceived discreet categories of race and sexuality become more complex when combined. Because of John's sexuality and race, he is both similar and different from both his father and William but he wouldn't be similar or different from either of the other men if it were not for both his sexuality and race, which students find difficult to unravel.

Given the ways that race, gender, sexuality, class, and nativity collide in the play, *Porcelain* is particularly useful in exploring intersectional identities. Within the larger social imagination, categories of race, gender, sexuality, class, nativity, etc. are often perceived and discussed as if they were mutually exclusive and discrete. Even more problematic is the tendency of classes that teach race, gender, sexuality, and class in a "topic" method where one "topic" is discussed one week followed by another topic the next as if they were discrete categories of analysis that can be examined in isolation from one another. However, intersectional theory argues that these categories, rather than distinct, are experienced simultaneously by those who inhabit multiple "categories" (Crenshaw). Rather than attempt to examine the lived experiences of marginalized groups through the lens of discrete, singular differences, intersectional analysis promotes the need to examine their experiences through an examination of the interlocking systems of oppression (Collins) in which members of subaltern groups are socially located. That is, members of subaltern groups don't simply experience racism, sexism, homophobia, etc. as additive systems of oppression where they experience these types of oppression individually, one at a time, but rather they are experienced simultaneously and the matrix of domination that these systems collectively create influences how each is felt. In the case of John Lee, he does not experience "racism" in the same way that straight Asian American men might experience it, he does not experience "homophobia" in the same way that a gay white man might experience it, but experiences being gay and Asian, a differently racialized and sexualized experience precisely because his race influences how his sexuality is experienced and vice versa. More importantly, how one comes to see themselves, and their place in the larger society, is simultaneously influenced by the "mutually constitutive relations among social identities" and the multiple social positions that individuals possess and occupy (Shields 301). To explore these questions, students are asked to discuss what factors may have influenced John's actions. Routinely, some students answer that it was his sexuality, others answer that it was his race. The follow up question is then why neither William nor John's father is presented as possessing the same types of angst as John. Exploring this question, students come to see how both John's race and sexuality intersect to create a unique experience that cannot simply be attributed to his race or his sexuality. More importantly for the discussion of intersectionality, they come to understand that John's experiences as a gay Asian man is greater than the sum of his experiences as a gay man or an Asian man. That is, students come to see that neither his race or his sexuality alone was enough for John to feel the angst he feels in the play. Yet when combined, John's experience as a gay Asian man leads to an experience that is "greater than" the sum of being an Asian man or a gay man.

As covered in the previous paragraphs, there are multiple ways to conceptualize and present an interactional analysis for class discussions. At the same time, Jones and Wijeyesinghe outline what they consider the primary goal in intersectional analysis in this way:

> An intersection framework complicates identity by highlighting the complexities of lived experiences when a person embodies multiple identities

simultaneously that interact and influence each other. These identities are in turn understood in relation to particular and evolving social and political context. Further, complicating identity draws attention to the significant diversity within groups and resists essentializing these groups such that this diversity is collapsed into one category [13].

In examining *Porcelain*, particularly the central character John, it is important to consider the way that his multiple identities come to interact and influence each other. As a gay Asian man living in a Western country, he is both a racial and sexual minority. But at the same time, because he is both a racial and sexual minority, he is not fully a part of a racial or sexual community. As Nancy Naples has pointed out, "the most powerful approaches to intersectionality also includes attention to the ways in which these interactions produce contradictions and tensions" (567). Clearly, John offers a number of ways that such tensions and contradictions can be examined. Fitting the "model minority" stereotype, John is headed to Cambridge University, one of the best university in the United Kingdom. Yet John's sexuality contradicts with this "model minority" image that he publicly performs and his private clandestine sexual behaviors are a direct contradiction of the stereotype of Asian Americans being sexually modest. Not surprisingly, when his crime is discovered, it is this contradiction in his sexual identity that leads to tensions between John and his father. Upon discovery, John is disowned by his father who vehemently shouts, "I have no son. Son is dead. Dead to me…. My son is no homo." Here, it is obvious that Mr. Lee's rejection of John as a son is rooted not in the murder but on John's homosexuality which does not "fit" with the way that Mr. Lee sees what it means to be Asian. One method of examining this contradiction is provided below on the discussion about power.

Reflections on Power

A central tenet of intersectionality theory is the importance of power relationships based on the way that individuals are located in the larger social structure. It is important to examine how "power" is presented in *Porcelain*, particularly examining who has power and the implication that the lack of power has on differently positioned individuals. To explore how power works along racial and sexual dimensions, students are asked to discuss how the relationship between John and William progresses. Despite John's higher socio-economic position (or at least the potential for it), William holds the power in their relationship based on his race. John's sexuality places him within the larger social structure where race is a more valued commodity than socio-economic status. It is race, particularly whiteness, that determines desirability in the gay community. The lack of whiteness places John in the inferior position to William. As Peter Jackson noted:

> When desirability is linked with race, and when certain races are ascribed a greater erotic interest than others, then to be a member of an "unsexy" ethnic group is to be equated with an inferior form of existence. Within the dominant Caucasian-focused gay sexual ideology, Asian homosexual men are simply "not worth a fuck" [184].

The differences in power that William and John bring to their relationship are obvious. As noted above, William grows increasingly aggressive as the relationship progresses while John becomes progressively more submissive. It is John who waits for William as he disregards John's feelings and emotions, it is William who decides when the relationship will begin and end, and it is William who dictates the nature of not only their sexual relationship but their sexual acts as well. In the end, William discards John because he is simply "not worth a fuck." This particular discussion leads students to challenge existing notions about race and wealth. Discussing the ways that "whiteness" buys power and privilege for William, students often discuss other avenues, such as education, where programs that don't specifically address race fall short.

Differences in power relationships can be seen in the relationship between John and his father as well. When asked about his son, Mr. Lee vehemently states that he does not have a son, erasing John from existence. Within the framework of the Asian diasporic experience, John has failed to meet expectations. More importantly, it is these expectations that force John into the closet of anonymous toilet sex.

At the same time, a discussion centered on how power is challenged and negotiated is also important for an intersectional analysis. A number of different passages from *Porcelain* can be utilized for class discussions about the ways that members of subaltern groups challenge the larger power structure. As January Lim (152) noted, the play's depiction of an Asian man committing a homicide "goes against the dominant culture's racial stereotypes of the 'model minority'" to which John is assigned. More importantly, the homicide works as a "perverse figure of resistance and offers an ongoing process of rethinking the power politics of race and sex in interracial relationships." In shooting William, John not only breaks from the expected cultural norms that has, up to that point, dictated his life, but also rejects the social, and stereotypically expected, [what?] behaviors attributed to Asian men. Rather than accept the fate of the butterfly, John becomes Pinkerton, the figure of power in the original Puccini opera by not only killing William but by "possessing" him, albeit in a macabre way. In the end, John states that, "He'll never be gone. Now I have him where I want him ... I've finally got Will all to myself now." Rather than accept his fate as the rejected and discarded "oriental lover" as butterfly had done, John rejects that fate and takes Will for himself. In the end, it is William who pays the ultimate price for stepping outside the boundaries of "normative" sexual behavior.

Similarly, the act of homicide is an indication of John's rejection of the expected diasporic Asian cultural norms that characterizes Asian immigrant lives. Lim (152) notes that this act, "represents radical, shocking behavior, unexpected from one who seeks social approval from the Asian diasporic community and the state." More importantly, his actions, when read as a rejection of the closet, can be read as a rejection of diasporic Asian cultural norms that demand a hidden (homo)sexuality in favor of group cohesion and maintenance of a public "face." Students often have a difficult time making the connection between John's actions and how these actions challenge larger beliefs about what it means to be Asian and how John's actions demonstrate that intersectional identities lead to contradictions and tensions as Naples noted. That is, they see John's actions as stemming from his "failure" to meet expectations rather than to any conscious act on John's part to challenge these norms and don't see that John's identity as gay and Asian leads to tensions between what it means to be "Asian" and what it means to be "gay."

One method of getting students to understand this perspective is to have students discuss why John's actions may have been "unexpected." Students often answer with stereotypical characteristics that hark back to the model minority myth, such as his future plans to enroll at a prestigious university. Then students are asked to examine why John's murder of William is "unexpected" but his plans to enroll at Cambridge is not "unexpected." I specifically ask students, "Wouldn't it be just as surprising to find out that a murdered was a Cambridge student?" When phrased that way, students come to see what qualities about John were expected and what qualities were not and which of his identities contradict with the other. This forces students to challenge their own assumptions about Asian Americans and realize that they do, in fact, hold a master narrative about how Asians "should be" and how John's sexuality contradicts this master narrative and creates tensions for John.

Suggested Assignments

To better explore the concepts discussed, there are a number of potential assignments that may help students examine their own lives as well as the lives of others. A few potential paper topics are presented below:

1. Students can learn to examine the ways that identities come to have "meaning" (that is, how are they socially constructed within the larger social narrative) in our society and how those meanings influence the way that these identities are experienced by those who make these identity claims by exploring various media products (such as films, magazine articles, television shows, etc.). For this potential assignment, students should be encouraged to critically evaluate how people who possess various identities are presented by various media products and how those representations influence the way that members of these groups come to be seen.
2. Another potential assignment involves students exploring intersectional identities. For this assignment, students should be encouraged to examine a media product that presents "diverse" members of a given social category (such as a movie with a black cast that includes both straight and gay characters or a movie about "gay" people with a multi-racial cast). Using such a media product, students should be encouraged to note the ways that different characters, who share one similar social category, are presented differently based on another social category.
3. Students can also be encouraged to explore their own social identities and the way that the different social identities they possess influence and impact each other. In this assignment, students can be asked to discuss what may be "expected" of them based on an identity they possess and explore how those expectations are either contradicted or strengthened by other identities. In this assignment, the goal is not simply to explore if their identities are contradictory but also how one identity comes to dominate the narrative surrounding another. For example, the experience of being a "straight man" may reinforce what it means to be "Asian," thus shedding light on how "Asian American" identity is largely constructed around a heteronormative and/or masculine "norm."

Conclusion

In *Porcelain*, Yew uses a story of the crow and the sparrows to demonstrate how identities are instersectional. Wishing to learn the sparrows' songs, a crow joins the sparrows, only to discover that "it will never truly belong with them." Finding his way back to the other crows, where he believes he "truly" belongs. While originally welcoming of the returning crow, the crow discovers that "the other crows found the crow distant. Different. Strange. Peculiar. Queer. They begin to avoid the crow [and] the crow was never more alone." Eventually, the crow comes to believe that it doesn't belong with the crows or the sparrows, different from both. As Richard Fung points out, for gay Asian Americans, their "families and [their] ethnic communities are a rare source of affirmation in a racist society" (1996 184). But their sexuality prevents them from feeling as if they truly belong. Yet the racism in the gay community leads them to believe that they do not belong their either. When confronted with a hostile gay community, many gay Asian men would be inclined not to risk losing that source of affirmation, finding it easier to remain in the closet (Chan). John's race, to some extent, traps him in the closet, leading him to search for love in a public toilet where his "true" identity can be better hidden through anonymous sex rather than an open declaration of his sexuality.

The central strength of Chay Yew's *Porcelain* is that the play offers a number of different pedagogical opportunities for examining intersectional identities as well as examining how such identities are socially constructed. Even in the classroom, race, gender, sexuality, class, etc. are often presented and discussed as if they were discrete categories that are inherent in the people who occupy these identities. Yet the lived experiences of people who encompass multiple different identities challenge the beliefs that there are universal and shared experiences among members of these groups. Also, the history of the way these identities are constructed challenges the very notion that there is a "natural" way of "being." Instead, these identities should be understood as having been, and continue to be, constructed in a complex social context. More importantly, the complex combinations of these identities interact in a way that is often contradictory. *Porcelain* allows for a more critical evaluation into the ways that identities are socially constructed, the ways that multiple identities interact and influence each other, and the implications that embodying multiple different identities has on individual lives.

Works Cited

Ayres, Tony. "China Doll: The Experience of Being a Gay Chinese Australian." *Journal of Homosexuality* 36 (1999): 87–97.

Berube, Allan. "How Gay Stays White and What Kind of White It Stays." *The Making and Unmaking of Whiteness*. Eds. Birgit Brander Rasmussen, Eric Klinenberg, Irene Nexica, and Matt Wray. Durham: Duke University Press, 2001. 234–265.

Boone, Joseph. "Vacation Cruises; or, the Homoerotics of Orientalism." *Post-Colonia Queer*. Ed. John C. Hawley. Albany, NY: State University of New York Press, 2001. 43–78.

Chan, Connie. "Issues of Identity Development Among Asian American Lesbians and Gay Men." *Journal of Counseling & Development* 16 (1989): 16–20.

Chin, Frank, Jeffrey P. Chan, Lawson R. Inada, and Shawn Wong (Eds.). *The Big Aiiieeeee! An Anthology of Chinese American and Japanese American Literature*. New York: Meridian, 1991.
Chen, Ciung H. "Feminization of Asian (American) Men in the U.S. Mass Media: An Analysis of The Ballad of Little Jo." *Journal of Communication Inquiry* 20 (1996):57–71.
Cho, Song. *Rice: Explorations into Gay Asian Culture and Politics*. Toronto: Queer, 1998.
Clum, John M. *Staging Gay Lives: An Anthology of Contemporary Gay Theater*. Boulder, CO: Westview, 1996.
Collins, Patricia Hill. *Black Feminist Thought: Knowledge, Consciousness, and Politics of Empowerment*. New York: Routledge, 1991.
Crenshaw, Kimberlé. "Demarginalizing the Intersection of Race and Sex: A Black Feminist Critique of Antidiscrimination Doctrine, Feminist Theory and Antiracist Politics." *University of Chicago Legal Forum* (1989): 139–168.
Diehl, Heath A. "Beyond the Silk Road: Staging a Queer Asian America in Chay Yew's Porcelain." *Studies in the Literary Imagination* 37 (2004): 149–167.
Drukman, Steven. "Chay Yew: The Importance of Being Verbal." *American Theater* November (1995): 58–60.
Eng, David. *Racial Castration: Managing Masculinity in Asian America*. Durham: Duke University Press, 2001.
Fung, Richard. "Looking for My Penis." *Asian American Sexualities*. Ed. Russell Leong. New York: Routledge, 1996. 181–198.
Hamamotoa, Darrell. *Monitored Peril: Asian Americans and the Politics of TV Representation*. Minneapolis: University of Minnesota Press, 1994.
hooks, bell. *Feminist Theory: From Margin to Center*. Cambridge, MA: South End, 1984.
Hwang, David. *M. Butterfly*. New York: Plume, 1986.
Jackson, Peter. "That's what rice queens study! White Gay Desire and Representing Asian Homosexualities." *Journal of Australian Studies* 65 (2000): 181–188.
Jones, Susan R., and Charmaine L. Wijeyesinghe. "The Promises and Challenges of Teaching from an Intersectional Perspective." *New Directions for Teaching and Learning* 125 (2011): 11–20.
Lee, Tom. "The Gay Asian American Male: Striving to Find an Identity." *Asian Week* June 22 (2000).
Leong, Russell. "Home Bodies and the Body Politic." *Asian American Sexualities*. Ed. Russell Leong. New York: Routledge, 1996. 1–20.
Lim, January. "Father Knows Best: Reading Sexuality in Ang Lee's Wedding Banquet and Chay Yew's Porcelain." *Reading Chinese Transnationalisms*. Eds. Maria N. Ng and Philip Holden. Hong Kong: Hong Kong University Press, 2006. 143–160.
McCulloh, T. H. "Chay Yew Mines Dark Side of Asian Life in Porcelain." *Los Angeles Times* January 10, 1993.
Murry, Stephen O. "Representations of Desire in Some Recent Gay Asian American Writings." *Journal of Homosexuality* 45 (2003): 111–142.
Naples, Nancy A. "Teaching Intersectionality Intersectionally." *International Feminist Journal of Politics* 11 (2009): 566–577.
Reyes, Eric. "Strategies for Queer Asian and Pacific Islander Spaces." *Asian American Sexualities*. Ed. Russell Leong. New York: Routledge, 1996. 85–90.
Said, Edward. *Orientalism*. New York: Vintage, 1978.
Shields, Stephanie A. "Gender: An Intersectionality Perspective." *Sex Roles* 59 (2008): 301–311.
Takagi, Dana. "Maiden Voyage." *Asian American Sexualities*. Ed. Russell Leong. New York: Routledge, 1996. 21–36.
Yew, Chay. *Two Plays: Porcelain and A Language of Their Own*. New York: Grove, 1997.

The Possibilities and Pitfalls in Teaching Sherman Alexie's *The Absolutely True Diary of a Part-Time Indian*

TEREZA M. SZEGHI

> What really gets me angry is that I write about [alcoholism], a lot, and people assume it's a stereotype. When anybody uses that word to describe alcoholism among Native Americans, as a stereotype, that's what really gets me angry. It's a disavowal of the truth. Alcoholism is *epidemic* among Native Americans and anybody who says otherwise is either drunk or they're lying or they're romantic fools, and so it's not the alcoholism itself that gets me angry, it's the denial that surrounds it.—Sherman Alexie, interview with Enrique Cerna, July 11, 2008

In March of 2007 Sherman Alexie addressed attendees of the Native American Literature Symposium at the Saginaw Chippewa Community Center in Mt. Pleasant, Michigan. Whereas other audiences I have seen him address included members of the local community, high school and college students, and a smattering of academics, this audience was comprised primarily of academic critics of American Indian literature. The first words Alexie spoke, as he gripped the podium, suggested that he had prepared a response to some of the dominant strains of negative criticism he has received from scholars and that he felt this was his moment to speak directly to his accusers. "I do *not* speak in stereotypes," Alexie asserted, with a hint of the anger referenced in the epigraph. He repeated this statement several times in staccato, each iteration separated by biographical details—memories of such traumas as the loss of family members to alcoholism, house fires, car accidents, and disease. In short, he performed the rejoinder he has offered frequently in interviews when confronted with the accusation that he harms American Indians by perpetuating stereotypes about them. Alexie has responded time and again by noting that his life experiences are not stereotypes; they are realities. The audience experienced Alexie's preface to his reading in stunned, or at least forbearing, silence.

In characteristic fashion, Alexie shifted smoothly into humor and moved back and forth between content regarding stark realities of colonization and American Indian life in the United States and comedic aspects of the same. He announced that he would be reading from his not yet released novel, *Flight*, and grabbed the book from the shelf within the podium. When the audience caught sight of the coveted book, they let out a collective gasp of anticipation—something Alexie clearly enjoyed and used as an occasion for another of his characteristic maneuvers: making fun of his audience. He hid and re-presented the book a couple more times, looking expectantly at the crowd for another audible response.

These two aspects of the reading, Alexie's refutation to charges of stereotyping and his relishing of his audience's hungry appreciation of his work, provide a snapshot of the critical conversation that has surrounded Alexie for over two decades. This conversation has been defined by praise for his formal skill—and, more specifically, his deftness in using and subverting literary conventions to communicate aspects of American Indian experience to a broad audience—alongside biting criticism regarding his representations of American Indians. It also points to the ambivalence many educators feel about assigning Alexie's books.

Students may not express their enthusiasm about Alexie's writing, humor, and worldview with a collective gasp upon spotting one of his novels, but instead do so with the disproportionate pace of their consumption of his pages and their animation during discussions of his work. Every time I assign Alexie's writing, whether in a first-year composition course, an American Indian literature course, or a survey of American Literature, students, on the whole, finish it well in advance of the deadline and arrive to class with more questions and discussion topics than time allows. As Tammy Wahpeconiah observes, such enthusiasm for Alexie's writing is no insignificant factor, particularly when you teach non-English majors (36). Further, I would add, the appeal Alexie's work has for students provokes them (with some nudging) to grapple with—rather than dismiss or otherwise gloss over—the complex issues he addresses regarding contemporary American Indian experiences as they are shaped by colonization and its legacies. Moreover, because Alexie is such a skilled writer, his work provides ample opportunities for developing essential analytical and critical thinking skills, along with other conceptual proficiencies.

The sketch I have just provided may sound like an English instructor's dream: a classroom full of prepared and enthusiastic students eager to look more closely at a text's formal features, thematic concerns, social justice interventions, etc. These are, indeed, some of the merits of assigning Alexie, and certainly among the reasons he frequents high school and university syllabi. However, this sketch would be neither complete nor accurate were I to conclude it here. The pedagogical challenges involved with teaching Alexie's work tend to surface once discussion ensues, as non–American Indian students are inclined to make sweeping claims about the hopelessness and alcoholism that plague Indian reservations—and about American Indians in general. Students from or heavily influenced by the dominant Euroamerican culture tend to lack exposure to American Indians outside of distortions perpetuated in Hollywood films and popular conceptions of the noble savage that saturate established U.S. mythologies.[1] Many students have internalized the myth of the Vanishing Indian and assume that American Indians died out with the horse and buggy. A smaller number of students, usually those who have lived in close proximity to or vacationed at or near a lucrative tribally owned casino, think that all American Indians are wealthy due to an influx of casino revenue. This backdrop of ignorance and misperception does not allow them a frame of reference against which to weigh or critically evaluate Alexie's representations of American Indians and their experiences. Moreover, because students generally love Alexie's writing and literary voice—his wit, his worldview, his invocations of popular culture, and his utilization of various formal literary techniques—they are quick to internalize his words and to do so uncritically. Particularly when teaching freshman, it is important to bear in mind that they tend to defer to external authorities and only gradually develop internal standards for evaluating information presented to them.[2]

My post-graduate school experiences with teaching Sherman Alexie's work have been at schools in which the Euroamerican student population comprises 83 percent to 86 percent of the whole and the American Indian population less than 1 percent. Consequently, the recommendations I offer in this essay and the statements I make regarding students' responses should be understood as particular to this teaching scenario.[3] I have found it useful, early in students' reading of American Indian literature, to ask them to complete an anonymous survey (see Appendix A) regarding their cultural backgrounds, prior exposure to and ideas about American Indian peoples and cultures, and their impressions of the novel thus far. The results of my most recent survey (a prior version of the appended version, administered in an honors composition course) are representative of student groups to whom I have assigned Alexie's work and illuminating in terms of the degree to which their prior expectations aligned with their impressions of the portrait of reservation life his 2007 graphic young adult novel, *The Absolutely True Diary of a Part-Time Indian* offers.[4]

All of the students in this class identified as "Caucasian" (though one co-identified as Cherokee). Most claimed little knowledge of American Indian cultures, and attributed the majority of what they did know to grade school or high school courses in which they learned of the mistreatment of American Indians—with Hollywood films serving as the second largest source of information and only a few students reporting any direct contact with American Indians. In the context of reading a novel that plays with the conception of being a "part-time Indian," it was particularly relevant and pedagogically useful to ask about their understanding of what it means to be an American Indian. A majority of students thought that having American Indian blood (many specified a 50 percent minimum) is necessary to identify as American Indian, while some cited living on a reservation as a necessary condition for self-identification, either in addition to or instead of blood quantum.

A recurrent theme in students' characterization of American Indian life today was connection to the land, arguably a function of the pervasive myth of the Ecological Indian. Many differentiated between reservation Indians (whom students associated with traditional dress and customs, poverty, and alcoholism) and assimilated Indians (those "catching up with modern society" who occupy a socioeconomic status between Euroamericans and reservation Indians). As to reservations themselves, students' impressions were mixed. Over half characterized reservations as land set aside for American Indians by the U.S. government, and about a quarter described the land as a space for commune-style living. A couple students emphasized that reservations are places where American Indians were forced to live in poor conditions, and only one described the reservation as land owned by a tribe, family, or individual of American Indian heritage. Students' prevailing conceptions of reservations from their reading of *Diary* likewise included descriptions of poverty, helplessness, alcoholism, inequality, and discrimination. One student wrote, "They are lazy because they believe nothing will ever go their way," while another remarked, "The people are like barbarians getting drunk and fighting all the time." However, all but one student, who was undecided and found the narrator biased, reported enjoying reading *Diary*.

These responses indicate that, on the whole, students in this class had little prior exposure to American Indian history, culture, and experience, and even less direct contact with American Indians. What ideas most of them had formed prior to reading *Diary* reflected common misunderstandings and generalizations about American Indians, perpetuated within many elementary and secondary educational settings and within popular culture. The survey results thus alerted me to the need both to provide important contextual information that would help students read *Diary* critically—rather than simply deferring to its portrait as representative, due to a combined deference to authority and a predisposition to see their prior impressions validated within the novel's pages—and to supplement the novel with multiple and divergent American Indian perspectives, as I detail below.

My interest in this article is not to litigate Sherman Alexie's guilt or innocence with respect to allegations of stereotyping but to address the responsibilities and opportunities educators have when assigning his work. This article takes as given Alexie's talent and the right of any author to draw from his/her own experience, as well as the fact that literature is more prone to be (mis)taken as representative of the author's entire cultural group by readers unfamiliar with that culture. I also take as given that, as educators, we have an enormous responsibility when it comes to the texts we assign. We not only must enable students to engage with them meaningfully relative to such common course outcomes as development of critical thinking, analytical, and writing skills; we also have a responsibility to assign a diverse range of readings to ensure, to our best ability, that students walk away from our courses with a better understanding of the cultures and perspectives such readings communicate.

My concern here is with the pedagogical possibilities and pitfalls *Diary* provides. With the aim of offering tools for teaching *Diary* responsibly (vis-à-vis American Indian communities and our students as citizens and ethical agents) and to maximum effect (vis-à-vis course outcomes) I will: identify the specific aspects of *Diary* that tend to provoke generalizations from students in order to assist educators in addressing and accounting for them; outline the potential gains of teaching the novel; offer classroom strategies for realizing these gains; and conclude with a brief discussion of how the pedagogical approach I offer for *Diary* pertains to the teaching of American Indian and multiethnic U.S. literature more generally, as well as to current pedagogical trends.

I have selected *Diary* as my focus because, since winning the National Book Award in Young Adult Literature in 2007, it has become a mainstay in high school and university classrooms across the country.[5] Further, this novel effectively showcases characteristic features of Alexie's oeuvre and thus provides occasions both for assessing what about Alexie's writing prompts students to make sweeping generalizations about American Indians and identifying why it is nonetheless valuable to assign it. I have taught *Diary* to groups of predominately Euroamerican students in first year college composition classes that I designed with the themes "coming of age across cultures" and "global perspectives on human rights." The novel is based on Alexie's own experiences growing up on the Spokane reservation and choosing to go to the primarily Euroamerican school just beyond the reservation borders.

Arnold or "Junior" Spirit, the novel's narrator and protagonist, discusses the impact of poverty, alcoholism, and internalized racism on the Spokane community and on his own identity. *Diary*'s humor, statements about the tensions between individual and collective identity, comments on the legacies of colonization (including multiple human rights violations on the Spokane reservation), and references to the awkwardness of emotion between teenage boys, led me to believe that the book would be ideal for these courses. Its hybrid form as a graphic novel that blends prose and cartoon illustrations also offers opportunities for developing students' abilities to analyze texts in multiple media as each uniquely and collaboratively creates meaning—which also can provide a relatively seamless transition to incorporating digital media for further context. Moreover, as a young adult novel, it is written in a manner that resonates particularly well with high school students, as well as students in their freshman and sophomore years. I therefore thought it would appeal to students in my composition classes while providing them insight into certain aspects of contemporary American Indian life. Though largely correct in my preliminary assessments of the novel's possibilities, I was disturbed by the generalizations and stereotypes about American Indians students articulated during discussions of *Diary*—derived through what I came to understand was a powerful alignment of their own preconceptions and the authority they located in the novel.

Confronting Alexie's Reservation as Prison

Junior is just one of Alexie's characters who articulates the view that "Reservations were meant to be prisons, you know? Indians were supposed to disappear. But somehow or another, Indians have forgotten that reservations were meant to be death camps. I wept because I was the only one who was brave and crazy enough to leave the rez. I was the only one with enough arrogance" (216–217). Reading *Diary* does, indeed, expose students to stark reservation realities, the truth of which are born out in data aggregated over the past several decades. For instance, according to the Centers for Disease Control and Prevention's assessment of data from 2001 to 2005, American Indians' age adjusted alcoholism mortality rate is twice that of the general U.S. population. Further, 65.9 percent of American Indians whose deaths were alcohol related were less than fifty years of age.[6]

Likewise, a Navajo prison inmate and poet characterizes his experience of reservation life thusly: "There is a battle going on behind the wall with the Native community. It's a battle against alcohol and drug abuse, against physical and mental abuse, against poverty and ignorance, against racism and anger. It is a battle for dignity, independence, freedom, justice, health, and happiness" (qtd. in Teuton 118). As this quote and the CDC report indicate, the traumas Alexie dramatizes are not particular to his own childhood experience of the Spokane reservation.

Notably, even fellow Spokane writer Gloria Bird, whose critique of Alexie's representations of the reservation as overly negative is now well known, decided never to return for many of the same reasons as Alexie himself. She writes,

> There is a subdued depression that manifests itself in high suicide rates, alcoholism, drug- and alcohol-related violence, and death, the effects of which are compounded by higher rates of cancer and economic instability. It is not the kind of place I would raise my children. In my heart, I carry many good memories of growing up in that place, but there are very real concerns that have led me to the decision never to return to the reservation [43].

The issue for Bird is not with Alexie's accuracy but, arguably, his disproportionate focus on negative features of reservation life at the expense of those features she recalls fondly and which Alexie himself has described as beautiful and magical (see his interview with Cerna).

Alexie's alleged failure to address the more positive aspects of Spokane reservation life—including community, tradition, and tribally specific culture—drew Bird's fire in her 1995 essay "The Exaggeration of Despair in Sherman Alexie's *Reservation Blues*." Three years later Choctaw-Cherokee-Irish critic Louis Owens issued a similar critique of Alexie and other American Indian writers who, in his view, achieve the greatest commercial success because they provide a "deficit model of Indian reservation life" (75). Owens concedes that poverty, alcoholism, and the generalized despair that accompany each are "unavoidable realities" of American Indian life and thus to avoid them would be a falsification. "However," he writes, "such portraits not only present just one side of Indian existence, but more unfortunately conform readily to Euroamerican readers' expectations that American Indians are all doomed by firewater; white readers find their stereotypes comfortably reinforced by sensationalized alcoholism and cultural impotence" (72). As Owens indicates, the reason why readers may walk away from an Alexie novel with an utterly despairing sense of reservation life is not only a consequence of the author's own views but also of their prior expectations.

Had Louis Owens lived to read *Diary* he would have found that Alexie has written a book that provides clear hope for American Indian survival. However, that hope resides decidedly outside the reservation boundaries and thus, I suspect, would cause Owens to double down on—rather than revise—his view that Alexie reinforces Euroamerican readers' assumptions about

American Indian life. In *Diary*, Junior must privilege his individual interests over his community's expectations. He must leave the Spokane reservation if he is to gain access to the resources, opportunities, and stability he needs. His daily efforts, from his long commute to Reardan High School to his scholastic and athletic commitments and his efforts to win friends among his new Euroamerican classmates, are painfully documented and well rewarded. Indeed, here we see evidence that the Ameritocracy works: if you work hard, you will succeed. Further, Junior's experience can be read as validation of assimilationist policies directed toward American Indians for centuries—which ostensibly were justified by the view that American Indians would be served best by assimilating into the mainstream and dismantling tribal structures alleged to mire them in a "backward" collectivist social order.

Junior's view of his daily commute as a routine loss and reacquisition of Indianness may represent to the informed reader the ongoing legacy of colonization (i.e., as a manifestation of internalized racism rooted in the assimilationist logic of early Indian schools that presumed to be able to erase Indian identity through education). However, students raised within an educational system that retains binary, colonialist conceptions of American Indians—and who themselves tend to think in binary terms—are prone to reading such a scene uncritically and to seeing Junior sacrificing his Indian self to survive as a logical, if lamentable, necessity. Many students equate reservation life with poverty and alcoholism, and many commented during class discussions on their difficulty understanding why some Spokane resent Junior for leaving and/or why anyone stays on a reservation. Further, students acculturated to the individualist ethos of mainstream U.S. culture can have difficulty appreciating the communitarian values present in much American Indian literature, including *Diary*. Teaching *Diary* to young college students in a fashion that exposes Alexie's subversive invocation of colonialist discourse (even as he ultimately validates leaving the reservation as being in the best interest of all Spokane people) requires educators not simply to work against the grain of centuries of U.S. cultural production, but also to find strategic ways of encouraging students to shift from binary to more syncretic levels of cognition.

Assessing and Unraveling Stereotypes Through Close Reading and Critical Context

Concerns about confirming stereotypes are shared by many who teach American Indian literature, and not just Alexie's work. For example, Helen Eikstadt and Francine Falk-Ross caution educators not to assign texts that contain stereotypes of American Indian peoples. However, as Bird and Owens indicate, part of the reason Alexie runs the risk of perpetuating stereotypes is because mainstream readers *expect* to encounter images of American Indians like those they have encountered previously. It would be easy, moreover, for writers like Alexie to avoid perpetuating stereotypes and for educators to disabuse students of them if they had absolutely no basis in reality. If alcoholism, for example, were not a real challenge in many reservation communities, the stereotype of the drunken Indian would have less force.

Another powerful convergence between students' presuppositions and Alexie's writing style pertains to his generalized language about American Indians and reservations. *Diary*'s language offers little tribal specificity, much less qualification regarding the subjectivity or limitations of individual experiences or perspectives. Junior frames his crossing of cultural boundaries and formulation of identity in terms that can confirm students' generalized and monolithic perceptions of what it means to be an American Indian. For example, one illustration depicts Junior standing beside a sign; the arrows pointing left read "Rez" and "Home," whereas the arrows pointing right read "Hope" and contain three question marks. Junior stands facing right toward a space of presumed promise, along with the unknown. This is just one place in the novel where Junior's dreams are located outside the reservation's borders. It is thus unsurprising that one student in my composition course themed "coming of age across cultures" gave a presentation that centered on the claim that the word "Indian," as defined in the novel, means hopelessness and crushed ambition, whereas "Part-Time Indian" signifies the realization of dreams.

Students in this composition course were tasked with developing their ability to craft and defend argumentative claims about texts through short presentations that functioned as oral performances of their literary analysis papers. Afterwards their peers were charged with raising viable counterarguments, requesting additional textual evidence, and asking any other questions they had. I then extended these conversations—as part of my effort to guide them in refining their arguments and carefully analyzing key textual moments—by identifying claims we might explore further and raising critical questions that might prompt students to revisit interpretations that rested on faulty or underdeveloped assumptions. Following the presentation on *Diary*'s definition of "Indian," I asked students how cultural identity is achieved and experienced in general—not just for American Indians. We then discussed the irony and logic embedded in the notion of being a "part-time Indian" and thereby engaged Alexie's portrayal of American Indian identity from the perspective of critics like Stephen Evans, who argues that Alexie uses irony to craft realistic survival literature. Evans writes, "much of Alexie's work to date comprises a modern survival document from which his readers gain strength by actively participating in the reflection of reality as viewed through Alexie's satiric lens" (52). Although Evan's essay predates *Diary*, his words apply to this novel as well and can help illuminate the ways in which Alexie presents unrealistic conceptions of American Indian identity as hurdles in the process of Junior's coming of age experience.

Like many high school and early college students, Junior begins the novel with broad, binary conceptions of racial identity. For example, he conflates whiteness and wealth, as illustrated by a cartoon split-screen of a white and Indian boy (57). The white boy's Ralph Lauren shirt and Timex watch are juxtaposed with the Indian boy's K-mart t-shirt and no watch at all. The non-material contrasts in the illustration include "A Bright Future" versus "A Vanishing Past" and "Positive Role Models" versus "A Family History of Diabetes and Cancer." Thus the material conditions of Junior's life are thinly contextualized and sharply distinguished from those of his Euroamerican peers. The reference to the Indian boy's "vanishing past" is representative of the challenges teaching this novel can pose. Students who presume that American Indian cultures have already disappeared are likely to overlook Alexie's satirical invocation of the myth of the Vanishing Indian. I have found it effective simply to ask students what it means to have a vanishing past, as part of the ongoing practice with close reading I pursue in composition classes. Students typically free associate with these words and often suggest that the phrase implies a personal disconnection with one's own history or a history that is irrelevant or even destructive in the present moment. I then explain that there is another possible reference point at work here that we might consider, and give them a brief encapsulation of the myth of the Vanishing Indian. Discussion of the myth and its role in Euroamerican-American Indian relations does help students to more critically assess the novel—and American Indian authored texts generally—but can sometimes be counterbalanced by the rhetorical force of *Diary* as they experience and interpret it firsthand.

One obstacle is what Bird characterizes as mainstream readers' trust of the American Indian-authored novel and their inclination to read any one text as representative of American Indian experience (49). When teaching first and second year college students, such trust converges with their tendency to defer uncritically to external authorities (as mentioned above). Because Alexie relies on generalizations—for instance, Junior's frequent statements about American Indians as a whole rather than more specific comments about the Spokane—students seem particularly prone to broad conclusions upon reading *Diary*. When I invited students in a composition course to weigh in on the allegation that Alexie perpetuates negative stereotypes about American Indian life, they observed that Junior's sister dying in a trailer fire after passing out drunk on another reservation solidifies the notion that Junior's experience of the Spokane reservation is representative of reservation life generally (205).

While Alexie's disinterest in romantic portraits of American Indian life, in addition to his own experiences on the Spokane reservation, may contribute to an overemphasis on reservation ills, it also yields a body of work that subverts some of the most abiding positive stereotypes about American Indians (e.g., stoic, mystical, noble/savage, nature-loving). In this way his writing offers occasions for critically examining the origins of such stereotypes and the aspects of Euroamerican culture that explain their perpetuation. In *Diary*, Ted the Millionaire is the go-to character for such analysis. Junior introduces Ted as a representative of a category of Euroamericans fixated on American Indians: "We'd expected this white guy to be original. But he was yet another white guy who showed up on the rez because he loved Indian people SOOOOOOOO much. Do you know how many white strangers show up on Indian reservations every year and start telling Indians how much they love them? Thousands. It's sickening. And boring" (162). This particular white guy appears at Junior's grandmother's funeral to return what he believes to be her beaded dance outfit, which he purchased and held onto for years, despite alleged feelings of guilt, because of its beauty. Ted claims to be devastated that he is too late to return it to Grandmother Spirit. Ultimately, what this scene underscores is the disconnect between romantic collectors like Ted—who, as Junior's cartoon illustration of him highlights, spends exorbitant amounts of money on alleged American Indian cultural artifacts, including "fringed buckskin pants purportedly worn by Geronimo ($150,000, from a private collector)"—and the material conditions faced by many American Indians today (including those on the reservation he claims to love), any actual tribal knowledge, or any direct ties to American Indian peoples (162–163).

When Junior's mother rises to accept the dance outfit on her mother's behalf, her comportment indicates her familiarity with the role a man like Ted expects her to play. Junior observes, "My mother's voice had gotten all formal. Indians are good at that. We'll be talking and laughing and carrying on like normal, and then, BOOM, we get all serious and sacred and start talking like some English royalty" (165). She goes on to inform Ted that the outfit cannot be Grandmother Spirit's because her mother was not a dancer and because, as the other Spokane present verify, the beadwork most likely is Sioux. Ted responds by rapidly placing the dress back in his car and speeding away. In response, first Junior's mother and then "Two thousand Indians laughed at the same time. We kept laughing. It was the most glorious noise

I'd ever heard. And I realized that, sure, Indians were drunk and sad and displaced and crazy and mean, but, dang, we knew how to laugh. When it comes to death, we know that laugher and tears are pretty much the same thing" (166). In the end, *Diary* invites readers to grapple with the realities Junior faces: e.g., the idea that a community can be sad and joyous simultaneously, or his father's offer of the five dollars he managed to save as a Christmas gift for Junior, after spending a week drinking the rest of the gift money away, being "a beautiful and ugly thing" (151). Confronting these seeming contradictions and seeing the truth of such a moment as drawing upon both beauty and ugliness, however, requires careful work to redirect students' desire to offer an up or down judgment on Junior's father—a desire arguably symptomatic of binary modes of thinking—and to help them develop the syncretic cognitive capacities most students achieve by the time they are seniors.[7] Asking students how they understand Junior's diagnosis of his father's gift as "beautiful and ugly" is one point of entry into an analysis that requires them to move beyond the binary and identify the meaning implied by this seeming contradiction.

Educators can further contextualize characters like Ted the Millionaire, along with other Euroamerican stereotypes about American Indians represented in the novel, by incorporating brief video clips accessible online. For a range of courses in which I assign American Indian literature, I organize and share short film, television, and advertisement clips through a course management system to increase students' familiarity with influential and persistent non–Native representations of American Indians alongside American Indians' own self-representations. My standard practice is to select a clip to show at the beginning of class as a means of drawing students into the work of the day, presenting information relevant to the assigned text, and framing the ensuing analysis we will perform of that text. Before offering any direction or context, I solicit students' impressions of the clip's core ideas and assumptions, rhetorical strategies, etc. I then build on these initial impressions by raising critical questions and offering relevant context. Finally, I ask them to identify connections with the assigned text, which moves us into our analysis of it. One video I use often is the 1971 Keep America Beautiful commercial featuring Iron Eyes Cody crying a single tear at the site of litter by the highway, which serves as a condensed representation of the idea that American Indians are born conservationists and that they live outside of contemporary time—as indicated by Cody's buckskin outfit, arrival by canoe to a busy highway congested with cars, and, as students observed, the fact that he seems never to have seen such littering before (given that he is moved to cry). Addressing the rhetorical context for this commercial also sets the stage for discussing why the makers of the commercial thought such an image would be so powerful to consumers, along with what this allows us to understand about just how ingrained and powerful the Ecological Indian stereotype had become by 1971. This commercial pairs nicely with Sherman Alexie's 2008 appearance on the *Colbert Report*, in which he makes fun of this same stereotype.

Showing Graham Greene's satiric commercial for "Dr. Greene's: The Ab-Original Pain Reliever," in which he mocks and calls attention to white Canadian actors who appropriate indigenous cultures, illustrates just how representative a character like Ted actually is. More importantly, the commercial represents indigenous humor and activism in the face of cultural appropriation, and thus *active agency* in an ongoing conversation about the relationship between indigenous and Euroamerican peoples. To further contextualize assigned texts and demonstrate their broader relevance, I find it useful to incorporate regularly into class discussions references to relevant current events in popular and political culture, whether it is the Fall 2012 scandal regarding Victoria's Secret dressing their models in headdresses, or supporters of then Massachusetts Senator Scott Brown's campaign staff mocking Elizabeth Warren's claims to American Indian ancestry by making war-whooping noises and tomahawk-chop gestures outside one of her campaign events. The blog "Native Appropriations: Examining Representations of Indigenous Peoples," maintained by Adrienne K. (Cherokee), is a good resource for such recent information and a forum where students can engage with American Indians addressing appropriation issues.[8]

Of course, several critics argue that Alexie's use of stereotypes validates, rather than transgresses, negative preconceptions of American Indians. Bird, for example, contends that historical tidbits are sprinkled into *Reservation Blues* for effect, not to function as substantive moments in and of themselves. Bird writes, "This is the dilemma for not only Alexie, but native writers in general: to accurately represent our communities without exploiting them. The buffer in *Reservation Blues* is to sugarcoat the picture with enough sidetracks and comic scenes to tone down the real issues" (51). Bird's concern is not just that historical and cultural context be provided but that such context be adequately emphasized. She expresses concern about colonialist influences on the novel, which she sees as reproducing—not subverting or critiquing—colonialist stereotypes. However, Alexie sees the boundary between exploitation and representation differently. In a 2001 interview, he noted, "My tribe drew that line for me a long time ago. It's not written down, but I know it [...] I feel a heavy personal responsibility, and I accept it, and I honor it" (Fraser). Alexie operates with an unspoken understanding of and commitment to his tribe's expectations regarding appropriate textual content—though one that clearly is different from Bird's. These statements regarding tribal accountability thus illustrate that there is not a single agreed upon ethical standard within any one tribe and that the issue of appropriate representation is complex, contested, and significant.

In a 2009 debate about *Diary* on the listserv of the Association for the Study of American Indian Literature, one point of contention pertained to whether or not the novel confronts non-Native readers with the persistence and consequences of colonization. Jane Haladay argued,

> By not contextualizing the historical circumstances of colonization that have created much of the brutal reality of Spokane Reservation life that Junior and his sister try to flee, Alexie doesn't push readers who are unaware of these histories far enough to feel any role in it, any responsibility. I think a non-Native reader could easily put down "Diary" without feeling the slightest bit implicated by the reservation dysfunctions as Alexie outlines them, with the added "bonus" of believing that white teachers and white schools are the only way out for "smart" Indians[9] [ASAIL Listserv].

Haladay's point resonates with Bird's earlier claim regarding *Reservation Blues* that, "Despite the verisimilitude of Alexie's portrayal of alcoholism and its impact upon individual lives, he does not attempt to put the social problems of economic instability, poverty, or cultural oppression into perspective" (51). I see throughout *Diary* references to the context Bird and Haladay require—regarding land loss, forced assimilation, external and internalized racism—but concede that these references are fleeting enough that readers unaware of the referents may gloss over them easily and thus see the reservation simply as a hopeless space from which American Indians must flee for survival. Again, this is the view that Alexie himself has espoused, and one that accords with his own experience. However, it is not a view shared by all American Indians and thus students should not be left with the impression that it is. For example, a statement like "reservations are where Indians were sent to die" indicates that *someone* sent Indians to these spaces. Although, as others have charged, Alexie does little to contextualize this reference, as educators we can do this work—and help students develop their close reading and contextualization skills in the process. Below I detail some strategies I have used to draw out the context to which *Diary* alludes productively.

Developing Multidimensional Readings Through Rhetorical Analysis

Junior's repeated, sweeping, and totalizing assertions equating the reservation with despair often overshadow the more positive dimensions of reservation life also referenced in *Diary*—as a discussion in one of my composition courses demonstrates. Recall that this was the class whose survey results I summarized above; the survey results indicated that the combination of a general lack of background knowledge and students' primarily negative view of reservation life played a clear role in shaping their interpretations. We read *Diary* in preparation for their rhetorical analysis papers, and were analyzing it accordingly—with an eye toward explicating the relationships between the novel's formal features, meaning, and its audience/s. A rhetorical analysis of the novel helps students to appreciate that what they bring as readers to the text shapes their interpretations and that the text likely will read differently for another group of readers. Moreover, this mode of analysis raises the possibility that they may not be the target audience for any particular text.[10] For instance, I asked the students to assess how different audiences might interpret the following passage and why.

> The Spokane Tribe holds their annual powwow celebration over the Labor Day weekend. This was the 127th annual one, and there would be singing, war dancing, gambling, storytelling, laughter, fry bread, hamburgers, hot dogs, arts and crafts, and plenty of alcoholic brawling.
> I wanted no part of it.
> Oh, the dancing and singing are great. Beautiful, in fact, but I'm afraid of all the Indians who aren't dancers and singers. Those rhythmless, talentless, tuneless Indians are most likely going to get drunk and beat the shit out of any available loser.
> And I am always the most available loser.
> "Come on," Rowdy said. "I'll protect you" [17].

I directed students to identify key phrasing, imagery, and other literary devices that might have significant and perhaps distinctive meaning to one or more audiences. It was in the course of this analysis that we discussed the passage's representation of reservation life as multiple audiences might interpret it. One student commented that his eye was drawn most to the negative statements about the powwow, in part because they speak to the "fall of a once great people," whereas other students said that, lacking direct experiences of powwows, they were reminded of similar aspects of their own experience (BBQs, State Fairs) in which most of the features of the powwow were also present, both positive and negative. This observation of similarity served as an effective mechanism for helping the class as a whole consider just how common such a blend of traditional events and poor behavior are at such large gatherings—across cultures—rather than seeing this moment as wholly culturally specific or, worse yet, as an indicator of a culture in irrevocable and pitiable decline. Another student said that when she first read the list of things that happen at the Spokane powwow, she did not focus on the negatives, but once Junior claimed that he wanted none of it, she redirected her attention to them. Several students agreed and commented that they followed Junior's lead in noting but then dismissing what was beautiful about the powwow and concluding that, on balance, it is a negative experience (and not just for Junior).

As we moved into a consideration of audience interpretation students observed that American Indian readers and others familiar with powwows might better understand the significance of the powwow's positive features (e.g., singing, storytelling, and war dancing). This observation provided opportunities for discussing each of these practices and what, with reflection on each, students without prior knowledge might now understand about what it might be like to attend the powwow. Taking each item on the list one by one and discussing their implications also is a method of training students to read closely and critically. Once more, the fact that we were practicing rhetorical analysis also offered opportunities for paying more attention to how Junior's specific subject position shapes his representation of the powwow and what else the passage might communicate relative to the novel's larger themes. For example, students noted that *Diary*'s large youth readership could relate to Junior's attachment to Rowdy given that most youth experience vulnerability of some sort and can connect emotionally to the feeling of being helped by a peer. This is just one example of how teachers and students can read against the grain of the novel by recovering and attending to the positive aspects of reservation life that can be overshadowed by the combination of Junior's emphasis on and students' presuppositions about the reservation's social ills.

Such a consideration of *Diary*'s multiple audiences can be developed effectively by incorporating into class discussion Alexie's own comments about his readership and a variety of responses the novel has received to date. Alexie stated that he aimed to reach young American Indian kids on reservations. Later he conceded, seeing they are the largest reading demographic, that Euroamerican women are his core audience. Still, he more recently measured his success by observing, "My audience is getting browner—that's great. And the age group from kids to old people. That's great, so I'm obviously doing something right" (Torrez). Deborah Miranda (Esselen and Chumash), in turn, weighed-in on the debate about *Diary* on the ASAIL listserv as follows:

> I loved *Diary* precisely because it didn't pretend to any cultural knowledge or experiences that a kid that age at that time, in that situation, would have had access to or would care about. It reminds me of Alexie saying "You know you're really an Indian when you suddenly wish you weren't."[11]

Miranda's comment calls attention to the young adult aspects of the novel—not just that Alexie writes it for young adults, but that his protagonist's worldview and understanding is limited by his own youth. Thus Miranda's words, when presented in the classroom, can function as an effective springboard for critically evaluating the scope and limitations of Junior's point of view while alerting students to a stock literary device and its implications. Indeed, the novel's statements about alcoholism are charged with pathos that results from the narrative perspective of a fourteen-year-old boy who suffers, in rapid succession, the alcohol-related deaths of his grandmother, close family friend, and sister. Once more a stark divide appears before Junior between the Euroamerican and American Indian worlds as he notes that most of his Euroamerican peers have never attended a single funeral. He repeatedly laments the barrier alcohol places between him, his community, and his cultural heritage. Yet, he also notes that many American Indians, including his grandmother, do not drink. Part of coming of age for Junior is learning to negotiate relationships strained by alcohol. Junior comes to appreciate that his father "may have loved me imperfectly, but he loved me as well as he could" (189). Again, Junior's coming of age is marked by the eventual achievement of a syncretic mindset that reconciles the suffering inflicted by his father's drinking along with his father's displays of love.

Transcending Cultural and Cognitive Binaries Through Analysis of Junior's Coming of Age

One of the most significant aspects of Alexie's writing is that it provokes students to confront the simple fact that American Indians did not vanish and are, in fact, participants in modern U.S. society with identities that draw upon a variety of cultural influences. Here *Diary* undoubtedly succeeds. Junior reads and draws comics, plays basketball, and envies his Euroamerican classmates' iPods; he also attends the Spokane powwow, measures risks he takes against the standard of past warriors, and ultimately conceptualizes multiple tribal identities for himself—from being a member of the Spokane tribe to a member of the tribes of "chronic masturbators," "small-town kids," "bookworms," and "tortilla chips-and-salsa lovers" (217). Living on the reservation while attending Reardan, in hopes of attaining a quality education, Junior's coming of age culminates in the realization of a multifaceted, hybrid identity that defies the colonial, binary logic of Euroamerican versus American Indian, civilized versus savage—but, importantly, without collapsing material and historically-rooted differences between groups to which the novel testifies.

Indeed, *Diary* contains numerous explorations of racialized, binary logic—frequently rendered absurd through a young boy's overly literal conception of it—which educators can highlight through analysis of key textual moments and, in the process, work with students to develop their analytical skills. For example, returning briefly to Junior's sense of daily loss and restoration of American Indian identity, of his daily migrations from the reservation to Reardan he reflects: "I woke up on the reservation as an Indian, and somewhere on the road to Reardan, I became something less than Indian. And once I arrived at Reardan, I became something less than less than Indian" (83). Junior hereby offers an extremely narrow, geographically based conception of Indian identity that arguably attaches to colonialist oppositional discourse of Euroamerican versus American Indian and reinforces the association students can have between American Indian identity and living on a reservation (see the survey responses outlined above). However, the idea that an individual might daily lose and regain his cultural identity in this fashion invites readers to interrogate the assumptions behind such thinking, rather than take Junior's assertion at face value. Educators can draw students into such an interrogation by asking them what we can infer, based on this passage and other relevant moments in *Diary*, about Junior's understanding of what it means to be "Indian" and how his understanding compares with their own sense of cultural identity requirements.

Highlighting and Contextualizing the Legacies of Colonization

Diary subtly undercuts the idea—which many students take as the novel's overarching message—that success requires Junior to assimilate into the Euroamerican world outside of the reservation. Significantly, Junior is strongly connected to a close-knit family. Although other members of the community see Junior as a traitor for leaving the reservation, Junior's extended family supports and aids him in achieving this goal. Further, when his grandmother dies, Junior comes to appreciate anew the bonds of his community—which I referenced in part above: "I realized that, sure, Indians were drunk and sad and displaced and crazy and mean, but, dang, we knew how to laugh[…]. Each funeral was a funeral for all of us. We lived and died together" (166). This portrayal of community cohesion, particularly the emphasis on living whole lives together, is in tension with Junior's view—which he continues to articulate after this point—of the reservation as a place where people go only to die. It is Junior's estranged friend Rowdy who comments that Junior is like nomadic Indians of old and thereby locates an indigenous precedent for Junior's response to his contemporary life as a Spokane boy.

I have found that students often are prone to overlooking the anti-assimilationist aspects of the story, but discussion of them—in conjunction with Junior's previous ideas about geographically rooted or partial American Indian identity—can prompt students to assess how/if the novel ultimately asserts a more syncretic understanding of cultural identity as a part of Junior's coming of age experience. To this end I provide students with a list of questions to consider as they read *Diary* and in preparation for class discussion, including: What is Junior's conception of Indian identity and culture? Does his conception change over the course of the novel and, if so, how and why? These questions set-up an interpretive arc that calls attention to key aspects of Junior's coming of age experience, inclusive of his development of a more nuanced and flexible understanding of his cultural identity. When I ask students to account for some of the shifts in Junior's thinking about American Indian identity, they frequently note that it develops in tandem with his ability to view the Euroamerican world in a more three-dimensional fashion upon firsthand experience. They note, for instance, the literal and figurative absence of fathers in Reardan in comparison to his own father's flawed but genuine efforts to raise him well (153–154).

Of course, fundamentally, *Diary* is a story about growing up in poverty. In our efforts as educators to steer students away from generalized thinking about American Indians, it is equally important that we not misrepresent or gloss over the stark realities of reservation life for many American Indians. As Deborah Miranda commented in an email to the ASAIL listserv, "There is so much negativity in his book because there was so much negativity in the reality of the life he is describing. The brutal truth is that when you are living with severe alcoholism, depression, poverty and racism, you don't have time for or give a damn about your 'cultural heritage.' You care about staying alive, getting out, and just trying to let the scars heal!" Indeed, one might argue that Junior's primary concern is survival—particularly finding a way to escape poverty. Junior observes, "Almost all of the rich and famous brown people are artists[...]. So I draw because I feel like it might be my only real chance to escape the reservation"[12] (6). Poverty is the lens through which he sees the world, a lens that generates sweeping and potentially dangerous conclusions, including Junior's repeated assertions that hope resides in the Euroamerican world. However, Alexie does make reference to significant, albeit rarely tribally specific, periods in American Indian history to which we can call students' attention and thereby shift their thinking about social ills on reservations—from a sort of impotent pity to phenomena with specific historical causes and thus the possibility of being redressed. We can consider identification and explication of these socio-historical traces as another method of reading against the dominant grain of the novel.

One such reference to a critical era in American Indian history occurs in the context of a conversation Junior has with a Euroamerican teacher from the reservation, Mr. P, who recalls being charged as a young teacher with killing the Indian in order to save the child: "We were supposed to make you give up being Indian. Your songs and stories and language and dancing. Everything" (35). Mr. P attempts to compensate for the generations of children he wounded by marking Junior as an exceptional Indian, deserving of a life apart from the poverty and despair of the reservation. He says, "You're going to find more and more hope the farther and farther you walk away from this sad, sad, sad, reservation" (43). Here students can gain insight into the state of the educational system on the reservation and the original assimilationist aim of reservation schools. With a small amount of historical context regarding American Indian educational history,[13] students quickly make connections to Mr. P and shift from reading him as an exemplar of white redemption to seeing his presence in the story as a more complex trace of a colonial legacy that explains many of the challenges Junior faces (challenges for which many students in my composition class wanted more context). Further, the exchange between Mr. P and Junior culminates in a moment of cross-cultural understanding and a celebration of individual opportunity—both elements of United States' mythos that mainstream students tend to embrace.

One way that educators can draw students' attention to the socio-historical traces present within *Diary* and, in the process, help students appreciate that Alexie's voice is just one of many American Indian voices is by pairing it with other American Indian authored texts. Most articles on teaching American Indian literature rightly suggest that we assign multiple American Indian-authored texts to disrupt students' conceptions of a homogenous, singular, or static American Indian culture. Indeed, it is safe to say that any time students encounter only one American Indian-authored text there is a tendency for them to read it as representative of all American Indian cultures and experiences.[14] Given that there are 566 federally recognized tribes within the U.S. today, in addition to many unrecognized tribes, such a reading of one text invariably will be a distortion of the complexity and heterogeneity of American Indian life. Although reading two or three texts will not necessarily avoid such distortions—particularly given that students' presuppositions about American Indian life can lead to a disproportionate focus on social ills in many American Indian texts (not just Alexie's)—strategic combinations can do a great deal to help students dispense with monolithic thinking about

American Indians and to read each text in a more nuanced fashion than they might otherwise.

For instance, whereas the context for alcoholism on reservations is not forefronted in *Diary*, and thus can be read by students as a function of a biological predisposition rather than a social ill with specific, historically rooted causes, both N. Scott Momaday's 1969 Pulitzer Prize winning novel *House Made of Dawn* and Leslie Marmon Silko's *Ceremony* (1977) feature protagonists, Abel and Tayo, respectively, who struggle with alcoholism clearly associated with Post Traumatic Stress Disorder (PTSD) and various colonial legacies (e.g., forced assimilation, mixedblood identity, and land loss).[15] These novels also feature strong American Indian characters who are not alcoholics and who, through their deep tribal knowledge, are able to aid the protagonists in their struggles to recover a place within their communities. Importantly—given students' predisposition to seeing traditional American Indian practices as locked in a nineteenth-century stasis and uniformity—what allows these characters to guide the protagonists effectively is their fluid understanding of American Indian culture. As the medicine man Betonie, himself mixedblood, tells Tayo, "long ago when the people were given these ceremonies, the changing began, if only in the aging of the yellow gourd rattle or the shrinking of the skin around the eagle's claw, if only in the different voices from generation to generation, singing the chants. You see, in many ways, the ceremonies have always been changing" (116). Here Betonie offers Tayo, whose PTSD both Western doctors and a traditional Laguna Pueblo medicine man failed in remedying, the possibility of recovery within an American Indian context. In other words, an ever-evolving view of American Indian cultures can accommodate new experiences like Tayo's wartime trauma, whereas a static understanding cannot. Thus, even on its own terms, *Ceremony* asserts that the vitality of American Indian cultures lies in their capacity for necessary adaptations over time; when paired with *Diary* it contributes powerfully to a much more varied representation of American Indian cultures than most students have encountered previously.

Ultimately, Tayo's and Abel's social and cultural recovery signals their physical and mental recovery as well. Whereas Junior struggles with his decision to leave the reservation and his conviction that he must leave to survive, Abel and Tayo struggle to find ways of assimilating their experiential and ancestral differences as mixedbloods into the heart of tribal life. Consequently, pairing *Diary* with either of these novels communicates the variability of reservations and any one American Indian's view of identity and survival, while calling students' attention to *Diary*'s subtler indications of the causes of alcoholism on the Spokane reservation and the positive aspects of Spokane tribal life.

Another way of both expanding students' critical frame of reference and providing them with useful analytical tools is by incorporating relevant American Indian literary theory and techniques, and engaging debates about Alexie's work. Even if it is not possible to assign many American Indian writers, it is possible to position their work within a large and varied conversation. In composition classes I find it works best to encapsulate a critical concept for students and begin discussion by asking them to identify connections with the assigned texts. I am always prepared to model at least one application by walking them through detailed analysis of a passage from the assigned text that reflects the critical concept I have offered. Afterwards students seem better prepared to do some of this work themselves, and often begin extending the application during discussion of the passage I select. In upper level literature courses, by contrast, it is more feasible to require short presentations in which students present their research on an assigned theory or literary technique and model close readings of literature in which they explicate how the theory or technique applies therein. I include below some of the theories and literary techniques I have incorporated in composition and literature courses:

- Jace Weaver argues that the most defining feature of American Indian literature is a commitment to American Indian community that works in opposition to five centuries of colonization (43). His term "communitism," which combines community with activism, can be used to illuminate such aspects of *Diary* as the Spokane community's response to Ted the Millionaire's misidentification of the beaded dance outfit's tribal origins as not just as a moment of solidarity and comic relief in the midst of grief, but also as an assertion of tribal specificity that reveals the acquisitive nature of his interest in American Indian cultures and the limits of his knowledge of them.
- Gerald Vizenor's "survivance" (survival and resistance). When asked in an interview about survivance, Alexie dismissed the idea—as well as survival alone—as being a low-level goal (Nygren 282). However, his body of work is threaded through with references, explicit and implicit, to multiple forms of survival, from simply persisting to actively resisting colonial threats. For example, his 1993 poetry collection *Old Shirts & New Skins* contains poems about drinking as a means of survival ("Sundays, Too") and as a threat to survival ("The 35th Annual Yakima Nation All-Indian Basketball Tournament"), survival as Crazy Horse's retort to Custer, and statements about U.S. Indian policy being designed to

ensure American Indian destruction, e.g., "*How do you explain the survival of all of us who were never meant to survive?*" (90, emphasis original). Incorporating Vizenor's concept of survivance into analysis of Alexie's writing thus provides a productive analytical framework. Indeed, Junior's coming of age experience as a whole can be read as a form of survivance—not just surviving at a basic level but resisting the racist practices Junior at times internalizes, as when he asserts that "Indians don't deserve shit" (56), and insisting on a high quality education and socioeconomic well-being.

- Indigenous appropriation and repurposing of colonialist discourse as anticolonial acts, as Deborah Miranda models in her tribal memoir entitled *Bad Indians* and on her blog "Bad NDNs."[16] By presenting those who were labeled "bad Indians" by Europeans and Euroamericans as models she can emulate today in the interest of her own survival and cultural recovery, Miranda upends the Eurocentric and colonialist norms behind the original negative diagnosis. In her "Novena to Bad Indians," for example, she writes, "Oh unholy pagans who refused to convert, oh pagans who converted, oh pagans who recanted, oh converts who survived, hear our supplication: make us in your image, grant us your pride. Ancestors, illuminate the dark civilization we endure. Teach us to love untamed, inspire us to break rules, remind us of your brutal wisdom learned so dearly: Even dead Indians are never good enough" (99). She presents her pagan ancestors (who, by the standards of the Spanish missionaries who attempted to convert them forcibly, were "bad Indians"), as well as surviving converts, as guides who can illuminate her present experience and give her courage to resist oppressive norms by breaking rules. Notably, although a resistant paganism threads throughout this passage, the portrait Miranda paints of this group of ancestors as they interacted with Catholicism is highly variable. To be among the wise, prideful, resistant group of California Indians Miranda invokes for guidance, and likens to God through her request to be created in their image, does not require one "correct" response to Catholicism.

Pairing "Novena to Bad Indians" with *Diary* can help call attention to the ways in which Alexie invokes and satirizes assimilationist discourses and non–Native representations of American Indians, from the educational policies Mr. P regrets perpetuating to the bright red American Indian mascot wearing a single feather who is the only American Indian at Reardan besides Junior (56). Throughout *Diary*, Alexie exposes the reductive logic of stereotypes. Junior's early days at Reardan, for instance, contain numerous illustrations of the influence of colonialist logic on Euroamerican perceptions of American Indians. Initially Junior suffers the twinned shame of being ignored or called such racist names as "chief," "tonto," and "squaw boy"—names derived from old Westerns. Junior's own comparison of himself as a star basketball player to a warrior, illustrated in a cartoon as including a feathered headdress, a loin cloth, and a widely aggressive stance, is just one indication that that his emergent sense of identity as a Spokane boy in a nearly all-Euroamerican school involves a dialectical relationship with stereotypical expectations about American Indian identity.

Further Pedagogical Applications

Although my primary focus in this article has been on teaching Sherman Alexie's *The Absolutely True Diary of a Part-Time Indian* and the particular opportunities and challenges it poses, many of the pedagogical techniques I offer can be adapted for teaching many works of American Indian literature, and Multiethnic American Literature more generally, in classrooms where students have little prior exposure to the cultures, histories, and experiences showcased therein. Although my experience teaching *Diary* has been in composition classes, my techniques are relevant to and can be developed in more advanced ways for the literature classroom. Targeted close reading practices not only help students develop their analytical skills but prompt them to confront the subtleties of what the text itself argues, thereby directing their attention away from a surface level response that may say more about their presuppositions than the text itself. Incorporating relevant contextual content that students may not have been exposed to in their prior educations, minimizing the risk of one minority voice being read as representative by selecting complementary texts from the same cultural group, drawing upon internet resources in the interest of time and students' responsiveness to multimedia content, and using relevant cultural criticism and literary theory, also are effective techniques for teaching a range of Multiethnic American literary texts.

As many colleges and universities embrace a "learner-centered," rather than "teacher-centered," approach to education, educators frequently are advised not to lead by offering information but instead to mentor students into uncovering what they already know. I concur that students should be active agents in their own learning and that such agency can be activated by empowering them, on the front end, to see themselves as having valid and productive perspectives to offer. Unfortunately, however, when it comes to teaching courses on American Indian literatures, histories, or cultures, the majority of students in U.S. classrooms (especially at what Eduardo Bonilla-Silva terms HWCUs, or Historically White Colleges and Universities) have little accurate contextual knowledge. Withholding cultural and historical context, or refraining from exposing fallacious stereotypes, thus involves unnecessary risks and dangers. Because of how widespread and powerful such stereotypes and misunderstandings about American Indians are, once students voice these ideas and are echoed by peers, the ideas can take on a truth status that "student-centered" educators can be caught on their heels addressing. Moreover, in a culture in which facts increasingly are taken to be subjective (as in the media discussions of political debates in which factions operate with competing "facts" that are left to stand as such), many freshman and sophomores operating at a binary level of cognition can feel justified in holding fast to their presuppositions, even when presented with contradictory evidence. For this reason, offering selected contextual information and targeted reading practices for engaging primary texts, such as those I model above, are vital pedagogical tools that must not be discarded in tandem with the adoption of student-centered learning practices—lest we perpetuate colonialist violence in the classroom.

Appendix A: Classroom Survey of Students' Background Knowledge Concerning American Indian Peoples, Cultures and Histories

200H Survey (Honors Composition)—*Anonymous*
Your cultural/ethnic identity: _____

1. Prior to reading *The Absolutely True Diary of a Part-Time Indian*, how would you characterize your experience/knowledge of American Indian cultures? Be as specific and detailed as possible (commenting on such things, as relevant, as your direct interactions with American Indian peoples, time spent on tribal lands, books read, etc.).

2. Where do your impressions of American Indians come from? Approximate using percentages next to each of the items below (e.g., Hollywood films 50 percent, School 20 percent etc.)
    a. Hollywood Films
    b. School
    c. Interactions with American Indians
    d. Family Stories
    e. Other: please specify: _____

3. What characteristics must a person have in order to identify as American Indian?

4. How many federally recognized American Indian tribes are there in the United States today?
    a. 3   b. 58   c. 100   d. 566   e. 987

5. As of the 2010 U.S. census, approximately how many people identified solely as American Indian/Alaska Native?
    a. zero   b. 1,000–2,000   c. 5,000–10,000   d. 1 million   e. 3 million

6. As of the 2010 U.S. census, approximately how many people identified as American Indian/Alaska Native in combination with one or more other races?
    a. 10,000   b. 500,000   c. 2 million   d. 5 million

7. How would you characterize some of the defining features of American Indian life today?

8. Identify one significant moment in American Indian history.

9. Identify one U.S. policy designed to assimilate American Indians into the mainstream.

10. What are reservations?

11. What impressions do you have of American Indians and reservations based on your reading of *Diary* so far?

12. Do you like *Diary*? Why/why not?

13. What questions has *Diary* raised for you so far? What do you want to know more about?

Notes

1. See also Wahpeconiah and Zitzer-Comfort.
2. See Baxter Magolda, King, Taylor, and Wakefield's analysis of the results of the Wabash National Study concerning authority dependence in college students. I cite here only the general trend the study documents rather than commenting on precise percentages due to the authors' concluding cautionary statement about the limitations of the survey sample.
3. For a discussion of teaching Alexie in classrooms that contain a sizable number of American Indian students, see Berglund.
4. Students were informed verbally and on the survey itself that I was conducting research on teaching *Diary* and that the survey results might be cited in my future publications. They were asked to complete the survey, without credit or penalty, during class time. All survey responses were anonymous.
5. *Diary* is also winner of: the 2008 Boston-Globe Horn Book Award, the 2008 American Indian Library Association Youth Literature Award, the 2009 International Book on Books for Young People Sweden Peter Pan Prize, and the 2010 California Young Reader Medal. It was a finalist for the Los Angeles Times Book Prize in 2007.
6. See the CDC's Morbidity and Mortality Weekly Report of August 29, 2008.
7. See L. Lee Knefelkamp, Patricia M. King, and Strohm Kitchener for discussion of the development from binary to syncretic thinking throughout most students' four years in college.
8. http://nativeappropriations.com/.
9. Reprinted with permission from Jane Haladay.

10. I find that calling attention to the fact that students from the dominant culture may not be the privileged audience for texts, and thus must do the work to understand the culture featured in these texts—and accept that there may be certain things they cannot understand—has a significant impact on students' cross-cultural competencies and understandings of alignments between race and socioeconomic power.

11. Reprinted with permission from Deborah Miranda.

12. Reprinted with permission from Deborah Miranda.

13. After students have had some time to engage with the novel, I provide them with a two-page handout that contains overviews of key eras in American Indian history, inclusive of the basic aims, scope, and duration of the boarding school system. I also show them clips from the documentary *Our Spirits Don't Speak English*, which contains testimonials from former boarding school students.

14. This issue of representation also tends to occur when we assign only one text from another underrepresented cultural group.

15. Following Louis Owens and other American Indian Studies scholars, I use the term "mixedblood" to refer to peoples of both American Indian and non-American Indian descent.

16. http://badndns.blogspot.com/.

Works Cited

Alexie, Sherman. *The Absolutely True Diary of a Part-Time Indian*. New York: Little, Brown, 2007. Print.

———. *The Business of Fancydancing*. Brooklyn: Hanging Loose, 1992. Print.

Baxter Magolda, Marcia B., Patricia M. King, Kari B. Taylor, and Kerri M. Wakefield. "Decreasing Authority Dependence During the First Year of College." *Journal of College Student Development* 53.3 (2012): 418–435. Print.

Berglund, Jeff. "Facing the Fire: American Indian Literature and the Pedagogy of Anger." *American Indian Quarterly* 27.05 (2003): 80–90. Print.

Bird, Gloria. "The Exaggeration of Despair in Sherman Alexie's *Reservation Blues*." *Wicazo Sa Review* 11 (1995): 47–52. Print.

Centers for Disease Control and Prevention. *MMWR (Morbidity and Mortality Weekly Report)* 57.34 (August 29, 2008): 938–941. Web. 6 January 2014.

Cerna, Enrique. "Enrique Cerna Interviews Author and Poet Sherman Alexie." Interview by Enrique Cerna. KCTS 9 News. KCTS Television, 11 July 2008. Web. 4 June 2013.

Colbert, Stephen. Interview with Sherman Alexie. *The Colbert Report*. 28 October 2008. Web. 8 June 2013.

Eikstadt, Helen, and Francine Falk-Ross. "Native American Literature as a Component of Multicultural Education." *Illinois Reading Council Journal* 36.1 (2007): 10–13. Print.

Evans, Stephen. "'Open Containers': Sherman Alexie's Drunken Indians." *American Indian Quarterly* 25.1 (2001): 46–72. Print.

Fraser, Joelle. "Sherman Alexie's *Iowa Review* Interview." *Modern American Poetry*. 2001. Web. 6 June 2013.

Greene, Graham. "Dr. Greene's: The Ab-Original Pain Reliever." *You Tube*. 19 July 2006. Web. 8 June 2013.

K., Adrienne. *Native Appropriations*. Web. 8 June 2013.

Keep America Beautiful. "The Crying Indian." Advertisement. *You Tube*. 22 April 1971. Web. 8 June 2013.

King, Patricia M. "Learning to Make Reflective Judgments." *New Directions for Teaching and Learning*, 82 (Summer 2000): 15–26. Print.

Knefelkamp, L. Lee. "The Influence of a Classic." *Liberal Education* 89.3 (2003): 10–15. Print.

Miranda, Deborah A. *Bad NDNS*. Web. 8 June 2013.

———. "Novena to Bad Indians." *Bad Indians: A Tribal Memoir*. Berkeley: Hayday, 2013. Print.

Momaday, N. Scott. *House Made of Dawn*. 1968. New York: HarperPerennial, 1999. Print.

Nygren, Åse. "A World of Story-Smoke: A Conversation with Sherman Alexie." *MELUS* 30.4 (2005): 149–169. Print.

Our Spirits Don't Speak English. Dir. Chip Richie. Rich-Heape Films, 2008. Film.

Owens, Louis. *Mixedblood Messages: Literature, Film, Family, Place*. Norman: University of Oklahoma Press, 1998. Print.

Silko, Leslie Marmon. *Ceremony*. 1977. New York: Penguin, 2006. Print.

Teuton, Sean. "The Callout: Writing American Indian Politics" *Reasoning Together: The Native Critics Collective*. Ed. Womack, Craig. Norman: University of Oklahoma Press, 2008. Print.

Torrez, Juliette. "Juliette Torrez Goes Long Distance with Sherman Alexie." *(Sic) Vice & Verse* 31 August 1999. Web. 6 June 2013.

Wahpeconiah, Tammy. "Navigating the River of the World: Collective Trauma in *The Absolutely True Diary of a Part-Time Indian*." *Critical Insights: Sherman Alexie*. Ed. Leon Lewis. Pasadena, CA, Hackensack, NJ: Salem, 2012. Print.

Weaver, Jace. *That the People Might Live: Native American Literatures and Native American Communities*. New York: Oxford University Press USA, 1997. Print.

Zitzer-Comfort, Carol. "Teaching Native American Literature: Inviting Students to See the World Through Indigenous Lenses." *Pedagogy* 8.1 (2008): 160–70. Print.

Section II: Focus on the Method

Reflect and Act
Using Applied Learning Projects to Engage Students in Text and Community

Helane Adams Androne

As an undergraduate student at a highly ranked university in southern California, I did not come from the same sort of communities from which many of my peers emerged. I had experienced the kind of upward mobility that occurs when a recently divorced single parent struggles through poverty into working class married life. I lived in a community whose lives and values were impacted by racism, gang violence, and classism. While many of my friends lived on campus and managed the full experience of college life, I did so living at home, working three jobs. I do not consider this a point to elicit sympathy; despite circumstances that could have counted me out, I was marked by privilege every time I stepped foot back into my neighborhood, every time I spoke to certain family members, and certainly every time I reflected on the loss of a friend to violence or found myself lamenting the blatant and obvious racism experienced by so many I knew.

My privilege included the reality that I had been raised with the expectation of success and was ambitious enough to pursue it. But my experience in these seemingly completely different worlds, worlds that used different jargon, different ways of negotiating, that had different daily concerns, led me to understand the way that worlds collide and permeate one another. I began to feel keenly the difference between the world of academia and the world of my "minority," working class community and I often found myself trying to find ways to connect the concerns and objectives of the two. Often when I teach American literatures written by ethnic populations, students have extreme responses to them—of deep engagement and connection, of gaping separation, and even of fearful confrontation. One way I have come to attempt to bridge what I consider a similar experience of distance and difference that occurs for students that occurred for me as an undergraduate, is the development of an extended project by which they could mine their own interests and experiences to find connections between the literatures and emerging concepts within those literatures to apply their insights in real communities. This Applied Learning Project has come to characterize my American literature classes and has grown and developed into a learner-centered device that demands personal reflection, audience assessment, creativity and community relevance.

When I was hired to teach African American writing at an open access regional campus of a public liberal arts university, it was clear that there was an open opportunity for me to reach students that shared my world-straddling reality. My background was comparativist, between African American and Chicana fiction, and I had experience teaching Asian American studies at a prior university. As I began teaching this non-traditional population, with students varying from above average high school students to stay at home mothers to war veterans, I still faced what many teachers of more traditional American literature face in the university environment today: a sense of extraordinary distance between what students understood in the classroom and what they experienced in their various communities. This distance was not to be blamed on the more traditional reasoning that our students were young, that they had not quite developed the sort of understanding of the value of literature and its inquiry for its use in the world. It has been for me quite the opposite in most cases: many of my students have certainly done some living and know quite well much of what the patterns, stories and forces are that are operating in their own communities; their connection to the kinds of texts I teach is the problem. They have not yet drawn the connections between what happens in American ethnic texts and what happens in rural Appalachia, small town America, and certain contemporary isolated and gentrified urban cores.

But the issue is not that they are unaware or unwilling. The real issue is that many of the students I encounter have not necessarily considered the variety of perspectives, histories, and issues in the kind of depth or breadth expected in a typical college-level literature classroom. Some have never taken a literature course at all, much less one that is not allowed to escape weighty discussions about race, gender and class. And yet, they strongly understand and can articulate the significance of their presence in the university as it relates to their very real, tangible needs outside the classroom. They harbor very few misconceptions about what a degree will mean for their lives. In fact, they are typically knee-deep in the reality of what getting an education at the stage of life they are in means for their families and communities in the very clear and present terms of the financial burden that sitting in the classroom, rather than standing at a job, is on their households and families. More often than not, they are eager and committed, but completely unwilling to pretend their innocence by engaging in lofty discussions without acknowledging the connection between those discussions and their sometimes severely localized perspectives on the world around them.

Engaging in discussion with my students means that conversations are rich, varied and real; the tone can fluctuate from that of the town hall meeting to the book club to the dinner table. Regardless of the moment we are in, however, there is the clear and present need to make this conversation relevant, to make it matter beyond the academic spaces so that my students can indeed connect and fully experience the transformative power of literature. Needless to say, my desire is to assist them in finding the connections, the opportunities for making their literature education relevant to their walk outside my classroom—not only for the skills they can develop, but for the very literal application of their knowledge, what my university had determined an important requirement for all its students: the ability to reflect and act.

Foundations

I had dabbled enough in the scholarship of teaching and learning to say that my approach was informed by the same principles that direct problem-based learning, community-based learning and service-learning. These foundations, a commitment to the more general process of inquiry as a direct attack on the more and more strategic training of students to master testing rather than problem-solving, despite overwhelming research that supports the use of the latter, produced what I call the Applied Learning Project (ALP). The ALP was initially in direct response to the overwhelm I felt about constructing the kind of scaffolding necessary to really successfully apply some of the most attractive possibilities of the previously mentioned methods. In some ways, the project was my stand-in for the application of the larger constructs I longed to apply in my literature classroom. The ALP actually grew out of my attempts to create a problem-based learning situation for students and transitioned into something deeply individualized, personal and, in many ways, relevant to the variety of students I typically encounter. It emerged from a particular situation: for my students, a traditional problem, even in its very real opportunities, would most certainly leave many of them disinterested and under-prepared, either based on their lack of experience or based on the fullness of their experience. My literature course students vary more than just disciplinarily; they vary radically in terms of their backgrounds, preparation for study, and motivation. This could seem a complaint about inadequacies were I not to clarify that my students are most often extraordinary in their motivations for being in my classroom. As one student once remarked, "I know what's out there already. It's working with my body. That's hard work and I can't do that forever. I'm ready to work with my mind." Their preparation for study has been both traditional and seasoned by life experience. They are "diverse" in the way that a community often is—by age, experience, opinion, perspective, preparation, ethnicity, class, gender, ability. I distinctly remember a student in one of my classes, who was a war veteran, warmly chatting with me, only to reveal that the other students didn't "see" things the way he did, at least because he had the "benefit" of choosing the eye he would wear to class. Would he wear the one with the American flag or the one with the marijuana leaf? He had lost his eye in combat and had since acquired a large selection of glass eyes with designer pupils; only those who really looked closely into his eyes long enough to notice, would see that the pupil had a message that was important to him. He had a selection of ways of "seeing" things and I was deeply inspired by the perspectives he shared.

I want to acknowledge the difference in the ways that my students view the world, even as I help them to add to that vision through the views of the world offered in literature, not by undermining their vision, but by highlighting it and adding another, asking them to consider the relationships between them, and then asking them to act on what they discover. Even as I hope to avoid being crass about the rather obvious metaphor in the student's story above, I can't avoid pointing out that it has come to frame my thinking about students in my classes. Is it possible to assist students in such a way that their individual perspectives are retained, valued and supplemented by another way of seeing? That they are able to see the world they live in, the small and unique spaces that are important to them, the spaces that are not lofty or academic or even beyond the state line in many cases, in ways that they, not I, find a way to change because it is their community and they belong to it and it belongs to them? Shouldn't they choose how to apply their knowledge to change it? As one student from the "hollers" of Appalachia told me, "I'm from there. These are my neighbors, I know how they are, how they do things, and I know how to talk to 'em."

And so I found myself with the question: How do I facilitate an inquiry process whereby each one of these students can find their own pathway for the application of what they've learned from our interrogations of these literatures in their own communities? There is a keen difference in the way my veteran student and my stay at home mom, and my Appalachian student connect to their various communities and why they might choose to do so in that way and how they might approach bridging that connection. I cannot help but think that my job is more than ushering my students into the skilled use of literary language and theory, into the complexity of cultural studies, in ways that always created language barriers between me and the people I cared about. I cannot help but think that helping to somehow create a bridge between their study of literature and their communities of practice is part of what I am doing here.

It is important to note, too, that my expectation coming into my literature classroom cannot be that these students will emerge with a greater sense of the historical and stylistic complexities found within our texts and then go into their communities preaching the merits of contemporary ethnic fictions. I know that even as they move through the material, they are imagining how singularly important and incredibly difficult it is to convey their learning in real situations outside academic contexts in ways that matter. Realistically, they might muse, when would such conversations come up and how prepared could they be after our survey course to do more than expound upon why they enjoyed some particular text that those in their audience might never have encountered? Would the ensuing conversation about larger issues within those texts be approached in similarly random ways that would then alienate them from their communities?

Of course the value of reading literature is not just in the book club opportunities that many students enter imagining. As teachers of literature, we know the kind of critical thinking and contextual learning and craft appreciation that comes with reading; however, our students are not often provided the opportunities to express what they've come away with in ways that move them and would somehow alter those they encounter in their various communities. I intend for the ALP to be that opportunity in that it asks students to consider their own interests in choosing their project focus, whether those interests are centered on career pursuits, hobbies, or the values they hold dear. Through this project, I expect them to ask a question that matters to them and their communities, to use the literature as inspiration for reflection on their question, and to act on what they find out in a way that is appropriate for their chosen audience, whether that audience is their family or their employer. I want to get them to engage the literature personally, which means building a relationship between them and the texts.

Fortunately and unfortunately, the texts I teach are not usually familiar to my students. Even those students who share ethnic background with the authors I choose are not typically familiar with the texts or the extent to which complex issues that we will discuss mingle and diverge from their own.

Certainly they are aware of what it's like to be them in a particular context, but they too are discovering what it means to consider the literature in community with other literatures that, taken together, enlighten them about the complexities of racism, sexism, classism, and all manner of sacrifice related to the larger themes of freedom and democracy to which conversations they have indeed been privy and participant.

Students in my classes will encounter texts from a variety of genres in a variety of modes; they will be introduced to ways of reading these texts that require a forthright dealing with complex issues. I teach a number of literature courses that not only involve the recognition of complex intersections between race, class and gender, but more often than not they will also find that we focus on spirituality/religion, politics and history. I have taught African American writing courses divided chronologically, Latino/a literatures envisioned broadly, American ethnic literature surveys, Integrative Studies seminars, and women's studies courses within which I employed the ALP and its corresponding scaffolding as a method for creating a richer experience for me and for my students, who clearly need an opportunity to make the kinds of connections between the concerns of the literatures with which we were dealing, the issues in their own communities, and the interests they wanted to nurture.

What Is the Applied Learning Project?

The Applied Learning Project allows for student choice for the direction of their research and the audience for which that research is meant. It means that students will engage in developing something that contributes to the thinking in their community in some specific way. And, it means that we get to acknowledge student interests and communities of practice even as we engage in a model of inquiry, generative thinking, and critical application of knowledge. It means that students are engaged from the outset of the course in the understanding that they are to remain keen to the issues and topics that move them, to attend to those and begin to plan their pursuit of them as a culminating response to their encounters with the literatures we examine. It should be said outright that students are not required to somehow create a less distant relationship with the literature itself; rather, they are to allow the literature to inspire them to act on an issue or concern that is already relevant to them.

The ALP is built as a project. It is not a paper; in fact, the majority of the writing is reflective and analytical, but not of the literatures we study necessarily; literary analysis happens all along the way. The project typically occurs as a final and is made up of the following elements and is articulated thusly in my syllabus to students:

> *The Applied Learning Project* (ALP) is an opportunity for you to apply your learning more personally by engaging creatively with the issues presented in class discussions and texts. This is a project, not a single paper, so there is a process involved with its completion. There will be idea-generating activities, drafts and revisions as we go along to assist in your thinking about and the completion of the project. These activities are extremely important to your successful completion of the project expectations. In this way, your work during the semester will rather naturally build into the final project; therefore, you cannot wait until the last minute to begin thinking about this project, so your class participation in activities and discussions is essential. More detailed instructions will be provided in class. The elements of the project include:
>
> **I. Project Proposal with Annotated Bibliography** (500 words). Now that you've located some resources, take some time to annotate them and cite them. That simply means you need to list the source in its MLA citation format and explain what the source argues as well as how that argument assists in progressing yours or your project more generally. I will provide more detail on what this looks like. *You must get approval on your proposal prior to completing the following project assignments.*
>
> **II. Applied Learning Analysis** (1250–1500 words). This is a reflective integration of your existing Discussion Notes. Go back and look at what you've noticed in the course material. How do your notes answer the question: *What are the most intriguing issues/concepts within the course material and why?*
>
> **III. Applied Learning Reflection** (750–1000 words). This is a look back at your project process and direction, including an interpretation of text(s), event(s), or moves that mattered to accomplishing your goals. The Reflection should consider more than just what you did, but also why you made the choices you made and what the impact of those choices may have been. *In your own words, tell me what you've done to complete this project, how and why.*
>
> **IV. Applied Learning Reveal.** This is the sharing of your project in whatever mode is appropriate for the audience of your Artifact. It should be shaped by the idea that this project is for real use outside the classroom; therefore, it should take on the look, feel and shape of something fitting the context of your chosen Artifact. We have practiced using a number of technologies that you can utilize to frame your work. The Reveal is essentially the appropriate "packaging" of the map of your project. It might be a Prezi, a Powerpoint, a Screencast, a website, blog or other format. This is the format for your audience to encounter your Artifact and the reasoning for developing it. *What is the best way to frame your message to your specific audience to achieve the most impact? What elements should be included to help convince your audience of the relevance and usefulness of*

your Artifact? How would that Artifact be packaged and presented to your audience?

V. Cultural Artifact. This is the "piece" that develops from the work of your project. This piece is the core of your project. It is the product you wish to put into use. It emerges from the understanding of a specific audience and its attending genres. You should choose an Artifact that appropriately matches the actual public audience and the associated context. What kind of piece is actually useful for impacting your audience?

In this way, I convey to students in their syllabus the most basic direction and scope of the project. Because it is a culminating project, most often it acts as their final exam for the course.

Each portion of the ALP progresses from the experience of the course, but the proposal is the place where students are asked to begin the integration of their thinking about the course material and their own interests. It is imperative that they begin that process relatively early because it helps not only to focus their thinking on their project, but also to frame their discussions of the literatures along the way, a point of scaffolding I will return to later. The Proposal is a relatively low-stakes assignment that allows for freedom in their thinking even as it provides them with a requirement to take a few first steps to act on their interests and begin to educate themselves on the larger conversations that are occurring on their chosen topic or issue. In the Proposal students must review the choices for projects and choose their direction, with the understanding that they can merge, intersect and re-develop the suggested projects as they see fit. As they determine their project, they must also determine their audience because the ALP requires that they produce some relevant Artifact[1] that is meaningful and/or useful for or to their selected audience. The choices of projects further articulate possibilities for these Artifacts:

Interest: Interviewing, Journalism   Project: Oral History
Research focus: Interviews, historical relationships between people and events

Oral history is information collected and verbally passed on by or about participants in an historical event. In traditional societies, without either written language or widespread literacy, oral history is passed down from one generation to the next and serves as a vital and reliable record of significant events in that people's past. In contemporary society, oral histories can discover and record valuable first-hand information from people that have experienced important events. So, what is the relationship between people groups and oral history? Choose a person or group to interview based on a significant topic, theme, or event. You will submit approximately 10 questions you intend to ask your informants prior to any scheduled interviews. You must get permission to record and transcribe the interview(s).

Interest: Politics, World Events, Activism *Project: Political*
Research focus: Localized politics and events & their affect on people, wildlife, environment

What is the relationship between culture and politics? This assignment gives you an opportunity to engage in social activism pertaining to relevant issues. You can develop an appropriate text (brochure, letter to a politician, poster, etc.) through which you argue your perspective to a well-defined and specific audience. Choose an issue/problem that emerged for you from the material in class, including lectures, discussions, films, etc.

Interest: Commercial TV/Radio, *Project: Media Marketing*
  Advertising, Business
Research focus: Advertising culture and structures, demographics, specific products

This assignment is an opportunity for you to study the trends associated with media and marketing of products to, for, and/or about a particular group. How is culture reflected in the media? Your project will consider research in the field, historic relevance of, and commentary on, the topic.

Interests: Nursing, Traditional/Alternative *Project: Wellness*
  Medicine & Therapies
Research focus: Health concerns, medicines, therapies and their effects on health, well-being

This assignment is for those of you with particular interest or concern with the health and well-being of members of society. This can be broadly defined; you might consider physical, mental, emotional, or spiritual well-being. What aspects of cultural identity are most significant to issues of wellness?

Interests: Visual Art, Instrumental Music *Project: Artistic*
Research focus: Popular and/or historically significant art/music, artists and themes

This project is to be presented and preserved as a statement or consideration of some aspect of a group's experience. You can create a visual or aural piece using whatever material suits your purposes. How do elements of culture inspire your artistic production?

Interests: Creative Writing, Literary Analysis *Project: Literary*
Research focus: Popular and historic writers and significant themes

This is a compilation of your own writing in whatever genre suits you (fiction, non-fiction, historical fiction, children's literature, poetry, etc.) directed to address and respond to aspects of a group's experience, your consideration of it, and reflection on it. How does your understanding of culture influence your literary choices?

Interests: Theater, Dance, Singing   *Project: Performance*
Research focus: Popular and historical productions and performances and themes

This is an opportunity for those who are comfortable with creative performance to incorporate those talents in a class presentation that articulates some issue or reveals some truth(s) about literature, culture, history, and/or politics. This project is broadly defined, so it can encompass a variety of modes, including but not limited to acting, cooking, and performance art. How is culture performative?

Interests: Teaching, Educational Policy   *Project: Curriculum*
& Leadership
Research focus: Current and historically significant issues and debates, curricular expectations

Okay Education majors, this project is intended to facilitate the introduction of culture and literature into a primary or secondary curriculum. You will design and implement an organized program for including what you determine are appropriate and relevant literary and cultural elements into a classroom. This could be in the form of a teaching philosophy statement, a lesson plan, a unit plan, etc. You should take into consideration current state standards as they pertain to the Common Core. How should culture be represented within a primary or secondary curriculum?

Interests: Travel, Museum Curation,   *Project: Site Project*
Historical Preservation
Research focus: Cultural production, its representations and historical connections and meanings

Where does culture happen and how is it imagined and preserved? This is an opportunity to encourage you to immerse yourself in the history and culture of a particular region/group, to visit a new place, or to explore that museum you've always wanted to visit. Choose a representative site to visit at least three times for at least two hours each time. Dates, times, and duration of the opportunities will vary, so it's necessary to check with the institutions for up-to-date information. *You must obtain approval for your site visit prior to any official visitation, regardless of your history with the location or area.* Imagine yourself a reviewer as you visit. What are the key elements of the site and how do those elements affect its audience?

I have also translated this narrative into a chart for my online students:

Chart of Project Artifact and Audience Examples

Context/Discipline	Audience	Possible Artifact *(not an exhaustive list)*
Journalism, Public Media, Communications	Specific demographic of the public (e.g., those who listen to hip hop music, those who watch mainly comedies, etc.)	• 5–10 minute documentary video • Video/Audio interview with person of interest

Context/Discipline	Audience	Possible Artifact (not an exhaustive list)
Politics, Activism, Community Organizing/ Education	Members of locally specific community/ region, particular political party of voters within a particular party, those concerned with or impacted by a particular issue	• Propaganda poster, brochure, or bumper sticker • Billboard • Community meeting presentation/speech
Literary, Philosophy, Cultural Studies	Theorists in the field, Readers of theory, teachers of theory	• Article • Website • Blog
Advertising, Marketing, Business	Advertising, marketing investors, consumers within a specific demographic or using a specific kind of product (e.g., sales agents & consumers of a certain kind of product)	• Magazine or newspaper advertisement • Commercial • Economic report • Enhanced product (real or inventive)
Health, Fitness, Spiritual well-being	Medical technicians and professionals, Age-specific care-givers, local healthcare workers/ hospital staff, Fitness program managers, Local clergy	• Brochure • Postcard advertisement • Billboard • Sermon • Recipe book • Culinary presentation
Visual Arts	Local community arts programs, Art museum staff/docents, local artists of a particular style, consumers of visual art	• Original piece • Artist focus for public use
Literature, Creative Writing	Book clubs, Genre readers	• Original piece • Analysis • Detailed recommendation list • Book Proposal
Performance Arts	Local/regional performance group, Producers, Casting agents, Performing arts supporters, Theater groups	• Audition video • Advertising poster • Portfolio • Production schedule/plan • Script
Education, Academic Leadership	K-12 Teachers, Principals, Early Childhood educators, Higher education administrators & Instructors	• Lesson plan • Syllabus • Philosophy statement • Article

Context/Discipline	Audience	Possible Artifact *(not an exhaustive list)*
Cultural Events, Historical/Memorial/ Museum Curation	Museum enthusiasts and curators, memorial organizers, non-profit organizers, academic program organizers	• Historically specific curator information • Program proposal • Site Review
Other?		

The project choices are meant to emerge from the students' interests, personal and/or professional, and I take pains to make sure that they understand this point most clearly. I talk to them about how their passions can translate into artifacts that matter to their communities and to their own future goals. The artifacts themselves vary widely based on their interests of course. The point is to make sure that they understand that their interests are to frame the inquiry question they ask and therefore the direction of the project, but their audience and purpose are to guide the development of their Artifact. The key question I typically ask students is: What is it that you think is important to convey about this issue you care about and to whom should that message be conveyed?

At times the audience and purpose merge into multi-layered artifacts, the most obvious type of which occurs most often among my education majors who often choose to create a lesson plan for their students. When we consult, I help students see how the various parts of their assignment can intersect with their audience and purpose such that their knowledge is applied to their interest. We talk about the culture of teaching, its inherent challenges, and the demographics of their desired classrooms. We discuss how their assignments within the ALP can lead to a deeper understanding of their desired field, and how they can shape their project to best fit their needs. I ask students to do some foundational reflection work to get at certain details:

ALP Foundation Work Instructions
Time to do some reflective writing that will develop the foundation for your project work.
I. It's time to begin thinking about how the course material reaches into the spaces of interest to you. What issues have stood out in the texts as most interesting to you? What patterns do you find most intriguing? Construct a topic list of interesting subjects, themes, characters, events that stand out most to you from the course material and discussions. We'll call this your *Topic Interest List*.
II. Take a moment and consider the *Topic Interest List* you've developed. Who are the people most interested in and impacted by the topics/issues on your list? This is your potential audience with whom you might enter into

public discourse or conversation (because they, like you, care about those topics and issues too).

III. What are the connections between those items on your *Topic Interest List*, the audience for that kind of public discourse and your own personal passions, hobbies, interests, or career goals? How are messages conveyed in their contexts? On your list, begin to match up topics with audiences and contexts. Now add to that the kinds of communication that happens within those contexts. This will help you think about the Artifact you might use for your project.

Consider these examples:

Example1: If you're deeply interested in music, and so are producers and musicians, you might consider their context to determine how messages are conveyed in that arena. In the case of this example, you might say that people into blues, like producers and musicians, might communicate messages through their music, through music posters, through music advertising, through jam sessions, etc. *An Artifact could be a music poster or advertisement or original piece.*

Example 2: If you're deeply interested in health care issues, and so are healthcare workers and community organizers, you might consider their contexts—perhaps within hospitals or in community health care situations. Perhaps they communicate through brochures, how to videos/training, handbooks and such. *An Artifact could be a brochure, training video, or handbook.*

Once students have done the reflective work, they can begin the actual Proposal. The Proposal helps them to take the time to familiarize themselves with the public discourse about their issue so that they are prepared for how they might articulate their argument within their Artifact. For example, when future teachers find out about the real conversations about standardizations and testing expectations, they can begin to construct their argument, which inevitably is about how to either provide for focused instruction on certain ethnic texts, or on how and what to appropriately integrate into the established American literary canon at their desired teaching level. The Analysis for such a project still addresses the basic criteria provided in their assignment:

> This is your opportunity to reconsider your discussion notes in another way. Go back through your discussion notes and consider the following questions:
>
> 1. What is the significance of the texts you've read to your understanding of the issue you care about ? (How and why?)
>
> 2. How will you apply your understanding, thinking, and experiences with these texts outside the classroom?
>
> 3. Which texts were most significant to your thinking about the complexity of American identities and why?
>
> Use your notes to recall specifics about your thinking and about text

details. Be sure and refer to specific texts, characters, notes you made for discussion, films, etc. to discuss the questions. This is your opportunity to both analyze and reflect on the course material and how it has reinforced, challenged, inspired and troubled your thinking. Be honest and be specific. Your analysis should result in a 1000–1250 word essay.

At this point, students use the notes they have constructed for our in class discussions, for which I provide "Guiding Questions" and role assignments,[2] to reflect and recall what has moved them throughout the semester. This sort of reflection is important to help students focus on the details that have provoked them most, those pieces and ideas and conversations that have given forth to their deepest questions and concerns. From this mode of thinking students are better able to focus their thinking on the connections they have noticed along the way. This assignment is best addressed in a draft within a couple of weeks of the Proposal deadline, but in final draft, it is most telling after the majority of readings and discussions of the semester are accomplished.

For most students, once they return to their notes from the readings, they discover that there are patterns in their responses to the texts; they have, in one way or another, asserted their opinions and concerns in ways that can guide their research and thinking. Taking an inventory of their thinking can lead to greater clarity for their project. For example, students interested in the politics associated with the environment might find themselves often inclined toward the environmental characterization in stories (as in African American naturalism), the way that authors critique and engage their environments (as in Nuyorican poems about the lower east side of New York), or their noticings of authors' dis/connections and responses to the implications of changing spaces (as in novels such as Viramontes' *Their Dogs Came With Them*).

Sometimes students interested in seemingly divergent fields find themselves in a position to learn from each other within their discussions on a complex issue; while students interested in health and well-being find themselves thinking about the healthcare implications of an entire population too afraid to go to the doctor, students with a business bent tend to find themselves asking questions about the economic implications of a growing undocumented immigrant population. The exercise of moving through their own musings and concerns that emerge from the stories we read, as expressed along the way, along with the noted questions and concerns of their peers, about the issues about which they care, most inevitably leads to focused yet nuanced perspectives on their world, their communities and the issues that matter most to them. Through the Analysis, students take that important inventory that typically points to their passions, interests, and larger core beliefs with which they can better focus their project, and therefore better understand its audience and purpose.

Once students have a clear audience and purpose, the Artifact emerges from their understanding of the culture of their audience and the genre that best allows them to address that audience. The Artifact sometimes becomes part of the plan itself, as in the case with future teachers, who tend to combine the elements of planning with the models they develop for their classrooms. These future teachers typically create a way to convey their information visually to their students (as in bulletin board, handout or website designs) and to argue their curriculum ideas to the other obviously important part of their audience: their department colleagues, including their curriculum directors and principals. In doing so, these future teachers are creating useful documents that apply their knowledge from the classroom in realistic, deeply authentic ways that can serve as stepping-stones for their thinking as professionals. Similarly, those deeply interested in learning and preserving voices and cultures find that their Artifact for an oral history focus is best as an audio/visual collection for researchers or that it is for more personal use in their families and communities as an album or presentation, which becomes a meaningful archive of their own histories, further connecting their experiences with the texts in our course.

The Reflection assignment of the ALP is perhaps the most telling of the assignments. In this assignment, students are asked to reflect on the entire process of the project, from beginning to end. I ask them to honestly assess their choices, what worked and what did not, and how the pieces of the project emerged for them. I ask them to consider commenting on the direction of the project, the assignments themselves, and whatever else mattered to getting them to completion. These assignments elicit the feedback I find most useful in determining how students made the connections that determined their final project and to what end. I get to hear about how the perceived recurring theme of acceptance influenced a future teacher and how she decided during the course of the project that she really wanted to be in early education rather than secondary:

> The stories and movies we watched often had people coming to America and facing the challenges that accompanied the move. Often, I noticed that acceptance was an issue many faced. In the movie *El Norte*, there were issues finding jobs due to being "illegal." The video that definitely showed the struggle for acceptance was *The Other Side of Immigration*. This film was following some Mexican workers who traveled to the United States to find jobs. The husbands would travel (and live) in the United States and work anywhere they could to make money. All the money they made, they

would send back home to their families to help support them. Again, these men talked about how hard it was to communicate with people and how they felt like they had to hide so they wouldn't be sent back home.

Her teaching philosophy was transformed as a result of both the issues that impacted her most and the process of developing a project that was meaningful to her life:

I started by making my teaching philosophy [include] my top three concepts: (1) Our classroom should be a safe, inviting area. Students should all be able to ask me questions, interact with peers, and be treated with respect. (2) Everyone should be treated equally. I want my students to view each other as equals and to try to help each other rather than hinder. (3) Encourage lessons that also can be related to real life. I want my lessons to have meanings that go beyond just the common core standards. I want my students to remember what I've taught them rather than know it just for a test.

She chose a topic and developed a lesson that would work in a first grade classroom.

In another project, a future science and math teacher expressed his concerns about the purpose of his project:

In doing this applied learning project I had several goals I wished to accomplish and features I wished to maintain. Primarily, beyond just accomplishing the assigned task, I wanted it to be something that was relatable to my chosen field of study, but also something that would be easily identifiable as my tastes, aesthetics, and style. It also had to be something I was not only proud to show my oldest son but that I felt he would benefit from, as enrolling in this course was as much for him as it was for me ... I rather enjoyed this project as it not only let me explore [a] subject that I found interesting, it also gave me a chance to share that with someone I care about.... It also allowed me to look at cultural and political aspects I had not really examined until this point, like the political situation in Argentina through the years, and how young men from around Latin America find themselves all around the world, aiding people in the world they have never even met, nor ever will.

This student articulates the ways in which the project takes on a personal meaning, particularly for non-traditional students.

Another student interested in sports studies found a way to integrate his passion and his project:

Since I am a sports management and coaching major, I figured I should focus on something that I could be potentially dealing with in the job market. My choice to focus on baseball in Cuba came as a result of the recent uprising trend of Cuban baseball players in the Major Leagues.... Being a baseball guy, I thought I knew a lot about baseball players from Cuba coming into the project, but I was surprised at how much I learned. It was a great experience to be able to do a project that I am passionate about, and it made me excited to be able to present it to others to show them my knowledge. I have honestly thought about using this experience to my advantage and learn more about Latin American culture while I am in school ... I also felt that my piece could have been used as a resume builder because it shows my previous research and specialization with Latin American cultures.

The vast majority of students express similar responses to this project. I have had students who were previously victims of domestic violence, now in school for social work, conduct interviews and construct Artifacts to educate and encourage their future clients (and friends) out of dangerous situations. I have seen students take on the cause of international feminism by creating a website to provide access to information and resources for women in other parts of the world. There have been more than a few creative writing students use their project to inspire and more deeply consider the details of their own stories and poetry. In fact, twice creative writers have gone on to publish the work they initiated or revised based on our course material and the feedback they received during the process of developing their ALP. I have known business and marketing students who examined, critiqued and developed relevant media to reflect their perspectives on the direction and scope of media attention to minority communities, geared of course to an audience of stakeholders and decision makers they intended to be in contact with once they stepped out into their careers. Visual artists have created text and character-inspired Artifacts; performing artists have written and performed poetry and music. I had a student who had begun a deep interest in the other side of the Hilton Head vacation destination and decided to pursue her interest in the Gullah peoples with visitations, interviews and a curated display that critiqued representations of the island as solely a tourist location rather than a place of deep cultural roots and ties to the land there. The result of ALP completion has been indisputably the best culminating experience in my classroom that I can remember.

The Final Reveal of the ALP can be staged in a number of ways. Usually, it is best to determine the staging of the reveal based upon the logistics of the class period. I have determined that our two hour final exam period works well enough for the Reveal if it is a small to medium sized class, but it is important to consider the time allotted per student for the sharing of their work and how that sharing will be most conducive to student engagement. For example, I have come to use a "tabletop showcase" or "poster session" style in the classroom for fuller classes. I have also broken the class into groups that shift in order to take turns as audience and presenters during the Reveal, but this does not always allow for every student to hear from each other. It is certainly best if the Reveal can happen across the span of several days during which students can respond to their peers' work and there can be a more relaxed atmosphere for the kind of community sharing that happens.

Scaffolding the ALP: Maps, Notes and Ritual Reflections

It is important to note that students do not care to jump into weighty projects without proper scaffolding any more than we do. In the beginning, I used this project as a distinct experience, but I have learned that it is important to connect and develop a number of assignments aimed at preparing students for the project process. In my own estimation, the scaffolding of the project best develops within a culture of inquiry, one in which students are from the very beginning, made to understand the value of their own experiences, communities and concerns. This can begin from the first day of classes and helps to develop a sense of community in the classroom. Brief opportunities for students to write and share with each other their thematically connected experiences works quite well. When we discuss sensitive issues, I often use a ritual reflection[3] to help students engage in the core principles of a text, such as asking students to write about a time when they realized they had to work, or a time when they realized they were poor/rich/neither, or a time when they realized they were a girl/boy/neither, or a time when they realized they had been the victim of some form of prejudice. Getting students connected to the themes within the texts is imperative to helping them see beyond the strictures implied by the particularities of context. It is much more difficult to separate themselves from the experience of racism, sexism, classism and so on when they point to a similar principle working within their own lives. The level of connection and empathy is important for beginning their journey into how these texts comment on their particular communities of interest if, in fact, they intend to make meaning of their time delving into them.

Another scaffolding exercise I have used is the Collaborative Interactive Map. This assignment is an opportunity for students to work together as they consider the intersections of their combined interests. I articulate this to students in their syllabus:

> The *Collaborative Interactive Map* involves determining the knowledge or interest you already have and locating that knowledge or interest spatially and contextually. You will collaborate with others who have similar or inter-

secting interests (culinary, musical, literary, business, educational, etc.) and decide on a region or area of focus using a map. You won't have to create the map (just use a ready made one). Your group will collaborate to determine the appropriate legend for guiding the reader through the group's interests via the actual locations for events, people, and/or important contexts for that topic of interest.

I group students for this assignment based on their interests as determined by some quick writing about themselves and their communities. They ultimately decide whether they want to focus on culinary, historical, scientific, musical, literary, educational, or business locations of note. I provide some chronological resources for their work, but it is largely up to them how they as a group want to proceed in the creation of a collaborative map. The mapping exercise is an effort to take the hysteria out of a mapping "test" and to create a situation in which students are actually doing what comes quite naturally: associating places and spaces with significant events, memories, and peoples. In the end, students knew more about a particular region of the world than any map test would have elicited—and it was a much more engaging experience when they presented their material (informally), again based on their own interests. What results is that rather basic interests in certain dishes or musical traditions enable students to present to the rest of the class its origins, its economic impact on the region, its variety of expressions and how it interacts within the world. What begins as distant, uninformed interests become visual journeys through several regions and results in conversations about farming, industrial access, and the development of certain stereotypes. At its best, this exercise offers students an opportunity to discuss the connections they find, to develop a visual representation of space and place, to determine what is of most interest to the audience exploring the region. The maps students produce indicate a different kind of cultural knowledge that is not easily employed when only asked to locate a city on a map. I am confident that my students have something to associate with particular regions they explored through the people, events, dishes, and music of those regions, making the map memorable and applicable to their own lives.

Perhaps the most important scaffolding I have done has been using a particular method for helping students prepare for in-class discussion that is a vigorous nod to the literature circles as developed by Harvey Daniels for use in K-12 teaching years ago. I was introduced to the model some years ago at a Lilly Conference on Teaching. Always one willing to try something new and shake up the classroom experience a bit, I immediately appropriated the role-based discussion group model for my college students. This role-based discussion process has never failed to provide the kind of focused analysis and interesting conversation that real engagement with texts brings. My roles have transformed over time, but they remain relatively consistent in the kinds of expectations I provide to students:

> **Director:** provides open-ended questions for discussion, helps keep group conversations on track
> **Locator:** locates and shares specific passages notable for their style, tone, topic, or other intellectual value
> **Connector:** provides interesting connections between author, event, contextual information on topics in our texts and issues, events, topics outside the text
> **Contextualizer:** locates information about people, events and authors that are of significance to the text

The Director is the person who presents opportunities to discuss the text through questions that elicit deeper thinking and consideration of the text's characters, themes, and so on. The Locator is the person responsible for making sure that the group returns to the text over and over again to identify, question and consider meaning through the poetics and conventions involved in the text. The Connector is the person responsible for what I like to consider the necessary distraction. I see this role as one that draws a group's thinking out of the text and into the thematic and contextual such that students are allowed to have a response to the reading that stems from their own interests and experiences. The Connector's role is vital in my mind to the scaffolding of a process that invites students to consider their interests and passions as valid and important to the conversation about texts. The Contextualizer dives into the details of authors' lives and interests and motivations, the reception of particular works, and how artistic movements and politics might be interacting with the text and what the implications of those interactions might be. Most often I give students the option to decide within their groups what their roles will be, though I sometimes change groups, ask that students switch roles and so on so that they can experience the difference in information collection and resulting group discussion. I also want them to have a variety of perspectives within their prepared discussion notes, which they will return to in order to complete their analysis within the Applied Learning Project.

The discussion notes that students prepare are due for each reading and are to be ready for discussion in class on the date we discuss each text. I encourage students to take notes within their groups as well so that they can add their peers' comments into their thinking when they reflect on their notes for the ALP. The notes provide a cache of reflections, details, and information for students to mine from and analyze when they are ready to focus on their projects. As many teachers have come to note, literature circle designs are fruitful, engaging and student driven.

The larger purpose for constructing this project is to engage students in the kinds of issues that develop from reading American ethnic literatures. As such, this project can elicit a number of responses from students, including empathy, frustration, and revelations about their organizational and research skills. Because the ALP arises from students, it is also constantly refreshed by students. I add and re-think project descriptions, scaffolding measures, and opportunities to help them connect with the material. In doing so, I have to remind myself that these are their projects, through which they will come to their own conclusions about the world within which they live. It is important that students do not lean too heavily on the ideas of the instructor, that they are reminded often that this project has to matter to them and their communities somehow. I have found that students do not often believe the initial instructions for this project because they are not at all used to being validated. Often my students come into the classroom having felt a sense of failure, desperation, and or necessity for change and specific answers. Helping them develop questions of their own, guiding them through a real/relevant research process, and applauding the Reveal of this project is so often a transformative moment for adults who need to recover a bit of their confidence—in themselves and in the connections between their educations and the communities that they are hoping to affect.

Notes

1. I refer to this as an Artifact rather than a "product" because there is often a necessary critique of the sort of commodification that is associated with products meant to be for or about the communities my students might represent. I find that referring to their piece as an Artifact opens the space to greater understanding of the cultural relevance of what they are creating.
2. The role assignments are inspired by the literature circle work of Harvey Daniels. I will return to these in more detail later.
3. See Androne, H. "Birth, Death and Transformation: Ritual as Inquiry in the Classroom." *Pedagogy: Critical Approaches to Teaching Literature, Language, Composition, and Culture* 14 (2013).

Works Cited

Androne, Helane. (2014) "Birth, Death and Transformation: Ritual as Inquiry in the Classroom." *Pedagogy: Critical Approaches to Teaching Literature, Language, Composition and Culture.* 14.2:317–341. Print.
Germano, Roy. *The Other Side of Immigration* (2009). Film.
Viramontes, Helena María. (2008) *Their Dogs Came with Them: A Novel.* Washington Square Press. Print.

The Answer Is the Story
Teachers and Students Authoring American Literature to Understand American Literature

Mary F. Dulworth Gibson

> "We were the people who were not in the papers. We lived in the white spaces at the edges of the print. It gave us more freedom. We lived in the gap between the stories."—Margaret Atwood, *The Handmaid's Tale*

It's the story that connects us. It's the adventure, the experiences, the trials, the joys, and the everyday that shapes a text that becomes our lives. We connect through that inner text to every other human being we meet. In teaching, that text comes from the lives of our students. This idea is not taught in our undergraduate classes with our children's literature and reading diagnostics, but it is the one lesson that I studied early, in the inner city of Cincinnati. My inner text was older, drastically different, and had no real connections to the young souls that waited for me that first day of school. But from the begining, I wanted to know, I wanted to understand, and I had no choice but to listen and *read*. Authentic American literature comes from many sources. You have the beautiful texts from authors who have lived the African American or Chinese American experience, but there is more. There is an inner text, even in the minds of junior high students, that tell of a life we may not recognize from the surface. The stories I heard, the stories written and spoken, were not in Pulitzer Prize winning novels but maybe they should have been. Pulling these rich inner texts from the minds and hearts of our students doesn't come with a difficult formula or strategy. It requires a lot of pencil and paper, a lot of room to mess up, time to let it sink in and settle, and most importantly, a willingness to really listen and respect the inner text that happens when it all comes out. In our twenty-first century world, a place where quick and now are the most important of qualities, this process seems archaic. Many of us schooled folks would say there is plenty of real text out there for students to read and learn from. Due to the constraints of testing and results, many of us simply don't have the time or room to allow for this process, or so we think. If we as teachers are here to promote the love of life learning, what better learning than to acknowledge the story that is within all of us and then share those stories with each other? How can we do this in a twenty-first century world that demands results and percentages? And, perhaps more importantly, why should we care about that inner text? It is through that inner text that we build a community, a family of students that feel safe and free to share their lives—that is American ethnic literature at its best.

I

> "Stories—individual stories, family stories, national stories—are what stitch together the disparate elements of human exsistence into a coherent whole. We are all story animals."—Yann Martel, *Beatrice and Virgil*

The morning of 9/11 started as any other morning. How many times have we heard that? My overfilled classroom of eighth graders were working on a writing piece, folks were up moving around, asking questions, getting peer edits complete, and it was hot—I remember because our windows were open and we were all still sweating. The rest of the morning is etched like a lithograph in my head even now, almost 13 years later. Someone came in and said "Turn on the TV." Someone else came in and said there had been an accident. We were busy so the screen simply stayed still and unnoticed as the first tower billowed smoke into that terribly beautiful blue sky. Even I stayed busy talking to folks, looking at work, and didn't give a second thought to that restaurant Windows over the World that I had visited every Christmas with my grandmother for as long as she had been alive. Our lives, for that moment were focused on work and productivity. And then it all changed. The decision to keep the television on after the second plane hit is still one I grapple with to this day. The emotional punch to the stomach caused not a sound in my normally loud and bustling classroom. We sat huddled together on my garage sale couches and chairs, glued to the TV. There were people falling, people looking up, people running, people calling, people confused, people in shock, people angry, people dead, and people desperately hoping. The hours went by so slowly. The first tower fell, the Pentagon was burning, the second tower fell, a plane crashed in a field somewhere. Where? Even as the final bell rang to go home for the day, no one moved. I realized that all of us were scared and everyone wanted to stay together. I remember thinking it strange that my very tough, very independent, very thick-skinned students were taking all of this really hard. It was of course a blow to our American pride, our sense of "nothing-can-happen-to-us," but my kids, from this neighborhood, with their life stories? The evening passed even slower. We all watched hours of news hoping someone would come out of the buildings okay or that our worst fear wasn't really true and all of it had been a mistake. But with morning, and a new day to teach, that wasn't the case. We had been instructed to leave televisions off and also told it probably was not a good idea to bring it up in class. With little sleep and a dazed expression, I walked in to the classroom that just a day before had been busy, bustling, and loud. The kids sat quiet, many absent, and most looking extremely tired. There was no loud lightning bolt or great revelation but it made sense, at that moment, to tell a story. I began by telling them about my grandmother:

> "What a fantastic lady," I said, "nails always done, hair perfectly in place, and always dressed to the nines. She was worldly, she loved theatre and music, but also watched every Detroit Lions football game during the regular season. She smoked long cigs that made her red nails even longer and she introduced me to New York City."

With a pause I asked if anyone had a relative like my grandmother? The folks around me started talking about aunts, grandparents, even relatives they only saw at Christmas and all of the interesting things that made them … interesting. We laughed a little and everyone kept listening. There was humanity and family in the stories and we could all understand that. I continued to tell them about my grandmother and our yearly visits to New York. It was with a theater tour and it included shows, shopping, really great food, but most importantly, a trip to the very top of the World Trade Center to the Windows over the World restaurant. I explained that this restaurant was filled with folks from all over the world. Your server may be from China and the chef may have been from Guatamala. There was a wooden dance floor that I always liked to walk across so I could hear my shoes. They brought you cherry Cokes in martini glasses so you felt as fancy as everyone else around you. It was time to share the point. The first plane hit the first tower so that the folks in the restaurant that morning had no chance of escaping. Years later we would all learn that many of the good folks who jumped that day probably came from the restaurant. I told the kids that although I missed her greatly, I was glad my grandmother had passed before 9/11. I think she would have been devastated to see the place she loved end up in the rubble of that day. I told the kids that I was mad and sad at the same time, that I didn't know how to put it in to words. It was like I wanted to hit someone for taking so much away from me. And then, "Ms. D., you're just pissed girl. I was there when my brother got shot. You want someone else to hurt. It doesn't make any sense so you just get pissed. I hit a wall outside the funeral home. It hurt, but I felt better." And that was it. In the days and weeks that followed that wrenching day of emotions, my students and I healed by writing our stories, our connections, our understandings and our heartbreaks that are still tied to the sights and sounds of that day. We were connected with people we didn't even know. The man that fell from the windowsill, the flight attendant who called her husband, the widow with three kids, the confused public, we were all of that.

There have been beautifully written memorials to that day etched so deeply in our hearts. Years later I used *Extremely Loud and Incredibly Close* by Jonathan Safran Foer in a freshman college English class. The novel is about a very unique young man who loses his father in the Trade Center disaster but begins another journey in hopes of learning more about his father. Along the way, he meets all kinds of New Yorkers, including his mute grandfather, and the interwoven text somehow helps heal the heartwrenching loss of that day. Students connected to the loss in their own lives and wrote narratives and poetry about the search for answers when things don't make sense. Nine-year-old Oskar is the main character and keeps the answering machine that saves the five messages from his father as he is trapped in the Trade Center on 9/11. Students wrote five messages to loved ones, themselves, or others that would be important to leave if they themselves knew it would be the last thing they would say. The result, a powerful narrative about love, loss, and the importance of saying what we need to say when we can say it.

II

> "After a while it occurred to me that between the covers of each of those books lay a boundless universe waiting to be discovered while beyond those walls, in the outside world, people allowed life to pass by in afternoon football games and radio soaps, content to do little more than gaze at their novels."—Carlos Ruiz Zafron, *The Shadow of the Wind*

My education in American ethnic literature continued. It didn't take place in the classroom of a university, but in the four walls of my classroom, the four blocks of the neighborhood, and the lives and interpretations of the young folks in front of me. My first step in this education was a hard one, I didn't share ethnic or class identity with my students and I needed to accept that. My students were white and black, most Appalachian in descent, and on the surface did not show any real ethnic links. But poverty was the great leveler. My students were registered as 99 percent economically disadvantaged. They received free lunch and services. They lived in government housing and lived off food stamps. Their parents, most of them high school dropouts, could not help with homework because they did not possess the skills themselves. The neighborhood surrounding the school was filled with drugs, prostitution, and violence with many of the victims and perpetrators being family memebers of my students. By twelve and thirteen years old, school was not the first priority for most of my students. Homework was not going to get done at home because most either worked, took care of younger siblings, or had to watch over parents. Many times students spent the night in emergency rooms, homeless shelters, or a neighbor's place. Conditions and circumstances were often beyond my comprehension or control but they were still my students, and understanding where they came from was a high priority. For a rich, white, Catholic girl from the South, the decision to teach in the inner city was not only frowned upon but met with bewilderment by family and friends. My upbringing kept me away from those who sat in my classroom and I was bred to travel down a different path. Ironically, the inner text of human experience can bring us all together.

By the time I finished my degree and started teaching, I was a single mother of three children under the age of 3. I had to apply for government insurance for my girls and I sat in the waiting room of the welfare office. I remember the nights sitting and wondering how I was ever going to make this work, worrying my girls would be different somehow because of my poor decisions. I remember worrying where the money would come from and the looks I often received at the grocery store or doctor's office when it was time to pay. I remember how I was treated asking for help, looked upon as if I were nothing. I came to understand that if I was treated that way, the long lines of other mothers behind me were receiving the same treatment. It was that life experience, that connection with others, that allowed me the space to listen and encourage the voices within my own classroom. Through the years I realized that my students really only wanted to be heard, really heard. They had spent most of their young lives under the assumption that they didn't matter, that what they had to say wasn't good enough, and they had no one speaking to them that looked or sounded like them. When given the freedom, the permission, the space, and the stage to speak to those experiences, their words created the dialogue that taught me authentic literature.

> "Forty three years old, and the war occurred half a lifetime ago, and yet the remembering makes it now. And sometimes remembering will lead to a story, which makes it forever. That's what stories are for. Stories are for joining the past to the future. Stories are for those late hours in the night when you can't remember how you got from where you were to where you are. Stories are for eternity, when memory is erased, when there is nothing to remember but the story."—Tim O'Brien, *The Things They Carried*

Using novels, real books with pages and spines, is an important piece of my classroom. The experience of reading a story and sharing those experiences with each other continued the lessons my students taught me. Many titles I picked up were frowned upon (by other collegues) with some asserting *your students couldn't possibly understand that*. That was clearly all the encouragement I needed. I spent hours looking for the stories I felt connected with my students. This required a more academic approach to American ethnic literature. What were the best examples I could bring into the classroom? What did I need to choose to make the work a success since we may or may not understand the schema the author brought to us as readers? What is *schema* and how do I explain that to my students? Did I need to front load or just let it happen? Is the reading level too advanced? Didn't I read that in college? There were different answers to all of those academic questions but the bottom line was … to let them read.

What came from their reading of these classic (and not yet classic) works was more than a connection with the authors and their stories, it was a connection between the lives of the characters and themselves. Take for example Tim O'Brien's *The Things They Carried*. I remember being forced to read this in high school and quite honestly, I answered three pages of rote questions, typed a ridiculous book report, turned it in, and received my grade. I knew Vietnam through Oliver Stone and Stanley Kubrick; what did I have in common with any of the characters and much more importantly … who cared? Handing out copies to my eighth graders however, changed the "who cared" into "why didn't I see it that way in the first place?" If you remember the first chapter, O'Brien does a brilliant job of describing what these young men *carried* using the word figuratively and concretely. He talks about all the baggage these soldiers carried before they went to war, while they were there, and when they came home. He descibed their attachments to *things* real and imaginary. He talks about the emotional connection to things before he tells the rest of the story. What I thought would take two class periods to discuss, led to two weeks of writing and analyzing what *we* carried. It clicked; there was an instant connection. It wasn't the academic theory of the novel or the diagnostics we were all taught in college. This was real, real connections made to a book that talked about a war fought long before my students were born—connections to soldiers three times their age living during a time they only saw in old movies. In my academic clarity my thoughts were that the war aspect of the novel would be the great connection. My students understood war, they understood fighting to live; to me, that was going to be their big connection and the jumping off point I needed to get them interested. But as they have through the many years of my teaching career, they taught the lesson and were much more connected than I could have imagined.

It happened again when I challenged them with *Flowers for Algernon* by Daniel Keyes. I found myself searching for 30 copies of the novel overnight. Again I worried about language, reading ability, vocabulary acquisition, all the things they taught me in school when choosing a novel for your class. None of that mattered to my eighth graders. From page one they completely understood the message, "Ms. D. people judge you all the time. They judged him because he was slow, didn't talk right ... I get it. I wish he had someone that believed in him. Maybe he wouldn't have fucked himself up like that." Well put and so true. We did a lot of the reading together. Once students discovered that the book read as if the main character was talking, that point of worry disappeared (I see high school students struggle with the way the book is written). They read to each other correcting each other in a way that was supportive, not condescending or rude. Once the main character begins his "improvements," they noticed the change in language, in dress, in attitude, and they missed the old character. They questioned what made the more intelligent character *better*. Why do we judge people on their language, dress, or academic level? I looked forward to every single day because I knew someone else would have it all figured out. They understood stereotypes and being judged; they knew how people looked at them and what people thought when they heard "8th and State." The connections to these characters brought forth an inner text from them that gave the work a whole new meaning. It wasn't academic anymore, it was far beyond a book report. It was life, real life that they were living and their experiences took the place of the character charts and vocabulary walls. It was a lesson only they could teach.

III

"2 a.m. and I'm still awake/writing this song If I get it all down on paper/it's no longer inside of me/Threatening the life it belongs to...."—Anna Nalick, *Breathe (2AM)*

The stories can now fill volumes. I have a student who lives on death row but asks about his journal he left with me many years ago. I have a student who is on her third degree calling to remind me of every graduation. I have a student who came out to his classmates in a poem, not an easy choice in the hood, but classmates gathered around him hugging him with acceptance. I have a student who works the streets for drugs (I see her every morning and every afternoon on my drive home). I have a student who is a single mother of three and loves her children more than herself. I have a student who was shot and killed in his driveway after a long battle to get his life together. I have a student who wants to teach. I have a student who wants to be the president of the United States. I have a student who performed his own music in front of the class and asks me if I remember the video we posted

The Answer Is the Story (Dulworth Gibson)

to an out-of-date AOL account. I have a student who wrote a letter to God apologizing for his "messed up life." These stories are not yet written in volumes labeled "American Ethnic Literature," but they are the true essence of that genre. As their teacher, I have had a front seat to this work and the opportunity to pull even more of their stories out of their hearts. With such an emphasis on the new Common Core State Standards, the allowance we give our students in the creative writing genre is fading fast. The ability to write freely, laying it all down, does not fit the five-paragraph model of claim to conclusion. For many of my students, the conclusion was never in reach, it was the story of their lives, and it wasn't over. It was their experience, their world, their voice, their emotions—no scientific evidence or literary rhetoric to back it up.

Whether a college classroom, an inner city middle school, a room of adults, or the Montessori experience, one thing never changes the story. When folks are allowed the opportunity to write about themselves, their experiences, their thoughts and feelings, and don't fear the red pen and rubric of a standard essay, magic happens. My biggest surprise, as I continue teaching, is the lack of that opportunity in classrooms everywhere. I remember my first week teaching freshman English at the college level. The assignment: the six-word memoir. Your life in six words along with a brief summary of the choice you made. I had a young lady approach me after class in tears. "I just can't wrap my head around this. Can you give me a rubric or format?" I felt horrible and asked her why it was so difficult. "We didn't write like this in high school. I can write research papers, anything you want, but I don't know where to start for this." I do not have an advanced degree and am in no way an expert, but I do know this: when students are not allowed to write from their heart, with their voice, about their own life experiences, the world misses out. We, as teachers, miss out on understanding where students come from, what they love, what gets them going. We miss all of that and more. As a good Catholic schoolgirl (not really), I spent 13 years in a parochial setting. There was not a lot of room for creativity there; I could appreciate that on tests. When I didn't know the answer I often wrote, "Because God said so." It never really worked until I finally met my match.

My eighth grade teacher was a woman who refused to give up on me. She was a Dominican nun, one of many who taught me about life, the love of teaching, service, and the art of grammar. The majority of my schooling, especially writing, focused on perfect grammar, excellent handwriting, and form. I was not a grammar princess by any means, but I loved to write stories. I wrote pages and pages and honestly, it sucked, bad, but I loved what I was doing. I would share with Sister Michael Anne my finished chapters, and she took it very seriously. She didn't grab her red pen right away; she just got into my story. Then she would talk to me about it, asking questions, and making my mind go even farther. Looking back, she was encouraging that writer in me. I still had to diagram sentences and take my weekly grammar quiz on Fridays, but secretly, I started to believe I was a writer and that was good enough for me. We have to do the same for our students.

> "Without a human voice to read them aloud, or a pair of wide eyes following them by flashlight beneath a blanket, books had no real existence in our world. Like seeds in the beak of a bird waiting to fall to earth, or the notes of a song laid out on a sheet, yearning for an instrument to bring their music into being. They lie dormant hoping for the chance to emerge. They want us to give them life."—
> John Connolly, *The Book of Lost Things*

Many great folks have written about and produced excellent writing models to help students write. I have used many in my classrooms and still do to this day. The most important thing to remember when you set out on this journey to discover American ethnic literature is that one size does not fit all. Thus, many of the rules and stipulations on our teaching styles are also not one size fits all. Our biggest challenge as teachers of writing is to know our students. Standard labeled writing does not fit this criterion but we all do it because of percentages and portfolios we have to produce. Students will not trust you with the technical stuff if they don't trust you with their writing guts. The "writing guts" of our students have to be penetrated for them to write at all. They have to get stuck on something, they have to drag through it like mud, and they have to feel some success in their endeavor. As teachers, we have to find those activities that do that for our students. I have found some that really work and I have also tried some that have really bombed. Things work differently for different folks, but when people are encouraged to write from their inner voice, there is an explosion.

We are here in the twenty-first century with the Internet, YouTube, music on demand and media to help us look for these treasures. In recent years, some of the best writing moments came from the inspiration of these new technologies. A *CBS Sunday Morning* segment on regret was one of these. "Things You Wished You Had Said" aired the Sunday after the Boston bombings and all of the drama of the days afterward. I stood in front of folks who couldn't remember 9/11 or the uneasiness of that day, but they knew this. I wasn't sure how they would react. I knew many of them had lost family or friends but the segment didn't just lend itself to those in our lives who had gone. My students taught me this. After viewing the 7-minute segment, they were all asked to write to someone to whom they wished they had said something. The result was the writing guts I was searching for. A student wrote to her father, who had spent most of her young life behind bars. Another student wrote to God in search of forgiveness for the mistakes he felt he had already made, including his mother leaving him and his father months before. Students wrote to parents struggling with addiction, they wrote to grandparents they never had the chance to meet, one wrote to me asking me to stop smoking because he worried I wouldn't be around to teach other folks. The connections these students made to a seven-minute segment blew me away. They even asked to read some aloud. No one was pressured, but before I knew it, all of my students were reading, *they had to* they said, *they had to get it out.* They hugged each other or clapped in response; there were "right on's!" and "I know what you means." It was powerful stuff, and not in my standards or curriculum map for those few days. If we miss these opportunities or trudge on through curriculum and miss these writing moments, we have deprived our students of what we are there to do for them. We don't get to acknowledge that voice and they don't get the opportunity to connect with others around them. They don't see how everyone else around them has a story and how that story can connect them together. That's the community we look for in our classrooms— whether we teach the college bound or the second grader.

IV

"The more closely the author thinks of why he wrote, the more he comes to regard his imagination as a kind of self-generating cement which glued his facts together, and his emotions as a kind of dark and obscure designer of those facts. Reluctantly, he comes to the conclusion that to account for his book is to account for his life."— Richard Wright, "How Bigger Was Born"

Using ethnic literature in my classroom became very obvious during my first years teaching. The binder said *Sounder* but my students were in no way going to be led to actually *read a book about a dead dog.* They were used to working out of the ten year old textbook that had snippets or parts of literary works, none of which connected to their lives in any way. In my teacher brain I argued with myself, "Well, you had to read those same boring books, they were good enough for you. They are classics, so who are you to judge what's best for students?" I think we made it through barely a chapter of *Sounder* when a student looked up, and as respectively as she/he could said, "Ms. D. this is bullshit. Who cares this much about a stupid dog?" Perhaps in my blinded realization I retorted, "Then what do you care about?" The room was so quiet I started thinking about escape plans. I felt I had truly stumbled onto something important but the way it came out, the students felt that by disrespecting the novel, they had somehow disrespected me. What followed was probably one of the most important conversations I had with a class of students.

It was a seminar, a type of honest back and forth, that finally made sense. The same brave soul who had argued about the importance of the dog took a breath and continued, "Here's the thing. We aren't living in those times. Dogs aren't that important. I have family that fights them in their basements so why would I cry if one died? All I'm saying is this ... if you want us to read these stupid books why can't we read one that has something to do with us?" You have to love students. The power they feel when we want to know about *them*. That night, I took on the challenge and to this day I read more than I ever did as a nerdy child. When you know your students, know what moves them, know where they come from and what they believe in, you can find the work that connects them and drags them through that mud I spoke of earlier.

For my folks in the inner city, Walter Dean Myers and Sharon Draper were big hits. At the college level, we took on a whole semester of graphic novels. Historical fiction for social studies? Forget *George Washington's Socks*, how about *Extremely Loud and Incredibly Close*? We read and kept reading. The *Cirque De Freak* series gave me serious cool points with my gentlemen. This series about a young man and his vampire friends took me out of my comfort zone but gave students an opportunity to write their own scary stories, create a graphic novel based on the given text, or start a conversation about how being different is never easy. The ladies loved *The Awakening* and *The Bell Jar*. Although heavy with emotional pain, my ladies understood the problems of "growing up girl"; they saw the pain in the words, the excitement in the adventures, and the acceptance of how the world is. The writing that emerged became volumes of feminist literature written by young ladies who had not yet experienced the fullness of a life but had many years of trials before their time. We read bell hooks and Nikki Giovanni. We wrote like George Ella Lyons and sent her "Where I'm From" poems because the kids were so proud. The reading of this work encouraged writing pieces that carried students through their best writing yet. We read opinions from Kathy Wilson's *(Not) Your Negro Tour Guide* column, and philosophy by Dr. Cornel West. We watched movies like *Boyz In the Hood* and *Do The Right Thing*, movies I had seen on my own and appreciated but couldn't fully understand until I watched it with folks who lived many of the situations daily in their own neighborhoods.

Many educators may frown on these titles and work because of the content, language, or expression presented but the *connections* they made to other learning in my class has been key. You watch a Spike Lee film, or discuss an opinion piece on black youth and suddenly it's personal, it is what is real for students, and they open up as if someone has finally validated their world. "Changes" by the late 2Pac was a lesson in what it meant to grow up black. I could not understand the lyrics or their power until that discussion with my students who could articulate racial nuances better than many scholars. It became more about the connecting and the fact that these stories were *theirs*. There was a sincere swell inside them that said your story is important and relevant and if you share that with others, you may have an affect on them too. This was the case when the late Aralee Strange entered my classroom one year on a grant from somewhere.[1] This incredible lady with a tattoo of a lightening bolt on her cheek confused students at first but then she read and wrote beside them and their work was genius. She told them about her plays and poetry and why it was important to speak from your heart. She showed them and sat with them and encouraged them. She came from Over the Rhine and had a real love of the neighborhood and the people in it. Many of them were from OTR too and they finally heard about their neighborhood in a loving light rather than a newspaper headline. Through this reading and writing students wanted to do more. They wanted to understand the world and they wanted to change it for the better. We volunteered at the church behind school at Thanksgiving and I watched students pack food boxes many of them would receive themselves. We cleaned corners and created gardens. We went to the theatre and had fancy coffees. It was empowering when they knew they mattered. It unfolded through their own remarks about the world around them and places they wanted to see. It was how it should be; their education was built around them.

V

"When people talk, listen completely. Most people never listen."— Ernest Hemingway[2]

Sometimes we forget that we should all still be learning. We attend required professional development, we sign up for a class or two because we need the hours, but real learning often happens when we least expect it. It doesn't cost anything or always happen in a classroom, but the opportunity to learn and hear American literature can happen anywhere. When we experience these moments, we can take them back to our classrooms and share those with our students. That sharing encourages students to share their own stories and see the value and power in the human experience.

Every Fourth of July my family has spent time at a campsite in Hillsboro, Ohio. Honestly, years ago, the idea of spending nights in a tent and roughing it was not my idea of a relaxing weekend (I blame that on my city upbringing). I am assuming with age that has changed. There was another reason ... the stories. This particular camp, like many across this country, is filled with characters whose stories you collect with every visit. Whether it is the fish they caught that was so large it couldn't be measured, or the war stories they share with each other, it is a treasured collection of life, family, sorrows and happiness.

I can't find a book of these stories so I listen carefully and take them all back to my classroom. I have to describe the characters, explain the settings, and try to tell the same story with the same inflections and tone they do.

Oral tradition has always been a unique way to preserve story. There is something in *telling* a story that connects us yet again to a bigger human family. When students are given the opportunity to tell a story, there are no rules, no real structure, it just flows. It often goes in many directions, gets off track, but somehow always come back to the ending they remember. Students will use voices that resemble the characters they tell us about; grandfathers, next-door neighbors, crazy aunts who have too many cats, all of these characters come to life to people who have never met them. In that telling, there is always a connection; students see their own lives in the words and actions of others. It was in this spirit of collecting stories that I was invited to a fascinating afternoon that I would share with my students.

There is a large population of Amish in Hillsboro. They live and work among the "English" but very rarely associate with them as friends. Every year the campsite has a Fourth of July celebration and a particular family of 12 arrives, in their horse and buggy, as if they just left a place that is still 100 years behind. The children run barefoot in their handmade pants, dresses, and hats. Mom walks holding the newest addition and Dad settles in with the rest of the men discussing work and the weather. I have always been interested in teaching children, whether from the inner city, rural farm area, high income to highest concentration of free and reduced lunch, so when I was offered a tour of the three local schoolhouses in the area, under the condition of no pictures, I didn't ask too many questions and realized I was going to be told a story that I would really need to *listen* to and retain. We arrived at their home; the children quickly grabbed books and sat with me to read. I was given the tiniest member of the family and was able to sit and hold him while the girls read. They were much more talkative than they had been at the campground around the other adults. Children do not start learning English in the home until they attend school but these young ladies could read and couldn't wait to grab another book. I was taken to the barn where a cow, their horse, several chickens and bunnies, and a brand new calf stood in the stall looking right at me. They told me about when it was born and of all the things they do around the farm daily. They easily picked up the animals for me to hold and I was amazed at their ability to accept me right away. I was in a bright orange bandana, shorts, and a T-shirt, muddy from a weekend of rain and camping, a far cry from their dresses, aprons, and head coverings. After a few minutes with the children, we pulled out of the short driveway waving to 11 other little souls who seemed to be covering every square inch of the yard. Hillsboro and surrounding counties have many Amish families and while driving to the first school house we pass several homes and farms with no electrical lines connecting their homes to the internet or CNN. Dad explained that Amish men have a trade; usually they are raised practicing that skill. Due to an accident, Dad had to switch from farming (heavy labor) to sewing and he and the boys have an awning and tent shop where they sew covers for boats, beautiful backyard tents, and build porches for campers who flock to the lake. It's beautiful work and he has kept busy. The boys all work with their father in the small shop next to their home. Mom was the teacher at the schoolhouse before she was married. Once women are married, their responsibility is now family and home.

We arrive at the first schoolhouse and I am transported to an episode of *Little House on the Prairie*, complete with the bell. The area right outside the schoolhouse has three large poles with two pieces of rope and a wooden 2 × 4—a swing set for recess time. Each of the schoolhouses we visit has two stories. The lower story seems to be for coats, jackets, a wood burning stove for winter months, and a sink for cleaning dishes after lunch. The wooden hooks on the wall are empty of coats now but seems very organized and reminds me of the Montessori classrooms I toured during my training. I am told later that the bottom floor is also where punishments are given. Each teacher has a strap and students are punished accordingly. We move to the top floor of the schoolhouse where a dozen or so old wooden desks, attached at the chair with metal desks, sit looking very empty. There is one bulletin board with the Golden Rule posted. There is beautiful hand written penmanship lines above the board. There are four lines: one for English letters, cursive and print, and two for German letters, cursive and print. It reminds me of second grade when we were finally taught the cursive we were so proud to write. The teacher's desk sits right in front of the room at the chalkboard and off to the side is a small area for supplies. The only other posters are grammar rules about punctuation and the use of conjunctions that still clings to the walls in the heat. I am allowed to open desks, to look at textbooks and the content of the large wooded desks. These books were old and contained mostly Bible stories (most books were copyrighted as Christian books). Students study math, reading, and some geology/history during their years of school. All students complete school at the eighth grade. There is no high school or higher education for anyone. I couldn't help but think of my own very full, over stocked, over visual classroom with drawers of pencils, pens, and markers, paper and other very unnecessary items. These teachers still used chalk and chalkboards. Classrooms were multi-age where eighth graders sat with kindergarteners every day. Mom explains that there are some children who are 'slow' and they have now set aside part of the classroom for them; a small space divided by a curtain. Mom continues to explain that teachers are highly respected in the community. I ask whether children who get in trouble at school also get in trouble again at home; she smiles and says, "Of course." As the men walk downstairs, I turn to Mom and ask quietly, "Do you miss teaching?" She takes the baby, smiles and quietly nods her head yes. The rest of the afternoon is spent touring the other two schoolhouses, both very much like the first. Families, I am told, pay for their children to attend the schools. There is an auction/dinner every summer to raise money for supplies and wood for the stoves during the winter, but families are responsible for the payment to teachers. It's a community organization that focuses on the student and although there are no computers or state testing requirements, it is a model of cooperation.

At the last schoolhouse I ask Dad about his concerns of the outside world and his family. His reply is matter of fact, "I had a three month subscription to the local paper and couldn't wait for it to end. Unless they overhear things in the shop, my children do not know of the outside world and, therefore, have no interest in what is happening." As we drive back to their home, I think hard. In this world of 24/7 cable news, Internet, Facebook, and Netflix, what are we missing? What affect has all of this had on the students in our classrooms? With so much at our fingertips, have we actually lost out on anything? As we arrive back at their home, the children gather around the car with a guinea, a small bird that I had mentioned I had never seen before. They put it in my hands and laughed as it pecked me softly and I grimaced. These children crowded around me as if I was from another world— eager to show me what they were doing and what they loved. Their world revolved around family and work; that is what they did, what they knew and, although many of us would see their way of life as ancient or suffocating, there is a communication that they have that we have lost. The children tell me the story about the calf being born. Their parents tell me about the school, showed me the classrooms, and relate their experiences as teachers. It was not written on line or put on the web. It wasn't financial or prideful. It was their contribution to the dialogue that is multiethnic American literature and it was a lesson well taken. I shared this experience with other teachers after our summer break. I was disappointed at their reactions; no one seemed as impressed as I was. I felt as though I had discovered some obsolete puzzle. My students however listened and understood the importance of story. They understood that I was doing exactly what I ask them to do all the time. Look around, listen, and chat with that person at the bus stop or that gentleman who cleans the classroom at your school. Look at lives that are different from your own and understand why that shared experience is important. The writing and inspiration comes naturally after that, but the life lesson of truly *understanding* this human connection that loops through us all is the real reward.

Students were given several different writing assignments after this adventure (note: Your students will love you when you have your epiphanies. They may not even enjoy writing but because of your excitement, the buy-in is high!) We talked about learning from others and so students were given the "creeper" assignment. Choose someone in the class who you may or may not know well. Watch them, catch a brief conversation in the hall with them, just *sneak* around them for a week. They then wrote these good folks letters about what they observed and the lessons they learned from them by just watching and speaking every once in a while. Later students wrote full on biographies of friends or family by deeply asking the questions that go beyond *where were you born?* or *what was your most important life lesson?* Students heard the stories, listened to the circumstances, and appreciated the connections they could make with people they thought they knew or the people they seemed so divided against. *This was real* work, *real* writing, with fascinating results.

VI

> "So folks understand the challenges that exist for African American boys, but they get frustrated, I think, if they feel that there's no context for it or—and that context is being denied. And—and that all contributes, I think, to a sense that if a white male teen was involved in the same kind of scenario, that, from top to bottom, both the outcome and the aftermath might have been different."—President Barack Obama addressing the death of Trayvon Martin

The essence of authentic American literature is the story. But what happens when that story comes in from two different, emotionally charged perspectives that cause people to pre-judge and decide based on life experiences and/or opinions? This summer, millions of folks sat glued to their televisions as George Zimmerman was put on trial for the death of Trayvon Martin. Most of us would have never heard of the case but when civil rights attorneys demanded justice for the hooded teenager returning from the store with Skittles and tea one rainy night in Florida only to be shot dead by a neighborhood watchman, lines were drawn and the delicate issue of race and class was once again in play. I too sat, day after day, listening to what, in the end, was the story with all of its characters and plot twists played out before America and the world every day. And the story didn't stop there. Late night news relived the daily events of the trials, Twitter and Facebook lit up with armchair attorneys weighing in on who had won that day. The judgments on those who took the stand even took on a life of its own. The young lady who was the last to talk to Trayvon, on the phone with him the night he died, shocked all of America because of her matter-of-fact, unreserved commentary of "crazy-ass crackers," and what some saw as disrespect as she was cross-examined by defense attorneys. It was a circus only mirrored by the O.J. Simpson trial of the nineties. As the trial and its commentary continued, I found myself sitting in judgment of the events, the people, and the young man who will never go to college or get married.

As the weeks of commentary and play-by-play continued, I realized that we were all missing the most important thing ... the story. Between switching channels, posting a comment, or yelling at the TV, we all lost sight of the story behind the mess in front of us. I don't know how many relevant conversations were had in churches, classrooms, or coffee shops about the real issue behind the high profile mess we were watching. I know I didn't have many; I was just sitting in judgment and awaiting the high drama of a verdict. When that verdict was announced late on a Saturday evening, there was a silence that I couldn't explain. Whatever your feelings about the case, it was over, and once again with judgment the story was supposedly finished. President Obama surprised the White House press corps a little over a week later with what many called very charged and highly personal remarks about the case. He is quoted trying to explain the disconnect African American families have with the judicial system and how if young Trayvon was white, how different an outcome we may have had. There's the story. As teachers, what responsibilities do we have to our students when it comes to issues of race, class, and gender? What's off the table or too taboo to discuss? How can we understand that inner dialogue if we don't ask?

I was in my second year of teaching when Timothy Thomas, an African American teenager, was shot in an alley while running from police. The city of Cincinnati erupted into riots for days. It happened to be spring break so I once again sat glued to my television watching the feed come in. I saw students, I recognized faces, and I saw the tear gas and bean bag bullets sprayed on their anger that poured into Over the Rhine for several days and nights. I was terrified and disgusted. What good are they doing? Burning their own homes and businesses? Getting hurt being arrested ... what is happening? In my own upper class, white, southern upbringing, their actions were no way to handle things. I just didn't understand. That next week as folks slowly came back to school, several students were still locked up or missing, news of the riots hit national news desks, and people were still angry. My students were exhausted, they were heightened with rage, and I too sat in bewilderment as to what had just happened. I remember distinctly the conversation going something like this. "Folks, we are missing people today and no one wants to work or even move. Could someone tell me what the hell is going on?" There was a brief moment of silence until the hands shot up and I was the student that day, for hours. "Miss D., don't you understand what happened?

They shot him for no reason, because he was black, because he looked a certain way. It was wrong!" My grown-up logic took hold and I spat back exactly what they thought I would say. "So how is violence and destruction helping matters? All of these people watching it on television? You are proving to them that what they think about you is true!" And then came that very long, awkward silence when I should have known I was dead wrong. "Miss D., what you don't understand is that you are those people. You are white, you live in a nice area, you don't have to worry about the police following you or assuming you are doing something wrong in a store. Every day they drive past, they smirk, they assume we are all thugs and thieves. Why does it matter what we do? They assume it anyway." Honestly, my feelings were hurt. I was just like *them*. But it was the education of their stories that helped me understand where they were coming from. For the next few weeks we wrote. We wrote about our own experiences, we wrote about absent fathers and the lure of the street. We talked about our anger, our rage, and more to the point, our disbelief and sadness over what had happened. Had the conversation not happened, and we went along like nothing happened, we would have all missed out on the revelations of *their* stories and how it connected to *them*. It is of the utmost importance that that dialogue is in classrooms everywhere so that we all better understand where our student's hearts and minds are coming from.

> "It takes courage to interrogate you. It takes courage to look in the mirror and see past your reflection to who you really are when you take off the mask, when you're not performing the same old routines and social roles. It takes courage to ask—how did I become so well-adjusted to injustice?"—Dr. Cornel West from *Hope On A Tightrope*

You know that moment right before a storm whips through a neighborhood? You may be on your porch, you see the lightning and the thunder shakes the ground. The wind is bending the trees in your background, even the squirrels are running for cover but ... there is something beautiful about it. You ease off your porch, away from the safety of shelter and you stand there. You look all around and know it's a dangerous spot and that you have no business pressing your luck but ... you still stand. You watch everything run, you listen to the wind hitting everything in its path, and you just stand. I feel that teaching American literature is the same type of storm. When you teach it, when you allow students to really dive in, what you receive in return is powerful. It is truth; it is their story, their lives on the page, their spoken word as they read that truth out loud. As teachers, this journey through authentic ethnic literature can be scary, like a storm, things whipping at you, thunder pounding, and squirrels running. In the end, it is an education that you can't buy. It turns our students into storytellers with unique stories that are all their own. The novels and media we share in class encourage the dialogue and provide the trust they need to become these storytellers. As educators we must do our homework: listen, watch, read, investigate, be willing to completely bomb, but do something that connects you to the lives, the families, the hearts of those students sitting in front of you day after day. Have the courage to look in the mirror, have the courage to share that mirror with your students, and then sit back and enjoy the storm.

Notes

1. Aralee Strange (1944–2013), poet, playwright (*Dr. Pain on Main*), activist, mentor, teacher, and friend. Owner of Word of Mouth poetry house in Atlanta, Georgia.

2. Hemingway reported in Malcolm Cowley, "Mister Papa," *LIFE* magazine (January 10, 1949), Volume 26, no. 2, p. 90.

Works Cited

Armstrong, William H., and James Barkley. *Sounder*. New York: Harper & Row, 1969. Print.
Atwood, Margaret. *The Handmaid's Tale*. Boston: Houghton Mifflin, 1986. Print.
Boyz n the Hood. Dir. Laurence Fishburne. Perf. various. Columbia TriStar Home Entertainment, 2003. DVD.
Brien, Tim. *The Things They Carried*. London: Flamingo, 1991. Print.
"If Only: Dealing with Regret." CBS Sunday Morning. *CBS Sunday Morning*. CBS. 21 April 2013. Television.
Chopin, Kate. *The Awakening*. Charlottesville: University of Virginia Library, 1997. Print.
"Cincinnati Riot of 2001." *Cincinnati Enquirer* 15 April 2001, sec. Local: Front Page. Print.
Connolly, John. *The Book of Lost Things*. New York: Atria Books, 2006. Print.
Do the Right Thing. Dir. Spike Lee. Perf. various. MCA Home Video, 1989. DVD.
Foer, Jonathan Safran. *Extremely Loud & Incredibly Close*. Boston: Mariner Books, 2005. Print.
Full Metal Jacket. Dir. Stanley Kubrick. Perf. various. Warner Home Video, 2001. DVD.
Keyes, Daniel. *Flowers for Algernon*. 1st ed. New York: Harcourt, Brace & World, 1966. Print.
Malcolm X. Dir. Spike Lee. Perf. Denzel Washington. Warner Home Video, 2000.DVD.
Martel, Yann. *Beatrice and Virgil: A Novel*. New York: Spiegel & Grau, 2010. Print.
Obama, President Barack. "President Obama Speaks on Trayvon Martin." *President Obama Speaks on Trayvon Martin*. Whitehouse.gov. Washington, DC: 19 July 2013. Television/Video.
Plath, Sylvia. *The Bell Jar*. 1st U.S. ed. New York: Harper & Row, 1971. Print.
Shan, Darren, and Takahiro Arai. *Cirque du Freak*. New York: Yen Press, 2009. Print.
West, Cornel, and Tavis Smiley. *Hope on a Tightrope: Words & Wisdom*. Carlsbad, Calif.: Smiley Books, 2008. Print.
Wilson, Kathy. "(Not) Your Negro Tour Guide." *City Beat Magazine* Summer 2000. Print.
Woodruff, Elvira. *George Washington's Socks*. New York: Scholastic, 1991. Print.
Wright, Richard. "How Bigger Was Born." *The Saturday Review of Literature* (June 1, 1940). Print.
Zafón, Carlos Ruiz. *The Shadow of the Wind*. New York: Penguin Press, 2004. Print.

Teaching *Spidertown* in the Blended Classroom[1]
Dulce María Gray

I started teaching Abraham Rodriguez's *Spidertown* in 1994 (a year after it was published) not just because I grew up in the Bronx (albeit far from the south section of the borough, and the experiences, he writes about), not just because I had recently completed a doctorate with an area of expertise in contemporary U.S. Latino/a literature and was drawn to anything published in the newly commodified genre, and certainly not just because he agreed to visit and chat with my graduate students. I taught *Spidertown* the first time mainly because I wanted my graduate students in that American literature class to encounter the great themes of spiritual and intellectual growth and self-discovery present in a Bildungsroman as lived by a sixteen-year-old in an impoverished Puerto Rican community a mere five hours by car from the privilege of the university where we sat and talked. I wanted my students to extend their traditional study of literature beyond Arnoldian concepts and to engage in discursive analysis of *Spidertown*—as well as to use the novel as a forum for wrestling with interdisciplinary disjunctive conflicts, the limitations of interpretive communities, and their own growing self-awareness as active agents.

I have continued to teach *Spidertown* in various other academic settings. Its genre-bending part thriller, part love story, part barrio fairy tale, part cinematic/TV/music video drama makes it easily adaptable. Despite it being twenty years old, when I teach *Spidertown* as part of a (sometimes "ethnic") literature class, or a composition class, invariably, students are still drawn by the urban setting, the rhythmic language, Miguel's party-sex-drugs-fast-driving life and the questions his situation poses for self-determination. Yes, my students and I have our gripes about the plot, structure and content (e.g., "Miguel and Cristalena's conversation about what to call themselves—Latino, Hispanic, Puerto Rican, Nuyorican—is forced, as if Rodriguez had a charge to include items in a list of political issues!"[2]). But even those gripes serve as departing points for productive discussions about American literature, the development of Latino/a literature in particular, and the writing process and product—especially. That's the focus I want to address in this essay: I want to describe my experiences teaching *Spidertown* in composition courses, even more specifically, teaching this novel in composition classes that are blended,[3] classes where I deliberately weave technology and a balanced combination of the pedagogies used in face-to-face (f2f) and online modalities (Dziuban et al.).

I started including *Spidertown* in my composition classes about ten years ago when I began to teach at a community college in affluent, highly literate, and hyper connected Silicon Valley. I based that decision on various reasons, among them the fact that the college serves a substantial number of low-income students from the fringes and underbelly of the valley, and that I remembered the lasting impact of reading Piri Thomas' eviscerating memoir, *Down These Mean Streets*, and Paulo Freire's *Pedagogy of the Oppressed*; these texts helped to spark my long-time intellectual fascination with the ties that bind race/ethnicity, literacy (particularly writing), power and agency in American society—a fascination that I nourished in graduate school by consuming the works of critical theorists such as Henry Giroux and Ira Shor. These authors, along with feminists such as bell hooks, helped shape my pedagogical approach. My decision was also influenced by the very real fact that unlike my university teaching, community college teaching feels like being in the front lines (and I say that with all due respect to soldiers and with the acknowledgement that I spent the first ten years of my life in the midst of a war): every semester I teach four sections (often just composition, since teaching literature decreases the contractually required load) with 33 students in each. That kind of teaching demands that students take greater control of their learning (Anson). And my students, they were, and continue to be, the main reason why I decided to include *Spidertown*: they are either very familiar with the world depicted in *Spidertown* or completely oblivious to it. And, since almost all of my students are wired, I make sure that my teaching happens in a blended/web-enhanced learning environment (Carpenter et al.).

I teach in a beautiful park-like campus of about ten thousand students that is situated in an exclusive residential area of Silicon Valley. Forty-eight percent of the students are Caucasian; eighteen percent are Latino/Hispanic (connected mostly to Mexico and Central America); thirteen percent are Asian; and slightly more than three percent are African American. Over twenty-six percent of the students range in age between twenty and twenty-four; twenty-one percent are over age fifty. Fifty-four percent of the students declare that their main intent is to transfer to a university; overwhelmingly, they transfer to California State University campuses. Almost fifty percent of incoming students assess into non-transferable pre-collegiate composition courses—courses that used to be called "basic skills" and are now generally known as "developmental"; and those who test into freshman writing are significantly underprepared. That mix is muddled further by the fact that many of the students in both the developmental and freshman composition classes are not economically prosperous. They are the sons and daughters of, and those who work at, McDonald's and Taco Bell, those who cut the grass, clean houses, babysit, and do construction. Quite a few are new immigrants struggling with language and acculturation impediments. Some are challenged by learning disabilities, mental illness, substance abuse and gang-related issues. Some are undocumented, recently out of prison, on probation and/or court mandated to complete some kind of training program; most have at least two jobs. Their lives are busy, cluttered, and demanding.

And yes, most of my students are also mobile and wired. They change residences often, attend more than one college at once, and even those who can't afford to buy their own laptops own a smart phone (and are reluctant to sit in the college's computer labs). They expect to access information—and education—easily, on demand, from their fingertips anytime anywhere. They text compulsively and are active users of social media. Like most students today, they crowd source, meet new people and maintain friendships and family bonds, often across geographies, cultures, and time zones through Skype, WhatsApp, Facebook, Twitter, Instagram, YouTube, and Tumblr (Kupperman and Fishman). Few take notes with paper and pencil; instead, they jot truncated words on their phones and tablets, or they use their hand-held devices to take pictures and videos of the information they want or need. (Those who can't afford to buy *Spidertown* photograph the entire novel rather than go to the college library where I place copies on reserve.) Most are at least familiar with (if not adept at) using the college's course management system (CMS) and its tools (discussion forums, drop boxes, chat sessions, video conferencing, calendar, email, podcasts) as well as with web-based applications (such as Prezi, Google Docs, SlideShark, and Flowboard) that allow them to collaborate synchronously and asynchronously in cyberspace. A few also complete free Massive Open Online Courses (MOOCs) especially in Coursera and Edx. Students being busy and wired are salient reasons for the rapid growth of Distance Education/online course offerings at the college; currently, twenty-five percent of all enrollment is completely online or hybrid. (Data for blended classes are not disaggregated.)

Yet, like many others, a few of my colleagues still uphold the stance Andrea Lunsford posited in 1979: basic writers have not "attained the level of cognitive development which would allow them to form abstractions or conceptions" (38). And those colleagues also support Linda Stine's assertion (made in 2010):

> Internet-based learning is not a natural fit for basic writing students. Online learning places heavy demands on such students' weaker skill areas—reading and writing—rather than building on their oral and aural strengths. It requires a level of technological skill that basic writers, especially older non-traditional students, often do not possess. It assumes a sense of independence and self-confidence that developmental students almost by definition have not attained. It also demands disciplined time management, which is an ongoing struggle for developmental students even in traditional class settings [33].

Hence, these colleagues assume, pairing a blended or completely online modality with a demanding text like *Spidertown* sets up developmental and underprepared freshman writers to fail (Del Principe). I grant that national statistics recurrently underscore that online students have a dramatically lower rate of retention and success (especially in writing classes) than f2f students (Anderson and Elloumi; El Mansour and Mupinga). I see that statistical trend across disciplines in the college and in my own online classes. But, research confirms that students in blended classes have as high retention and success rates as, and often higher than, those in f2f classes (Bonk and Graham, Picciano and Dziuban); that is corroborated by my experiences during the last ten years. I often answer these colleagues by reminding them that the vast majority of students in our classes tend to be older than the traditional freshmen and that (partly consequently) they are not basic thinkers; they are not cognitively underdeveloped students. Generally, even the younger students are already survivors of demanding life conditions that spur maturity. They wrestle daily with the same and similar circumstances as those described in *Spidertown*; or, if they don't have such dire lives, their neighbors do. They are street-savvy and resourceful. While a few are indeed straight out of the neighboring high schools, living with their parents, and in search of themselves, on average, twenty per cent of the students in my classes are over age thirty, with children and plenty of life experiences. Some may have the memory of crossing the desert to get into California. Increasingly, many of them are returning veterans who have seen the horrors of war in Iraq and Afghanistan, and still may be dealing with post-traumatic stress syndrome and other effects of battle.

On the other hand, it is true that my students are disconnected from the specificities of the South Bronx during the nineteen-eighties. But that's yet another excellent reason for including *Spidertown*: the novel exposes students to a reality that may resemble some of their own life experiences but it is different enough to prod them to pose questions and to use their reflexive habit of reaching for their electronic devices to seek answers. It is also true that my students also lack consistent opportunities to be "initiated," as David Bartholomae and Anthony Petrosky termed the process in the late nineteen-eighties, into the conventions of academic life generally and in cyberspace. Frustratingly, the traditional means for "initiating" students (e.g., support services such as bridge programs, counseling, and financial aid) continue to dwindle. But that too is an impetus for pairing a blended modality with *Spidertown*. Since my ability to affect federal, state, and institutional-level change is limited, and since as a professor my power to make a difference is located mainly in the classroom, pairing technology and this text is an imperative. That combination helps me to transform my developmental and freshman writing classes into active sites for "initiation," since, as Ellen Wagner clarifies:

> Evolving blended learning models provide the essential methodological scaffolding needed to effectively combine face-to-face instruction, online instruction, and arrays of content objects and assets of all form factors. For example, in such a blended learning scenario, a student may find him or herself participating in a face-to-face class discussion; he or she may then log in and complete an online mastery exercise or two, then copy some practice exercises to a PDA to take advantage of what David Metcalf calls "stolen moments for learning"—those times between classes or meetings, while on the train, or waiting for an appointment [qtd in Bonk and Graham xix].

Rodriguez's *Spidertown* is a socially relevant and personally engaging novel that demands discussion, and therefore it fits my students' tech-centered predisposition to communicate, collaborate and build communities (Dooley and Wickersham). As one of my students put it: "*Spidertown* serves as a window into a place that is alien to many people. It is an educational piece that teaches the sheltered student that pain and suffering exist in our country, and that yet there are people who stand by and do nothing about it." Of course, there is still the perennial objection to using novels and literature in a composition class—at least since 1992 when the idea was formally introduced by Erika Lindemann at the Conference on College Composition and Communication, her contention being that students "remain poorly prepared for the writing required of them in courses outside the English department" (311). Gary Tate's response clarified that literature needs to be included because composition is not just a "service course" for other disciplines, and because literature hastens students to consider big ideas and the function and role of writing beyond the realm of academia. Michael Gamer's subsequent argument underscored that "imaginative texts are suitable [for composition classes], if not desirable because they hold multiple points of view and are by nature multidisciplinary" (282), and, because literature allows students to "make use of their own experience while simultaneously seeing the limits of that experience" (283). More recently (2009), Emily Isaacs affirmed that using literature in the composition classroom is productive, especially if it is read with an emphasis on cultural rather than aesthetic concerns; she added that "the truly forward thinking have turned to second courses in digital literacy, hypertext, writing for the World Wide Web, or, more broadly, writing with digital media" (97).

My own stance on this debate has been constant: yes, literature (especially socially relevant texts like *Spidertown* that are pertinent to students) needs to be included in the composition class (Gamer). However harrowing the story, *Spidertown* provides for my students an example of a powerfully familiar "contact zone"[4] (as Mary Louise Pratt named it), and a kind of "borderland" and "mestizaje"[5] (as Gloria Anzaldúa called it)—a demarcated sliver where affluence, poverty, race, ethnicity, violence, identity, and the palpable promise of the American Dream abut. That cordoned sliver where the action takes place, the Bronx during the nineteen-eighties, abounds with seemingly relentless and inescapable crises, disenfranchisement and marginalization, but also with survival, intellectual and spiritual growth, love and transcendence. The main character's search for meaning and guidelines to do what is right when engulfing necessity precludes honor and dignity beckons students to consider their own circumstances, and the scalding slang-ridden street dialogue requires that they pay attention to language.

Yes, teaching *Spidertown* in a blended classroom can be intimidating for pre-collegiate and underprepared freshman writers who may be accustomed to being force-fed information and rules about composing essays. Hence, I make it a habit to be transparent. I include a statement in the syllabus listing my general expectations,[6] and on the first day of class I discuss my pedagogical approach in greater detail. I mention the critical and feminist scholarship that has helped to shape my teaching strategies; I explain how and why I emphasize "connected learning" and students' transformation from being passive recipients of knowledge to active participants in the making of meaning, and how and why, essentially, my role is to be a facilitator, a mentor and provider of expertise, information, and guidance who helps them become more effective writers. We talk about how and why their engaged voices are vital in the student-centered dialogic and collaborative community that we build during the semester,[7] and about how and why all of us need to respect each other's differences[8] and help each other to accomplish the objectives and student learning outcome of the course. I organize and populate the course with content for the entire semester following (and customizing some of) the CMS's tabs.[9]

I automate the weekly assignments and lessons in the Modules folder so that they're linked to the calendar and grade book, which means that students can review their performance at any time. In fact, the Report tool allows them to configure their attendance, milestones, progress and grades in graphs and charts. I describe assignments and activities in individual weekly modules, and I note due dates in the calendar and in each of the DFs and DBs. I organize the content by establishing a pattern, so that each week is clear and predictable. For example, I outline and number my instructions and lessons. That allows students to refer to a particular item by number.

I systematically deliver content in various modes, so that I can reach kinesthetic, auditory, visual and other kinds of learners. For example, students work individually, in pairs, and in small groups. We engage in f2f discussions; we use the Discussion Forums. I administer both written and oral exams. We read together. We review the notes I post online and students contribute texts of their choices (Wikipedia being one of their favorite sources). We watch videos and screen films, listen to pertinent music, examine art, eat different kinds of food, attend special events such as lectures, and even go on field trips (to a museum or to a Latino enclave, for instance). Invariably, I function as a facilitator, particularly as they conceptualize and complete their student-initiated inquiry-based projects.

A week before the official start of the semester, I reveal the course in the CMS, and I email a welcome message to all registered students. I emphasize that they must pay particular attention to the Modules, exhort them to read the detailed syllabus and warn them that they must complete a brief quiz about the syllabus, and I provide information about where to find technical and academic support as well as the assurance that I aim to be flexible and responsive to their personal needs, level of academic skills, and interests. I request their feedback and then make adjustments. (I continue to make adjustments through the semester.) I explain that our class is paperless, and that there are alternate accommodations if anyone needs them.[10] I repeatedly clarify the course's student learning outcome, each assignment's objective, and most importantly how the objective of individual assignments and activities connects to and helps students arrive at the course's learning outcome (Kirtman). Such transparency upfront tends to filter students who are not ready, for whatever reason, to commit, so that generally the students who start the semester do so with a measure of interest, engagement and investment.

I design individual assignments so that students learn and practice—recursively during the entire semester—major objectives which together help students to achieve the learning outcome for the course. Those learning outcomes follow California educational code and are established by the English department in the community college where I teach. These two charts describe the student learning outcomes and major objectives for assignments in each of the developmental and freshman composition courses.

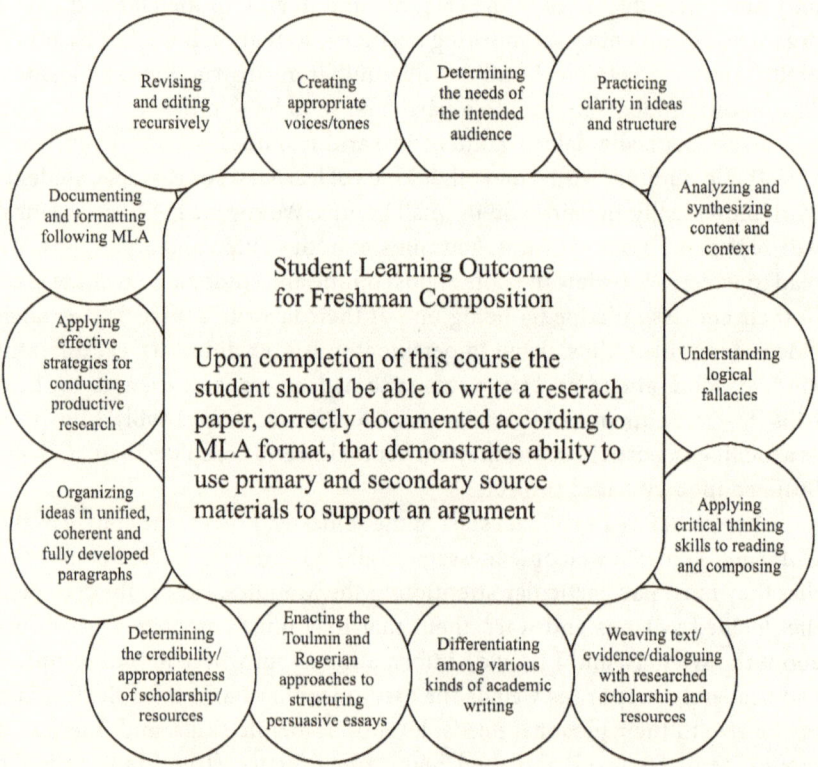

The next flowchart describes sample assignments and activities I design for the developmental writing and for the freshman composition students. Each version of the assignments is incrementally demanding (since it builds on the skills learned previously) and thus recursive—not just repetitive—in its use of the fundamental skills/rhetorical "moves"/objectives students must learn and practice in order to meet the student learning outcome.[11]

Usually, I don't start the course with *Spidertown*; I include it in the last half of the semester, when students feel more confident and empowered to

Aim: Have students understand and reflect on the importance of practicing effective reasearching skills

Sample assignment: Now that you and your partner have identified, read and discussed two scholarly articles that help you to support and/or refute, as well as develop, the theses in your essays, prepare a five minute Prezi presentation for the class where you examine the hurdles and successes you encountered in the research process.

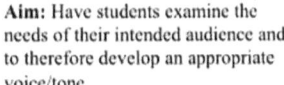

Aim: Have students practice revision and editing skills

Sample assignment: Now that you and your partner have revised your first drafts following the feedback you gave each other, take the questionnaire that I posted in the Lessons tab and, using the tracking tool in Word, answer each of those 10 questions for your partner's essay, and then for your own essay.

Aim: Have students understand the basic differences between the Toulmin and Rogers approaches to building a persuasive essay

Sample assignment: Consult the Prezi presentations archived in DB #10; that will refresh your understanding of the elements both Toulmin and Rogers use. Then, read your partner's essay and compose an outline of the elements he incorporated. At the end, explain how your partner is/is not successful in using those elements.

Aim: Have students examine the needs of their intended audience and to therefore develop an appropriate voice/tone

Sample assignment: Compose a list of 20 words and phrases that describe the needs of your intended audience. Review that list with your partner and give each other feedback. Then, compose another list of 10 words or phrases that describe the voice/tone that you will use in this essay--and, of course, HOW you will create that voice/tone

Aim: Have students analyze and synthesize content and context

Sample assignment: Review your notes and the archived DF where you discussed the videos we watched about the Bronx in the 1970s and 1980s. Review the notes that you took while reading the first scholarly article. Review the notes you jotted during the first discussions about *Spidertown*. Once you have considered all of that, compose a 250 word position paper examining the one issue that stands out to you.

Aim: Have students understand the importance of MLA conventions; practice applying them.

Sample assignment: Review the videos I posted in the Lessons tab. Review how to use the Online Writing Lab (OWL), and remember the lessons we discussed in class. Then, take your partner's essay and, using the tracking tool in Word, apply all MLA conventions and correct any mistakes.

tackle a challenge, after they have built a community, after they have been to a library orientation and have practiced looking up credible and scholarly articles and information, after they have wrestled with formulating questions and identifying main points, and after they have written at least two formal essays (up to 2,000 words in the freshman composition class) and the required revisions of each. I delay the inclusion of *Spidertown* also so that my students and I can discuss and understand that our class is not about analyzing literature; it's a class where they learn to compose non-fiction essays following academic conventions and MLA formatting. I begin by guiding students to "contextualize" the novel—to find information about Puerto Ricans in New York and elsewhere, about the plot, setting, author, and anything that glares at them. As starting points, I embed or post links to relevant articles, movies, documentaries, art, music, and I open a Discussion Forum (DF)[12] with two or three generative questions, and with details about my expectations (e.g., length of initial entries and responses, due dates, and criteria for grading). A jumpstarting-sort of question prompts students to start thinking and to produce ideas and text more freely.[13] From there, it is their task to offer more texts and questions to help contextualize the novel. (One semester, several students were thrilled to find Rodriguez's web page and Facebook profiles.) The conversations are threaded and remain visible to all of them throughout the semester, so that they can trace their developing insights (especially when they are formulating theses).

The aim in this "pre-writing" warm-up-type of assignment is to get students to gather evidence, exchange ideas with one another, and increase the potential for each of them to research, contribute and arrive at new understandings. Everyone in the class is required to read everyone else's entries, so that when we meet f2f their conversations are fluid, a continuation of what has been happening online. This activity is productive not just in equipping students with what they need to "enter" the novel and to start writing, it also, as Sherer and Shea affirm, helps them to practice "strategies for meta-learning ... inductive and creative models of reasoning and problem-solving" and "horizontal (peer-to-peer) learning and contribution" (57).

Students find that *Spidertown* is immersive; the plot and quick-tongue vernacular "suck you in," they say. Nonetheless, invariably a few students feel daunted and "lost." One student's comment during our f2f meeting echoed others' sentiment: "When I first opened the novel I thought, what are they saying? How do you read this? This is crazy!"[14] An older woman emailed the entire class: "When I first began reading the novel, I felt extremely uncomfortable. How is it possible, I asked my husband, that a sixteen and a half year old boy could be living this life?" A man wrote in a DF: "It's a bit shocking and depressing, mindboggling." Another man said: "I cringed when reading *Spidertown*. I would postpone reading just because it was so much to take in." One very young woman wrote in a chat: "Could that be true? It was like in another country. Nooooo, that can't be real. No way." But there are also students for whom the story in *Spidertown* is very familiar: "I don't have to look far from my own family to see a few examples of what happens in *Spidertown*" many students claim. One semester, four different students wrote the following:

> I am not a stranger to living on the streets, as I also dropped out of school when I was sixteen years old and ran away from home. I managed to find a place to live temporarily and moved in with a friend's older sister and slept on the couch. Although I did recreational drugs, I did not sell them. I even got a job at Kmart getting paid minimum wage so that I could eat and have money for bus fare. Now thirty years later reading *Spidertown* as a mother of two young boys I need to know what I can do differently to avoid this ever happening in my family.
>
> My nephew has been in prison since he was seventeen years old. His problems started at an early age. His father left when my nephew was young. My sister had three children on welfare. Unfortunately, because of my sister's economic situation, similarly to Miguel, my nephew was growing up in a bad part of town. Drugs, alcohol and gangs were everywhere, including school. The education was also substandard. After getting involved in drugs my nephew was shuttled from one school to another. Eventually he quit school. It was a downward cycle from there on.
>
> In *Spidertown* the stories are very similar to the way I grew up in the east side of San Jose, California. It is no place for the weak. It's a tough world where dope slanging, gangs thriving, and murder of people are an everyday routine. It's an everlasting struggle to survive. In order to survive sometimes you must be part of the rough world. You must adapt to this hell on earth to have an opportunity to live.
>
> Where I grew up was filled with abuse—people selling drugs to young and old people, women exchanging sex for money, and kids being on their own while the parents partied or were uninvolved because they were busy just focusing on themselves. It was hard living in the ghetto. It was a constant power struggle between the environment and yourself. You must show that you're tough enough to keep going forward.

As students begin to offer their own experiences, they also begin to commiserate and to provide solutions: "This novel reminds me of the 'tragedies' counselors and family members warned me about while I was growing up, like ending up with a bum, un machista, getting knocked up, losing my 'honor' … I YouTubed and I found an interview from someone who lived in the South Bronx at that time. He explained that every day he woke up and always knew it could be his last day because the crime rate was so high … I read an interview with Rodriguez where he says that his prose is like people shooting each other. I mean like, I'll get you the exact quote from Rivera's article, wait ... I saw Rodriguez on a Vimeo video and he is from the South Bronx, so I just know he's telling the truth in *Spidertown* ... OMG, did you know he's a musician too? Go to his webpage." Sometimes, students also post pictures or videos of something they've created (a sculpture or a performance of a song) in response to an idea that's touched them. As a matter of course, conversations extend beyond our physical meetings, beyond time constraints, beyond the oral, and into synchronous and asynchronous written encounters. Since they are archived, students can return repeatedly to these written exchanges. Consequently, students strengthen alliances and feel more invested in the class, the novel and each other—and that's a good thing, especially in the middle of the semester when students feel most compelled to drop the class. As Revere and Kovach affirm, infusing technology fosters "student engagement in the learning process," and that engagement helps "to decrease attrition, enhance learning outcomes, and improve student satisfaction" (124).

And yet ... blended teaching and learning, and *Spidertown*, receive little academic attention individually; no one has written about the combination. Hence, following I describe the major impacts of teaching this novel in blended classrooms: (a) students ask and answer crucial questions; they practice research skills (b) students become genuinely engaged in writing as a process; they are prompted to reflect. Combined, these impacts help students to learn rudimentary writing skills such as choosing an audience, shaping tone, generating ideas, identifying a main point, composing a thesis, developing and supporting it, reconsidering the function of a conclusion, and organizing an academic essay cohesively. That is, they practice reading, writing, and making more critical meaning—using the tools they "own," tools that are familiar and part of their everyday lives. Those impacts give students greater awareness of the rhetorical "moves" they must make in composing: what do I want to say, why do I want to say it, how will I say it/what mode and evidence will I use, to whom will I say it/who's my audience, and so what that I said it? Consequently, students think more pointedly—more self-consciously—about pre-collegiate and freshman composition-type skills such as finding an authentic voice, being acutely aware of the audience, providing and substantiating textual and other evidence to develop and support their points, and thinking about their own relationship with the content.

Students Ask and Answer Crucial Questions; They Practice Research Skills

Rovai and Jordan affirm that "blended courses produce a stronger sense of community among students" than either traditional or fully online courses

(1). Blended learning helps to create a familiar, fertile, egalitarian and safe environment that promotes community inquiry; for starters, students can't see facial expressions and body language while online, which pushes them to ask questions and clarifications; plus, the "asynchronous computer-mediated conferencing supports flexibility, reflection, interpersonal and teamwork skill development, motivation, and collaborative learning environments—resulting in deep and meaningful understandings and communities of inquiry" (Garrison and Kanuka 98). Blended learning helps to meet the classroom goals identified by Osguthorpe and Graham: pedagogical richness, access to knowledge, personal agency, ease of revision, increased engagement, safe, respectful, and robust social interaction among students (231). When paired with a socially relevant text like *Spidertown*, blended learning can be transformative for students, particularly in getting them to ask crucial questions, and to practice sound skills in researching (Garrison and Vaughan 11).

Spidertown prompts a catalogue of questions that require beyond the surface-level meaning making. Those questions take students outside of the fictional world of the novel and lead them to learn about the realities of the South Bronx. That kind of questioning is precisely appropriate for writers in my developmental and freshman composition classes. Through the years, aside from details on language, story development and specifics in the text, my students' most recurrent queries include these: "What causes that kind of poverty? Where do you start solving a problem like that? How does such a situation exist in the wealthiest country in the world? Why didn't the rest of New York City also become like the South Bronx? How is it possible that even police officers were selling drugs? Miguel has $8,000; why doesn't he get in the car and drive out of the Bronx to escape Spider's web? Why don't all those people just get out of that ghetto? Why don't they go back to Puerto Rico? Why don't they all come together and clean up their neighborhoods and get rid of that horrible and dangerous situation? Is it that Puerto Ricans don't work very hard (you know, they like to siesta a lot)? Most are smart enough to run a business, but why do they only blame white people, like Amelia does? What leads these parents to abandon and mistreat their children? Why do the kids drop out of school? Why do they join gangs? Why are these teens so homophobic and sexist? Does Firebug have mental illness? Why does he treat all his women like bitches and hos? Where does Miguel's desire to change really come from; is it because he falls in love with Cristalena, a good girl? Or is there something deep inside him that makes him want to be better? Why should we read this novel? Is it Rodriguez's biography? Why should I care about a place and time so long ago? What should I do with what I learn by reading this novel? Spider and Miguel talk about writing like it can do magic; does writing really matter in our lives? Why does Rodriguez use so much filthy language? Why is Amelia so needy? Why doesn't Spider care that he's using children and selling them dope? Aren't those scenes with Cristalena pornographic; why does Rodriguez include them? It's true: selling drugs is like running a business, so what's wrong with making money from selling drugs? Is the ending real—it's like ... devastation from page one and then bam: hope—is that real?" And, consistently, the most recurrent question from students has been: "why are they burning the buildings?"

As students begin to read, it is very productive to gather and post their questions and to request that they work in teams to find answers. Their collaborations generate more questions and answers, and result in written insights about the plot in the novel, the layered complexity of the real place and time in United States history, their own experiences and life stories, the writing process, and each of their own written pieces. In those collaborations they learn and practice—recursively—critical reading and writing skills. From there, I guide students in the research process; actually, it is their engagement with the novel that propels them to seek substantiating information. One student said it best: "to better understand the world depicted in *Spidertown*, to put things in perspective, and to figure out what I want to write about, I have to research." Students definitely prefer to conduct research electronically, from the comfort of their spaces, devices, and on their time—not by visiting the college library, or any physical library.[15] Their reluctance has to do with time, as this student explains: "I have two jobs and two kids. Researching in a library is an obstacle, as I have to schedule my day around the library's hours. It's a no brainer. Because of technology I am able to access the college's databases conveniently from my home computer, or my smart phone, at a time that is suitable for me." Invariably, students start researching by clicking on videos because they want to see—and validate—for themselves. These two students explain what happens:

> Troubled by the images running through my mind, I needed a clearer picture of Rodriguez's young men running the streets with drugs in their pockets and guns in their hands. I went directly to YouTube, and began searching for videos on the Bronx in the 1970s. To my disbelief, the videos prove that *Spidertown* depicted these men and women accurately. And then I watched the documentary *80 Blocks from Tiffany's*. Abraham is not lying. He is telling true stories just with made up characters. There were really worn down buildings, prostitutes on every corner, policemen drinking their coffee in their cars while 15 year olds are dealing cocaine and risking their lives. After seeing the videos the characters seemed to become real people in my mind, and that made me want to know more about them.

While watching the documentary *Man Alive: The Bronx is Burning*, I saw a strikingly similar resemblance to scenes from the war in Afghanistan. I found it nearly impossible to comprehend that such a place exists in the United States, this land that I have come to love because of its abundant freedoms and overall sense of security. I became increasingly interested in the background of such a place. How did it develop into such a harsh environment? How does one survive and prosper in such a place? Why would someone want to stay there? I needed to find answers.

There are indeed various shortcomings in resorting instinctually to videos—among them the minimizing of imagining, and the exacerbating of the tendency to determine "truth" solely on the basis of appearance. Nonetheless, since aside from wanting to do nothing more than Google their questions, students absolutely want to see, and since at that point it is also imperative to encourage self-reliance, I include plenty of opportunities for them to review videos, films, and documentaries. Students affirm that such inclusion is productive; they note insights such as these: "To be able to see exactly what it looked like at the time fundamentally shifted the way I think now about this novel. It is no longer just some fiction to me ... I prefer reading this novel, instead of some history about the Bronx, because there's a sweet hopeful ending; that's not the case in reality ... Rodriguez's novel and the videos are a harsh juxtaposition to my life and views. I grew up in a quiet and safe neighborhood. I grew up without an understanding of the plight of many of my fellow humans.... Watching the videos I was confronted with images I have always ignored. That led me to wonder: why do I hide in my comfort? Are those poor people happy? Are they ashamed? Are they proud? What about love? Do they feel like there is anything missing? Would I be lazy like them if I happened to be born in the South Bronx in the 1970s? Would I be terrified if I were to be under those circumstances.... Some of those scenes remind me of living in East Los Angeles ... Detroit ... my home city before coming to the United States."

By this point, students are at ease analyzing, synthesizing, and reflecting recursively. Then, I prompt them toward greater meta-awareness of their own growth as writers by having them make live Prezi presentations on the development of their research, and having the entire class give feedback (both during the live presentations and later when they are deposited in the Drop Box). Those presentations bridge what students learn from the visuals and from reading scholarly articles, thus guiding them to focus, develop and substantiate their theses. These students describe part of their presentations on researching:

> The films and historical photographs that I researched gave me the idea to look up scholarly articles about graffiti. A chapter in Dalleo and Machado Sáez's book gave me an overview. Two different articles let me see both the positive and negative aspects of graffiti in the Bronx during that time

period. One article says graffiti was commonplace and a public nuisance. The gangs used it to mark their territory and caused the South Bronx to look unkempt. The other article said that graffiti was a new art form. I saw the graffiti as young people expressing themselves in a peaceful and artistic fashion instead of channeling their emotions into violence. I would not have been able to grasp these aspects of graffiti in the Bronx without finding those videos and articles.

I consider myself a feminist, maybe because there are so many machos in my family. I found myself becoming angry reading the slang and the abusive language towards women in Rodriguez's book. I almost wanted to stop reading what I thought was a trashy novel. I could not wrap my mind around the oppression, how the men think they were raised above everyone else. As I began diving further into the videos, I realized that machismo is connected to abusing women. I chose to dig deep into the factors that create machismo. At first I wanted to see if I could understand the characters in *Spidertown*. I wanted to get inside their heads. But then I wanted to figure out machismo and how it abuses a woman. I found so many articles that my head is spinning. A chapter in the book by Allatson is like reading Greek! Now I have to make sense of all the explanations and I have to figure out my thesis.

At first I thought the fires were set by bored teenagers looking for a show, and then I thought why is Firebug acting like he was getting good at his job? How can burning buildings BE a job? I saw the videos and I was disturbed. How can there be so many burned buildings in one place? I read chapter three in Allatson's book. He explains that Firebug's fascination with fire is a reflection of his dad's attitude towards him, that Firebug becomes an arsonist because his father was hung up on fire, and because his father punishes him by burning parts of his body. Okay, I thought, that's just one crazy abused kid. Who burned all the other buildings? I had to find out, so I went to Wikipedia (I know! That was just to start) and surprisingly I learned that it is very complex, like a web of contributing factors. I learned about government projects that helped destroy the Bronx. There was an explosion of building low-income housing for the new waves of poor Puerto Ricans and southern blacks that came in the 1950s. "Slumlords" did not maintain those buildings and by the 1970s they lost value and the owners started paying arsonists like Firebug to burn them so they could get the insurance money. Another article said that the owners of the buildings were white people who had invested when the industry in the South Bronx was booming because of many manufacturing companies in that area. After the relocation of the manufactures and the decline of the price of the properties, arson was the only possible way for the building owners to gain some money on their properties. Another article said that sometimes even the tenants burned their own buildings to be eligible for welfare money.

For both developmental and freshman writers, the tasks of formulating questions and researching to find the answers allow students to practice essential writing and academic skills that help "initiate" them into academe and that propel them into being more self-conscious critical thinkers. That process is facilitated by *Spidertown*'s appeal and rich content and the fingertip-access to information inherent in the blended modality; they emphasize the import of healthy inquiry and need to support stances with sound evidence. Of course, these skills benefit students beyond their writing classes and beyond college itself. These skills also stimulate and nurture greater student engagement and reflection. This student describes the transition:

> There came several instances I consider to be jumping off points, times when what I was reading or writing jarred and disconnected me from what I knew and understood about the world so significantly that I felt compelled to research more. I felt more than just curiosity; what I felt was compulsion. I felt the need to put down the book, or to stop writing, and to fire up my MacBook Pro, and start looking for additional information.

Students Become Genuinely Engaged in Writing as a Process; They Are Prompted to Reflect

Today, more than ever before, students in our overcrowded classrooms include "different generations, different personality types, and different learning styles," therefore, in order to engage them in general it is imperative for our pedagogy to incorporate multiple approaches "including face-to-face methods and online technologies that address the learning needs of a wide spectrum of students" (Picciano 4). Engaging students so that they care about writing as a process specifically, and prodding them to reflect on how the content connects with their own lives, anchors them; when students feel that they belong, they are more likely to stay and succeed in the class (Peck). Engagement and reflection are a bit easier to accomplish in blended teaching, since inherently the environment is student-centered (Warnock). The professor is not the sole holder of knowledge: she is a facilitator, a more experienced coach and mentor, a leader who sets the tone and also knows how to include students in the practice of decision-making. Blended classes place learners in active roles thereby nudging them to take greater ownership of their learning. That's a fertile setting for fostering the practice of judging the quality of each other's written pieces by following defined guidelines and criteria about the thesis, supporting evidence, organization, and grammar, and for encouraging deep engagement and reflection on the intellectual, cognitive emotional, body and soul levels (Ginns and Ellis).

In addition to using a pertinent text like *Spidertown* and the blended modality, in order to grow engagement and reflection, I also practice the following: (A) I am accessible, sometimes even vulnerable. I often give students a piece that I'm writing, and they workshop it. Then I bring them my revision with explanations as to how their suggestions directed my changes. That kind of accessibility models what I'm teaching and helps me to bond with students on a professional basis. Plus, I get to practice Holmberg's theory that personal relationships promote student motivation and learning. (B) I make students feel that each of them matters by prioritizing quick, frequent and individualized feedback on their writing. I prefer using the Word tracking tool, to highlight what they do well and to show them how to build on their successes. (C) I conduct at least two in-person or video conferences per semester (Hewett; Edmundson). Given the huge number of students I teach, conferencing is a very demanding task. But I minimize the impact on my time and energy by doing small group, partner, and focused conferences. I ask students to plan: they arrive in my office, or we Skype (or talk on the phone), and we discuss what they deem to be important in their essays, in their order of preference. If I see that they're off target, I veer them toward recognition by asking questions. Such conferences are excellent opportunities for demarcating stages in their writing processes, and for helping them comprehend that in assessing—in reviewing their partner's or their own essays—they are intrinsically developing their internal reflective skills. (D) I include fun out-of-the-classroom-norm activities that help decenter the power in our community, and that humanize me (so that the relationship between "professor" and "student" becomes more fluid, and so that the revision process becomes less of a "me against the professor" situation). For example, in a classroom like this one where we examine *Spidertown* so closely, I may have students Skype with my friends, or the children of my friends, who live in the Bronx; or, I may ask the author to visit or to Skype with us. Sometimes, students research and cook a Puerto Rican meal and bring it to the classroom, or we go out to eat, or we attend a pertinent art exhibit, a performance or a film at the cinema. Those experiences help students to "re-vision," (see again, and again), to return to their drafts with fresh information and attitudes, and to find connections outside of *Spidertown*. Invariably, after participating in an out-of-the-classroom activity, they listen to a Podcast on a tangential topic (chosen by any of us), and they use a DF to compose a brief analysis about what the event adds to the content of their essays; thus, they enact revision recursively on various levels. (E) I definitely practice Peter Elbow's "how-to" for writing "with power" by focusing on revision substantially more than on the final product (240).

Generally, students find it difficult to give equal time to prewriting, drafting, revising, and editing recurrently. They're not used to it and certainly not inclined to thinking and rethinking an issue, or evidence, or organization. Therefore, I start revision and reflecting activities by taking one of their written drafts and modeling how to use screen-capture tools such a Jing, Snagit, and Camtasia that allow me to record voice messages that students can access with one click (Gouge; Halverson et al.). Students who are primarily auditory learners, especially, respond very positively. But almost all students prefer to compose revision feedback by using screen-capture tools, especially Jing, because it is free and easy to use. However, at certain stages, I require that they also use the tracking tool in Word, or that they answer guided questions, so that they are forced to inscribe their reflections (Gilbert et al.). The process of inscribing lends a heightened sense of reverence, per se, that is missing in the oral; because of writing's permanence, it also leads to more frequent revisiting and thus further reflection. Written and archived revision feedback is particularly effective when students arrive at personal insights that can be—for them—momentous.

For some students, consistent systematic revision offers the first opportunity for grappling with disorienting dilemmas and contradictory information; for other students, it offers a place and occasion to disentangle, maybe even recognize, the impact of some very emotional issues.[16] They may arrive at new understandings about what it means to inhabit other people's perspectives, to be empathetic, to gain expanded awareness about our interconnectedness, and to reach a more powerful conviction about their civic duty. Meyers calls this aim "transformative pedagogy" and describes it as encouraging "students to critically examine their assumptions, grapple with social issues, and engage in social action" (219). These students describe instances of those transformations:

> I was writing about when Miguel remembers the most recent instance of Firebug's arson. He recounts the rolling clouds of smoke and the dazzling flames that came out of the buildings and he describes the fire engines' red lights as strobes in a disco (Rodriguez 3). Casually, Amelia comments, "He's gettin' better," and passes Miguel the bag of popcorn they are sharing (Rodriguez 3). My emotional reaction was surprising. All I thought about was the people in the buildings. I didn't know I could feel so deeply for strangers.
>
> At first, I could not relate to *Spidertown*. I had no sympathy. My peers are not dying daily. I do not live in a ravaged neighborhood and no one directly close to me is affiliated with the drug trade. It was not until I began researching and writing my essay that my heart broke and the story came alive. It began to affect me, the fact that most young people in Miguel's situation were parentless and running around and shooting people. Seeing the names, pictures, homes and statistics of real children who were in essence surviving a war, writing about those faces, it occurred to me that if circumstances were different, I could be them.
>
> As I wrote my essay, it humbled me to realize that my good fortune is

rare in the large scheme of things and that poverty, crime, and unhappiness are more common than how I grew up. That changed my negative assumptions into empathy.

Writing about Rodriguez's fascinating characters, then figuring out that real people live like that, that helped me develop and find reason in my own life. His depiction of the horrors of life and love, of a world so radically and fundamentally different from my own, encouraged me to figure out their connections to my own life, to how poverty affects me, and to how I can help to change that kind of situation.

After I saw the videos and the poor conditions in the Bronx, how life truly was there, and after I began to write about it, I began to sympathize more with the main character, Miguel, and to better understand why he felt there was no way out. I learned that what causes poverty is very complex, and that stopped me from being impatient with poor people.

Most of my family lives like the characters and I want no part of them. I went through seven foster homes since I was six and I just hate the way my family is. Too many are in prison. Some are always high. My parents did meth. I used to hate them all, but as I wrote about *Spidertown* I realized that I was learning about why my family lives that way. It is not just a choice. They are not just lazy. It's complicated. Now I see my family very differently and that makes me feel different.

I found that in writing my essays I started to understand Miguel's life. That made it possible to expand my personal opinion on a lot of things and to increase my desire to learn.

These transformations happen most often when students make personal connections with the content, their peers and the professor—and, symbiotically, when there is improved general engagement in these three areas: behavioral, emotional and cognitive (Chen et al.). Behavioral engagement entails involvement in social and extracurricular activities; that impacts persistence and retention. Emotional engagement includes connecting with professors, peers and the content in the class; positive connections strengthen students' willingness to work diligently. Cognitive engagement necessitates motivation and commitment to do the best work possible; that usually results in success. Recurrent revision hones students' ability to make connections, arrive at insights, and take greater interest in performing increasingly complex compositional tasks such as self-assessment, peer-assessment, and wrestling critically with their own feelings, attitudes, and decisions (Mezirow).

Parting Reflections

In this essay I aimed to highlight how and why teaching *Spidertown* in a blended classroom helps students to improve their writing and critical thinking skills. The pairing is productive particularly for "non-traditional" students like mine who are "connected" to new technology and therefore, as Sherer and Shea note, "expect that teaching and learning will be more interactive, collaborative, and experiential" (56), and for professors like me who are fully invested in, as Dailey-Hebert et al. affirm, understanding and embracing the "shifting paradigms in higher education," that "acknowledge the new generation of learners and the symbiotic relationship between their learning and technology" (128). Indeed, students today are at the center of an exponentially increased exchange of information and knowledge: they "are clamoring for more technology; technology for building relationships, communicating in real-time, collaborating within an online community, and engaging in the learning process" (Revere 114). Infusing technology in our classes is not just about being trendy; it is about being responsive to students' lives; it is about meeting students where they are, and about, as Menchaca asserts, using various technologies to personalize the learning process and to meet students' multiple learning styles—especially given the continual retrenching of programs that have historically helped students to succeed in college. The blended environment is productive for freshman writers generally, and specifically for pre-collegiate writing students, since it "allows an exploration of the new world of online teaching and learning opportunities while, at the same time, retaining the structure and personal connection that adult developmental students tend to need and value" (Stine 50).

Pairing the "interactive and engaged learning experiences" of a blended classroom with a socially relevant and formidable text like Rodriguez's *Spidertown* enables intrinsic opportunities for students to access information, as well as to practice evaluating, summarizing, comparing, contrasting, analyzing, synthesizing—all of the traditional modes in non-fiction writing—and therefore to also strengthen the critical thinking skills they need to function effectively in our globalized societies: communicating in a culturally mixed audience, collaborating and negotiating with different types of people, and confronting and addressing a wide range of potentially contentious views and issues. This pairing helps students to become adept at sifting complexities, feeling comfortable with dissonance and ambiguity, backing up their stances, and perpetuating the transformative work of coexisting peacefully. It helps them to take greater ownership of the writing process, and to use writing beyond traditional academic functions—to use writing to get to know themselves as "linked" citizens in a "globalized" world, citizens who must address multifaceted rights and responsibilities on both the local and global, and the individual and collective, levels (Rhoads and Szelényi).[17]

My goal in pairing the blended classroom with Rodriguez's *Spidertown* is to create a writing environment where students learn academic conventions and also expand their critical thinking skills. I want them to practice "posing real-world problems that address societal inequalities" and also to "implement action-oriented solutions" (Meyers 219). Students with highly literate backgrounds may take this notion for granted, and others may be too busy surviving to stop and think about how effective writing can be a tool for arriving at greater consciousness or for combatting inequity. But, my experience clarifies that the result of this pairing is a vehicle for inducing students in the writing classroom to move toward greater overall and cultural awareness, intellectual agility, deeper sense of responsibility, participation, and active agency. Those skills, as Schattle explains, form the cornerstone of what defines "global citizenship." Global citizens are people who understand "complex issues from multiple vantage points," who recognize "sources of global interdependence" and the "shared fate" that implicates humanity and the planet—those who look "beyond distinctions" between "insiders and outsiders in order to view the human experience in more universal terms" (Schattle 29). At the end of the semester, students habitually concur that focusing on *Spidertown* through the use of technology leads them to improved writing skills and greater awareness of themselves. These students explain:

> When I started this class, I never imagined that I would be writing about some of the things I am writing about today, but the story of *Spidertown*, the videos and the digital documents have provoked me to think long and hard. The changes that I experienced while reading *Spidertown*, in conjunction with the web tools we used, assisted me in transforming a fictional story into a huge opportunity to learn things I had not imagined. It made the process of reading *Spidertown* a richer more meaningful experience that gave me new insights. It impacted how I view writing, formal education in my life, my responsibility as a parent and mentor, and my ability to feel empathy in my community and in the world.
>
> I initially had reservations and questioned the choice of *Spidertown* for reading material, as the language and topic offended and troubled me. But being in a web-enhanced class helped me understand the reality of people in the Bronx at that time, and why Rodriguez had to write the novel this way, and why writing is so important to begin with. It also helped me understand the necessity to question and research issues that create internal conflict. I now understand that if I am to evolve as a student and a woman who lives in two cultures, it is important to use writing and researching as a catalyst for growth.
>
> This novel made me think about writing, myself as a Latino, and what I want to do in my future. It transitioned me from ignorance and fear of certain things and ideas, to empathy and understanding, and ultimately to thinking about my place in the United States and Latin America. I learned to ask questions and to get answers and make new knowledge that is going to help me in my career and in raising my bi-racial son.

Being in this blended class and studying *Spidertown* has reignited my interest in learning by transforming school from an uncomfortable environment to one that is personalized and distinct. I don't feel afraid of writing anymore. I feel that writing is about my ideas and that I have to figure out what my ideas are all about. I had never thought so much about myself, my culture and what I'm supposed to do with writing. I did not know I could use writing for that!

Finally, it is important to affirm that successful teaching of *Spidertown* in developmental and freshman composition classes delivered in a blended mode is dependent on key factors, among them the following: students need context, visuals, and to hear the dialogue. They need to discuss the plot development in person and virtually. They need multiple and varied opportunities to write and to practice as many rhetorical modes as can be squeezed in a semester. Group projects and other opportunities for peer collaboration are essential. Interaction between students and the professor must be robust. Professors need to remember that teaching and learning extend beyond the confines of regularly scheduled f2f meetings and into the virtual classroom. Teaching and learning take place at different times of the day and night, and not necessarily during concentrated and focused times. In fact, with busy adult students, completion of assignments is usually apportioned in between daily life routines. Technology evolves rapidly and therefore tools and practices must be reviewed and updated routinely. Impeccable organization, immediacy in responding, sustained tech support, and consistent and frequent assessment is absolutely necessary.

Notes

1. I thank all of my students, especially those in the four composition classes I taught during spring 2013 semester, for allowing me to walk with them for a short distance in their educational journey, and for presenting their strengths and weaknesses in ways that prod me to continue to learn. I am humbled by their resilience and determination! Writing this essay is for each of them.

2. All of the student passages I quote are just as they were written, including some grammatical and other types of errors. I leave out students' names to protect their privacy and to emphasize the similarities in their responses across time and types of courses where I have included *Spidertown*.

3. Today there are several terms used to describe my approach. Some might call it "hybrid" learning, an approach that requires students to learn independently mostly online. Some might call it "flipped" learning, an approach that requires students to complete foundational work online and then apply the lessons in the form of problem-solving and discussions during the f2f portion of the class. It used to be that the "blended" approach was defined by the online component being "additional" and "complementary" to the f2f component. But my "blended" approach integrates all of the con-

tent, activities and pedagogy into a cohesive learning experience delivered by two equally important modalities.

4. Pratt defined "contact zones" as "social spaces where cultures meet, clash, and grapple with each other, often in contexts of asymmetrical relations of power, such as colonialism, slavery, or their aftermaths as they are lived out in many parts of the world today" (1).

5. Anzaldúa defined the "borderland" as the physical and epistemological space between the United States and Mexico, a space where cultures, classes, genders, and identities meet and clash; she defined "mestizaje" as inhabiting multiple worlds, as a process and a state of being that shifts, transcends duality and emphasizes plurality.

6. Here are my expectations; understanding them will help you to succeed in this class:
- I will deliver the content of this course in a thorough and professional manner.
- I will help to create a dialogic, safe and fun student-centered environment where you can take charge of your learning and where generative discussions and activities can happen respectfully and insightfully.
- I will evaluate all of your work critically, conscientiously, and following established criteria.
- I will maintain a reasonable but challenging pace, and I'll be consistently open to your needs.
- You **will dedicate at least 6 hours per week solely to the work required in this class**. That's the Andrew Carnegie Rule, which is affirmed in Title V (California educational law) for college students. If your life circumstances do not allow you to dedicate 6 hours per week to just this class, this may not be the class for you—please take my caution seriously.
- You will read the syllabus very carefully and check the CMS consistently, so that you can stay informed and therefore better prepared.
- You will submit all work on time, in a Word file, and in the assigned place. (Again, I do not accept work that is submitted late, but if at any time you foresee a problem, please speak with me in advance and we will work together to solve the problem.)
- You will keep up with the readings and assignments and participate fully in all discussions.
- During discussions you will show/prove that you have read and considered the texts very carefully.
- You will complete all essays following MLA style format.
- You will make absolutely sure that you know how to use the CMS by the end of the first week of class.

7. I also include this statement at the beginning of the syllabus: "Welcome! This class is an educational safe zone. It welcomes and respects the viewpoints of students of all sexual orientations and genders, as well as all races, ethnicities, nationalities, religions, social statuses, sizes, learning styles and abilities. All members of this learning community are expected to treat each other with respect and dignity."

8. In order to create what I call an "educational safe zone" in the virtual classroom as well, I post the core rules of netiquette:
- Remember that you're interacting with humans who have feelings.
- Address your peers by name.
- Always re-think before clicking send.
- Adhere to the same standards of behavior in both the virtual and actual classrooms.
- Respect your peers' time and needs, especially when you work in pairs or small groups and depend on each other even more.
- Make it an instinct to offer your help.

- Minimize potential contention with patience and respect.
- Respect your peers' privacy.
- Be forgiving of other people's mistakes.
- Be ethical at all times.

9. Tabs include "Calendar" (where I post due dates for individual assignments), "Announcements" (where I provide links and other relevant news), "Syllabus," "Communicate" (where students can email individuals or everyone in the class), "Report," and "Lessons/Assignments" (where the content of the course resides in folders). I make sure that the content of the course is no more than two clicks away; I arrange it in folders titled "Modules" (one for each week in the semester), "Lessons," "Quizzes," "Discussion Forums," and "Drop Boxes" (where they submit the formal versions of their work).

10. It is necessary to comply with Americans with Disabilities Act (ADA)'s recommendations so that students (especially while in the virtual component of the class) have what they need in order to access content and to participate fully.

11. Note that the actual assignments are embedded in a great deal more description and background information, for instance when and where they are due, how many points (out of a possible one thousand during the semester) each is worth, and how they are linked to the assignments and activities before and after.)

12. I also give them the option to start a blog or use the CMS's chat tool.

13. A sample question for the DF: "How do *Spidertown* and the videos we watched this week create opportunities for writing?" One student's entry in the DF: "The sad truth is, surprisingly places like the South Bronx depicted in the videos and *Spidertown* are very real. There are numerous places around the world where our conventional ideas of society simply do not hold up. These places are such a stark juxtaposition to what I personally, and I think many of you, have ever experienced. However, this is precisely why they create so many opportunities for writing: they give us insight into something many of us have never known to exist, except maybe in movies and our imagination. The dialogue that can be raised from these videos and Rodriguez's novel is very important. It concerns everything we hold dear. We must be aware of the truth of what goes on in other areas of the world and writing about issues has always been an effective way of combating them. The conditions of being human will always be difficult, and these places show what can happen without necessary foundations to uphold our higher ideals. The real question is, why aren't more people writing about the reality of the videos and *Spidertown*?"

14. In order to help students in reading, I recently started using Balabolka, a free downloadable text-to-speech engine that reads content from documents (such as DOC, HTML, ODT, PDF and RTF) and then allows students to save text as an MP3, MP4, OGG, WAV or WMA. This application lets users choose the type of reading voice they want to hear, and it has a timer that can be set to read at bedtime, for instance. Students who are primarily auditory learners tend to benefit most from using such text-to-speech applications.

15. Nonetheless, I schedule an orientation during a f2f meeting so that, at least, they learn how to distinguish between scholarly and non-scholarly sources, why it is imperative to document, and how to document following MLA. That visit is followed by a short assignment requiring that they complete the virtual library orientation and learn to use the databases available.

16. Keeping a journal is very effective for this purpose. I used to require that students keep a journal, but given the reality that I don't have the bandwidth to respond to their entries on a frequently consistent basis, now I explain why journaling is productive and I recommend it highly.

17. Here I refer to Giddens' definition of globalization: "the intensification of world-

wide social relations which link distant localities in such a way that local happenings are shaped by events occurring many miles away and vice versa" (64).

Works Cited

Allatson, Paul. *Latino Dreams: Transcultural Traffic and the U.S. National Imaginary.* New York: Editions Rodopi, 2002. Print.
Anderson, Terry, and Fathi Elloumi, Eds. *Theory and Practice of Online Learning.* Athabasca, Canada: Athabasca University, 2004. Web. 18 April 2013.
Anson, Chris M. "Distant Voices: Teaching and Writing in a Culture of Technology." *Cross-talk in Comp Theory: A Reader.* Ed. Victor Villanueva. 2d ed. Urbana, IL: National Council of Teachers of English, 2003. 797–818. Print.
Anzaldúa, Gloria. *Borderlands/La Frontera: The New Mestiza.* San Francisco, CA: Aunt Lute Foundation, 1987. Print.
Bartholomae, David. "Teaching Basic Writing: An Alternative to Basic Skills." *A Sourcebook for Basic Writing Teachers.* Ed. Theresa Enos. New York: McGraw-Hill, 1987. 84–103. Print.
_____, and Anthony R. Petrosky. *Facts, Artifacts, Counterfacts: Theory and Method for a Reading and Writing Course.* Upper Montclair, NJ: Boynton/Cook, 1986. Print.
Bonk, Curtis J., and Charles R. Graham, Eds. *The Handbook of Blended Learning: Global Perspectives, Local Designs.* San Francisco, CA: Pfeiffer, 2006. Print.
Carpenter, Trudy G., William L. Brown, and Randall C. Hickman. "Influences of Online Delivery on Developmental Writing Outcomes." *Journal of Developmental Education*, 28.1 (Fall 2004): 14–35. Web. 12 April 2013.
Chen, Pu-Shih Daniel, Amber D. Lamber, and Kevin R. Guidry. "Engaging Online Learners: The Impact of Web-Based Learning Technology on College Student Engagement." *Computers & Education* 54.4 (2010): 1222–1232. *Academic Search Premier.* Web. 4 May 2013.
Dailey-Hebert, Amber and Emily Donnelli-Sallee, Laurie N. DiPadova-Stocks, Eds. *Service-eLearning: Educating for Citizenship.* London, UK: Information Age, 2008. Print.
Dalleo, Raphael, and Elena Machado Sáez. *The Latino/a Canon and the Emergence of Post-Sixties Literature.* New York: Palgrave Macmillan, 2007. Print.
Del Principe, Ann. "Paradigm Clashes Among Basic Writing Teachers: Sources of Conflict and a Call for Change." *Journal of Basic Writing* 23.1 (Spring 2004): 64–81. *Academic Search Premier.* Web. 1 May 2013.
Dooley, Kim E., and Leah E. Wickersham. "Distraction, Domination, and Disconnection in Whole-Class, Online Discussions." *Quarterly Review Of Distance Education* 8.1 (2007): 1–8. *Academic Search Premier.* Web. 5 May 2013.
Dziuban, Charles, Joel Hartman, and Patsy Moskal. "Everything I Need to Know About Blended Learning I Learned From Books." *Blended Learning: Research Perspectives.* Eds. Anthony G. Picciano and Charles Dziuban. Needham, MA: Sloan Center for Online Education, 2007. 265–286. Web. 24 April 2013.
Edmundson, Andrea, ed. *Globalized E-Learning Cultural Challenges.* Hershey, PA: Information Science, 2007.
80 Blocks from Tiffany's. Gary Weis, dir. United States: Above Average Productions, 1979. Online documentary. *YouTube*, 12 March 2008. Web. 3 March 2013.
Elbow, Peter. *Writing with Power: Techniques for Mastering the Writing Process.* New York: Oxford University Press, 1981. Print.
El Mansour, Bassou and Davison M. Mupinga. "Students' Positive and Negative Expe-

riences in Hybrid and Online Classes." *College Student Journal* 41.1 (March 2007): 242-248. *Academic Search Premier*. Web. 20 April 2013.

Freire, Paulo. *Pedagogy of the Oppressed*. New York: Continuum, 1970. Print.

Gamer, Michael. "Fictionalizing the Disciplines: Literature and the Boundaries of Knowledge." *College English* 57.3 (March 1995): 281-286. Web. 25 April 2013.

Garrison, D. Randy, and Heather Kanuka. "Blended Learning: Uncovering its Transformative Potential in Higher Education. *The Internet and Higher Education* 7.2 (2004): 95-105. *Academic Search Premier*. Web. 3 May 2013.

____, and Norman D. Vaughan. *Blended Learning in Higher Education: Framework, Principles, and Guidelines*. San Francisco, CA: Jossey-Bass, 2008. Print.

Giddens, Anthony. *The Consequences of Modernity*. Stanford, CA: Stanford University Press, 1990. Print.

Gilbert, Jennifer, Susan Morton, and Jennifer Rowley. "E-Learning: The Student Experience." *British Journal of Educational Technology* 38.4 (2007): 560–573. Web. 18 May 2013.

Ginns, Paul, and R. Ellis. "Quality in Blended Learning: Exploring the Relationships Between On-line and Face-to-Face Teaching and Learning." *The Internet and Higher Education* 10.1 (2007): 53–64. *Academic Search Premier*. Web. 1 May 2013.

Giroux, Henry. *Teachers as Intellectuals: Toward a Critical Pedagogy of Learning*. Westport, CT: Bergin and Garvey, 1988. Print.

Gouge, Catherine. "Conversation at a Critical Moment: Hybrid Courses and the Future of Writing Programs." *College English* 71.4 (2009): 338- 62. Print.

Halverson, Lisa R., Charles R. Graham, Kristian J. Spring and Jeffery S. Drysdale. "An Analysis of High Impact Scholarship and Publication Trends in Blended Learning." *Distance Education* 33.3 (2012): 381–413. *Academic Search Premier*. Web. 18 April 2013.

Hewett, Beth L. *The Online Conference: A Guide for Teachers and Tutors*. Portsmouth, NH: Boyton/Cook, 2010. Print.

Holmberg, Børje. "A Theory of Teaching-Learning Conversation." *Handbook of Distance Education*. Ed. M.G. Moore. London, UK: Taylor and Frances, 2007. 69–76. Print.

hooks, bell. *Teaching to Transgress: Education and the Practice of Freedom*. New York: Routledge, 1994. Print.

Isaacs, Emily. "Teaching General Education Writing: Is There a Place for Literature." *Pedagogy: Critical Approaches to Teaching Literature, Language, Composition, and Culture* 9.1 (Winter 2009): 97–120. Web. 10 May 2013.

Kirtman, Lisa. "Online Versus In-Class Courses: An Examination of Differences in Learning Outcomes." *Issues in Teacher Education* 18.2 (Fall 2009): 103–116. Web. 24 April 2013.

Kupperman, Jeff, and Barry J. Fishman. "Academic, Social, and Personal Uses of the Internet: Cases of Students from an Urban Latino Classroom." *Journal Of Research On Technology in Education* 34.2 (2001): 189–215. *Academic Search Premier*. Web. 5 May 2013.

Lindemann, Erika. "Freshman Composition: No Place for Literature." *College English* 55.3 (March 1993): 311–3116. Web. 23 April 2013.

Lunsford, Andrea. "Cognitive Development and the Basic Writer." *College English* 41.1 (1979): 38–46. Print.

Man Alive: The Bronx is Burning. Bill Morton and Desmond Wilcox, Eds. United Kingdom: BBC TV/BBC2, 1972. Online documentary. *YouTube*, 21 April 2012. Web. 5 March 2013.

Menchaca, Michael P., and Teklu Abate Bekele. "Learner and Instructor Identified Success Factors in Distance Education." *Distance Education* 29.3 (November 2008): 231–252. Web. 6 May 2013.

Meyers, Steven A. "Using Transformative Pedagogy When Teaching Online." *College Teaching* 56.4 (Fall 2008): 219–224. Print.

Mezirow, Jack. *Transformative Dimensions of Adult Learning.* San Francisco, CA: Jossey-Bass, 1991. Print.

Osguthorpe, Richard T., and Charles R. Graham. "Blended Learning Environments: Definitions and Direction." *Quarterly Review of Distance Education* 4 (2003): 227–234. Web. 7 May 2013.

Peck, Jennifer J. "Keeping it Social: Engaging Students Online and in Class." *Asian Social Science* 8.14 (November 2012): 81–90. *Academic Search Premier.* Web. 5 May 2013.

Picciano, Anthony G. "Blending with Purpose: The Multimodal Model." *Journal of the Research Center for Educational Technology* 5.1 (Summer 2009): 4–14. Web. 22 April 2013.

_____, and C. Dziuban, Eds. *Blended Learning: Research Perspectives.* Needham, MA: Sloan Consortium, 2007. Web. 23 April 2013.

Pratt, Mary Louise. "Arts of the Contact Zone." *Profession 91.* New York: MLA, 1991. 33–40. Web. 1 May 2013.

Revere, Lee, and Jamison V. Kovach. "Online Technologies for Engaged Learning: A Meaningful Synthesis for Educators." *Quarterly Review Of Distance Education* 12.2 (2011): 113–124. *Academic Search Premier.* Web. 5 May 2013.

Rhoads, Robert A., and Katalin Szelényi. *Global Citizenship and the University: Advancing Social Life and Relations in an Interdependent World.* Stanford, CA: Stanford University Press, 2011. Print.

Rivera, Lucas. "Bronx Author Shakes Up Latino Literature." *Hispanic* 11 (April 1998): 16.

Rodriguez, Abraham. *Spidertown: A Novel.* New York: Hyperion, 1993.

Rovai, Alfred P., and Hope M. Jordan. "Blended Learning and Sense of Community: A Comparative Analysis with Traditional and Fully Online Graduate Courses." *The International Review of Research in Open and Distance Learning* 5.2 (August 2004): 1–13. Web. 10 May 2013.

Schattle, Hans. *The Practices of Global Citizenship.* Lanham, MD: Rowman and Littlefield, 2007. Print.

Sherer, Pamela, and Timothy Shea. "Using Online Video to Support Student Learning and Engagement." *College Teaching* 59.2 (Spring 2011): 56–59. ERIC. Web. 2 May 2013.

Shor, Ira. "Illegal Literacy." *Journal of Basic Writing* 19.1 (2000): 100–112. Print.

_____. "Our Apartheid: Writing Instruction and Inequality." *Journal of Basic Writing* 16.1 (1997): 91–104. Print.

Stine, Linda J. "The Best of Both Worlds: Teaching Basic Writers in Class and Online." *Journal of Basic Writing* 23.2 (2004): 39–59. Print.

_____. "Teaching Basic Writing in a Web-Enhanced Environment." *Journal Of Basic Writing* (CUNY) 29.1 (Spring 2010): 33–55. ERIC. Web. 5 May 2013.

Tate, Gary. "A Place for Literature in Freshman Composition." *College English* 55.3 (March 1993): 317–322. Web. 24 April 2013.

Thomas, Piri. *Down These Mean Streets.* New York: Knopf, 1967. Print.

Warnock, Scott. *Teaching Writing Online: How and Why.* Urbana, IL: NCTE, 2009. Print.

Performing Community
Teaching Ethnic American Literature Through the Short Story Sequence

David Magill

I always start with punctuation. It puzzles my students in African American literature (or Native American literature, or others courses on literatures of racial and ethnic groups) when I note on day one that there is no hyphen in "African American," which I have written on the board. I do this partly to avoid having to correct the mistake multiple times on their first paper, but also to start a discussion about the term "African American." The hyphen, I tell them, is a bridge which connects two words to make one concept, easily defined, such as "action-packed"; "African American," on the other hand, is two distinct terms yoked together, as W.E.B. Dubois describes in *The Souls of Black Folk*: "One ever feels his two-ness,—an American, a Negro; two souls, two thoughts, two unreconciled strivings; two warring ideals in one dark body, whose dogged strength alone keeps it from being torn asunder" (11). To study African American literature requires keeping those two terms in tension, seeing them as in conflict as well as cooperation and understanding how they work to define a particular relationship to the notion of community. There is no easy bridge to connect those two sides; rather, the individual creates identity in the middle, between the two terms, negotiating and constructing selfhood from the sociocultural ideals of race and nationality at work in the United States.

This opening discussion, which also arises in my other ethnic literature courses in slightly different forms, offers a small way of giving my students a different vision of racial and ethnic identities as a means of understanding how we might view these terms within the tensions of individual and community. This becomes particularly important at a school where the student body is mostly white and middle class. But as we progress into the literature, I have found that a compelling means of getting students to understand this idea more fully is through the use of the short story sequence. In what follows, I will argue that the short story sequence represents inherently in its form the social construction of communities and ethnic identities. Using Sherman Alexie's *The Lone Ranger and Tonto Fistfight in Heaven* and Jhumpa Lahiri's *The Interpreter of Maladies* as representative examples, I argue that the choice of short story sequence as a genre is a social act that not only undermines "naturalized" ideals of community but also highlights the ethical implications intrinsic to building a community, be it a nation, a town, or a readership. The sequence allows authors to give voice to marginalized peoples, to allow the subaltern to speak from within the interstices of dominant culture. Teaching these texts allows the instructor to foreground notions of identity and community as well as examine the interplay between form and content that these sequences use in creating meaning. As such, this genre represents an important locus point for the teaching of twenty-first century ethnic American literature, whether in individual classes on ethnic literature or in a section of a class with a focus on American literature or even the short story.

The short story sequence, also referred to as short story cycle by some critics, is a unique form that has gathered increasing attention in recent years.[1] Robert Luscher, for example, defines the short story sequence as "a volume of stories, collected and organized by their author, in which the reader successively realizes underlying patterns of coherence by continual modifications of his perceptions of pattern and theme" (148). While other definitions might alter slightly, what they share in common is a focus on the tension between the individual story and the communal text and the meaningful possibilities that generates, particularly for ethnic writers who have gravitated toward the genre as a means of depicting their relationship to the larger national community of America. James Nagel notes,

> Writers from a wide variety of ethnic groups have used the form for the depiction of the central conflicts of characters from their own race or nationality. As "American" narratives, these stories often involve the process of immigration, acculturation, language acquisition, assimilation, identity formation, and the complexities of formulating a sense of self that incorporates the old world and the new, the central traditions of the country of origin integrated into, or in conflict with, the values of the country of choice [15].

The short story sequence thus highlights the difficulties of merging those two terms not only in its content but also through its form, allowing authors to critique simplistic notions of community formation and nationalist assimilations. As such, they interrogate facile notions of belonging to country or community by exposing the multiple possibilities for identity within a group configuration.

J. Gerald Kennedy ends his collection *Modern American Short Story Sequences* with an essay in which he articulates the short story sequence's work as creating a "semblance of community" (194). He further describes, "The genre embodies an insistently paradoxical semblance of community in its structural dynamic of connection and disconnection. The simultaneous independence and interdependence of stories in a sequence fosters a corresponding awareness of both the autonomy of individual stories and the elements that conjoin them" (195).

I highlight the use of this term because it indicates how authors have used the short story sequence as a social and political tool. In fact, I would argue that these authors go beyond a "tacit social or cultural gesture," as Kennedy argues, to both create a definition of community and highlight the fictional nature of that construction. The form of the short story sequence is crucial to this project; the disjunctions between individual stories as well as the connections are important in making meaning through narratological and characterological linkages.[2] The sequence thus highlights the readerly role in performing community through the imposition of meaning in the spaces between stories. The reader is kept autonomous even as he or she is invited to make connections, to forge a communal relationship with text and writer.

As a result, the short story sequence implicitly defines the reader's interpretation as the social construction of a community within stories but simultaneously foregrounds this process by introducing the gaps and disjunctions that deny easy meaning. As Jeff Birkenstein notes,

> As readers, we begin to draw inferences about characters within a given story that we *could not draw* if we had but a single story. Upon progressing (reading critically) through the cycle, we simply cannot approach each successive story with a clean slate, an empty mind; quite naturally in a short-story cycle we make connections, see patterns, impose order and meaning retroactively, and begin to anticipate themes and possibilities to come. We know, or sense, that a community is forming, and in our mind we create our own meta-text, making connections progressively *and* regressively [498, emphasis his].

The reader must create meaning in the spaces between the stories, must write that meta-text, and the habitation of that liminal space allows for students to experience vicariously the cognitive dissonance ethnic American authors depict in their works.[3] The short story sequence thus becomes a crucial form for the literature teacher to demonstrate the multiplicity of ethnic identities and cultures as well as the social constructions of communities, including the classroom.

To return to my beginning, I always end my discussion of the absent hyphen on day one with a response assignment which asks my students to write about a time when they felt in between two places, times, or events and explain how they saw themselves in that moment. As the majority of my students are freshmen and sophomores, I get a number of stories about high school graduation and the transition to college. But I also get stories about the shift from youth to adolescence, and tales of families moving from one state to another. Our second day together, then, begins with a discussion of their writings where I ask them to describe their feelings when in that liminal space. The students offer up words such as "confused," "unsure," and "scared" but they also toss out phrases such as "excited," "curious," and "determined, and we list these on the board in two columns—positive and negative feelings. Many of them, upon seeing the larger list, reveal that they felt emotions from both sides of the equation. They begin to see how that space can feel full of possibility and also anxiety, with individuals feeling that tension as they move away from one identity or community toward another. And as I question them, now "safely on the other side," I point out how many of them describe themselves as part of their new community but also connected to their past group. We can see how they learn to negotiate the different identities that belong to each community, constructing themselves so as to connect to each in a comfortable way while also having to deal with the conflicts between the two, from issues as simple as curfews at home versus freedom at school to the more complex ones such as intellectual growth and learning that changes one's relationship with family members and friends.

We end this discussion with the students more aware of the complexities of community membership and identity formation so that they are more open readers of our authors' confrontations with the same issues on a larger scale. This cognitive exposure is an important precursor to the short story sequences we will read because it engages the students with this idea of the contradictory nature of ethnic community and identity. As Kennedy notes,

> Lacking a continuous narratorial presence, the sequence—like the decentered modernist novel—places the reader in a strategic position to draw parallels, to discern whatever totalizing meanings may inhere in the composite scheme ... but this glimpse of connection, we must remind ourselves, forms a partial and problematic view, ordinarily achieved by the suppression of those fissures and incongruities that complicate the reading of the sequence and expose the gulf between one text and another [196].

Students, as we move forward, can build upon this thought process and begin to see the ways in which the ethnic short story sequence uses form to critique and develop its content. Of course, my simple exercise does not replicate the larger difficulties of racial and ethnic identity in a nation of white privilege, but it does allow the students a heuristic for understanding the liminal spaces that the short story sequences manipulate in order to examine ethnic American identities and communal definitions. And this work can occur in a multitude of classes, from courses on individual ethnic groups to multiethnic literature surveys. I have even successfully used these strategies in a course on the short story. In all of these courses, having been exposed to such ideas, the class can begin its examination of a short story sequence in earnest and explore why this form has been so attractive to ethnic American authors.

Sherman Alexie's *The Lone Ranger and Tonto Fistfight in Heaven* is a short story sequence that works particularly well following the response assignment I describe above because he articulates his characters' positionality between two cultures so evocatively.[4] Alexie's stories are always, as Birkenstein notes, exploring "Spokane/Coeur d'Alene Indians and their desire to reclaim the ancient traditions of an oral culture as well as their paradoxical rejection of that culture for the Anglo trappings of Diet Pepsi and basketball, both on and off the reservation" (488). They are in-between, and my students begin to recognize that space. To further this examination, we read "A Drug Called Tradition," a tale where Alexie explicitly defines this state of being when he writes, "Your past is a skeleton walking one step behind you, and your future is a skeleton walking one step in front of you. Maybe you don't wear a watch, but your skeletons do, and they always know what time it is. Now, these skeletons are made of memories, dreams, and voices. And they can trap you in the in-between, between touching and becoming" (21–22). Alexie demonstrates our placement between history and imagination vividly, and we can see how his Indians are trying to negotiate their identities temporally as well as culturally. But this passage also articulates the anxiety of being in that liminal space—the feeling of entrapment that Alexie shares when he writes, "That's what Indian time is. The past, the future, all of it is wrapped up in the now. That's how it is. *We are trapped in the now*" (22, emphasis his).[5]

Important as well to this moment in the story is the fact that the narrator prefaces these insights with the claim, "*There are things you should learn*" (21, emphasis his). The statement addresses the reader directly, implicating him or her in the lesson. Susan Berry Brill de Ramirez notes, "Alexie incorporates strategies from oral storytelling into his written story so that his readers take on actual roles within the story" (155). I stop at this sentence and ask the students why Alexie might make this choice –and after some discussion, we decide that this narrative act blurs the lines between reader and character in a manner that forces us to engage with the text. We become both hooked on the drug of tradition and learn the lesson of historical awareness that might cure our addiction. Alexie teaches us to read differently in order that we may accept the blurry lines and create our own agency to move between and among the spaces and identities that so often bifurcate into us and them, white and Native, urban and reservation. Jerome Denuccio states that, for Alexie, "the self is positioned in a social space replete with memories, dreams and voices that invite attention and response, that must be accommodated and negotiated if the self as an individual and a tribal subject is to emerge" (87). Alexie's stories show us that, while his characters often struggle to sit on one side of that binary or the other, the fact is that they are always and already both Native and American culturally—their happiness lies in being able to claim both sides of that identity and live in the middle.

Armed with these ideas, my students and I enter the space between "A Drug Called Tradition" and "Because My Father Always Said He Was the Only Indian Who Saw Jimi Hendrix Play the 'Star-Spangled Banner' at Woodstock." The third story in the collection, this tale depicts a father and son relationship where the father believes, "That's all there is.... War and peace with nothing in between. It's either one or the other" (29). But Alexie shows us the dangers of this bifurcated thinking throughout the collection, and the previous story allows us to see the necessity of critiquing this statement. Alexie's narrative asks us to look backward and forward, so I ask my students to think about how the lesson learned in the previous statement might fit here. We discuss character motivations and actions, as this father ends up leaving his son and wife behind—the story is narrated as the son's remembrance of his father. But we also discuss how Alexie asks us to both sympathize and critique his characters as we consider their visions of the world. Molly Winter notes of Alexie's collection that "each story ends in a fragile moment, teetering on the brink of history, failure, forgiveness, and redemption. The presence of love, music, memory, and traditions promises continuance, though, as Junior says at the end of 'A Good Story,' 'there is just barely enough goodness in all of this' (144)" (476). After focusing specifically on these two stories, my students can see how Alexie positions us as readers to find our own space of interpretation, and defines that space as imaginative: "Survival = Anger × Imagination. Imagination is the only weapon on the reservation" (150). We can discuss, then, how Alexie understands individual agency and see how he reveals Native Americans both controlling and constructed into their identities.[6]

At this point, I hand out their writing assignment, where I ask each student to write a short essay in which they choose two stories from the collection and write from in between them to explain how the two stories inter-relate and define each other's meaning. I inform them that, while they can take two consecutive stories for this assignment, they may also choose two non-consecutive stories so long as they can define the connection that would allow these stories to speak to one another. "Jimi Hendrix," for example, pairs well with "Witnesses, Secret and Not" in terms of looking at fathers and sons; but "Witnesses, Secret and Not" (the last story in the collection) also works well in conjunction with "Every Little Hurricane" (the first story), a juxtaposition that highlights the cyclic nature of the collection as well as the focus on emotional pain in Native life. My students and I spend several days in class discussing Alexie as they work on this assignment, and their reading habits shift toward looking for connections and links across stories; however, I also caution them that we must remember the disjunctions and differences, for those also contribute to the creation of meaning. We work at making sure that they can discuss each story individually as well as make connections between them. I always find these days full of lively discussion, and that more students participate as they explore and develop their consciousness of this form of reading, this reading of form. Student papers from this assignment can vary widely, as you might imagine, but the best ones avoid the traditional comparison/contrast model and instead view the stories as dialogically interconnected. Students are able to see how they, too, can escape the formal binary of the comparison and find meaning in the space between stories. I often receive papers that contain self-aware statements of the reading process, which suggests that the students understand their own position in relation to the two stories.

We end our unit on Alexie with the students more aware of how form and content inter-relate; how identity arises from social constructions that combine history, culture, and personal vision; how ethnic identities in particular require negotiating across traditional divisions of race, gender, and culture; and how community arises from the interrelationships between individuals and/or groups. Alexie's Indians can pursue traditional identifications with their Native culture *and* drink Diet Pepsi while watching basketball. They can build communities across allegiances to histories, groups, and traditions, but conflicts can arise as well. Alexie shows us how culture constantly morphs and changes across boundaries not only through the content of his characters and their lives but also through the form of his stories, which combine, merge, split off, fight, and witness to the myriad possibilities for imaginative interpretation.

Another text that I use when teaching ethnic American literature is Jhumpa Lahiri's *Interpreter of Maladies.* Lahiri presents a formal challenge for students in that her collection does not follow the pattern of Alexie's, or other traditional sequences, which use recurring characters and landscapes as a means of signaling to the reader a need for connection. Lahiri's stories seemingly have no connection, which leads some students to question whether *Interpreter of Maladies* why I refer to the collection as a short story sequence. But Noelle Brada-Williams has persuasively argued for reading Lahiri's work as a short story cycle, stating, "A deeper look reveals the intricate use of pattern and motif to bind the stories together" (451). Brada-Williams traces the thematics of community, communication, and care and neglect through all nine stories of Lahiri's cycle, suggesting that they comprise the connective tissue that links the cycle together. She notes, for example, how the first and last story serve as bookends, with "the Third and Final Continent" reflecting and reversing the plot of "A Temporary Matter." Such linkages across the text undercut linear reading strategies and emphasize the multiple connections possible between stories; they ask the reader to alter reading strategies and make links between radically different stories without regard to linear sequence or plot development. But these stories can also stand alone, allowing the reader to parse the individual meanings as well as the collective focal points. That tension is important, as Michelle Pacht notes of Louise Erdrich's *Love Medicine* and Maxine Hong Kingston's *Woman Warrior*: "Both are made up of text-pieces that can be read alone but a full understanding of the endemic and often uncomfortable clashes that are commonplace between mainstream American and the communities represented in these texts becomes apparent only when one reads the text as a whole" (113). Lahiri similarly represents these clashes in both the content of individual stories and the formal work of the short story sequence. Using Lahiri's work, then, allows me to show students how an author can marry form to content and depict the individual's relation to community and development of ethnic identity in the United States.

Take, for example, "A Temporary Matter." Shoba and Sukumar, a struggling married couple in the story, find themselves without electricity each night for five days. They use this time in the dark to tell each other truths they had previously hidden as they eat dinner together; these secrets escalate from day one's revelations of innocent early dating mishaps to the final night when she announces she is leaving him and he responds by telling her about his moments holding their stillborn son. The story ends, "They wept together, for the things they now knew" (22). Shoba and Shukumar gain illumination in the dark, and their relationship is both at an end and a new beginning. Shukumar realizes that while they are living together, "he and Shoba had become experts at avoiding each other in their three-bedroom house, spending as much time on separate floors as possible" (4).[7] The story sets up such tensions internally to teach the reader how to approach Lahiri's text and its external connections to identity and community. The story reminds us of Shoba and Shukumar's Indian heritage but also highlights their status as new Americans, from Shoba's comparisons of Indian and American weather to Shukumar's remembrances of Shoba's Indian and Italian cooking. As we watch them interact, we learn of their assimilation to American culture but also their adherence to traditional Indian customs. Shukumar is earning his doctoral degree, a choice that reminds us of America's status as land of possibility and upward mobility. But their relationship has suffered, re-defining their marriage and their identities over time—they have stopped cooking and marketing, and Shukumar realizes that if he does not cook, Shoba will eat cereal for dinner.

Interestingly, every time I teach the story, one student will ask, "But what about the Bradfords?" Shoba and Shukumar's older neighbors, Lahiri includes them as an image of marital bliss—we see them walking arm-in-arm, or walking their dog to the local bookstore. They seem the "perfect couple," and some students argue that they stand as a counterpoint to Shoba and Shukumar, with their physical affections and general goodwill standing as the example of happiness. Others chime in to point out that, since the Bradfords do invite Shoba and Shukumar to join them at the bookstore and did respond to their lost child with a sympathy card, they symbolize an ideal of inclusive community. By the end of the discussion, then, we can see that Lahiri's opening story offers us important ideas about community and ethnic identity.

I ask students, after discussing this story, to explain how it might connect with "When Mr. Pirzada Came to Dine," the next story in the sequence. In basic details, this story could not be more different from "A Temporary Matter": the focus is on a child and a family visitor, and there is no discussion of marriage or relationships. But, having read the previous story, the students quickly identify Lahiri's focus on community. Mr. Pirzada comes to America to earn his doctoral degree, and Lilia's family takes him in as a regular guest; however, Mr. Pirzada is both part of their community and estranged from it. We soon learn that Mr. Pirzada is from Dacca, a city bordering Pakistan and Bangladesh and, at the time of the story's setting, invaded by Pakistan. The international conflicts between India and Pakistan stand in sharp contrast to Lilia's family and their warm welcome of Mr. Pirzada. He eats dinner with him, watches the news with him, and even helps Lilia carve a pumpkin and trick-or-treat on Halloween. He becomes part of their community even as their homelands war over land and border rights. Lahiri offers a vision of cross-cultural communication and friendship that transcends the national and ethnic divisions of their peoples.

In contrast to this vision of connection comes "Interpreter of Maladies." Mr. Kapasi, a translator who presumably speaks Hindi and English, is accompanying Mr. and Mrs. Das on a tour and as they travel, he becomes infatuated with her. At a crucial moment in the story, as Mr. Das takes the children to see some monkeys, Mina Das confesses that her son is the result of an afternoon encounter with her husband's friend. When she pushes Mr. Kapasi to respond because "he is an interpreter," he can only ask her whether she feels pain or guilt. Her anger and disappointment combine with his vision of her depression to separate them; she heads to join her family and he becomes emotionally distant, noticing only that she loses his address to the wind. When I ask the students to consider this story, we start with the question, "What is an interpreter?" They can quickly identify the literal position of interpreter that Mr. Kapasi—a translator. But then I ask them to consider why Mina Das, after confessing to Mr. Kapasi, asks him, "Don't you have anything to say? I thought that was your job.... As an interpreter" (65). I ask my students to explain how Mrs. Das might be using that term differently, and we move from the idea of literal translation—one word for another—to a more figurative version—defining meaning of words. From there, the students can easily see how that definition mirrors our work as readers, and we can discuss how Lahiri marks this story as important by making it the title story in the sequence. Our job as readers is to interpret the maladies of the characters and understand their conflicts and correspondences, but also to glean meaning from them. We are not just to summarize in other words but to interpret meaning; ironically, the difference between those two actions is what drives Mr. Kapasi and Mrs. Das apart but what should bring us closer to the story. Their conflict of morals and ethics alienates them from one another but gives us meaning as we ponder the importance of connection and the barriers that frustrate or interfere with it.

Having reviewed these three stories, the class can now discuss Lahiri's overall vision of community and identity. Students can identify the struggle that occurs in each story as the individuals seek connection in relationships of family, marriage, and friendship, and how the barriers of language, culture, and circumstance make connection difficult, fragile, and ephemeral.[8] Further, they are excited to discuss the ways in which lack of knowledge, whether through ignorance, deceit, or unfamiliarity, breeds such disconnection. We can then extrapolate to their own lack of historical and cultural knowledge, such as with the India-Pakistan disputes that I invariably have to parse before we discuss "Mr. Pirzada." As we talk about the ways in which readers of these stories are positioned, students begin to understand how their knowledges (or lack thereof) might influence their interpretations, how their culture and language defines their reaction to Mrs. Das's infidelity as much as their moral beliefs. I also introduce the critical idea of cosmopolitanism, which Susan Koshy and Elizabeth Jackson have connected to Lahiri's work.[9] I ask my students to consider, after defining the term, whether Lahiri's cosmopolitanism is uncritically accepted, limited in some fashion, or explored as a contradictory space of identification.[10] At this point, I also hand out their writing assignment, which asks them to choose two stories that we have not yet connected and discuss their vision of community or identity. The idea of cosmopolitanism offers them a language for discussing those ideas, but I assure them that it is not the only discourse they may choose when writing about Lahiri. Similar to what happens when I teach Alexie in this manner, the papers I get often seem more aware of their own comparative structures as well as more complex in their engagement with Lahiri's content.

With this structure in place, we continue through the rest of the text, returning to these notions as we encounter other characters. The discussion through the rest of the stories centers on how Lahiri portrays her characters living in the space between, much like Alexie does. For example, we read "Mrs. Sen" and see how she can be physically living in the United States but culturally clinging to her Indian lifestyle and beliefs, to the point that she cannot drive a car and feels isolated and trapped in her apartment with only the young Eliot to keep her company. Her conflict of identity arises from her desire to maintain her cultural connections in a country where she cannot do so easily. My students argue for her need to be able to do so, articulating Lahiri's critique of American assimilation, but also note that Mrs. Sen's story does not end well because she cannot find agency in that middle space. Thus, they determine her to be in between and anxious about that placement.

Similarly, "This Blessed House" depicts the uneven cultural positioning of Sanjeev after his marriage to Twinkle, with him wanting to balance between the two cultures while Twinkle sees their new house, with its eccentric architecture and hidden treasures left by the previous inhabitants, as support for her American worldview. The story ends with their finding an enormous silver bust of Christ, which Sanjeev hates for "its immensity, and its flawless, polished surface, and its undeniable value" (156–57). Sanjeev's mental rejection of this Christian symbol, despite his earlier assertion that "there are Christians in India," reflects his distaste for Twinkle's optimistic materialism but also for her resistance to his cultural beliefs. The assumption that he will acquiesce in displaying the Christ bust is only the latest in a strong of actions she takes to connect him to the house and her adventurous spirit. Yet what makes the story interesting is its refusal to support Sanjeev completely; though told from his view, the story does not necessarily support his conclusions about Twinkle. Instead, Lahiri foregrounds the conflict between them and the ramifications, and readers are conditioned to understand this conflict and see how both sides struggle to negotiate their identities within its cultural matrix.

We then turn to the two stories set outside the United States: "A Real Durwan" and "The Treatment of Bibi Haldar." Both stories portray women living in India who are on the borders between spaces. My students point to descriptions such as one of Boori Ma, the durwan: "Knowing not to sit on the furniture, she crouched, instead, in doorways and hallways" (76). Boori Ma may be an Indian woman in India, but she assimilates no better than Mrs. Sen or Mr. Kapasi. She is critiqued for not guarding the new toilets and ostracized unfairly. At this point, we can discuss the ethics of the community and its definition through exclusion—and my students debate the means of exclusion as we define community. Bibi Haldar is similar to Boori Ma in that she is physically part of the community but socially ostracized in a manner that the title highlights—our focus is on her treatment and the question I ask the students is, "Does the story support the community's treatment of Bibi Haldar?" The students think I want them to say "No," but our discussions complicate the answer as we discuss what their treatment entails and where it goes wrong. Both these stories, juxtaposed because of their setting despite their distant placement within the collection, force students to go beyond American views and consider community more comprehensively and culture more forcefully.

The unit ends with "The Third and Final Continent," which I mentioned above as a bookend for "A Temporary Matter." One reason the story works so well as a bookend is its depiction of a successful Indian marriage and assimilation—but at the same time, that also raises questions for my students who have read several stories of adjustment difficulties. But this couple has its issues as well, and so the discussion turns toward the question of what skill set offers these individuals success. Partly, my students decide, it is simply that these two do the hard work necessary to maintain a relationship. But partly it seems as well to be the blessing of Mrs. Croft—their visit to her serves as a turning point for Mala and the narrator. Judith Caesar notes of "The Third and Final Continent," "When Mala and the narrator enter Mrs. Croft's house, her exterior walls shut out the world of 1969 America and her interior walls create new arrangements of distance and closeness, intimacy and privacy, rearrangements of external and emotional space that make love possible" (57). That certainly seems to be true, but it is important to see how Lahiri re-defines that ideal to show us the inter-relationship of the internal and the external, the private and the public. Mrs. Croft's house does seem like a space of escape from the world, but that world still exists in the story, even if temporarily dismissed. The narrator remembers it, and follows the news of the moon launch and other events even as he lives there. But more importantly, the reader remembers it both from inside the story and from other stories such as "When Mr. Pirzada Came to Dine," a text which likewise focuses on the domestic space of happiness but never erases completely the external politics of nations at war and the effects those tumultuous events have on the internal dynamics of the family and the community. Thus, the story embodies for us the reading practices necessary to understand the cycle and its depictions of identity and community as always being redefined and always fragile, reminding us again to move between the binaries and find the space of "both/and." Speaking of "The Third and Final Continent" in comparison to "Nobody's Business," Caesar claims, "the stories are two versions of the American spirit of place, one utopian, one dystopian; the materials of the two places are the same. The difference is in the imaginations of the characters or in their inability to find the space in which to imagine one another and construct a set of values for themselves that respects the humanity and the differentness of others" (66). For Lahiri, the importance of this space is to construct those values but also to recognize the constructedness of those values. We must respect humanity and differentness, as Caesar claims, but we must also engage critically with the discourses that separate us.

I teach Alexie and Lahiri because I find them superlative texts that engage with the difficulties of ethnic identity in the United States in provocative and compelling ways. But I also turn to them because they merge form and content through the short story sequence, and thus expose us to new ways of listening. There are, of course, many other examples that would work well in such a course—Louise Erdrich's *Love Medicine*, Maxine Hong Kingston's *Woman Warrior*, Sandra Cisneros's *The House on Mango Street*, Jamaica Kincaid's *Annie John* immediately come to mind, and there are many others. One could teach various configurations of these texts, but what remains constant for me is the productive use of formal tensions to examine specific contents, whether it is Erdrich's exploration of Native history and gender politics, or Kingston's mythic heroics and feminine agency. I chose Alexie and Lahiri because of their accessibility for my students and their focus on community as a central theme. But mostly, I chose them because of my enjoyment and love of their writing. Alexie's and Lahiri's short story sequences offer us a cognitive space to develop our faculties of listening and thinking by creating a formal structure that pushes us to read in new ways, to make different connections, and to hold contradictory ideals in place. They allow us to contain multitudes.

Notes

1. For definitions of the short story cycle and sequence, see Ingram, Luscher, Kennedy, and Nagel.
2. Michelle Pacht notes, "the spaces in between the stories are often as crucial to understanding the larger meaning of the text as the stories themselves" (1-2).
3. Rocío Davis notes, "the dynamics of the short-story cycle have converted it into a form that is especially appropriate to the kinds of conflict presented in ethnic fiction" (4).
4. Andrew Dix, for example, notes that the "predominant effect [across the stories] is one of dispersal rather than concentration" (158). He asserts the tension between the desire for connection and meaning that we share with the characters and the difficulties inherent in maintaining tribal meaning in a nationalist framework.
5. Jerome DeNuccio and Kathleen Carroll both argue persuasively that Alexie, while promoting connection to tradition, is not trying to return Indians to a prelapsarian past but rather to articulate ways to bring those traditions into the present so they are spiritually connected and temporally located.
6. DeNuccio states, "the term *Indian* names a subject position traversed by competing claims" (87).
7. Judith Caesar notes, "In her short stories, Lahiri uses the architecture of old American houses as an emblem of the emotional spaces between the people who live in those houses" (52).
8. Susan Koshy reads Lahiri as asking us to "imagine an impossible hospitality from the position of the other who cannot feel at home" (594).
9. See Koshy and Jackson's discussion of cosmopolitanism. Koshy's vision of minority cosmopolitanism is particularly compelling.
10. Koshy argues that Lahiri "makes apparent divisions and affiliations that can be folded neither into multiculturalism nor into Western cosmopolitanism's identity-bracketing universalism" (598). Her claims fit well with the reading I am making here.

Works Cited

Alexie, Sherman. *The Lone Ranger and Tonto Fistfight in Heaven*. New York: Harper-Perennial, 1993. Print.

Birkenstein, Jeff. "'Should I Stay or Should I Go?': American Restlessness and the Short-Story Cycle." In *A Companion to the American Short Story*. Ed. Alfred Bendixen and James Nagel. London: Wiley-Blackwell, 2010. 482-501. Print.

Brada-Williams, Noelle. "Reading Jhumpa Lahiri's *Interpreter of Maladies* as a Short Story Cycle." *MELUS* 29.3-4 (Autumn/Winter 2004): 451-64. Print.

Caesar, Judith. "American Spaces in the Fiction of Jhumpa Lahiri." *ESC* 31.1 (March 2005): 50-68. Print.

Carroll, Kathleen L. "Ceremonial Tradition as Form and Theme in Sherman Alexie's *The Lone Ranger and Tonto Fistfight in Heaven*": A Performance-Based Approach to Native American Literature." *The Journal of the Midwest Modern Language Association* 38.1 (Spring 2005): 74-84. Print.

Davis, Rocio G. "Identity in Community in Ethnic Short Story Cycles: Amy Tan's *The Joy Luck Club*, Louise Erdrich's *Love Medicine*, Gloria Naylor's *The Women of Brewster Place*." *Ethnicity and the American Short Story*. Ed. Julia Brown. New York: Garland, 1997. 3-23. Print.

DeNuccio, Jerome. "Slow Dancing with Skeletons: Sherman Alexie's *The Lone Ranger and Tonto Fistfight in Heaven*." *Critique* 44.1 (Fall 2002): 86-96.
De Ramirez, Susan Berry Brill. "Learning to Listen to Stories: Sherman Alexie's 'Witnesses, Secret and Not" in *Short Stories in the Classroom*. Ed. Carole L. Hamilton and Peter Kratzke. Urbana: NCTE, 1999. 153-62.
Dix, Andrew. "Escape Stories: Narratives and Native Americans in Sherman Alexie's The Lone Ranger and Tonto Fistfight in Heaven." *The Yearbook of English Studies* 31 (2001): 155-67.
Dubois, W.E.B. *The Souls of Black Folk*. Ed. Henry Louis Gates, Jr. and Terri Hume Oliver. New York: Norton, 1999.
Jackson, Elizabeth. "Transcending the Politics of 'Where You're From': Postcolonial Nationality and Cosmopolitanism in Jhumpa Lahiri's *Interpreter of Maladies*." *Ariel* 43.1 (2012): 109-126.
Kennedy, J. Gerald, ed. "From Anderson's *Winesburg* to Carver's *Cathedral*: The Short Story Sequence and the Semblance of Community." In Kennedy 194-216.
———. "Introduction: The American Short Story Sequence—Definitions and Implications." In Kennedy. vii-xv.
———. *Modern American Short Story Sequences: Composite Fictions and Fictive Communities*. London: Cambridge University Press, 1995.
Koshy, Susan. "Minority Cosmopolitanism." *PMLA* 126.3 (May 2011): 592-609.
Lahiri, Jhumpa. *Interpreter of Maladies*. New York: Houghton Mifflin, 1999.
Luscher, Robert M. "The Short Story Sequence: An Open Book." *Short Story Theory at a Crossroads*. Ed. Susan Lohafer and Jo Ellyn Clarey. Baton Rouge: Louisiana State University Press, 1989.
Nagel, James. *The Contemporary American Short-Story Cycle: The Ethnic Resonance of Genre*. Baton Rouge: Louisiana State University Press, 2001.
Pacht, Michelle. *The Subversive Storyteller: The Short Story Cycle and the Politics of Identity in America*. Newcastle: Cambridge Scholars, 2009.
Winter, Molly Crumpton. "The Multiethnic American Short Story." In *A Companion to the American Short Story*. Ed. Alfred Bendixen and James Nagel. London: Wiley-Blackwell, 2010. 466-81.

Problem-Based Learning and Landscape Perspective in a Jewish-American Fiction Course

Jeff Sommers

In this essay I report on a course in Jewish-American fiction that I taught by using Problem-Based Learning (PBL). I found three major advantages to the PBL approach in this course:

- The students had to become a part of a communal effort to shape the course in a meaningful way.
- The students had to create knowledge rather than receive it because they had to answer a complex question that had no single correct, factual answer.
- The students had to learn how to take what one of them termed "a landscape perspective" on the course, meaning that they had to step back and take a broader view of the work rather than a "portrait perspective" of examining individual, discrete artifacts and experiences.

My decision to take the PBL approach culminated a journey that commenced in the 1980s when I first began to teach general education literature courses at an open admissions, two-year campus. That journey led me to invite my students to take an increasingly larger responsibility for designing the course, a direction that I want to argue has been entirely appropriate and productive. The students on my campus were generally first-generation college students, usually working part- or full-time while attending classes, commuting from five to 60 minutes to the campus, with a median age of 26. My 1980s Major American Writers syllabus (see Sommers 1995) was a comprehensive one: it assigned a thick literature anthology and a novel as required reading; it designated specific daily reading assignments on the course calendar; and it specified a final grade based on assigned papers (40 percent), exams (40 percent) and class participation (20 percent).

By the time I came to teach a course in Jewish-American Fiction in the mid-'90s, however, my view on teaching general education literature courses had changed, thanks to theorists such as Bruce Kimball, who advocated "shifting the emphasis in the classroom away from what the faculty member knows and toward what the student learns.... The liberal arts teacher should stimulate and facilitate the student's learning and cannot, in fact, teach in the traditional sense of conveying or informing" (96), and especially Robert B. Barr and John Tagg. Barr and Tagg argued that colleges should be more focused on how to "produce learning" rather than how to "deliver instruction" (16). They noted a number of ways in which change would occur with a shift from an "instruction paradigm" to a "learning paradigm": by acknowledging that "knowledge is constructed, created, and 'gotten'" rather than clinging to an older notion that "knowledge comes in 'chunks' and 'bits' delivered by instructors" (17), teachers would move away from covering materials to designing "specified learning results"(17). They concluded that the implications of these ideas necessitated shifting the role of the teacher from professing to designing "learning methods and environments," and they urged faculty to find ways to design classrooms in which "faculty and students work in teams with each other and other staff" (17).

In my '90s literature course, my syllabus dramatically changed: it listed only a single short novel as a required text, the calendar indicated a due date for the assigned novel but left the remainder of the calendar as "To be determined," and a contract grading system required students to establish goals for themselves in the course including a list of completed readings and assignments that would enable them to reach those goals. I had re-designed the course to become "inquiry-based." "The students—and I—would construct the course collaboratively in the process of inquiring into the culture of Jewish-American writers" (275). In my course a decade earlier, the inquiry that drove the course had been mine alone and had been completed before the semester began, codified in the course syllabus. "My own rhetoric in the two syllabuses ... clearly changed from a legalistic, distant prose based on an overtly one-sided power relationship to a less-formal, more conversational prose based on a conception of negotiation between student and teacher" (277). If the 1980s course described a journey, I wrote, that journey was "not to be an exploration but a guided tour" (278). My original literature course had not acknowledged "that individual students might be different; it sketched out a course that would be identical for every student" (285). These kinds of moves paralleled other teaching moves described in the same essay collection in which my analysis was published, moves described by Gerald Graff as a "problematizing" of the literature teacher's authority. Graff urged teachers to present "literary knowledge not as a set of correct answers (or right readings), but as a conversation whose terms are always open to renegotiation and challenge" (325). At the time, I was satisfied that my new approach had led to "renegotiation and challenge."

A Continued Journey

However, I subsequently came to realize that my redesigned course had emphasized the students as individuals embarked on private journeys when they were actually members of an interpretive community whose journeys were not solitary at all because we regularly made communal decisions about the reading, and we came together to discuss those readings. The individualized contracts seemed to work against the notion of community. This realization troubled me.

Similarly, Marcia Baxter Magolda's longitudinal research into student academic experiences leads her to the realization that the students in her study had had a college experience that "reinforced listening to authorities rather than developing self-authorship" (xxii). She advocates instead a pedagogy that would link "existing knowledge to student's experience and development, engaging the messiness of working through knowledge claims, and engaging in a genuine mutual construction with learners" (215). Echoing Baxter-Magolda, Hugh Mercer Curtler argues "education requires information, but more importantly, it requires that a person be able to *process* that information, to make informed choices and wise decisions" (29). I was convinced by these theorists that I needed to effect further change in my teaching.

I read other theorists advocating similar positions specifically focused on teaching literature: the goal of teaching literature should be "moving students into a more active and 'generative' position" (Podis and Podis 119); "we need to make changes so that our students can, after taking a literature course, explain what literature professors do and why it is important. We need to find a pedagogy that invites our students to participate in the profession" (Valenza 259). Gerald Graff presented an agenda that might move literature instruction in this direction:

> One of the most necessary things about a community ... is the opportunity it gives you to hear your own points played back to you in somebody's else's terms. Arguably, we don't know our own thoughts until we hear them translated and altered by somebody else ... I think our students and colleagues would probably write better if they wrote in dialogues with each other rather than in solo performances [qtd in Tompkins and Graff 25].

But how could my Jewish-American fiction course be revamped to accomplish these goals? That became the problem with which I had to grapple.

My teaching strategy developed partially in response to reading Randy Bass's seminal essay "The Scholarship of Teaching: What's the Problem?" Bass argues for reconceiving the idea of a "problem" in teaching as an opportunity rather than as a failure (8). His idea is to study the problem and produce scholarship, but the revelatory moment for me came when I realized that an opportunity was presented by the central "problem" that all literature teachers faced every time they designed a course: what should the class read? I had already converted my syllabus from one that provided all the answers to "What shall we read?" into one that invited the students to participate in answering it. The next step I would take was to center the course on that question, bringing the students into the fray in the much-contested arena of canon formation, albeit the canon of a single course.

The "problem" of what to read seemed to me to be of pressing importance in an ethnic literature course. My 1990s class had encouraged the students to select the reading list, but it had done so more as a gesture toward decentering the classroom than a planned approach to teaching Jewish American literature. My idea for the course that I describe and analyze in this essay was to involve the students in trying to meet the very challenge I faced as the instructor of the course by requiring them to solve the problem themselves. Thus, I turned to Problem-Based Learning (PBL). PBL is "focused, experiential learning organized around the investigation, explanation, and resolution of meaningful problems. In PBL, students work in small collaborative groups and learn what they need to know in order to solve a problem" (Hmelo-Silver 236). Effective PBL models incorporate two crucial features: a rich problem that spurs the students into free inquiry, and learning that is student-based (Hmelo and Evensen 2). This pedagogy fit very nicely with the concept I had for my course because the problem I wished to present to the students was not only a "rich" one but also a real-world problem, one that I would have faced alone as the instructor of the course if I had not decided to include the students as active participants. Such an approach challenges students, and that is precisely what I wanted to do. During this period I was selected as a Carnegie Academy for the Scholarship of Teaching and Learning (CASTL) fellow and spent a year developing a research project that studied the use of PBL pedagogy in an introduction to literature general education class. That project resulted in two publications that demonstrated the positive effect of the PBL approach on students' critical reading skills (See Sommers et al.; Sommers 2005). With the experience of using PBL behind me, I decided to extend its use by engaging my students more directly in the problem of designing the course itself through the creation of the course reading list.

My newly designed syllabus was quite different from my '90s Jewish-American Fiction course. The new syllabus offered this course description:

> In this course we will read a variety of texts to map out the changing role of identity both inside and outside of the literary texts. We will examine how the presentation and definition of identity is tied to individual ways of understanding the relationship of the self to ethnicity, gender, race, and nation. In addition, we will consider the politics of identity both in and outside the text, taking up the question, "Why do groups choose to identify themselves in particular ways?"

Additionally, I outlined a number of specific course objectives, the two most relevant of which were "You will be able to understand that college literature courses ask students to read literature that has been chosen by a reader or readers and that the choices made reveal the value systems of those who make the choices" and "You will understand Jewish-American culture more fully. Reading Jewish-American fiction will provide many opportunities for you to learn more about yourself and American society through learning more about Jewish-American culture." I wanted my students to understand that the syllabus was a construct, not a given, an understanding that I thought they would come to know best through the experience of helping to construct it.

In the newly designed course, I only assigned a single novel and a short story anthology. Student groups were to select three additional novels for the class to read with each group responsible for leading the class discussion of their chosen novel. Students in these same groups would also determine the short stories to read from the anthology and lead discussions of those selections as well. Near the end of the course, the students would produce academic posters that presented their own suggested reading list for a future iteration of the course, based on all of the readings we had completed; I would invite other faculty to attend that poster session. Forty percent of the final grade was determined by these collaborative activities with a reading journal and class participation (30 percent), and quizzes and a take-home final essay (30 percent) fleshing out the course requirements.

The first assigned reading was *Girls* by Frederick Busch, a well-received contemporary detective novel. The novel had no discernible Jewish content or characters, but in an interview about his book, Busch mentioned his own Jewish background. I assigned the novel because I wanted the class to confront the course question immediately. Was it sufficient reason to select this novel solely because its author was Jewish?

As for the students in the class, they were typical of the student population I was accustomed to teaching: a number were in their late twenties and thirties with one student in his forties. They ranged from first-year students to students with several semesters of college experience. All commuted to school; most held jobs during the day before our evening class meetings. Some students were full-time while others were part-time. No student in the class ever self-identified as Jewish although one student reported in a class survey that he had studied "some of the history regarding the Holocaust as well as some limited study of Judaism." No one else mentioned having such a background. I identified myself as Jewish, explaining, however, that I would not be presenting myself as "the expert" on Judaism, which would have been an exaggeration of my knowledge, but that I was willing to share what I could in terms of background I had experienced or learned as I prepared for the course.

In the analysis that follows, I draw evidence from materials produced by the students, including their final essay exams, reflective writing produced periodically throughout the course, completed surveys administered during the semester, and interviews with four of the students after the course had ended. A colleague visited the class and gathered signed permissions from the students in my absence. The interviews were conducted by the same colleague in her own office. It was explained to students that they could choose, at any time, to withdraw their permission and that their names would be changed if I wrote about their work. All of these materials finally came into my hands several months after the course had concluded.

What Did the Students Learn?

First a proviso—I can generalize to some extent about what the students reported and demonstrated in their work, but obviously their experiences varied. I offer evidence here that illustrates varying levels of sophistication and insight on the part of the students—as well as disagreement with one another and with me. In some ways, this lack of unanimity was precisely what I wanted to see happen because it replicates the ongoing debates over canon in our field. The students' materials demonstrate that the course was "messy," to use Baxter Magolda's word. As I observed at the outset of this essay, there were three major advantages to the PBL approach that I took in this course: the students' communal effort, the students' creation of knowledge, and the students' taking a "landscape perspective."

The Communal Effort

The course demanded that the students select the readings, a feature of the previous course I had taught. This time, however, the decisions were made by three groups with each one selecting from a list of six contemporary works of fiction. The course was to conclude with a final take-home essay exam on a novel chosen by each individual student from the group of novels not chosen for class discussion. Each group created a brief thumbnail description of all six novels that I posted on our course website as a resource to facilitate the students' personal choices for their final papers. With the short stories, I assigned several, but I left most of the decisions to the students, only asking that each group select three stories from the remaining unassigned twenty. The groups were responsible for designing and leading class discussions of their selected novel and short stories.

So the work of the course compelled the students to rely upon one another to make choices, produce materials (the brief reports on the novels), and plan class discussion sessions. The students also participated in a late-semester poster session. I provided them with a list of our chosen course readings, and asked each student to create a poster that identified four selections that would constitute the assigned reading list for their own course in Jewish-American fiction, offering a rationale for their decisions. At the poster session, the students took turns presenting to one another as well as to three of my faculty colleagues whom I had invited to join us. Finally, each student wrote a final essay, evaluating her or his chosen novel to determine whether it would be an appropriate novel to assign in a Jewish-American fiction course.

One result of these communal efforts is that the students learned the value of referring to our other readings as they discussed individual texts, and they referred to other readers, i.e. the teacher, their classmates, even the visiting professors, as well. One student, Carl, explained in his interview that he had answered the final essay question by recalling his response to the poster presentations: "I sat down and thought about 'How would I go about presenting this to the class?'" Thus, the community of the class provided him with a context for critical thinking.

The students also began to rely upon resources beyond their own reading experiences. At one time or another, more than half of the class members indicated in their work or in their interviews that they had relied upon research materials in their deliberations and choices. One student related how she had been torn between two novels for her final essay and decided only after reading reviews of both. Another student quoted from three reviews she had located, one in *The New Yorker* and one by the editor of our short story anthology. That same student reported in a commentary on her essay exam that "I went down the list of novels available and looked up information on each one (author background, theme of novel, novel content, difficulty of reading, and so forth)" before making her decision. A classmate visited an author's website in an effort to learn more about his background, and read it closely enough to discover that he had listed his date of Bar Mitzvah in a timeline, thus identifying himself as a Jewish-American writer.

One student's take on using research materials was notably different, however. In his interview, Dwayne observed that he could have researched the book and the author and that he did in fact visit Amazon.com to read commentary about the book. However, he then consciously decided against relying upon critics of his selected novel because, he said, "The teacher could have found them on his own." Dwayne wanted to write about his "own ideas," he asserted. "I could have done more research on the war [World War II], about the bombing. But honestly I wanted to see what I could dredge out of the book on my own without using other sources." Both of these comments are quite revealing. Of course, any final essay exam is going to be read by the instructor, yet Dwayne's construction of me as a reader in his interview is not so much as his judge as it is as his colleague, someone who could very well perform the same research that Dwayne had done. In referring to the content of the novel—World War II and the London Blitz—he makes one of the very few remarks by any of the students about the chosen novel's subject matter. His comment forcibly made clear to me that the students had rarely discussed the possibility of learning more from other sources about the *content* of the novels. In future iterations of this course, I plan to offer more such materials myself when we read my few selected readings in hopes that it will serve as a demonstration that investigating the factual basis of the novels can be valuable.

Some class members found the communal nature of the poster session to be influential. Carl pointed to the value of the poster session, which he termed "a presentation to other English faculty." He used that session as a launching pad for his final essay, he reported, testing out his concerns with intertextuality, a point to which I will return. Another student, Nancy, in referring to the poster session, makes this striking commentary in her final essay exam: "I had a very intense conversation with one of the women [guests] about someone believing that the literature for any given cultural class had to be written by an author of that culture for it to be appropriate. That is not my opinion, however." This student's essay is not particularly strong, but her comment suggests that she has indeed been grappling with a genuine and important issue and viewed her exam as an opportunity to continue a conversation with me, the *professional conversation* that she had begun with another literary scholar, positioning herself as a member of that conversation. She stumbles in her essay, but her effort is to invoke the kind of "self-authorship" described by Baxter Magolda, as she embraces the role of the literature professor, albeit momentarily and somewhat unconvincingly, as advocated by Valenza.

Dwayne also commented on the poster session in his interview. "I hated that Poster Project," he said, explaining that he felt deficient in creating a visual representation of his ideas, even though he had been provided with exemplars and templates. He concluded his observation, however, by exclaiming to the interviewer, "I think it was wonderful that he made us do this." His explanation for this apparent contradiction lay in his metaphorical description of the course. The professor, he said, "was honing us down like a blade." He explained that all of the many activities during the semester had made him practice the kinds of thinking needed to complete the later work. For him, the course apparently unfolded as it progressed, one activity building on another as he constructed his own knowledge with the skills he was developing.

In short, there is evidence to suggest that the students were not operating in the atomistic, individualistic way that my students in the 90s version of this course had been when they each doggedly pursued self-designed personal course goals. The two concluding assignments in my new course may well have been authored individually by each student, but the poster session was presented to an audience of peers and faculty, and the final essays uniformly took notice in one way or another—by reference to class activities or researched materials about the chosen novels and authors—of a larger community than just the student alone.

Creating Knowledge

For the final take-home essay I asked the students to select one of the novels from the three lists I had shared with them earlier in the term, novels that we had not read as a class (meaning that they had a choice from among fifteen works of fiction). The question I posed was the following: "What makes your chosen novel appropriate reading in a college-level Jewish-American fiction course?" The assignment sheet elaborated by asking "How do we define 'Jewish-American' when describing a novel?"

One strategy that the students used in their final exams was to reformulate the essay questions to suit their own approaches. In her interview Evvy explained the importance to her thinking of changing my question to these variants: "What makes this class Jewish? Where did that come from?" She continued, "And as the time went on through the course you realize why. It's not just like a religious course, but it's set up to make you think about different cultures and the way things are thought of by different people." (Note that Evvy, like Dwayne earlier, hints at the unfolding nature of the course as time progressed.) Evvy recognized that the essay questions were genuine, not merely artificial test questions, but she also felt confident enough to replace them in order to reflect her own understanding of the course.

Another student, Lewis, notes in his final exam that the essay question is "somewhat subjective. Different people will have different opinions about if a book is appropriate." But he does not use "subjectivity" as an excuse to shirk his responsibility or adopt a convenient relativistic stance. He answers the question about his book by writing that it offers insights into Jewish religious observance, and its lack, and concludes, "For a person that is not a Jew, the novel will educate them [sic] on these topics that they may not have been privy to. This is important, as I believe that insight into the Jewish religion should be a major goal in this course." Lewis has decided on a purpose for the course, and his observation about non–Jews is certainly a reflection of our own class, where none of the students was in fact a member of the ethnic group whose literature was being read, as everyone in the class knew. Similar to Lewis, Patti voices her opinion in her final essay: "I feel that the literature must contain some educational details, whether directly or indirectly. What I mean by this, 'directly and indirectly,' is that ... in the case of a Jewish-American fiction course, the material must have some kind of educational benefit." Lewis and Patti are effectively changing the essay question by adding "And why?" and then thinking about the reasons for their decisions.

Carl's essay also modifies the exam question by adding ancillary questions. He, like Evvy, recognizes that the question is an important one to the course, not just an assessment question. He decides to modify it to read "Does the work contribute to the study and understanding of the course focus?" and then poses two follow-up questions: "Does the work cause the reader to think critically about identity (here specifically Jewish-Americans) and how literature explores the questions and struggles as we try to understand identity (and how that pertains to the Jewish American cultural focus)?" and "Do readers gain a better understanding of the culture being studied and are they able to find similarities in the culture that are universal with their own backgrounds?"

Carl, like Evvy and Lewis, ultimately decided that his chosen book was appropriate for the course. In fact, only one student, Ursula, determined that her selected novel, Sherri Szeman's *The Kommandant's Mistress*, was unsuitable. She reluctantly admits that "despite my best efforts," she could not find the novel appropriate. She writes, "For a novel to be effective in a Jewish-American fiction class, I feel that there must be some evidence of Jewish culture within. In order to understand what being Jewish entails, I would have needed to see more of the culture of the Jewish characters," and then she notes that the novel did not involve Jewish-American characters. Ursula devises a rather narrow and rigid definition in response to the question and takes the adjective "Jewish-American" literally: she expects the book to provide "knowledge of the struggle of Jewish people to assimilate, especially in America. As I have learned, being Jewish-American is an adjustment, and I saw no details of what a struggle that can be."

Because the novel is set in a World War II concentration camp, the characters are not American. "This novel's main focus is the culture within concentration camps, not the culture of the Jewish people," she points out. About the Holocaust setting, she makes the point that "Although there is something to be gained by understanding the impact of the Holocaust, it is not what defines the Jewish community." The novel simply does not address "the Jewish beliefs, customs, or daily rituals that we have learned about through other readings this semester. I was unable to gain any understanding of what being a Jewish-American meant in terms of identity, position, or family background by reading this novel." I was pleased that Ursula had read her novel in the context of the course we had created jointly, but I was surprised at her narrow definition of appropriate subject matter. After all, one group had chosen Art Spiegelman's *Maus* for the class to read, but perhaps Ursula's thinking was that the graphic novel was set in America, and the Holocaust scenes were flashbacks based on one survivor's memories. In a literal sense, the main characters were "Jewish-Americans" because they had immigrated after the war.

Despite her rigid standards, Ursula is actually an adept literary reader. She praises the novel's style, at one point offering a sophisticated analysis of light and dark imagery used in the novel to "portray the Jewish community as ... victims." But she reluctantly puts aside her admiration for the novel's fine writing because its "focus seems to be on women's sufferings and eventual revenge as well as dark sexual themes of dominance" rather than on Jewish-American matters as she has narrowly defined them. I can imagine having a spirited class discussion about Ursula's take on this book (one that another classmate decided in her final essay was indeed suitable for the course), with a close examination of her very rigid expectations for the reading. Nonetheless, she is thinking critically about the issues of course reading list design.

At one point, Ursula also notes that not only are none of the characters Jewish-American, but neither is the author, which she also sees as a strike against the book. The question of authorship is one that arose continually in the course. Because this was a general education literature course for non-majors, I chose not to introduce discussions of the "death of the author." Amy Lai recently notes, "One must be cautious not to take the concept of the 'death of the author' too far. In literary theory, the author's 'death' should be read metaphorically and not literally" (20). The members of this class clearly took the question of authorship quite seriously. And why not? Sherman Alexie's well-known critiques of Barbara Kingsolver and Larry McMurtry for writing stories about Indians (See Jaggi; Fraser) make clear that the question of who gets to tell the stories of minorities is a very real one. Those issues arise even within the minority group itself, as our class had seen. The editor of our short story anthology highlighted the "the tensions (and distance) between the religious and the secular" (Zakrzewski xxi) present in the fiction, and our class had seen some of these tensions after one group assigned Tova Mirvis's novel *The Outside World*. Commentator Wendy Shalit criticized Mirvis and other "authors who have renounced Orthodox Judaism—or those who were never really exposed to it to begin with" for their "unflattering or ridiculous" depictions of observant Jews. Mirvis responded to this critique, first by cataloguing her own qualifications as a life-long observant Orthodox Jew and then speaking as a fiction writer:

> But the fact that we are insiders to the Orthodox world is irrelevant. Since when must a fiction writer actually have lived the life he or she writes about? Since when must one be a murderer to write *Crime and Punishment*, a pedophile to write *Lolita*, a hermaphrodite to write *Middlesex*, a boy on a boat with a tiger to write *Life of Pi*? Yes, it seems, Shalit has outed the whole tawdry lot of us. She's revealed to the public the terrible truth: Fiction writers make up things.

There is something a bit inconsistent about Mirvis's sarcastic defense of the fiction writers' craft after she has vigorously defended her status as a knowledgeable Orthodox Jew when one could expect her to reject such a defense as unnecessary. Alexie's critiques had not critiqued non–Indian writers for "making things up" but instead challenged them for appropriating the stories of another culture, much as Wendy Shalit had done by denying that Mirvis possessed the appropriate credentials to write her novel. Nonetheless, the issue raised by the Shalit-Mirvis debate echoed in the students' memories, as 75 percent of the final essays dealt in some fashion with the question of the author's religious or ethnic identity.

A few students adopt a "hard-line position": only fiction by Jewish-American authors would be appropriate for the reading list. In his essay, Dwayne observes, "In our Jewish American writing class we ask the question how do we define 'Jewish-American' when describing a novel? The answer seems as elusive now as it did at the beginning of our class. I think that the answer can be tackled by saying that writing can qualify as Jewish American fiction if it is written by a writer that is Jewish." His use of "can" does not seem to rule out fiction by non-Jewish authors, but he clarified his position in his interview when he said, "We discussed could even a person who wasn't Jewish write Jewish books? ... For me personally, real Jewish literature should be written by Jewish authors because it springs from Jewish culture." In this position, he was not alone. Flora agrees, but notice how she does so—by positioning herself as the instructor making the reading list decisions: "If I were a professor and an instructor of Jewish-American Literature I would want my class to consist strictly of reading material that has not only Jewish American novels or short stories, but that the author had to be Jewish also." She explains that such an author would be better able to speak from "first-hand experience." Flora's position contests Tova Mirvis's defense that "Fiction writers make things up." Dwayne and Flora do not seem to see any nuances in the issue, but they do manifest careful thought about the subject, Dwayne by recognizing that this question drove the entire course, not merely the final essay, and Flora by recognizing that the problem is a very real one faced by a teacher selecting a reading list for an ethnic literature course.

Other students acknowledge the authorship issue, but decide to downgrade its importance. For Theresa, it is the topic of the fiction that matters rather than the author's background ("the author may or may not be Jewish," she writes). For Carl, the question is important but insoluble: he cannot find out through his research if his author is Jewish, but he puts the issue aside because her novel "certainly causes the reader to think critically about identity" in its examination of a future time when Jewish culture appears to have faded into obsolescence. "I think the idea of a lost Jewish culture is the biggest aspect which would make the novel appropriate reading...," he concludes. Also appropriate, contends Patti, is a novel that has been written by "someone who has been in or around, or has studied (extensively) the culture and religion of the Jewish community." Patti's take is a thoughtful response to the debate between Shalit and Mirvis and between Alexis and Kingsolver over who has "the right" to tell the story and perhaps a subtle rebuke to Mirvis by asserting that fiction writers can employ research in lieu of just making things up.

The flip side of the coin regarding an author's identity had been present from the semester's start when I assigned Busch's detective novel in which a Jewish-American author wrote a fiction unrelated in any overt way to the subject of Jewish-American life. And some students asked the question explicitly: "Does the author's identity alone legitimize a novel for this course?" Evvy is not troubled, it seems, as she simply observes about *Girls* that "One of the books was just written by a Jewish writer. It had no reference at all to Jewish-

American lifestyles or cultures." Her answer is disappointing because she seems to have acquiesced to my decision to assign the book. On the other hand, Patti refuses to choose a novel simply because of its author's identity as a Jew. She reasons that such a novel might not "offer any insight into the world of Jewish religion or culture."

But several students offer more complex discussions of the authorship issue. Wendy poses a series of questions that problematize the discussion: "What about a fictional book that has no relation to Jewish-Americans, such as book that is centered around life as a cowboy out on the range, but is written by a Jewish-American author? Can [this novel] truly be considered Jewish-American fiction? Ultimately it is a matter of opinion." However, Wendy does not simply stop there. She adds, "However, I believe that all can be fair game for the following reason":

> It has been my experience that whenever a person tries to write about something completely non-related to him/herself, somehow a small detail tends to find its way through. Therefore the Jewish-American author that is writing about something completely non-related to Jewish-Americans will still include some subtle hint of his/her life without even knowing it.

Carl's take is equally nuanced and insightful, in a different way. In his interview, he imagined himself as a writer. "Being a non–Jew, if I write a book that has a protagonist who is Jewish or a topic like what does it mean to be an Orthodox Jew, do I have a right to have my book included in that course or not because I'm not Jewish?" Although he did not answer his own question in the interview, he does answer it in his essay when he not only asserts that such a book would be appropriate to the course, but also argues for its value. "Excluding non–Jewish authors writing about Jewish subject matter or characters especially in a literature and identity course would detract from course content. Seeing how non–Jewish American writers think and write about Jewish culture and subject matter can be as important as how Jewish-American writers write and think about Jewish culture and subject matter." I think Carl has reconceived the course to some degree by imagining it to be a consideration of Jewish-American identity rather than an analysis of Jewish-American fiction, but then perhaps his conception is closer to the course description than the course I actually presented.

Nancy, the student who reported having engaged one of our guest professors in an "intense conversation" about authorship at the poster session, expands the issue in her essay to encompass other ethnic literature courses. She wants to contest the authorship question, arguing that if one insists that only ethnic authors be included, it would lead to more complicated considerations.

> So if I were to take an African American English course, then all of the books that we read will have to be written by black people. If I am taking the course, will it ever be said that an author may not be "black enough" to write for such a course? Will another author question the background of that author's blackness? What if that black author was raised by white people—would that pose a problem?

All of these discussions show attempts by the students to create their own knowledge about the course–and, in some cases like Nancy, about ethnic literature courses in general–rather than merely reporting back what they have been told by the instructor. The discussion seems "messy" and hard to pin down, because it is! The essays evidence serious consideration of the central course question, the inquiry upon which the course has been based.

Taking a Landscape Perspective

My concept of this course was that it would "unfold" as we moved through the work of the term, in contrast to my 1980s Major American Writers course, which presented the entire, already-formulated plan at the outset. This approach led one student, Carl, to describe the course as having taken a "landscape perspective." In his interview, he expatiated on this idea: "If you look at a painting as a landscape, it is encompassing what you see. So basically, an all-inclusive view of what you studied in the course. I need to look at the whole sixteen weeks not just the last 3-4 weeks." He talked about a "gradual change" in how he perceived the issues of the course not one "Eureka!" moment. As he considered his chosen novel in the final essay, he noted that "I wanted to get into the idea that you should see how a work contributes to the course." In other words, he did not want to focus on the novel as a discrete reading assignment but as one integrated with all that had preceded it. He made this point explicit in his interview: "You draw from other works to understand the work you're reading when you're not clear about it." He called this form of making connections "intertextuality," and he engages in this form of connecting when he discusses his chosen novel, Lisa Lerner's *Just Like Beauty* in conjunction with Tova Mirvis's *The Outside World*, which we had read in the course. He also links Lerner's book to Huxley's *Brave New World*. In short, he explains, switching metaphors as he does so, that he feels literature courses should take

> a broad view.... You have this broad question and you break the question down by using smaller pieces. You don't eat a meal in one bite. You have to take many small bites to finally consume what you have sat down to eat. It's the same way with studying literature. You don't swallow a whole book or three or four books at one time, you break it down and talk about them.

Carl is the most insightful student in the class in speaking about the architecture of the course, but he is not alone in noticing the effects of the course's inquiry strategy on how he understands the reading. Taking a "landscape perspective" required students to reflect on the impact of the course approach on their own reading and thinking processes. Dwayne called the answer to the exam question as "elusive now as it was at the beginning of the class," linking his efforts in the final essay to his ongoing challenges in the course. Lewis, on the other hand, reflects that "I had a really hard time answering the question about a book being suitable for a college-level Jewish American fiction course before this project [the final essay]. But, after writing the essay, I think I have a pretty good handle on it."

In her interview, Evvy observed that, "What kind of threw me off [about the final paper] ... was that this is not supposed to be a book report. We weren't supposed to regurgitate what we'd read." She went on to explain that she found that shift in reading "kind of hard," particularly because she had really enjoyed reading her chosen novel and wanted simply to "share with others" what she liked about it. That shift in reading compelled her to remember the question, "What is Jewish-American Fiction? How does that apply?" and to note that "'Why is it Jewish-American fiction?' was a question addressed in every class." And, as she adjusted her reading, "things started coming to me" about the cultural and religious aspects of the novel. Like Evvy, Ursula also reported challenges to her reading process. In Ursula's case, she "absolutely loved reading" her chosen novel, but she "struggled to find the importance of the novel itself in a Jewish-American fiction class." She describes how she used post-it notes to flag important passages in her reading, but halfway through the book, she discovered that all of her notes were focused on the author's style and use of fictional techniques. "I was unable to find any pages to mark that showed evidence of value to studying Jewish-American culture." And, reluctantly, Ursula thus rejects the novel, having determined it to be inappropriate for the course.

The discord between "normal" reading practices and the kind of critical thinking required by the course was not welcome to some students, Nancy most notably. In the journal assignment in which she was to explain to me which novel she would be selecting, she writes about her difficulties in making a choice. "I suppose as much reading as I have done this semester, I am getting worn down. I love to read, but I also do not want it to be repetitive or a routine that means nothing at the end of the book. I guess I feel there are way too many books out there to read, so why would I want to waste my time on one that I really wasn't going to enjoy." She chose the same novel that Ursula had thoroughly enjoyed but reluctantly rejected: Sherri Szeman's *The Kommandant's*

Mistress. Nancy's reason in part was that she had been "swept up" in reading about the Holocaust and could not resist selecting another book about events from that era. Unlike Ursula, Nancy is untroubled by the author's identity and by the European setting of the story, so she recommends the book. Her final essay begins with the statement "It is quite obvious to me after the course is over that there is not a right answer here" to the exam question. Because that is the case, she feels free to recommend a novel that she has enjoyed reading. Her discussion of her decision is disappointing in its superficiality, but her heightened awareness of her reading preferences as a response to the course's central question is perhaps a first step toward taking a landscape perspective of the course.

Two students even allude to the future, after this course. Dwayne ruefully told his interviewer that "In the future I don't know whether I'll enjoy literature more or less by looking at it critically." On the other hand, Carl, who not only embraced the "landscape perspective" concept but coined the phrase, even extended the "landscape" beyond the conclusion of the course. He comments in a written reflection on his final essay, "I hope that some of the students in the class this semester have written essays that compel you to include some of the final selected novels as required course reading should you teach this course again. I liked the fact that the students had a say in the selected novels." I interpret his final sentence to be a commentary on the group work that had determined most of our course reading list, but I also notice that he has embraced the collaborative nature of the course to the point where he can envision a future reading list also affected by the work of this specific reading community.

What seems to have happened in the course is that the students, to varying degrees of course, grew more aware of their discomfort. The uncertainty of the answers to the course's central questions–and the variants they themselves created–was a fact of the course. Making peace with the discomfort, recognizing that some, perhaps many, of their answers could be and would be contested became a central part of their experience as readers, thinkers, contributors to the course. Unlike my previous attempt to include my students in designing this course, the current iteration had not only made room for differences among the students, but had also made them conscious of being a part of a communal journey. The students provided provisional answers, and most realized to some extent that provisional answers were all that could be provided.

The Continuing Journey

As I plan my next Jewish-American Fiction course, I will once again focus on an inquiry-based approach, posing the same question about the reading list that I did in the course described in this essay. But I recall a comment made by Flora in a survey I had distributed near the end of the course. When I asked how our reading was different from or similar to the way the students read literature *outside* of school, she responded, "Outside of school I have no one to discuss my thoughts of what I read compared to what someone else got out of it." That observation did not surprise me, but when I read her comment *literally*, choosing to interpret "outside of school" to mean "away from this building," I began to see new directions in which I might take the communal inquiry of the course, extending its "landscape perspective" through technology. Encouraged by the effects of the interactivity of the course, I conjecture that I can now use newer technologies that will foster even more of a reading community.

- Using blogs lodged on the course website will enable me to offer occasional alternatives to a written reading journal. The reading journals served as one means of "honing the blade" for the students, but in its conception, the journal implies a dialogue between the student and the instructor. A blog, on the other hand, implies more interactivity among the members of the community, increasing the opportunities for students to contest one another's views by posting blog comments
- Using video journals as an occasional alternative to written journals or blogs can also expand the reading community. I have already begun to assign some of reading journals in the video format of TechSmith Jing© screen capture technology (a free download). The technology allows students to narrate whatever text or images they choose to display on their computer screens. These videos are limited to five minutes and are secured by password so that only classmates with the proper link can access them. Students have included biographical materials about an author, interview excerpts, video clips from filmed versions of a fictional text, images related to the text as they discussed their interpretations and questions, and annotated versions of the actual fiction itself. The video approach, like the blog, assumes a wider audience than just the instructor. Unlike the blog, however, it introduces the student's actual voice and expands the ease with which ancillary materials can be incorporated into the response.
- Using Voice Thread, another free download, to conduct mediated discussions would enable a group to post responses to a text or an image. It offers participants several options: written response, voice-recorded response, video response with sound. This

technology would facilitate "out of school" discussions among the members of the class community and might provide a virtual alternative to the in-person poster session as each student could convert her or his poster to a page in Voice Thread and then sit back and wait for posted responses.

I am not an advocate of using technology for the sake of using it, but options such as the ones I have just described would afford my inquiry-based literature class even greater opportunities for the kind of "dialogues" that Gerald Graff advocates rather than the "solo performances" (qtd in Tompkins and Graff 25) of my previous teaching model. Given the results of my latest course in Jewish-American Fiction, I am persuaded that the inquiry-based model should indeed continue to be the next step in my journey as a literature instructor.

Works Cited

Barr, Robert B., and John Tagg. From Teaching to Learning: A New Paradigm for Undergraduate Education." *Change* 27:6 (November 1995), 12–25. JSTOR. Web. 3 March 2013.

Bass, Randy. "The Scholarship of Teaching? What's the Problem?" *Inventio* 1 (February 1999). Web. 17 June 2013.

Baxter-Magolda, Marcia B. *Making Their Own Way: Narratives for Transforming Higher Education to Promote Self-Development.* Sterling, VA: Stylus, 2001. Print.

Busch, Frederick. *Girls.* New York: Ballantine, 1998. Print.

Curtler, Hugh Mercer. *Recalling Education.* Wilmington, DE: ISI, 2001. Print.

Fraser, Joelle. "Sherman Alexie's *Iowa Review* Interview." 2001. Web. 18 June 18 2013.

Graff, Gerald. "Afterword." Art Young and Toby Fulwiler, eds. *When Writing Teachers Teach Literature: Bringing Writing to Reading.* Portsmouth, NH: Heinemann-Boynton/Cook, 1995. 324–333. Print.

Hmelo-Silver, Cindy E. "Problem-Based Learning: What and How do Students Learn?" *Educational Psychology Review* 16: 3 (2004), 235–266. Print.

Hmelo, Cindy E., and Dorothy H. Evensen, "Introduction." Dorothy H. Evensen and Cindy E. Hmelo, eds. *Problem-Based Learning: A Research Perspective on Learning Interactions.* Mahwah, NJ: Lawrence Erlbaum Associates, 2000, 1–18. Print.

Jaggi, Maya. "All Rage and Heart." *The Guardian.* May 2, 2008. Web. 19 June 2013.

Kimball, Bruce A. "Toward Pragmatic Liberal Education." *The Condition of American Liberal Education: Pragmatism and a Changing Tradition.* New York: College Entrance Examination Board, 1995, 83–99. Print.

Lai, Amy. "The Death of the Author: Reconceptualizing 60 Years Later: Coming Through Amy the Rye as Metafiction in Salinger v. Colting." *USF Intellectual Property Law Bulletin.* 15:1 (Feb 2011). 19–52. Web. 15 June 2013.

Mirvis, Tova. "Judging a Book by Its Head Covering." *The Jewish Daily Forward.* February 4, 2005. Web. 20 June 2013.

Podis, JoAnne M., and Leonard A. Podis. "Beyond Fear and (Self-) Loathing in the Composition-Literature Wars: Contextualizing the Politics of Writing Assignments English Studies." Michelle M. Tokarcyzk and Irene Papoulis, eds. *Teaching Composi-*

tion/*Teaching Literature: Crossing Great Divides*. New York: Peter Lang, 2003.112–126. Print.
Shalit. Wendy. "The Observant Reader." *New York Times*, January 30, 2005. Web. June 20, 2013.
Sommers, Jeff. "The Hegemony of the Final Exam: Problem-Based Learning in the Literature Classroom." *Inventio* 7:1 (Spring 2005). Web. 21 June 2013.
_____. "Multiple Literacies and Inquiry-Based Teaching: The Two-Year Campus Literature Course." Art Young and Toby Fulwiler, eds. *When Writing Teachers Teach Literature: Bringing Writing to Reading*. Portsmouth, NH: Heinemann-Boynton/Cook, 1995. 273–286. Print.
Sommers, Jeff, Helane Adams Androne, Ellenmarie Wahlrab, and Angela Sneider. "Critical Reading Outcomes and Literary Study in a Problem-Based Learning (PBL) Literature Course." *MountainRise* 3:1 (2006). Web. 21 June 2013.
Tompkins, Jane and Gerald Graff. "Can We Talk?" *Professions: Conversations on the Future of Literary and Cultural Studies*. Donald E. Hall, ed. Urbana and Chicago: University of Illinois Press, 2001. 21–36. Print.
Valenza, Robin. "Symposium: Teaching the Conflict at Twenty Years: Gerald Graff at the Museum of Natural History." *Pedagogy* 3 (2003): 256–259. Print.
Zakrzewski, Paul, ed. *Lost Tribe: Jewish Fiction from the Edge*. New York: HarperCollins Perennial, 2003. Print.

Section III: Focus on the Philosophy

Using Ethiopian Healing Scrolls as Ethnomedicine to Read Healing in African American and Contemporary American Literature by Women

SHAWNRECE D. CAMPBELL

> Art is our one true global language. It knows no nation, it favors no race, and it acknowledges no class. It speaks to our need to reveal, heal, and transform. It transcends our ordinary lives and lets us imagine what is possible.—Richard Kamler

In my junior-level English seminar course, "Healing & Wholeness in Contemporary Literature: Writing as a Healing Art," I use Ethiopian healing scrolls to focus on how therapeutic reading and writing can be. Students and I discuss how as readers we often find ourselves entering the world described in the pages of a good book and becoming involved with the characters therein and close the cover of the book having gained new insight and ideas. I inform them that that is the purpose behind the use of bibliotherapy: to assist readers in expanding their knowledge and understanding of societal and/or world issues or the ways in which they may have been mis-educated or in overcoming the emotional turmoil related to a real-life problem by having him/her read literature on that topic. We then use the texts to serve as springboards for discussion and possible resolution of the issue(s) they address. We journey through contemporary literature, self-help books, popular literature and "chick flicks" written by African American, Asian American, Euro-American and Native American authors to analyze the resolutions offered for the real-life problems members of such groups often encounter.

Our first few weeks of class are spent telling our own healing stories about an object that has significant meaning to us, discussing what Ethiopian healing scrolls are and how they are created followed by discussions on the ways in which the authors of the texts under study in the course, particularly the Black authors of African ritual inheritance novels,[1] can be viewed as writers of transatlantic healing scrolls. We then discuss how knowing biographical information about the authors will help students to locate and define any similar characteristics they see between the texts of the authors under study in the course and those texts created by authors of African ritual inheritance novels that are used as examples during discussions on Ethiopian and transatlantic healing scrolls. I emphasize to students that it is the context into which the author is born and the context from which they write that infuse the context of the novels the authors create. This discussion helps students understand the identity location of individual authors so students can more accurately assess the authors' professed writing goals in relationship to the "evidence" found in the author's body of work. It also helps them to see that there are myriad types of journeys that are a part of healing and wholeness. We then have a discussion about why I am requiring the students to keep writing journals where they will respond to topics that have been chosen to promote their own healing through writing. I point out to students that they have shared a healing story orally, now it is time for them to experience the process of writing their healing stories. All of these discussions and the assignments/activities associated with them, which I will discuss later, provide students with tools to use as part of their critical thinking and reflection process. Thus armed, the students are now ready to examine the ways in which writing is used as a healing art in the texts under study in the course.

This pedagogical approach resulted in glowing student evaluations for the course. The three summative student evaluative comments below echo the general tone of all student comments:

- The class discussion on which the course is based is a great way to conduct the class. Even though there were individuals which I hated I learned to interact with him or her and learned how to better communicate what I thought and how to handle situations;
- This was a very different kind of course. Very unique in my education experience. I loved it. It was more like a meeting of friends, experiencing a journey, than just students in a class;
- I had never heard of writing as healthy or used to heal. Class taught me to appreciate another side of English;
- Courses like yours are the reason I chose to go to this university when I could have gone to several others.

It is the rigorous thinking and learning process upon which the course is built that enables a student to indicate that she/he was able to listen (empathize and understand) to someone they hated. They had to be exposed to opposing views on various issues and understand them by engaging in a deliberative thinking process (which included reading different perspectives on various course topics under study as well as participating in conversational debates) in order to reach a view toward acceptance of someone they did not like. Another student reaching the "aha" moment of learning how writing can lead to healing is also the result of deep thinking and critical insight that comes from a long process of deliberation, which resulted in the student being able to put the big picture together; he/she saw how the macro-system works—how one's life script as it is being lived can be a healing stories for others when it is shared. Knowing exactly how the structure of healing stories works is the first step into developing a personal theoretical framework that explains the world as the student knows it. Being in a course that fosters collaboration and camaraderie among students allowed them to form a strong support system for each other and to feel more comfortable engaging in discussions on taboo and/or politically charged issues. As a result, students genuinely enjoyed reading and screening the class works under study and spent more time doing so. This in turn led to many students being intrinsically motivated which resulted in one student using writing as a healing art as a theoretical framework for examining Virginia Woolf's *To the Lighthouse* in a 400-level English seminar course she took the following semester.

It is from this historical perspective of success in teaching this course that I share details about the pedagogical processes that I use in establishing a strong exploratory foundation for students to stand upon while journeying through the course. I begin by explaining the campus culture of where I work. I then explain an icebreaker technique I use with students, which unwittingly has them sharing a personal healing story, but is very important in helping students understand how Ethiopian healing scrolls work and establishing an atmosphere of trust among the students in the class and between the professor and each student in the class. Next, I discuss the nine writing topics students respond to in their writing journals as a way of furthering students' connection to healing stories and discuss the expected learning outcomes for each topic and the course text the writing topics are paired with. This is followed by explaining the Author Biography group assignment given to help students understand the healing processes the authors—*dabtaras (also spelled debtara)*/healers—use in their healing scrolls (texts) to achieve their literary goals. I follow this by explaining the role of Ethiopian clerics (*dabtaras*) in creating healing scrolls and how I see the authors under study in the course, particularly the Black women writers as transatlantic *dabtaras* who also create healing scrolls—texts with words and rhetorical imagery[2] rather than the pictorial/graphic images and written words of prayer that are a part of traditional Ethiopian healing scrolls. I then explore the intricacies of the Ethiopian healing processes in Paule Marshall's *Praisesong for the Widow*. I devote substantial time to examining Marshall's *Praisesong for the Widow* to enable a clear understanding of how to use the Ethiopian healing scrolls to read African spiritual inheritance literature. *Praisesong* is an exemplary text that allows the reader to see how ancestral inheritance rituals made it through the Middle Passage to immerse in African diasporic systems of healing despite colonial mountains that have long blocked ancestral views and closed ancestral pathways (Cartwright 130). *Praisesong* reconnects "North America with the Caribbean and Africa" through immersion in "continuing rites of spirit possession that have provided counter-cultural resistance to 'zombifying' forces of enslavement" (131). Africa's transatlantic descendants find freedom from the bonds within that originated from the outer bonds of slavery's legacy. Finally, I give special consideration to the concepts of writing the text of the body[3] as a healing story as well as the importance of maintaining connections with one's ancestral heritage in order to sustain one's health as it is historical disconnection that often makes an individual sick.

Campus Culture

I work in a picturesque setting full of nineteenth century historical architecture and southern charm. Many students who attend the university are first generation college students, come from working middle class families, and wouldn't be able to attend the university without financial aid and working full time while taking classes full time. However, quite a few also come from wealthy families and drive Mercedes and BMWs to school. Although still small, the numbers of minorities students are increasing, particularly Latino/a and Caribbean students of African descent, as is the number of openly identifying LGBTQ students. Domestic U.S. African American numbers remain relatively low. Yet, in this upwardly mobile diverse population, the shadows of institutional racism and cultural racism still dwell. Students of color routinely come to my office complaining about prejudicial treatment from white students, faculty, and staff. Faculty of color, as well as their allies, often lament the systemic disenfranchisement of faculty of color. Even though the new administration has hired over forty people in various executive, senior, and other academic leadership positions and greatly increased the visible presence of openly identifying LGBTQ leadership in these positions; as of this writing, there isn't one department chair, dean, senior administrator, or executive administrator of color on the campus. Yet, somehow, it seemed as though faculty and students of color were expected to throw a parade of kudos because the first black head coach had been hired in the history of the university. And of course in various ways, students and faculty are encouraged to let what happens on campus stay on campus—a quiet as it is kept "Morrison *Bluest Eye*" type of atmosphere. This is the environment in which I teach my healing and wholeness course. Consequently, as I revise and teach various iterations of the course, I work at making it a class that is useful for all those who take it regardless of their social-cultural background as I have found that every student—regardless of race, class, gender, or sexual orientation—who has taken my course has a healing journey that they are on.

Show and Tell Technique

This is an adaptation of an icebreaker that has been around for years. For the second day of class, I ask students to bring in an object that is significant to them and that relates to the theme of the class: healing and wholeness. They must be willing and able to explain why the object is significant to them as well as how they see it relating to why they signed up for the course. This allows students to get to know something about each other's healing journey and why being in a course like this matters to them. It also helps establish a culture of trust among the students as well as between the students and myself as I ask each student to honor the sacred space we create in the classroom by not sharing what happens in the classroom with those outside of the classroom.[4] Unlike the campus culture message of keeping silent that results in students feeling they are in an unsafe environment, invoking the mantra of silence in my course creates a safe space for students to pursue their journey of healing and wholeness as they know their confidences will not be betrayed. Accordingly, this show and tell technique opens students up to writing their own healing stories as part of the journal assignments they are required to do that are discussed below.

Journal Topics

According to Louise DeSalvo, the kind of writing that helps us heal is "writing that describes traumatic or distressing events in detail *and* how we felt about these events then and feel about them now," which, she says "is the only kind of writing about trauma that clinically has been associated with improved health" (25). She goes on to say that writing dear diary type entries or venting about traumatic events doesn't result in writing that heals (25).

Having learned from previous iterations of this course that students will write dear diary entries or just vent the entire semester if they aren't given other delimiters, I discourage them from writing about any particular subject matter or concept more than twice. This requires that students give more attention to the content of the assignment directions rather than using every assignment topic as a way of continually rehashing frustrations they may be experiencing in their personal lives. Students write journal entries on topics that have been linked to a class text that is also dealing with that topic. The table below lists the journal topics and expected learning outcomes. I develop the expected learning outcomes and select the texts the journal topics are paired with. The journal topic list and the detailed assignments relating to each journal entry topic are adaptations from the "Writing as a Way of Healing" course on Ksur.net. I only provide the journal entry topics in the table below as they are available to anyone who visits the "Writing as a Way of Healing" course homepage on the Ksur.net website. One must take the "Writing as a Way of Healing" course in order to access the assignments.

Learning Outcomes	Writing Journal Topics
• Learn how writing can be used as a positive tool for healing • Gain an understanding of how writing can bring about positive transformation • Learn how to tap the healing power of memoir writing • Analyze and make better sense of your thoughts and feelings in daily living • Explore ways to turn hard to manage emotions into logical, balanced, and healthy feelings	• Writing the Heart Journal Entry Paired with Louise DeSalvo's *Writing As A Way of Healing: How Telling Our Stories Transforms Our Lives*
	• Writing Anger Journal Entry Paired with DeSalvo
• Gain a deeper understanding of how writing can be used as a positive tool for healing • Gain a deeper understanding of the healing power of memoir writing	• Writing Love Journal Entry Paired with Elizabeth Gilbert's *Eat, Pray, Love: One Woman's Search for Everything Across Italy, India, and Indonesia*
• Explore what spirituality means to you and its role in your life	• Writing Spirituality Journal Entry Paired with Gilbert
• Learn to use descriptions, arguments, wild thoughts, and colorful emotions	• Writing Fiction Journal Entry One of two assignments that students can choose to significantly revise and turn in for their final paper.
• Learn to see a memory from someone else's perspective	• Writing a Memoir Journal Entry The second of two assignments that students can choose to significantly revise and turn in for their final paper.

Learning Outcomes
- Explore your innermost feelings about self-love and how it is shaping your present and future
- Understand the root causes of anger and how to deal with it in positive, healthy ways

- Writing plans to achieve a brighter future

- Gain a deeper understanding of what spirituality means to you and its role in your life
- Understand the power of forgiveness
- Learn to move on without bitter grudges

Writing Journal Topics
- Writing the Mind Journal Entry Paired with Toni Morrison's *The Bluest Eye*

- Writing the Future Journal Entry Paired with Joan Morgan's *When Chickenheads Come Home to Roost: A Hip-Hop Feminist Breaks It Down*
- Writing Forgiveness Journal Entry Paired with Marilyn Heavilin's *Roses in December: Comfort for the Grieving Heart*

Author Bibliography Group Assignment

I begin this assignment by explaining to students that whether crafting fiction or nonfiction, poetry or plays, writers use words to transport readers, and from the simplest blog post to the great American novel, it is a process—and it is hard work. So, why do authors do it? What healing journey are they on? What are their healing processes? Students are then directed to review the authors to be studied over the course of the semester and to email me a ranked listing of the authors indicating the student's desire to research the life and works of that author and present their research to the rest of the class.

At the next class meeting, I announce the composition of the groups, and I also send out the information in a Blackboard announcement. Student groups are determined according to class size and the number of primary texts to be covered over the course of the semester, but I have often found that groups of two or three work best for this assignment. During the presentation, students need to explain why the author wrote the particular book assigned for class reading as well as any other literature written by the author that is related to the class context. Groups are required to (1) paint a vivid portrait of the author, the author's intended audience(s) and their texts not under study in the class; (2) have an interactive component as part of their presentation; (3) use visual media as part of their presentation; and (4) be animated during the presentation. Every group member is evaluated individually on the area in which they present, and the group is evaluated as a whole on the synergistic qualities of the presentation. Students should plan to present their biographical research on the author for 20–30 minutes followed by or interspersed with class discussion.

African Ritual Inheritances

African ritual inheritances were the metaphysical practice of nearly all Africans transported to the Americas during slavery (Creel 69–97). Morrison's works tend to focus on African rituals as practiced within the new world boundaries of the Americas. So many authors articulate Africa as a pervasive center of wisdom and spirit; such representation occurs in many works by African American writers, including Morrison's. Consequently, Morrison leads readers to consider *Paradise* within a community of healing stories as the transatlantic version of Ethiopian healing scrolls. The authors are the dabtaras (healers) creating healing scrolls (their novels) with the potential of healing countless readers through visual rhetoric.

From antiquity, Ethiopians have considered art, medicine, faith and personal connections to be intimately and inextricably linked. Jacques Mercier equivocates in *Art That Heals* that "Ethiopian healing scrolls, which link art and medicine, challenge the West's narrowly conceived definitions of art and medicine…. "Can one cure with art by making, using, or looking at it?" (9) and "what can the image, or the plastic expression of a subject, supply that language cannot?" (11). In other words, what is it about the expression of a subject that supplies healing power when Western modes of medicine and/or language alone cannot?

I will postulate one answer to that question— what is it about the expression of a subject that supplies healing power when Western modes of medicine cannot?—as it relates to writing as a healing art by exploring writings that describe, define, promote, and maintain the spiritual, physical, and mental well-being of Black women throughout the transatlantic diaspora. Transatlantic *dabtaras*, as connoted by Ille's definition of ancient African healing knowledge in general, "preserve this knowledge, presenting it as relevant and viable and demonstrating in intimate detail how vestiges of that knowledge took root in the Western Hemisphere, in African American culture, and in American culture period" (ix). Thus, I aim to highlight the importance of women writers as health care activists on their own behalf while also emphasizing the medicinal communal effects that such self-care has on individual members of the reading community.

As we progress through the semester, the framework above, helps students begin to see the ways in which writing has been used as a healing art by the various authors being studied in the course. Knowing biographical information about the authors' helps students contextualize and then analyze the meaning of healing and wholeness to each author and the philosophical process each author employs to reach a place of healing and wholeness. I point out to students how the author's biographical information also helps to identify any tensions between the author's biographical cultural context and the cultural context of the text the author has created that we are studying. This in turn helps to explain to an outside group—readers of the texts— the emphasis, or lack thereof, that the author uses in depicting the elements of her biographical culture that influence the text she creates.

Dabtaras, Ethiopian Healing Scrolls, Ethnomedical Criticism

Using Ethiopian healing scrolls as an ethnomedical tool of analysis proves particularly useful for the study of African-based wellness narratives because it allows the reader to analyze a text from an ethnocultural point of view according to African-based explanatory models of traditional systems of healing instead of through the lens of Eurocentric biomedicines. Ethnomedical systems, healing practices based on the traditions—particularly spiritual practices—of a particular region and herbal medicines created from locally available plants, aim to cure illnesses and diseases through restoring a balance in the relations of the patient to self, the community, and the supernatural world. This mode of analysis, which I have come to call ethnomedical criticism, focuses on reclaiming wellness through self-worth and the "discredited" knowledge (to quote Toni Morrison) of a culture's healing practices (344).

Thus, in Ethiopia, when a person is ill, he or she commissions a *dabtara* to create a scroll to heal them. Mercier explains, "a *dabtara* is an unordained cleric who has studied singing, poetry, and literature; a cantor, a scribe, a teacher, he practices traditional medicine in its most varied aspects" (14–15). The *dabtara* will interview the patient in stages, "make a diagnosis, and prescribe a cure" (15). During the first stage of consultation, the *dabtara* will employ the two poles of Ethiopian medicine: (1) the first pole is the "use of prayers and talismans"; (2) the second pole is the "use of plant and animal medicines. In traditional thinking, these two techniques go together 'like honey and butter,' the first acting upon the spiritual cause of the disease, and the second upon its symptoms" (Mercier *Ethiopian* 14).

Because there is often a gap between the spiritual cause of the disease and the symptoms exhibited by the patient, the *dabtara* "will consider his or her past life in an effort to identify the cause. When did the sickness begin?

... Didn't this sick person" offend an elder, cut themselves off from their ancestral heritage, have illicit sex, have a spell cast over them, and so on (Mercier *Ethiopian* 14)? After interviewing the sick patient, using a complex iconographic system, a *dabtara* paints arresting images and prayers on the scroll, which are believed to combat the forces causing illness. The *dabtara* will also give the patient any sacrificial instructions that they need to follow. It is the sacrificial activity that produces the parchment upon which prayers and talismans are written. The parchment equals "the height of the person the scroll is intended for. This will mean that the client is protected against demons from head to foot.... The scroll is now ready to receive its prayers and talismans, which the *dabtara* executes using a pen ... and then copies the prayers" using various types of colored inks "to make the scroll more effective" (Mercier *Ethiopian* 16, 17).

Although there are wide variations, the traditional curing, healing process, used by *dabtaras* consists of two groups of rituals: the first ritual aimed at driving out the impure spirit and the second ritual aimed at restoring the patient to a spiritual balance (Mercier *Ethiopian* 15). "The sick person will still see them [the spirits] howling and threatening in his or her dreams, but they will not be able to approach" (Mercier *Ethiopian*15). Thus the images and prayers which appear on the scrolls are extremely important as it is the patient's personal connection with them that allows healing to take place. The prayers used often come from stories of Christ. The images which appear on the scrolls range from religious symbols, to the story of King Solomon— who learned from God the "constitution of the world and the operation of the elements"—from lions, birds, and abstract talismanic patterns to the most frequently depicted symbols, of colorfully rendered eyes (Mercier *Art* 48, *Ethiopian* 19). The patient looks fixedly at the scroll and enters a healing trance; by staring at the scroll, the patient is penetrated and cured through his or her eyes. Mercier states that one of the most remarkable qualities of Ethiopian healing literature "is the importance it gives to the Names (*asmat*) of God, the angels, devils, the *zar*. Knowing them gives the dabtara mastery over all spirits, and thus the power to heal, subjugate, and destroy" (20). I explain to my students that the names of God are kept a secret because they are full of power. Thus they are guarded judiciously because once someone knows one of God's sacred names they have access to the power contained in invoking that name. Similarly, once students become aware of and can name—discuss, share, write down—the name of their secret pain they are then in a position to invoke power over that named secret. I then remind them that the only kind of writing that has been associated with improved health is writing that names the pain, discusses how the individual felt about the pain then and how the individual feels about the pain now (DeSalvo 25). The journal assignment discussed above allows students to do this.

Black Women Writers as Transatlantic Dabtaras

Many Ethiopians, [as do many black women writers of African ritual inheritance novels], conceive of the body as a house in which illness may be provoked by the entrance of an unclean spirit (Mercier *Art* 106). For the authors of transatlantic healing scrolls, the unclean spirits are the myriad forms of slavery's legacy resulting in the oppression and destruction of the well-being of the individual and the community. The objective of both the transatlantic *dabtaras* and the Ethiopian clerics is to expel the unwanted spirit and to seal the body from future visitation. Just as traditional healing scrolls act as a double for the patient (Mercier 95), African ritual inheritance novels act as a double for the reader. For example, one interpretation of plate nineteen in Mercier's *Ethiopian Magic Scrolls* is that:

> The picture represents the net in which Solomon caught the demons like fish. The central face is a demon, identifiable by texts written on the scroll; they are angels watching him; the black arcs are the seals that imprison him.
> This talisman is also called "scissors" because of the X's placed in the four directions, serving as scissors to cut off aggressive spirits.... A talisman like this is meant to drive demons away, the eyes having a protective function apart from any other interpretation [76].

Mercier reveals in *Art That Heals* that the proliferation of the eyes is one of the most striking aspects of Ethiopian scrolls. Despite considerable compositional variety, the eyes are consistently rendered with such an overpowering force that in certain cases "the image has become all gaze" (94). Mercier goes on to assert:

> the gaze is central to the function of the scrolls. Talismans within the scrolls "cannot cure and close the body without making the possession explicitly— without activating the possession, making it signify. Outside Ethiopia, induction into a trance state is usually effected through music—through the sense of hearing. In the Ethiopian scrolls we find the rare case of induction into a trance through an image—through the sense of sight" [95].

As Z.S. Strother discloses in his book review of Jacques Mercier's *Art That Heals*, the transfixing gaze from the scroll "points to the eyes looking back at it from within the human host. The demon hiding in the dark recesses of the body suddenly has a spotlight of vision turned on it. Forced into focus, he is made to speak and to relinquish the patient" (13). This is reminiscent of the Christian story of Jesus sending the legion of demons into the herd of swine who rushed head first off a nearby cliff (Matthew 8:28–34 *Holy Bible*). Jesus comes upon a man possessed with a demon. He asks the demon its name. It responds legion because there are many demons inside of the man— not just one. Jesus invokes his authority over the demons through the use of their name and commands them to come out of the man and go into swine that are nearby. The demons obey, and once inside the swine, rush head first off a nearby cliff.

Berends (1993), Brinkman (2000) and Mugabe (2010) echo the following sentiment: "it is an incontrovertible fact that healing practices in the Old and New Testaments have more in common with African traditional healing than with modern medicine" (Mugabe 364). Modern medicine focuses on treating the body so that disease is no longer present whereas the focus of African traditional healing is in alignment with the World Health Organization's definition of health. The "World Health Organization ... states that health is a state of complete physical, mental, and social well being not just the absence of disease" (Mugabe 366). As a result, Berends, Brinkman and Mugabe believe that traditional types of African healing fulfill cultural functions that Western modes of modern medicine cannot (Mugabe 364) as Western modern medicine has separated religion (spirit) and science (body). However, "the underlying belief [in African culture] is," according to Nicole Monteiro and Diana Wall, "that in the community, mind and body must be incorporated into ritual systems in order to facilitate healing, as well as transform and empower the individual and the group" (235). An acceptance that echoes the purpose of Ethiopian healing scrolls as discussed above. Monteiro and Wall go on to assert, "ultimately, given their holistic structure, rituals benefit the society in many layers. They play an integral role in socialization, expression and communication; help to build and maintain a healthy sense of self-esteem; and also offer an alternative cathartic experience for not only individuals but for the community as a whole" (235). These are sentiments that echo Berends, Brinkman, and Mugabe and that are parallel to the self-care practices exhibited within the work of transatlantic *dabtaras*. As such, African inheritance novels mirror the types of healings Jesus performed through "cleansing, forgiveness of sins, through the faith of someone, through magical acts, by means of exorcism, and by touching and being touched" (Mugabe 263). Thus, healing practitioners who keep this African Christological worldview in mind when engaging in the diagnosis and treatment of their patients are using healing processes that will result in a patient who is whole physically, spiritually and socially. It is at this point that I remind students that their journal assignments help them individually progress through these processes, these stages of healing. At the same time that we are having this discussion we use ethnomedical criticism to identify, define and discuss the parallel processes we observe in the texts we are studying and how that affects the healing journey of the characters within those texts. These simultaneous conversations help students to understand how healing texts written by the authors we are studying aid a reader of the texts, such as themselves, in her or his healing process. The discussions also help students to see how the story arcs of the various African ritual inheritance novels discussed above represent the various African healing processes—ethnomedicines—used to cure a range of reader ailments.

Praisesong for the Widow as a Healing Scroll

In *Praisesong for the Widow*, Avey, short for Avatara, Johnson's sickness is revealed in the first section—"Runagate"—when Avey deserts two of her longtime friends during the middle of their cruise without explanation. Avey doesn't know that her illness is caused by slavery's legacy disconnecting her from the black community and the history of her ancestral roots but her friend Thomasina recognizes that there is something deep going on to cause Avey's hasty departure from "the suddenly zombifying experience of her Caribbean cruise" (Cartwright 132). Thus begins Avey's Gullah seeker journey, according to Creel, toward a "spiritual metamorphosis, symbolic death, and rebirth" that will develop her soul through metaphysical striving. As Elizabeth McNeil posits, "if the initiate rises to the challenge, she is led to healing and wisdom, which are powerful resources for survival and spiritual enrichment, not only for the individual but also for her family, community, and the greater community of the text's readers" (34).

In a dream aboard the ship, Avey finds herself back in Tatem in the Gullah area dressed to the nines and her Aunt Cuney is attempting to get her to take a hike in the woods to visit Ibo landing (32). Aunt Cuney's spellbounding story goes:

> 'Cause those pure-born Africans was peoples my gran' said could see in more ways than one.... And when they got through sizing up the place real good and seen what was to come, they turned, my gran' said.... They just turned ... and walked on back down to the edge of the river here ... chains didn't stop those Ibo none.... They just kept on walking like the water was solid ground. Left the white folks standin' back here with they mouth hung open and they taken off down the river on foot. Stepping [37–39].

The Ibos who had taken one look and knew at an instant of all of the past history, present history, and future history of Tatem up to the point in time where Avey was standing at the Landing in her dream, had decided to walk back to the water in mass and walk back home to Africa. For in that instant they saw slavery, emancipation, Jim Crow era, the four little girls bombed in Alabama, the Civil Rights Movement, and the abandoning of Africa and of connections to African roots of millions of their descendants and decided they would not stay and be a part of such a sickness. This dream caused Avey such discomfort that something became lodged in her bowels that she could not dispel but gave her great malaise whenever she thought about returning to her present disconnected life. However in this section of the novel, Avey does not know her life is disconnected, she only knows that she is ill and must leave the ship and return home at once, or so she believes.

Dabtara Marshall continues Avey's consultation stage into section two—"Sleeper's Wake"—where Avey confronts the dead as part of the initiation ritual and gains wisdom from that meeting that allows *dabtara* Marshall to reveal why Avey is sick and what she must do to be cured. This section of the novel focuses on how Avey and her deceased husband, Jay, became disconnected from their African heritage. There is also a name change in this section as Jay becomes Jerome Johnson to Avey and Avey cannot recognize or find Avey or Avatara in herself. Narratives where Avey catches a glimpse of herself in the mirror and doesn't recognize who the woman is are representations of this. It is also represented by Avey not recognizing her husband and seeing this superimposed tormenting image of him on his face whenever she fully looks upon him nor her husband recognizing her when his last words in his sleep to Avey are "Do you know who you sound like, who you even look like...?" (89) as he was having a stroke.

After this fateful day, gone is their practice in the artistic healing rituals they use to once enjoy, such as turning their living room into a pretend dance hall for two; Jay listening to 78s he had inherited from his father with songs of Mamie Smith, Ma Rainey, Big Bill Broonzy, and others as the lyrics enveloped him and "the tension could almost be seen slipping from him like the coat or jacket he would still have on falling from his shoulders to the floor" (95). Jay also cuts off his mustache which he had worn up until that time like his father did his mustache during the World War I era. It is in this moment that Avey senses that the last trace of everything that was distinctive and special about Jay had vanished also (131). In Avey's dream-memory:

> Moreover (and again she only sensed this in the dimmest way), something in those small rites, an ethos they held in common, had reached back beyond her life and beyond Jay's to join them to the vast unknown lineage that had made their being possible. And this link, these connections, heard in the music and in the praisesongs of a Sunday: "...*I bathed in the*

Euphrates when dawns were/young (italics in original)...," had both protected them and put them in possession of a kind of power....

All this had passed from their lives without their hardly noticing. There had been no time. Their exhaustion at the end of each day had been too great. Running with the blinders on they had allowed that richness, protection and power to slip out of the living room, down the stairs and out of the house, where it had vanished, along with Jay, in the snowy wastes of Halsey Street [137–138].

Avey finally realizes what she has lost and the price she has paid for that lost. When Avey looks into Jay's casket while dreaming and sees "in the face of her great loss" (133) what she had reared: "she and Jerome Johnson ... could almost pass for twins" (141). As she looks upon him, she sees no trace of the Jay she loved but only "that other face she sometimes thought she detected pale and shadowy over his" (132). Jay is not released from the haunting spirit representing the demonic central face discussed above in reference to plate nine. He dies from the sickness the pale face has caused and the novel closes with the image of Avey collapsed in total despair in her hotel bed raging as she slept: too much, too much, too much (143).

This section follows the sacrificial ritual for scroll preparation as *Dabtara* Marshall has Avey engage in the initiation rituals, which will create the parchment necessary to make a scroll. During this rite Avey finally allows herself to become awash in the memories of rituals she and Jay shared before they became disconnected from their African heritage. Avey's confrontation with her dead husband and aunt and the wisdom she gains from those confrontations are used as parchment for the scroll upon which Marshall adds the appropriate talismans and texts as well as the baptismal name of the patient, Avatara, to prohibit the return of the evils of capitalism.

The scroll having been prepared, in section three—"Lave Tete (Wash Head)"—Avey meets Lebert Joseph who convinces her to go to The Excursion—the middle passage back to ritual purification that happens once a year on the island of Carriacou. It is Lebert Joseph and his daughter Rosalie Parvay who will act as Avey's *dabtaras* within the texts as they both "possessed ways of seeing that went beyond mere sight and ways of knowing that outstripped ordinary intelligence (Li gain connsaissance) and thus had no need for words" (172), just as the Ibo's did at the Landing back in Tatem. Joseph tricks Avey into agreeing to attend by telling her the boat ride to Carriacou will be smooth when he knows the currents are such that those not familiar with the ride will most likely become sick. Yet, it is this cleansing sickness that Avey needs to vomit up and excrete the blockage in her bowels so that her head will be washed—cleared out of the blockages that have prevented her from reconnecting to the power and protection of her roots—so she will be prepared for healing.

In "The Beg Pardon"—section four of the novel—Avey's full understanding of her disconnection from her heritage and the price she has paid because of it occurs during the Ring Shout when she realizes it is the essence of the practice of remembering that brings power not the material sources that are a part of it. Avey promises herself that she will spread the message of The Excursion—of the healing processes—that reconnected her to her roots just as it kept Lebert, Rosalie and Aunt Cuney connected to their roots. She would explain how it drew its magnificence and power through telling healing stories. The Excursion was an event that healed participants through the telling of African ancestral histories and herstories just as the stories of Ethiopian scrolls were intended to help people to heal. Therefore, if an individual would "read" the text of their body, know their ancestral history, and write that text, in relationship to their ancestral history, they would be healed. However, in order to do this, that individual would need to understand that they know more about the message their illness is conveying, and therefore, the individual is the most important repository of knowledge about themselves and their illness, not a specialist in the care of the body or any other outside entity. Once an individual wrote the text of their body—their healing stories—not only would they be healed but those with similar illnesses whom they had shared their healing stories with would also be healed. This healing partnership would help to solidify the communal mind-body interconnectedness of individual members that make-up the community. Marshall's *Praisesong for the Widow* is a healing scroll that was created to expose the evils of financial gain at the cost of historical disconnection; to drive out the evil and seal the entries to the spirit so as to prevent it from returning.

This helps to underscore that the power of the scrolls isn't so much in the scrolls themselves as it is in the faith that the believers bring to the scrolls. So the scrolls, talismans, and other healing objects become a point of remembrance that keeps the believer connected to their faith, their source of power, because they always have a visual object as a reminder in front of their eyes. It is in this way that these objects work as healing artifacts; something that both Ethiopian and transatlantic *dabtaras* recognize, understand, and write.

By locating themselves in the traditions of African ethnomedical practices, my students derive knowledge, understanding, and voice-naming their pain and sharing their healing stories—from the transatlantic *dabtaras* that they study. Throughout the course of the semester, I remind my students that the visual objects from their "show and tell" activity on the second day of class operate as points of contact, images of faith, for their individual healing stories. Merely looking at their individual symbols transports each student back to the time and place of the object's significance—places which brought a sense of comfort and peace, places of healing. It is in this way that my students come to recognize their items of significance working as healing artifacts, parallel to the healing scrolls.

Notes

1. African ritual inheritance novels heavily incorporate African-based cultural and historic rituals, especially metaphysical practices, into their narrative.
2. I will use the terms rhetorical imagery and visual rhetoric interchangeably. Visual rhetoric is a theoretical framework used to analyze how visual images—including written words—communicate. The term is approached differently depending upon the academic field of study. My use of it includes the analysis of images as well as the images created by the narrative of the written word.
3. Text of the body is a termed I created to describe the stories that are only able to be written and shared as the person in need of healing untangles the chains within the mind that keeps one in various forms of pain and starts a journey that leads to wholeness.
4. I do make it clear to students in my syllabus and during the course introduction during the first day of class as well as through reminders throughout the semester that any remarks about harming themselves or someone else will be taken seriously, and that I will refer them to the campus Counseling Center should such an incident occur.

Works Cited

Berends, W. "African Traditional Healing Practices and the Christian Community." *Missiology: An International Review* 21.3 (1993): 275–288. Print.
Brinkmann, E. "Medical Ethics and the Bible." *Bible Today* 41.1 (2000): 25–32. Print.
Cartwright, Keith. "Notes Toward a Voodoo Hermeneutics: Soul Rhythms, Marvelous Transitions, and Passages to the Creole Saints in *Praisesong for the Widow*." *Southern Quarterly* 41.4 (2003): 127–143. Print.
Creel, Margaret Washington. "Gullah Attitudes Toward Life and Death." *Africanisms in American Culture*. Bloomington: Indiana University Press, 1990.
DeSalvo, Louise. *Writing as a Way of Healing: How Telling Our Stories Transforms Our Lives*. Boston: Beacon, 1999. Print.
Holy Bible, 2d ed. Carol Steam, IL: Tyndale House, 2007. Print. Authorized New Living Translation Vers.
Illes, Judika. "Foreword." *A Healing Grove: African Tree Remedies and Rituals for the Body and Spirit*. Stephanie Rose Bird. Chicago: Chicago Review Press, 2009.
Kamler, Richard. "Overview." *Seeing Peace*. RichardKamler.org. 2003. Web. 31 August 2009.
Marshall, Paule. *Praisesong for the Widow*. New York: Putnam. 1983. Print
McNeil, Elizabeth. "The Gullah Seeker's Journey in Paule Marshall's *Praisesong for the Widow*." *MELUS* 34.1 (2009): 185–209. Print.
Mercier, Jacques. *Art That Heals: The Image as Medicine in Ethiopia*. New York: Museum for African Art, 1997. Print.

_____. *Ethiopian Magic Scrolls*. New York: George Braziller, 1979. Print.
Monteiro, Nicole M., and Diana J. Wall. "African Dance as a Healing Modality Throughout the Diaspora: The Use of Ritual and Movement to Work Through Trauma." *Journal of Pan African Studies* 4.6 (2011): 234–252. Print.
Morrison, Toni. "Rootedness: The Ancestor as Foundation." *Black Women Writers*. Ed. Mari Evans. New York: Anchor, 1984. 339–45. Print.
Mugabe, Henry J. "Markan Healings Through African Eyes." Review and Expositor 107 (2010): 363. Print.
Samuels, Michael. "How Art Heals: Mind-Body Physiology." *Art as a Healing Force*. Web. 31 August 2009.
Strother, Z.S. "Review." *Art That Heals: The Image as Medicine in Ethiopia. African Arts* 33.1 (2000): 12–15. Print.

Engaging Rites of Passage in Performative Text
Using Ritual Poetic Drama as an Applied Theater Practice

Tawnya Pettiford-Wates

> "Art is the immediate intervener in the cycle of poverty of the human spirit. It opens the doors of the mind immediately and the bird of the human spirit can fly free. We've seen it. We know it works. What we need is to believe in it sufficiently enough to create a massive institutional instrument fully committed and mobilized to this end."—Ossie Davis

Eurocentrism and traditional classroom/studio spaces still dictate content, form and approach to text and literature within schools, university programs and conservatories. The traditions and standards of established practice continue to resist any change that would embrace or reflect inclusivity of diverse perspective and cultural location as players in analyzing, deconstructing and engaging in critical discourse around the styles and forms of the established paradigm. Arts education and training is not an exception; it does not represent the multiplicity of culture, race or class that exists in the social fabric and fiber of the American cultural landscape. The contributions of non-white artists and scholars have been systematically excluded from study in the practical form of the dramatic arts (the play/story itself) and from the theory or pedagogy of the dramatic form (how to do it), and from the methodology and practice of the form itself. As a student/artist, I found that I was missing my self and the artistic connections to my own power and potency after years of study and immersion in the theatre arts. This discovery was in dichotomous opposition to the promised outcome of my years of dedicated conservatory education.

The traditions of Stanislavsky, Chekhov and Grotowski may have prepared my physical instrument but they did not nurture my spirit nor feed my soul. In fact they consistently confused and alienated me from my artistic intuition and authenticity. I was navigating my journey through conservatory training as a foreigner awkwardly attempting to learn the language, embrace the social practices and "fit-in" to a form that intentionally excluded me from it. I was completely oblivious of unwittingly participating in the progression of my own alienation.

In response to such dis-placement and awkward casting as an outsider within my own artistic discipline, I have generated a new methodology, the use of Ritual Poetic Drama Within the African Continuum (RPD-WAC), as a tool for student/artists to access their individual authentic creative content, potency and power as citizens/artists and students. It engages the student/artist as a *creative* entity located uniquely within a specific and complex cultural location of experiences that influence and fertilize the personal treasury from which they make withdrawals towards the creative process. This is in contrast to the traditional classroom/studio models that continue to promote the process of becoming an empty "vessel" waiting to be filled by imitating someone else's experiences and/or life. The process of becoming an empty vessel or blank canvas, as it were, feeds into the false mystique and narrative that there is a "sameness" or "basic human" that we all aspire to become and on this common ground, we are all allowed equal access and participation without regard to race, gender, class or cultural location.

The lack of representation for people of diverse backgrounds, cultures, colors, class, race and gender distinctions should make it abundantly clear that equitable participation in the mass media marketplace may be an aspiration, but it continues to be a completely allusive reality. The dramatic arts industry and many other industries fall woefully short of being fully inclusive of the world in which we live. And yet, students/ artists are required by the traditional model to earnestly pursue a standard of speaking, being, and modeling behavior that simultaneously alienates them from themselves. In contrast, RPD-WAC—RPD for short—as a tool for student/artists recognizes them as uniquely located within their own cultural context and facilitates the artist's ability to "cover the ground on which they stand"[1] and take responsibility for who they are, what they bring to the space, and the contributions they are impelled[2] to make to their community as artists and citizens. And finally, the process recognizes what students as artists uniquely contribute to the space in which they create art. The methodology is designed to empower the artist and facilitate the process of self-actualization specifically to engage the artist, as citizen, vessel, and as practitioner, holistically connecting her/him to her /his own cultural continuum and context.

In creating this model with particular interest towards recognition of cultural identity and perspective as essential in performance arts training, I am engaging in a critical interrogation of Arts Education and "traditional" training models within the academy. This acknowledgement is imperative. Transformative processes within the academy must evolve if traditional and classical theatre arts methods are to ever truly embrace inclusivity. The progression of the contemporary artist and the contemporary arts community is one that points toward multiculturalism; therefore the pursuit of new theory and practice that acknowledges difference is increasingly essential to the health and longevity of the dramatic form itself. The infusion of cultural pluralism in thought and practice becomes paramount if the industry is to become relevant beyond the entertainment of elites. As teachers of performative texts, we must attend to and centrally locate within the artistic expression of the dramatic form those texts inspired by the cultural tapestry of our world rather than featuring them as *avant-garde* side dishes or exotic fringe experiences. We must ask: What is the relevance of theater arts and what purpose do theater arts serve in our society? This interrogation frames the discourse for truly engaging students in the relevance of performative texts. We have a responsibility, then, to move beyond a purely Eurocentric model and demand that perspectives, practices and theories located within a cultural continuum become an integral part of the theoretical and practical application of new and emerging forms, styles and modalities for arts training and standards of pedagogical implementation. We must allow our revelations to lead us to the recognition, acknowledgement, transformation, and inclusion of those pedagogical differences and distinctions that are authentically rooted within culturally relevant perspectives, contexts and experiences.

It was my own experience with a performative piece of American literature that changed how I understood my training and helped me to understand how problematic that training had been. *For Colored Girls Who Have Considered Suicide/ when the rainbow is enuf* written by Ntozake Shange, was not written in the standard of "the well-made-play,"[3] the standard that is held to be the best in the *traditional* American Theatre industry. No. It did not fit the model or the self-defined standard. It is poetic drama, a "choreopoem," as defined by the playwright herself. She claimed her own identity through her art, defined it with specificity and accuracy and made no apologies. Poetic Drama was not located anywhere in my formal training. Classic textual analysis and stage standard speech could not help me with the words and text by Shange. My education was deficient. I was ill prepared for my first Broadway audition after attending the best schools in the United States and the United

Kingdom. Despite my ignorance of the style and form, I got the job, joined the Broadway Company and soon after was out on the road with the New York Shakespeare Festival's First National Tour of *For Colored Girls* ... beginning at the National Theatre in Washington, D.C. I consider the eighteen-month tour and twelve-month extension to be my "unofficial" graduate training, formal introduction and prelude to the form I would later call Ritual Poetic Drama within the African Continuum (RPD-WAC).

Establishing and Engaging the Classroom as Community: The Components of Ritual Poetic Drama

> A story is impelled by the necessity to reveal itself; the aim of a story is revelation, which means that a story can have nothing to hide- at least not intentionally. This also means a story resolves nothing. The resolution of a story must occur in us, with what we make of the questions with which the story leaves us. Plot on the other hand answers all questions it pretends to pose.—James Baldwin, *The Price of the Ticket*, p 583

The Ritual Poetic Drama process is designed to facilitate the artist's journey towards self-actualization and authenticity. Participants move through a ritual process to access their own individual creative content and in so doing truly begin the process of becoming innovative artists, self defined, and courageously leading the pursuit towards bold and authentic self expression rather than imitative artists willing to recreate again and again a choreographed copy of what has been done over and over again in replicated fashion like some sort of factory assembly line. The simple goal is to guide the creative artist to tap into their uniqueness and special gifting as artists practitioners and then engage them in determining how their gifting can serve their community as citizen artists.

The process of using RPD-WAC requires, above all, a willingness to participate. It challenges and moves people outside of their comfort zone and can be very disarming. There have been occasions when people have chosen to step away from the process because it is a full-body, mind and spirit immersive practice and some have been unprepared or underprepared to go that far. It is not about your so-called "talent quotient" or that you need a special skill set in order to participate. No. I have facilitated the process with groups of people that have limited or no performance experience and have no intention of ever becoming an artist in any form as their vocational calling. The

RPD model has most effectively been used as a tool for Performances Studies and student/artists engaged in creative/artistic disciplines, however it has demonstrated an efficacy among other populations as well. The groups to which I refer above are student/artists and when given the opportunity, they are most often committed and engaged in, if not curious about, the RPD process and the challenges it presents. In the process of un-masking our vulnerabilities, and revealing our personal truths some find the intimacy of engaging in community too intense. Some find it necessary to step away from the process because non-participation as a community member is not an option. Withdrawal from the process is rare. If it happens, it is usually because the process of community building requires a type of transparency, an honesty and trust that many people have not experienced before and in some cases, they have too much anxiety to fully embrace the process. Most people can, however, overcome their fears and anxieties in order to fully participate because there can be no spectators. Any type of passive observation during the Ritual and community building process violates the sacred nature of the process itself and allows for a "fourth-wall" type experience that creates a class of voyeurs who vicariously live, feel and express through a different class of "subjects" who are then objectified by the outside group. No matter how sensitively you approach it, the work (in-process) cannot be watched; it must be experienced.

First, it is important to understand the terms of the process. **Ritual** refers to an altered state of consciousness. It is relating to the universal self and the collective rhythms and experiences of the universe. The truth of the universe is articulated in the familiar cycle of life/death/transformation. **Poetic** refers to the emotional internal truth as well as to the metaphoric and the dance. The Poetic lives within the symbolic. It is lyrical, rhythmic, flowing, expressive and elevated, it is emotive and its language encompasses representative, emblematic and figurative speech, sound and phrase. The complimentary duality of the metaphor in the language and the poetry of the movement create the text and movement poem and the rhythms within the Ritual Poetic Drama. **Drama** is the form, the content, and the style. The essence of the **drama** is the story. There is, then, a perfect marriage of the interaction of the drama (of the self) coupled with and shaped by inner knowing, creating Drama (for the society/community).

In western/European traditions of drama and art we think in terms of answers and solutions. There is a duality of self and society, but one does not seem to compliment the other. A magnification and glorification of the individual (self) makes the society (community) of lesser value and importance. A strange and fierce competitiveness almost requires the one to conquer or bring under submission the other. Thus, there is an either/or dichotomy between them. In contrast, with an African perspective[4] we see more of a complimentary and intrinsic connectedness between the individual (self) and the society (community). Since one cannot exist without the other, there is an expectation that one has an unquestioned responsibility to the other. In any pursuit of self-knowledge or gain one must pay homage to those who supported and provided for the individual and in that there is a shared achievement. In contrast to the western cultural continuum of detachment and debate in an oppositional dichotomy where winner takes all, the African-centered perspective embraces inclusion and dialogue in a both/and orientation of shared recognition, responsibility and largeness of spirit. Competiveness and the conquest seem less important than moving the whole of the community forward in the knowledge that we are the sum total of our collective parts.

The above comparison of western orientation as contrasted with African-centered orientation is something that must be explained to the class community before we can enter into the process of the use of RPD. The traditional models of university, college, conservatory classrooms and studio spaces are not generally given to an African-centered model of training and therefore it is with deliberate intentionality that we must have a paradigm shift as to how "we" enter into and also recognize exactly to what degree the very nature of our traditional Eurocentric learning/instructional/experimental space is about to be transformed.

What is often most challenging in beginning work within the Ritual Poetic process is the student/participant's inability (at times) to let go of the linear thought process and model. The influence of "Greek tragedy" and the legacy of the "well-made play" continue to hang around like old familiar ghosts. These elements, while being present in western theater traditions, are virtually absent from the African origins of drama. Initially the classroom space is disoriented and even confused as if they are learning a new language. In facilitating the work open and honest dialogue is of primary importance. It is called "house keeping" where we metaphorically "clean out the cobwebs and pick-up the trash." It is during this time when the class interrogates the traditional model of the dramatic form and compares and contrasts it with what they perceive about the Ritual Poetic model physically by listing their disparate characteristics on huge sheets of butcher paper sprawled out on the floor. This hands-on tactile exercise provides an opportunity for the student/artists to experience the distinctions between the two forms as they articulate their perceptions of the basic characteristics of each one and place the two side-by side.

TRADITIONAL WESTERN MODEL OF THE DRAMATIC FORM	RITUAL POETIC DRAMA FORM
Search for "rightness" the answer or results	Search for origins
A dichotomous orientation of either/or	A dialogic process based in Both/And
Technical training is emphasized	Personal growth emphasized as intent of the process
Dividing the actor/artist Into components – voice & speech/movement/acting	Bonding with the rest of the Community
Competition based	Improvisation as a strategy towards Transformation
Tension is expected and accepted	Homecoming/family/exploration of the familiar encouraged as an integral part of the artist's creative self
Lecture as the primary source of disseminating information	Recognition of others as a part of self and self as a part of something greater than self
Looking towards others for validation	Acknowledgment that if the artist/participant is to be complete and fully functioning in her/his role within the community they must work towards health balance and well being in their life
Asking for permission as a dependency	Spirituality emphasized rather than dogmatic or didactic paradigm
	It is a holistic process mind/body and spirit (in balance with one another)

When unpacking the concerns of the class community regarding the initial exploration of Ritual work, many feel dis-oriented by the process at first because they have not approached learning from this particular modality before, nor have they been given this much ownership or responsibility for their individual learning process. The traditional classroom space allows the learner to be content to "fit in" to a form rather than step out and explore or push down barriers that often limit participation within a traditional paradigm. Through opening up to the process, it becomes clear that participants must bring their thought patterns into partnership with their emotional and physical senses and in so doing there is a commitment of the self, willingly and wholly surrendering to the process. That is not an action easily accomplished within the framework of traditional western Arts Education that often rejects the idea of holistic arts training including mind, body and spirit.

The "spirit" in this kind of process is fundamentally missing from Eurocentric training. The intellect and the achievements of the intellect are highly exalted in the United States. In contrast, RPD provides a reverence of the intellect only as a fragment of something greater than, rather than being superior to or a superseding part of, the individual or community. As a culture, western society tends to approach things from a skeptical, individual centered basis; "What can I get out of it?" "What are my rights?" "How will it affect me?" These attitudes tend to separate the use of RPD from the western/western European expression of a perceived "higher" intelligence and/or self-centeredness rather than a "we" centered identity. Much of the confusion around the intellect as Primary/Supreme, rather than part of/ inter-dependent is the same confusion surrounding the differences in the plot and the story, the linear and the Continuum, the product/result and the process/transformation. James Baldwin's quote eloquently differentiates between the *story*, the vehicle of the Poetic Drama from the *plot*, the vehicle of the western/western European dramatic tradition.

There are several other distinctive variations between Ritual Poetic Drama and the western model. Ritual Poetic Drama incorporates a tri-unity of practice from a position of power—the word power, the music power and the dance power. It is presentational[5] and spiritual. There are no spectators. The audience participates in the drama much like the Black Church Experience. It is essential to participate if you are going to be present. The Western Model is primarily emotionally internalized, visually voyeuristic and auditory-spectatorship. It is narrative and representational.[6] It is something that "was" rather than "is." As Aristotle defines Drama, it is an imitation, not the thing itself.

This definition fundamentally challenges what it means to be a creative artist. The act of imitating, copying or simulating creative artistic expression ignites passionate critique, interrogation and analysis in the classroom space. The student/artists do not readily embrace the idea of imitation as a basic definition for the creative artist; to them it seems contradictory or counter intuitive. We are then presented with an opportunity to reference the side-by-side comparisons of the Traditional Western model and the RPD model we made on the butcher paper some time earlier. Revisiting the comparative analysis gives the student/artists a chance to discover for themselves one of many learning/teaching moments as we begin the process of transforming the learning environment into one that fully reflects the RPD model. In this moment the process of collective communal self-reflection and discovery makes an immediate shift (environmentally) in the classroom/studio space.

One of the fundamental problems in writing a story for the stage has been how to integrate and submerge the exposition of the storyline into the body of the drama so as not to impede the dramatic impact. Exposition is that information which constitutes the background of the action, with which the audience must become acquainted so that the play can proceed. Ideally, no single fact connected with the background is brought in until it can be of maximum dramatic service to the action itself (Grebanier 156).

Ritual Poetic Drama eliminates the need for exposition, thus freeing the creative artist to "be" the storyline rather than to "tell" the storyline. Ritual Poetic Drama approaches the drama in the present rather than in the narrative revealing the most intimate and immediate states of the human condition. The audience, therefore, become the writers of the exposition by their connection to that which is the universal human experience.

The audiences are no longer spectators but active participants in the drama and the connection between the audience/participant and the actor/participant is a spiritual communication whereby both are changed, moved or motivated by the experience. They have become witnesses. More importantly, they are responsible for what they have witnessed. Perhaps using a championship basketball game as an example can effectively illuminate further. The basketball court becomes the stage and the spectators the audience. The audience/spectator/participants come to the contest with the expectation and anticipation of witnessing the drama encapsulated in the competitive struggle of each team to overcome the obstacles presented by the opponents. While the drama begins with the toss-up, the exposition of the game began months earlier as the exploits of each team marched across the sports pages of daily newspapers and other sports media. We assume the audience is already armed with background information and that we need not reiterate what is already common knowledge. Ritual Poetic Drama engages the dramatic form in much the same way. We make the assumption that the audience is armed with essential information with which living life and collective experience has equipped them. They have an "inner knowing."

Within the RPD continuum, we begin with the most intimate details of the human condition, experiencing the soul, bone and marrow of the character. Through the course of the Word power (drama), the Dance power (movement) and the Music power (Sound) we can weave together the storyline. The auditory form of music and sound, the visual form of movement and dance, and the literary form of text and poetic imagery combine in order that the audience experiences the immediate pain, joy, fear, and uncertainty together with the artist. Just by its very nature (RPD) lends itself as a valuable tool for artists and non-artists alike to enhance the study and craft of performance and to illuminate life and the value of participation in it. But beyond that I see the use of RPD as a new pedagogy for arts education and training within the traditional classrooms and studio spaces of the academy. It has been used effectively to help students to access their own creative content, the unique genius and authenticity that is within them waiting to be released. When one can cover the ground they stand on fully present, without being compelled to minimize and deny who they are in order to "fit" the metaphorical costume they have been told they must wear, they seem to grow wings and fly. They begin to recognize their ability for self-determination in their art and within their spirit. They boldly question and give themselves permission to create their own artistic expressions with liberty and authority instead of being bound by traditions that generally do not recognize them.

Ritual Poetic Drama and/or the Well-Made-Play

The well-made-play, is a term used to describe logically constructed plays following the pattern of careful exposition and preparation, a series of complications that creates growing suspense and build to a climactic moment, after which all important questions are resolved (Brockett 442). This definition is the most widely used and universally accepted by artists and scholars. By the aforementioned definition, Ritual Poetic Drama is not qualified to be a "well-made play." Of course it is not the only form of drama that does not fit into the western model and system of validation however, it is one form of drama that has been most disparaged by the definition. By this definition, plays such as *For Colored Girls.... Ain't Supposed To Die...* and *The Colored Museum* were given their own categories when being criticized and evaluated by the Eurocentric press and theatrical awards committees. They could not be considered next to the likes of A *Street Car Named Desire* or *Who's Afraid of Virginia Woolf?*. Arthur Miller and Tennessee Williams' works are the masters and the standard by which "all" others are judged. Ritual Poetic Drama is not within the cultural continuum of Williams or Miller. Neither is it within the dominant culture's cannon that claims the title "Masters of the American Theatre."

The Ritual Process

> Whenever improvisation is a performative strategy in ritual, it places ritual squarely within the domain of play. It is indeed the playing, the improvising, that engages people, drawing them into the action, constructing their relationships, thereby generating multiple and simultaneous discourses always surging between harmony/disharmony, order/disorder, integration/opposition, and so on.—Margaret Thompson Drewal, *Yoruba Ritual*, 7–8

The Ritual Process begins with an acknowledgement that we are gathered together as a community with a common–Unity and an over-arching fundamental principle of harmony as our primary governing value. When embarking on the journey participants agree not to violate the rhythms of the community while at the same time embracing retention of its common humanity. This recognizes that our humanity not only includes love, joy and peace, it paradoxically also includes fragility, ignorance, jealousy, weakness and ironically distrust, dishonesty and dysfunction. No one is asked to be perfect but they are required to be present. It is a process. Navigating that process is as important and impactful as the learning/creative progression each participant will inevitably experience. The ritual process begins by calling upon the ancestors, present and past, which have contributed to the place where the students uniquely stand at that moment. The lights are dimmed and candles are lit. We gather together in a circle and they are introduced to the first of many distinct differences contrasting the Ritual Poetic Drama (WTAC) process with the traditional classroom space. There is no instructor/professor or guru present. There is a facilitator and guide. The smell of sage is present, and a large pitcher of water and a bowl sit in the center of the room. There is a small container of earth from the continent of Africa and the drum beats as we begin. Each student is asked to take an inward journey that will manifest outwardly, they are invited to willingly commit to the process, and the facilitator/faculty must make the same commitment. There are no spectators so the facilitator/faculty must practice and model a passion and explicit commitment during every step of the ritual process. There must be shared disclosure and experience. We each, in turn, call into the space the name of someone or some several people (ancestors) and pour libations for them as we acknowledge what they gave to us that allow us to be here present, right now. It is an opportunity for us to give thanks and to ask the ancestors that they help us as "we" embark upon our journey. It is a significant moment of vulnerability and transparency. There are always tears (more libation) and joy. Most have never engaged in this type of learning environment before but are intensely curious. We are preparing the space for the journey we will take individually and collectively. It is a powerful beginning. Form should follow content because the content comes out of the philosophy, and style then becomes the offspring of the perfect marriage between content and form (Pettiford-Wates).

In RPD as Applied Theatre Practice there are an abundance of teaching and learning moments. All are learners and all are teachers. With a deep sense of community, each student learns from personal experience and the experiences of others. We are truly greater together than we are individually. It in no way diminishes the individual. In fact the work must begin with each person one by one which provides an opportunity for each one to have experiences collectively they have not previously had. Contrasting western drama's fourth wall, which encourages voyeurism rather than participation, in this learning community watching without participating is a violation of community ethics. In our community, there is no fourth wall, no barrier between audience and artist. Each student-artist must be a witness, not a spectator. A witness has a responsibility for what they see; there is an emotional connection and identification with one's own humanity through the story/narrative of another (Pettiford-Wates and Waluconis).

Engaged student/participants, who witness, teach, learn and facilitate in the moments they are invited or requested to do so, are necessary in order to facilitate the individual and collective journeys of each community member. All share in small group; large group and individual guided and stimulated ritual journeys. Family of origin and childhood moments involving a rite-of passage experience is where each journey begins.

The drum is always present and there is a ritual process whereby participants enter into an altered state of consciousness to reconnect with a specific rite-of-passage moment in their life. These journeys often produce expressions of anger, pain, or hurt. Through the ritual process student/artists move in a cyclic manner from moment to moment until there is a discovery made. Many people only experience a partial understanding while they are in midst of the journey. We move from the immediacy of the moment, visualizing when and where the event took place, the initiatory event, to the next moment and the next, each symbolizing the Life/Death/Transformation that is the essence of the Ritual cycle. Once they come back to consciousness (from their altered state) they begin to write. Write without thought or plan, they write purely on impulse, without judgment to the ever-present beat of the drum. The drum is the heartbeat of life and the baseline of the African Continuum. There is an abundance of writing and space is given immediately for those who journeyed to "share" their writing (poetic drama) in a LOUD voice with strong emotion. They are impelled to speak, to move, to re-create their journey through improvisation spontaneously. Often this re-creation is when the authentic discovery or revelation is made. They are encouraged to treat it as spoken language instead of written language or literature. The words should not take on a literary orientation or spoken-word nature. Rather the words should live in the moments in which they were created, which can be very intense at times. Others within the community, the Witnesses, are often so profoundly affected by the narratives that they are impelled to write and share as well … at times there can be multiple voices in the space at once- a cacophony of sound, poetic drama and movement. There is only one rule and that is that the written pieces cannot make their way into the final performance piece/play unless they are read aloud to the community by the author. Once we begin the devising process of creating a work of performance that will frame this particular community's collective journey, the individual relinquishes any individual ownership, because all work is collectively authored. The original author, if their writing is to be included in the final work of art, willingly gives up their ownership and contributes their work to the whole for the greater good.

Engaged Community Building

The process described above does not takes place in the first week or even the second usually. We must work to create our community together. The Ritual Poetic Drama process requires that we create a community with families or Clans. Each Clan has shared responsibly and distinctive characteristics that illuminate the specific role and responsibility they have to the greater community. Together, we discuss what we need as a community to sustain us so that we can thrive, fully self-sufficient. Here we engage the theatrical principle of the suspension of dis-belief or the "magic IF."[7] What do we need from one another if we actually were to live together as a community? And what would we need if there were other communities like us out there? Through a ritual process using the drum and song we consider each Clan/family and then self-select into a community of five or seven families that usually include: Farmers-Nurturers, Hunters-Gatherers, Warriors, Elders, Scribes-Teachers-Storytellers, Healers, Builders and Artists. Once everyone has a Clan/family we begin to assign specific duties such as Openings/Closings for each class, rehearsal or studio session. Each session must have an Opening and Closing as a part of the Ritual Poetic Drama process. All performances are devised through a process that involves collectively authored work, depending upon topic or focus of the class or classes involved. The work is usually located within an Interdisciplinary or Coordinated Studies class model e.g. English Composition, Poetry, Theatre, Dance, and Intercultural Communication. This of course can be adapted to an independent singular class model as well.

Each family has distinct tasks and roles to perform in relation to the larger community; as well as shared responsibilities. There are research assignments and a reading list. Each Clan/family schedules group presentations of their assigned book/film or article. They also are responsible to facilitate a writing session each class day. Additional assignments include researching the time period, historical context and political/social events pertinent to the time, place or topic: then making presentations to the entire community. The work must be grounded in the intentional use of theatre and the dramatic form as a tool for social change. We want to apply theatre arts and the dramatic form to engage audience/participants through inspiration, education, activation or aggravation as the primary goal of our dramatic intention. Our form of engagement for both artist and audience is the Use of Ritual Poetic Drama Within the African Continuum.

In 2001, a coordinated studies class at Seattle Central Community College created a play called *uncle tom: Deconstructed* using the process explicated above. The play was based on the 1852 novel by Harriet Beecher Stowe titled *Uncle Tom's Cabin*.[8] We deconstructed the novel through the ritual process and rigorously interrogated the character of uncle tom and the formative role that character played in the historic legacy of racial caricature and denigrating stereotypes of African American people to the present. The play created a platform for open and honest dialogue about race in America and the damaging legacy of slavery, systemic racism and institutional bias that pervades not only the American cultural landscape but global perceptions as well. The dialogues after each performance ignited a community movement to create more space for dialogue and more opportunity to devise performances and plays like *uncle tom: Deconstructed.* Shortly after, **The Conciliation Project** (TCP), a social justice arts organization was born. The Conciliation Project is a 501c3 non-profit theatre company located in Richmond, Virginia, whose mission is: *"To promote through active and challenging dramatic work open and honest dialogue about racism and systems of oppression in America in order to repair its damaging legacy."* Since its inception, TCP has created many more plays about race and racism in America. Each play has been created through a collaborative writing process facilitated by The Use of (RPD-WAC) Ritual Poetic Drama Within the African Continuum and each play includes as a part of the play's epilogue a facilitated dialogue that is in the unique style of TCP, branded as a part of the methodology and audience engagement process the company uses. These plays are not solely for entertainment but more importantly to engage the audience/ participants in difficult dialogues in an entertaining and educational forum, or edutainment.

The Ritual Poetic Drama model and the plays created thus far through its collaborative process are about the history and cycles of racism, sexism and the intersectionality of oppression in America. The core premise and fundamental assertion of this work is that it has been successful in engaging audiences in the process of unpacking race, racism and privilege. We know that benign neglect has proven to be impotent in ending racism: If it is even possible to end it? To forget about racism and pretend it does not exist ensures that it always will exist. The word racism: can be an extremely divisive word. No one likes the word and it tends to be a trigger. However, through the infusion of Ritual Poetic Drama as a tool to create the plays/creative work as a platform and provide space for the audience/witnesses to interrogate the message, meaning and content of the work it has had some efficacy in moving those with whom it has intersected to a space where they can admit race, racism and institutional bias is so deeply embedded within every aspect of our national landscape ... it is enacted locally, nationally, and internationally in U.S. relations on every level. It is in our schools, jails, financial systems and institutions globally. This recognition alone creates significant transformation whereby it almost feels as if an intervention has been made.

"ART is an immediate intervener in the cycle of poverty of the human spirit...." And this intended outcome of the Ritual Poetic Drama process is to educate, motivate and activate the artist and audience towards social change and community engagement.

Applied Theatre Practice: A New Pedagogy and Engaged Community Model

This emergent pedagogy, the use of Ritual Poetic Drama can claim many disciplines in a transformative learning process that allows students to engage in a full body immersion that challenges them on every level. The desired outcome is to build a community of learners that become forever-committed citizen artists or citizen activists working towards massive social change through creative social justice initiatives. The work ultimately wants people to engage in a movement that challenges the meme that the more things change the more they stay the same. If this transformative process can engage a community of learners to become activated in the world in which they live, if it can facilitate learning through a process of intense interrogation and deconstruction of literature and of self, if it can open eyes and liberate spirits so that the citizen/artists can live to create again then it is worth the effort and worth the journey. No one who is an involved artist/participant or audience/witness remains unaffected or unmoved by what they see or what they do in the process. It is always a community event, a very human experience that touches the spirit and the soul. It is not just play ... it is the real deal. We struggle together. As a class/studio, audience/witness there is a sense of solidarity that takes great effort but also has great reward.

A story, within the dramatic form, is written as a play or a dramatic text. Until it is interpreted by performance/performer it remains literature or in its literary form. Performance is an act of outward demonstration, a display of behavior. For the performer, it is literally breathing life into the character created by the author on the page. The performance takes the literary form of story, most often written in play form and gives expression, emotional content and active motivation to that story and character allowing the audience to actually visualize the character and experience the story through witnessing the act of performance. The act of performance breaks barriers of time and space and allows the audience to be drawn into a type of time travel while they live the story with the performer and the performance.

Storytelling and telling a story seem like different examples of the same thing however, when examined through the lens of the dramatic form there is indeed a distinction. Telling a story focuses more on the one doing the telling or speaking the story. The *telling* has a narrative quality and the story is clearly about someone or something that is not present in the current time or space. Telling a story takes on the persona of the "teller" as the instrument or filter of the story. The audience is aware that a story is being told and depends on the teller to engage them through their senses and imaginations effectively leading them through the story to its conclusion. On the other hand, storytelling as performative attempts to actually become the story itself and challenges the audience to suspend its disbelief and embrace the "reality" that the story and the storyteller are one. What becomes instantly true is that what is being witnessed is, in fact, the story of the storyteller, and the audience is reliving the same in performance; an outward demonstration of the story as it actually happened or even as it is happening. So although time and space might challenge the audience's own knowledge and experience, the performance invites them to believe that they are actually present as the story reveals itself through the performer and the performance. Although there are excellent storytellers (Storyteller n., one who writes or tells stories), there is a distinction and qualitative difference between telling a story and storytelling when explored through the act of performance and performer.

In his 1926 essay "Criteria for Negro Art" W.E.B. Du Bois articulates what is the essential purpose for Art and the role of the artist within her/his community. He believed that Art for Art's sake was a useless pursuit and the goal of Art should be transformative because of its ability to challenge, present, agitate, preserve and affirm. Art is and should be propaganda was Du Bois' assertion but Art's first obligation in creative process was truth,

> "not for the sake of truth, not as a scientist seeking truth, but as one upon whom truth eternally thrusts itself as the highest handmaid of imagination, as the one great vehicle of universal understanding." Further Du Bois asserts that in telling the truth, the artist takes on the role of being used as an instrument of— "justice, honor, and right—not for sake of an ethical sanction but as the one true method of gaining sympathy and human interest."—Du Bois, 1926

In teaching performance and performance text, the art of storytelling is imbedded within the pedagogy of RPD. The ultimate goal in using this methodology is to facilitate the process for the student/artists to access their authentic and unique creative genius. Authenticity is grounded in truth and transparency and transparency evokes a state of self-consciousness and vulnerability. How then do we address the awkwardness and discomfort of the tension and lack of ease that is brought into the room when student/artists learn that we are going to explore a new methodology and approach to the techniques of performance through the process of personal story and rite of passage journey? The idea of becoming another (character) by putting on a mask and covering up your own truth or substituting a "created" truth of the character that you are playing is a way of approaching the creative process but it is not the way "we" are going to approach the process. We are going to first explore or own truths, our own stories in order to find our authenticity as creative artists, that we might bring that same authenticity and truth to each and every character that we present. This is a paradigm shift. There is nervous laughter and some concern as to the "how-to" and "what-ifs" of the process that undoubtedly arise. In order to calm nerves and allay fears we must first create a community where the process can happen creating an environment that promotes trust, respect, mutual disclosure and collaborative work. Building that community is essential and fundamental to the success of the RPD model. The model's most important function to the performer and the performance is as an application to access emotional vulnerability through personal story. All drama is based in story ... finding ones own story (as a performer) helps the artist to relate to and re–LIVE another's story as if it is their own. This is the fundamental challenge for the performer and the process of performing. How to become the story as a storyteller instead of just telling a story? The aesthetic experience of the audience and the effect the performance and/or performer has on them is profoundly different when they, the audience, become witnesses to the event rather than spectators.

Looking at specific texts and the particular challenges presented in reading and performing these texts we can draw some insights into the use of RPD as an applied practice.

Atol Fugard's *My Children, My Africa*, Ntozake Shange's For *Colored Girls Who Have Considered Suicide/When the rainbow is enuf*, Amiri Baraka's *Dutchman* and Lorraine Hansberry's *Les Blancs* all offer different challenges to the performer/storyteller. One distinction that cannot be underestimated is that many contemporary students have not ever seen these texts in performance or literary form. Although written by well established and award winning playwrights, these plays are not generally incorporated or required reading for "typical" classrooms. Most are old enough to be considered *classic* fare but not universally embraced as classic.

For Colored Girls... is the play that is most alike to narrative story, each performer has at least one stand alone story. The play is a choroepoem and stylistically it is (ritual) poetic drama. There is no exposition or time to get the audience all on the same page as the play begins. This is also true for the performer in approaching this work. As a ritual poetic drama, *Colored Girls* has no exposition or backstory for the performer to latch onto and there are no video versions of the play to mimic or imitate.[9] In the case of the creative arts, imitation is NOT the highest form of flattery. The student/artist must create an intimate connection with the text and discover the places where they find empathy and personal connection. They begin to search for the things they have in their personal story/reality that authentically connect to the story/reality of the character they are performing. This connection will become the pulse, the internal heartbeat and what impels the story to reveal itself through the vessel that is the artist/performer. In *For Colored Girls* all the characters are named for the colors of the rainbow. For this example we will use the love poem performed by the Lady in Orange.

The following is only an excerpt of *Love Poem* #1 from the choreopoem *For Colored Girls...* by Ntozake Shange

> ever since i realized there waz someone callt
> a colored girl an evil woman a bitch or a nag
> i been tryin not to be that & leave bitterness
> in somebody else's cup/ come to somebody to love me
> without deep & nasty smellin scauld from lye or bein
> left screamin in a street fulla lunatics/ whisperin
> slut bitch bitch niggah/ get outta here wid alla that/
> I didnt have any of that for you/ i brought you what joy
> i found & i found joy

Performer makes the above text the first cycle out of three. Cycle One establishes (1) the where: the physical environment for the story, (2) the who: a colored girl trying to shed the definitions and limitations of that and (3) the why: why I need to speak now through the use of the physical/emotional environment created with sound and movement impulse—who I am (the story) that is impelled ... why it has an immediate NEED to be told.

> /especially when i can make the music loud enuf so there is no me but
> dance/ & when i can dance like that/ there's nothing cd hurt me/but
> i get tired & i haveta come offa the floor & then there's/
> that woman who hurt you/ who you left three or four times/
> & just walked back/after you put my heart in the bottom of
> your shoe/ you just went back to where you hurt/ & i didn't
> have nothing/ so i went to where somebody had something for me/
> but he wasn't you/ & i was on the way back from her house
> in the bottom of your shoe / so this is not a love poem/ cuz there are
> only memorial albums available/

The above excerpt picks up in the middle of what would be Cycle Two ... reveals the conflicts/questions/concerns or problem presented by the story. It is during this cycle where the performer is interrogating the dilemma the story offers. This is a new cycle and has a new primary emotion that is first expressed through movement, then sound and finally text. Performer continues to explore through sound and movement the primary emotion in this cycle and the text is impelled through the need to reveal itself and is rooted organically in the expression of the artist's own voice and authenticity.

Performer picks up in the middle of the poem here as she continues.

> / but a real dead lovin is here for you now/ cuz i don't know anymore/ how
> to avoid my own face wet wit my tears/ cuz i had convinced
> myself colored girls had no right to sorrow/ & I lived
> & loved that way & kept sorrow on the curb/ allegedly
> for you/ but I know I did it for myself
> I cdnt stand it
> I cdnt stand bein sorry & colored at the same time
> It's so redundant in the modern world

The above Cycle Three is where the moment of CHANGE, Transformation, Revelation or Recognition occurs. The performer uses the above method of primary emotion expressed through sound and movement until text is impelled.

Below is an illustration of the RPD cycle of Life/ Death/Transformation. The performer goes around and around the cycle at least four times visiting each emotional/physical location growing and expanding each time they visit a specific moment in time on their journey (the character's journey.) Each time they visit physically a time and place on the continuum their experience becomes more and more connected to the reality and authenticity of the "lived" experience of the character or of the moment on the life continuum of the story/storyteller. This is in direct contrast to the linear model of exposition/plot/conflict/climax/resolution/denouement and distinguishes the RPD model from the western/western European model.

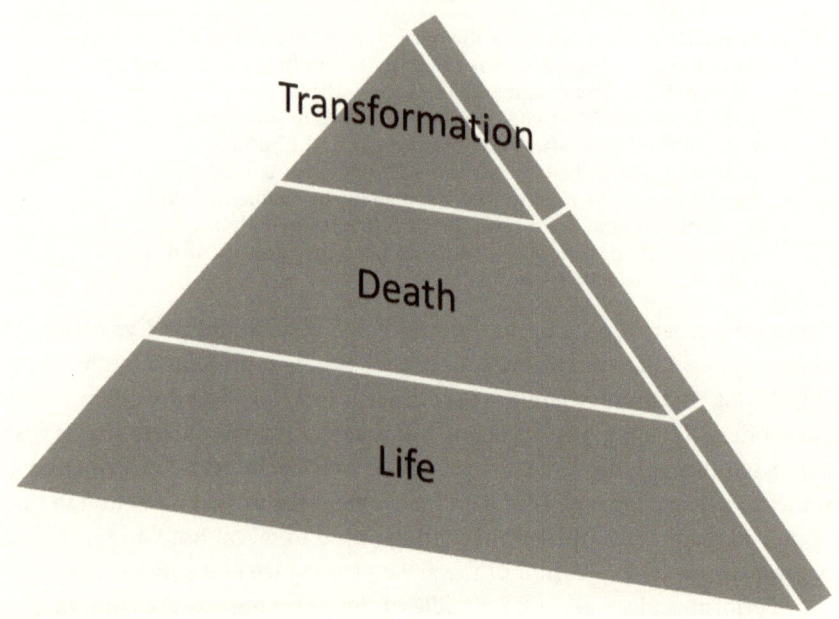

The Process Sequence is as follows:
1. Read the dramatic text at least three times—(a) understanding the story, (b) understanding your character (c) gathering information about your character from another character's perspective (this can also be "others" who do not directly speak to you in the text)
2. Translate the written word into spoken language: a process of using phrasing, emphasis, inflection and gesture (non verbal communication). Write out the text on a legal pad or another piece of paper to help make the text you are speaking your own.
3. Divide the text up into three cycles representing Life/Death/Transformation as explained in the examples above.

Using the above methodology the performer enters into a process of exploration whereby they can locate themselves within the parameters of the character they are becoming. The performer finds their personal and authentic connection to the character in order that they can become the story that is

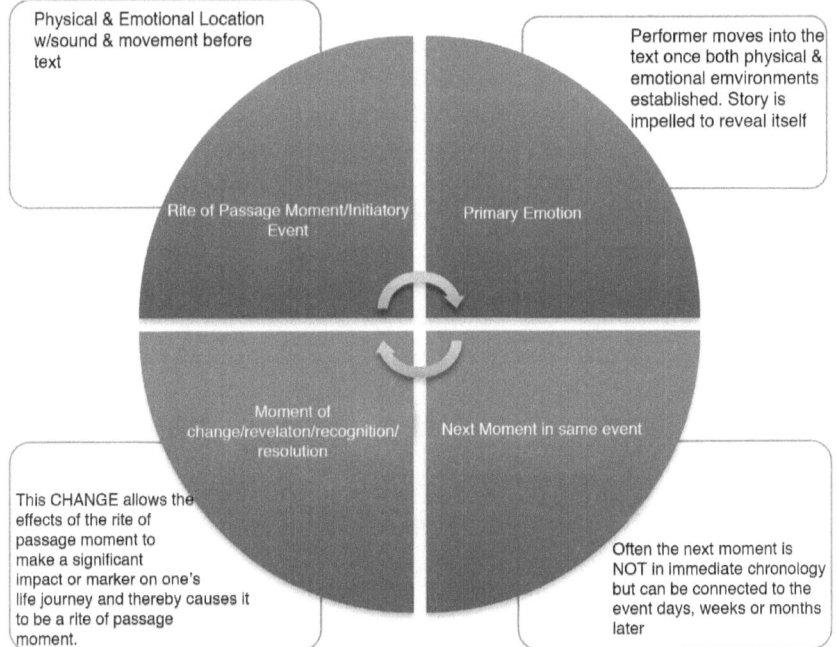

impelled to be revealed through them. They become the vessel of the story using an authentic self and voice. The journey then becomes what the performer reveals to the audience who then become witnesses of an authentic story instead of a passive group of spectators or voyeurs hearing a story told instead of a story lived in the moment.

In Closing…

> "The experiential process of performance facilitated the students' cross-cultural engagement—their "border-crossing" in ways that altered the manner of their understanding of themselves."—E. Patrick Johnson, *Appropriating Blackness* p. 244

Interdisciplinary learning is a potent and powerful model. It creates, for the student/artists an effective community of learners and engages them intimately as allies and advocates for their own education and process. It empowers them as students, teachers and facilitators within the learning community and inspires in them an unquenchable thirst for something more … something that involves not only developing a sense of self but an *inner knowledge* and a vision of themselves within a larger community and social context. The process has allowed them to recognize their own potency and infused them with a belief that change is possible. It is possible not only because they have personally experienced change/transformation but also because they have seen it happen! They have been a witness to its impact and its power. The Art of theater has an interdisciplinary approach as a core value. Ritual Poetic Drama Within the African Continuum uses a model of learning in community and models an interdisciplinary and collaborative approach to teaching, learning and artistic expression. It asks each person to become an active and conscious advocate in the process- and to begin a process of healing through self-knowledge and self-discovery. RPD as a methodology philosophically inspires each student/artist to take responsibility for the impact a transformative process can have on learning, (re)membering legacy and envisioning the future

The Dramatic and Performance Arts uniquely inspire its participants to build a community in order to facilitate its expression and the outcome of that expression is inextricably linked to the collective passion, power and potency found in community. All participants must find both the unique individual contribution they bring and the *common unity* they find in the topic, subject or purpose of their unique artistic expression. Shared knowledge and shared experience enriches both what we learn and how we learn it; additionally, it impacts and influences the choices we make in determining what it is we want to know. Although the process impacts each participant differently, the reflections of those who have participated in the RPD model, based on the creation and building of a learning community, unequivocally testify to its ability to enable transformative change and an empowered learning experience that unexpectedly influences how the participant envisions the potency of teaching and learning in community, empowers the participants to engage actively in the process and fundamentally transforms the classroom/studio/rehearsal space allowing the autonomy of active interrogation, collective collaboration and the liberty of the creative process.

Learning Communities based on collective study and a communal commitment to both teaching and learning have impacted and empowered my creative expression as a citizen, artist and educator. The emergent process and evolution of the RPD model serves to inspire a type of liberation. The process in community becomes one in which all participants work together to challenge the status quo and the roles and responsibilities found in the traditional or "classic" models of classroom and/or studio space. Fundamentally, our individual successes and failures are inextricably bound to our collective success or failure as a community. Our mantra becomes: *"Individually*

I know some things and you know some things but collectively we know a lot more."

Notes

1. "Cover the ground on which you stand!" is an expression that my grandmother, Georgia Pettiford used repeatedly throughout my childhood. Although it was years before I truly understood its meaning, I instinctively knew it to be a battle cry for self-determination and self-actualization. The expression and the way she shouted it out as an affirmation also served as an exhortation for personal responsibility and accountability. Grandma would stand up and say, "You see this shadow I cast and how it's covering this ground? Well? I don't know about you, what you believe or where you're standing. All I do know is I am COVERING the ground on which I stand."

2. To be impelled in this context means with much urgency; like projectile vomit is unable to be stopped or directed, so too the "story" MUST be told, it cannot remain unspoken, it must come out of the vessel and is unleashed in a manner that cannot be contained.

3. The "well-made-play" is a term used to describe logically constructed plays following the pattern of careful exposition and preparation, a series of complications that creates growing suspense and build to a climactic moment, after which all important questions are resolved (Brockett 442). This definition is the most widely used and universally accepted by artists and scholars. By the aforementioned definition, the result of Ritual Poetic Drama is not qualified to be a "well-made play." Of course it is not the only form of drama that does not fit into the western model and system of validation; however, it is one form of drama that has been most disparaged by the definition. This "well-made-play" model has been used to systematically devalue and marginalize the RPD process and practice. It was by this definition that plays such as *For Colored Girls.... Ain't Supposed To Die...* and *The Colored Museum* were given their own categories when being criticized and evaluated by the Eurocentric press and theatrical awards committees. They could not be considered next to the likes of A *Street Car Named Desire* or *Who's Afraid of Virginia Woolf?*. Arthur Miller and Tennessee Williams' works are the masters and the standard by which all "others" should be judged. Ritual Poetic Drama is not within the cultural continuum of Williams or Miller. In fact, neither is it within the cultural location of the dominant culture's cannon that claims the title "Masters of the American Theatre."

4. The concept of an African perspective is both discursive and distinct among African and African American scholars. The original ideology frames the Pan African movement of W.E.B. DuBois, Kwame Nkrumah, Jomo Kenyatta and Robert Mangaliso Sobukwe. Pan Africanism promotes a shared cultural continuity across all African peoples within the diaspora. This universal belonging was more important than the specifics of cultural practice across ethnicity and nationality. In contemporary discourse, post apartheid; migration, economics, warfare and globalization have broadened the scope and inclusiveness surrounding the critique of a unified continental African-ness. In the reference above, the intention is to locate the concept within a wide-ranging cultural continuum rooted within continental Africa that values community, core principles of humanity, contextualizes success differently than does western philosophy and spirituality and instinctively embraces the process of life, death and transformation. Race, ethnicity or political viewpoint does not intentionally provide any context. An African perspective is a philosophy that holds to both/and as compared to a dichotomous orientation of either/or.

5. Presentational acting is when the actor attempts to reveal real human behavior. It is organic. It works from the inside out. The actor has no preconceived outcome in mind but trusts that a result will occur.

6. Representational acting is when the actor works from the outside in. The actor uses style, form and fashion to imitate human behavior. They have a specific outcome in mind and employ the methods needed to achieve a specific result (Uta Hagen, 1973).

7. The "magic if" is a theatrical convention first articulated by Constantine Stanislavski and is a part of what has come to be known as the Stanislavski System, a systematic and articulated technique of acting which employs various methods and strategies that facilitate the actor's portrayal of characters for the stage and performance. The "magic if" suggests that actors put themselves in their character's shoes, with the character's given set of conditions and then ask themselves "what would I do if?" "How would I react to that? And so on. This technique creates a sense of reality for the actor.

8. The character of Uncle Tom from Harriet Beecher Stowe's novel *Uncle Tom's Cabin* is never capitalized in the work of The Conciliation Project. This character's name is intentionally not capitalized. He is a created thing, a prop, not a real and fully formed person/character. On the contrary he is "the creation of a white woman's fantasy."—Angela Davis

9. The 2010 screenplay version of *For Colored Girls...* was written by Tyler Perry and is based on the original play by Ntozake Shange but is not the play itself.

Works Cited

Baldwin, James. *The Price of the Ticket: Collected Nonfiction, 1948–1985*. New York: St. Martin's, 1985. Print.

Boal, Augusto. *Theatre of the Oppressed*. New York: Theatre Communications Group, 1985. Print.

Cliff, Michelle. "The Land of Look Behind." *Multi-Cultural Literacy*. Ed. Rick Simonson. Saint Paul: Graywolf, 1985, pp. 63–81.

Deirdre, Heddon, and Jane Milling. *Devising Performance*. New York: Palgrave Macmillan, 2006. Print.

Drewal, Margaret Thompson. *Yoruba Ritual: Performers, Play, Agency*. Bloomington: Indiana University Press, 1992, pp. 7–8. Print.

Du Bois, W.E.B. "Criteria For Negro Art," *The Crisis*, Vol. 32 (October 1926): pp. 290–297.

Fugard, Athol. *My Children! My Africa!* New York: Theatre Communications Group, 1990. Print.

Hagen, Uta. *Respect for Acting*. Hoboken, NJ: John Wiley and Sons, 1973. Print.

Hansberry, Lorraine. *Les Blancs: The Collected Last Plays*. New York: Vintage, 1972. Print.

Harrison, Paul Carter. *Black Theatre: Ritual Performance in the African Diaspora*. Philadelphia: Temple University Press, 2002. Print.

_____. *The Drama of Nommo*. New York: Grove, 1982. Print.

Johnson, E. Patrick. "Performance and/as Pedagogy." *Appropriating Blackness*. Durham: Duke University Press, 2003, p. 244. Print.

Jones, LeRoi. *Dutchman and The Slave: Two Plays*. New York: HarperPerennial, 1971. Print.

Oscar, Brockett. "Defining the Well-Made Play." *The Essential Theatre*. Austin: Harcourt Brace, 1976, 442. Print.

Pettiford-Wates, Tawnya. "Re-Vision: Towards a Re-Connection of the Dramatic Artist with the African Origins of the Dramatic Form." Doctoral Dissertation. The Union Institute. (1992):225 Web.

Pettiford-Wates, Tawnya, and Carl Waluconis. "New Pedagogy for Learning Communities." *Ritual Poetic Drama Within the African Continuum* Vol. 6, No. 10 (October 2003).

Schechner, Richard, ed. *Performance Studies: An Introduction*, 3d ed. New York: Routledge, 2013. Print.

Shange, Ntozake. *For Colored Girls Who Have Considered Suicide/ when the Rainbow is enuf.* New York: Scribner, 1997. Print.

Stanislavski, Constantin. *An Actor Prepares.* New York: Routledge, 1989. Print.

Finding Connections, Contexts and Ourselves
Strategies for Moving Beyond Generalizations in the Ethnic Literature Classroom

BEN RAILTON

One of the most significant and frustrating obstacles that confronts the teacher of ethnic American literature is the ease with which students can move, in both communal and individual work, from discussions of specific texts and individuals to generalizations about entire ethnic or racial identities and communities. An attempt to unravel the complexities of perspective and the presentation of identity in *The Autobiography of Malcolm X* becomes instead a conversation about African American history and literature and anger; group work with the ambiguities and ironies of Sui Sin Far's story "In the Land of the Free" turns into debate over immigration and assimilation and ethnic neighborhoods; a paper meant to highlight a close reading of rhetorical strategies in William Apess' speech "A Eulogy for King Philip" relies far too heavily on a set of stereotypical concepts of Native Americans' alternative, nature-centered spirituality and worldview and existence. None of the latter topics or questions are ones about which it would be impossible to have a strong and nuanced classroom discussion or write a successful analytical paper, given the right framing and sufficient available evidence. But I believe that it is not the role of most literature courses to provide that type of extensive supporting material, nor is the focus of those courses likely to be on the kinds of sociological and historical issues to which such topics connect. Instead, the real focal points of literature courses, the complex works and authors themselves, are in this pattern used as representatives for their ethnic identities and communities, as a means to discuss the broader questions rather than as the subjects of extended analysis on their own terms.

Leaving aside the irony of using individual texts as representatives—tokens, if you will—of entire ethnic traditions, such generalizing readings almost always move far too quickly past, if they do not altogether ignore, the specific content and form, the themes and choices, that constitute these literary texts and demand extended attention and in-depth analysis.

There are many factors that play into this tendency to generalize, but I believe that two of the most critical are a lack of shared contexts and a sense of the authors' identities as outside of and distinct from our own. For the former, since again it is neither the pedagogical place of nor realistically possible for an ethnic literature professor to provide extensive sociological or historical contexts for his course's primary texts, those texts and theirs authors can very easily become the class's only conduits to the much more general topics around which stereotypical narratives are always hovering (African American anger, immigrants' desire not to assimilate, Native American spirituality, and so on). For the latter, the more an author's or character's identity and experiences seem entirely distinct from our own, the easier it is to turn both him or her and the text into that "other" about whom such generalizations are usually produced; this problem is particularly exacerbated in classrooms that do not have any or many explicitly ethnic presences and voices (such as at Fitchburg State University, the predominantly [90-95 percent, depending on which source is consulted for the information] white non-Hispanic institution where I teach[1]), but of course will always be the case for every other ethnicity besides one's own, and so I believe it remains a prominent factor in the generalizing tendency whatever the exact demographics of an institution and its classrooms.

One strategy that I have found exceptionally helpful in resisting that tendency and creating more specific, nuanced, and meaningful classroom discussions and individual written work is to provide analytical contexts to the students. By that I don't mean information; I've already noted my objections to bringing much broad sociological or historical information into a literature course, and while more specific information about (for example) an author's biography and career can certainly help us frame and analyze a particular text, such info does not necessarily help with—and might even exacerbate—the broader problem of generalizations. Instead, I mean providing the students with the means to analyze multiple identities and texts in relationship to one another, ideally across one or another seeming border between personal and literary identities (such as generational, generic, or cultural differences), in order to allow for more specific and nuanced ideas and conversations. In this essay I will discuss two particular components of that pedagogical strategy, one involving the class's shared readings and one the students' individual written work: working with texts in pairs, in order to provide immediate analytical contexts for each text and discussion; and replacing more traditional academic papers and exams with a multipart, multigenerational family timeline and history project, in order to make the students' own identities another subject for our analyses and conversations. I first utilized both strategies in my Ethnic American Literature course at FSU in Fall 2007 (as part of a syllabus I developed in response to my first attempt with the course, in Fall 2005, the discussions and papers in which had included far too much generalization[2]), and will rely throughout on specific examples (both from our course work with the texts themselves and from the family history projects) to illustrate how these strategies helped us avoid generalizations and develop complex analyses of both our shared and individual materials.

Even—perhaps especially—the most complex and dense ethnic literary texts, when presented and read in a vacuum, can easily be turned into fodder for one or another generalized topic and conversation. One way to stall such generalizations, or at least to redirect onto a more specific and analytical track the tendency to link one text and author to identities and communities outside of them, is to construct a syllabus in which students read and discuss texts in pairs, and thus analyze them not only individually (which certainly remains the primary and central goal) but also in complex conversation with and relationship to one another. I have actually found that the second level of analysis often bleeds back into and strengthens the first—that is, that in order to develop the kinds of comparisons and contrasts that are the focus of the multi-textual analyses, the students look more closely at specific passages, formal elements, and themes in the individual texts than they might otherwise. Moreover, the professor can create and use the pairings to foreground, and thus help the class think about, various factors that contribute to and distinguish both identities and texts, what I'd call borders between different authors and readings, including generational, generic, and cultural categories; highlighting this attribute in the pairings allows for explicit conversations about continuities and changes across these lines, as I hope the examples below illustrate, and thus provides specific frames for both the comparative analyses and the course's ongoing, overall discussion of ethnic American literatures.

The first two (of four total) pairings in that Fall 2007 course exemplified the generational border—that is, they featured two texts written from the same general ethnic perspective and within the same literary genre, but published in and reflecting significantly distinct time periods. We began by reading two African American autobiographies from a century apart, Frederick

Douglass's first *Narrative* (1845) and Richard Wright's *Black Boy* (1945); and then moved to two Asian American works of fiction from the early and late twentieth century, Sui Sin Far's collection *Mrs. Spring Fragrance* (1912) and Amy Tan's novel *The Joy Luck Club* (1989). Our conversations about the two autobiographies yielded a very interesting, specific continuity: the importance that both Douglass and Wright place on learning to read and write, and the concurrent ways in which both foreground their dual roles as protagonists and authors of their personal narratives. When Wright details, midway through his long first chapter, his mother's "encourag[ing]" response to his first hesitant steps at "recogniz[ing] certain words" and so "learn[ing] to read" (25), any sense that such language acquisition and family support are to be taken for granted in any young boy's life is challenged by a turn to the opening paragraphs of Douglass's Chapter VI, where Mr. Auld forbids his wife to teach young Frederick to read, arguing both that the skill would "forever unfit him to be a slave" and that "as to himself, it could do him no good, but a great deal of harm" (57); Douglass resists these arguments and continues to teach himself, much as Wright will later illicitly use an employer's library card to check out books for his own reading and edification. While these passages and elements of the narratives are likely immediately familiar to scholars of American literature—as the quantity of scholarship on them illustrates—the students came to them not through such scholarship or even through any specific prompting on my part, but rather because they were asked (particularly in their brief weekly email responses to the readings) to identify moments or details in the two texts that seemed to relate to one another, and many highlighted those passages or others like them. To be clear, the students still connected such moments to Douglass and Wright's shared racial identity, but did so significantly in the opposite direction from a generalization: they first noticed the themes of reading and writing, and then began to think about and discuss the question of what these experiences and desires could tell us about the African American experience across the centuries (along with related questions such as the impact of slavery on subsequent, post-emancipation generations). That is, by focusing first on the texts themselves, individually but also in relationship to one another, they developed more organic and specifically grounded ideas about defining and persistent elements of race and identity in America.

On the other hand, our discussions of Far and Tan highlighted an equally complex and significant example of a change across the time periods. Many of Far's stories, in fact virtually all of them, focus on the struggles that her Chinese American characters and their families face in the new world, during and especially after the immigration process; however, the struggles that seemed to the students most prominent in Tan's novel are those faced by the mother characters in the old world of China, before their immigrations to America. And the students' analyses linked that distinction to a formal difference between the two texts: Far's use of a third-person narrator throughout her stories as opposed to Tan's shifts between the first-person perspectives of seven characters over the course of the novel. That is, when Far's character Lae Choo says to her young son, in the opening paragraphs of "In the Land of the Free," that "'twas for thee [she] left" her husband in America and returned to China, the reader is forced to extrapolate any further details of the mother's old world experiences, as the narrator and story turn instead firmly to her imminent struggles with the Chinese Exclusion Act upon her return to the new world (93); whereas when Tan's character An-Mei Hsu begins her first chapter of narration, "Scar," with the words "When I was a young girl in China," the story follows her perspective and memory into that old world and focuses entirely on her life there, with the reader left to extrapolate how the story's portrayal of mothers and daughters might be relevant to the characters' evolving relationships in the American present (42) . While the students did not initially have the critical language to describe these distinct narrations, they nonetheless recognized that we were hearing far more directly from Tan's characters and learning more about their identities and pasts as a result; I could then amplify their responses with a brief discussion of narration and perspective, one that tied these sometimes confusing theoretical frames to the students' specific takes on the two readings. There are a variety of possible explanations for these differences between the texts, but one broader factor to which the students connected them is a sense of immigration and assimilation as more difficult and challenging processes for Far's turn of the twentieth century immigrants than for Tan's late twentieth century ones—a generalization, of course, but one again produced through and grounded in specific analyses of these two class texts.

Our third pairing exemplified instead the generic border, as it included two Hispanic American authors working in roughly contemporary time periods but in different literary genres: we read excerpts from Sandra Cisneros' work of fiction (part collection of short stories, part novel) *The House on Mango Street* (1989); and a number of poems by Martin Espada (published in the 1990s and early 2000s). In this pairing, some of the most productive conversations about both continuities and changes were linked directly to formal elements; we talked a great deal, for example, about first-person narrators and poetic speakers, and how related elements such as perspective and structure are influenced by that fundamental question of voice and, in turn, impact our reading of themes of ethnic identity and experience in those texts.

Cisneros' choice to create and utilize a very young first-person narrator and voice, Esperanza, contributes directly to the short and seemingly superficial nature of the book's stories, the lines between which her audience must read to find her thematic meanings. This deceptive simplicity is exemplified by the closing lines of the book's titular first story, when Esperanza writes, of that less than ideal current home, "For the time being, Mama says. Temporary, says Papa. But I know how those things go" (6). By contrast, Espada creates, in his poem "Jorge the Church Janitor Finally Quits," a mature and (as that "Finally" implies) world-weary speaker, one who in the poem's opening four lines engages, much more explicitly than Esperanza, with thematic issues of home and place: "No one asks/where I am from,/I must be/from the country of janitors." The class's specific discussions of first-person voices in moments like those, moreover, led some students to think further about our earlier versions of such voices, both in another work of fiction (Tan's novel) and in the autobiographies—connections that I facilitated by asking them, in this pairing's open-ended final weekly email, to connect either Cisneros or Espada to any earlier reading in any way—and thus to anticipate, model, and ultimately strengthen the kinds of cross-cultural moves that our fourth pairing would entail.

In that fourth and final pairing, we focused on two texts from the same literary genre, the multigenerational family novel, and the same basic time period, the turn of the twenty-first century, but two quite distinct ethnic, cultural perspectives: Native American (Chippewa) Louise Erdrich's *Love Medicine* (the New and Revised 1993 edition) and Indian (Bengali) American Jhumpa Lahiri's *The Namesake* (2003). Having spent most of the semester discussing pairs of texts and authors that shared an ethnic and cultural framework was, I believe, a significant factor in our ability to compare across such frameworks in this case; that is, we had developed our ability to analyze the influence of ethnicity and culture on an individual's identity and perspective and experiences, and so could extend those analyses to the continuities and changes across different ethnicities and cultures. That was particularly relevant to some of the thematic concerns that we identified and analyzed in both novels, including the relationship between an immigrant family's old and new worlds and a Native American community's more traditional and more modernized aspects, and the questions of assimilation and resistance within and across multiple generations in each case. Moreover, our discussions of formal elements such as perspective in the generic pairing carried over nicely to these two novels, which utilize very distinct narrative modes in order to achieve a similar effect of shifting across a variety of characters' perspectives. Lahiri's traditional third-person omniscient narrator moves smoothly and easily across the perspectives of all her novel's main characters, even shifting, in the text's most surprising and complicating moment, for an entire chapter into the perspective of the protagonist Gogol Ganguli's wife Moushumi, at the moment when she begins an extramarital affair; whereas for Gogol, the son of Bengali American immigrants, the United States has always been his real and ideal home, Moushumi, herself a first-generation immigrant, feels a stronger link to Paris than to America, and thus her browsing, in the concluding paragraph of this chapter, through "an oversized volume of photographs of Paris" in the apartment of the man with whom she is having the affair is a deeply resonant moment (267). Erdrich's novel, on the other hand, lacks any overarching narrator, with each character providing his or her perspective directly (at times in first-person voice, at times through limited third-person omniscient narration) in the relevant stories. This element contributes a story-telling dynamic to the text and its themes, particularly at those moments when a narrator explicitly addresses us; in one striking such sequence in the final story, "Crossing the Water," the young narrator, Lipsha Morrissey, has just met his father for the first time, asks him about the criminal charges from which his father has spent much of his life fleeing, and then admits that he "just don't trust to write down what he answered, yes or no. We have entered an area of too deep water" (364). The formal and thematic elements of both novels, and thus our work as readers of them, are certainly deep throughout, but putting their characters and perspectives in conversation with one another, and with all those that we had encountered throughout the semester's pairings, helped us to gauge and navigate those depths much more successfully.

Those successes notwithstanding, I can't conclude my discussion of this reading strategy without admitting that it, like any pedagogical strategy and perhaps especially like any one with which students might not be familiar or experienced, certainly has its potential drawbacks. While I tried to spread our work with the texts out a bit more than I might in other syllabi—taking three weeks to read the full books rather than the two I would devote to them in most other literature courses, for example—it is almost inevitable that reading two texts at a time means asking students to read more pages for each class; even when that isn't quantitatively the case, seeing pages or chapters in two books for each class can feel intimidating for students and perhaps lessen the likelihood of the reading getting done. And even when the reading is done, there is of course the potential for confusion, for the two texts to blend together in ways that might make it harder for students to (for example) find evidence or passages in one or both. Yet I was at the time and remain absolutely convinced that the benefits outweighed these drawbacks, not only for the analytical reasons that I have tried to highlight in this section, but also in strengthening various classroom skills that are a part of any literature course. For example, I found group work to be especially interesting and productive with this course, as I could ask a particular group to highlight one interesting passage from the day's readings in each African American autobiography that deals with family relationships, and then to think about how each author constructs that theme; when that group came back to share their ideas with the class as a whole, we'd have models for both the analyses of individual texts and the comparative level of analysis. And in terms of individual student work, when I asked students, as one of the final exam's couple mini-essay questions, to create and then analyze their own pair of texts, across any two of our existing pairings, I found them significantly better equipped to produce such comparative analyses than has been the case when I have asked similar questions of other classes. Having developed this idea of paired readings in order to mitigate tendencies particular to ethnic literature courses—and still believing that it is a strategy ideally suited to such courses—I have now decided to bring it into other American literature courses (in which of course ethnic literature remains prominent) on some levels as well, such as likewise ending a second-half American literature survey by reading concurrently two turn of the twenty-first century multigenerational novels.

All of the communal work I've traced here, however, doesn't necessarily address the second significant cause of the generalizing tendency: the gap that students often perceive between their identities and perspectives and those represented by our authors and captured in their texts. As I mentioned in introducing that gap, its presence and significance does depend to some degree on the demographic makeup of an institution and classroom; and without question the distance between the students and certain especially underrepresented and thus over-stereotyped ethnicities or communities (with Native Americans often exemplifying both of those traits) is greater and more influential than other such gaps. Which is to say, this is an area in which one-size-fits-all remedies are likely to be particularly imprecise, or at least to need adjustment for the specifics of any given situation. But nonetheless, as I also argued above, any individual student, whatever his or her particular ethnicity or race or background, is likely to feel that the majority of the authors and texts on an ethnic literature course's syllabus are significantly distinct from, and outside of, fundamental aspects of his or her identity, experience, and perspective. This gap might seem to represent a problem with—and thus require efforts to increase—students' empathetic qualities, their abilities to step outside of their own perspectives and experiences sufficiently to appreciate and understand those of others. But while empathy is both an admirable and a valuable trait for any individual, and certainly creating it a worthy ancillary goal for any literature class, I don't believe it can be a primary objective, at least not in and of itself; moreover, I think the gap here is more directly tied to analytical difficulties, on two distinct but equally significant levels (both of which unquestionably do also make empathy less likely). It will always be harder to analyze something—at least something qualitative like a work of literature—if it feels entirely separate from, and thus less meaningful to, one's self. And if the majority of texts in an ethnic American literature course seem to fall into that category, one deeply problematic result is a vision of a very divided America, one containing a number of different groups and identities (multiculturalism having made it rightly difficult to get through University without recognizing the presence of those multiple communities) that do not, necessarily, have a great deal in common with one another.

While I am sure there are various effective methods through which to bridge a perspective gap like this in the classroom itself, I believe that it is especially important to do so in the students' individual written work, both because it is that work which every student (regardless of his or her level and style of contributing to class discussions, for example) will produce and because it is there that the individual stakes (in terms of grades) are clearest and instructor's feedback most possible and productive. The strategy that I employed in designing the syllabus for that Fall 2007 course, and one that I believe is uniquely effective at bridging the gap between students and material in any ethnic literature course, involves replacing the traditional academic work with a multigenerational family timeline and history project. As I will delineate more fully below, that replacement occurs both throughout the semester (with project stages in lieu of short, text-based papers) and in its culminating work (with the project itself in lieu of a longer, research-based paper; and then with final exam questions very much connected to the project as well).

I first encountered the idea of such a project through the UMass Boston American Studies program, and more exactly through the *Instructor's Guide* to the program's anthology *American Identities*. As the anthology and guide's editors—longtime UMB American Studies professors Lois Rudnick, Judith Smith, and Rachel Rubin—highlight, they decided at an early point in designing their introductory American Studies courses to include a timeline and history project, in order to require students to "become the historians of multigenerational processes that have shaped their American identities." They stress the initial resistance with which this request for personal analysis is usually met, but argue that "by the end of the course, the majority of students have a family story that they have at least partially anchored in history."[3] I would second both the goal and, in my experiences with the projects (which I have subsequently also included in a new Introduction to American Studies course at FSU), the results, and add that those results are even more pointed in an ethnic literature course. That is, it is unlikely that many students would dispute the claim that we are all Americans and thus a part of American history, but I believe a significant number might not describe themselves as ethnic Americans; working on the multigenerational family timeline and history project in an ethnic course, however, allows students to learn more about and then analyze their families' and ultimately their own complex, shifting, multi-part identities, and the multiple places and communities and cultures and elements that have comprised those identities. While the project's aim is not to collapse all such identities into one, nor to elide the specific and unique aspects of each identity and family—quite the contrary, it requires students to learn and write about precisely those aspects on multiple levels— it does highlight some fundamental similarities or at least connections across both individual and communal identities, and thus makes it substantially more difficult for students to perceive ethnic Americans (from any particular community or overall) as "other" in any absolute way.

As with any academic work, but perhaps especially when that work will be new to the vast majority of students, it is helpful to use the shorter, earlier stages to build a set of skills that the students will then utilize to produce the longer, culminating pieces. In my experience, the project ultimately requires the students to master three such skills (besides those of reading and writing that are common to all written literary analysis): research, reporting, and analysis. In the first and shortest stage, I ask the students to focus almost entirely on the research and reporting skills; they choose a photograph or item that is of particular significance to their family and both describe (as thoroughly as possible, for an audience who will likely never see it) and contextualize (with whatever information and history seems relevant) their chosen object. I have found that the students initially struggle with both skills—finding it difficult to describe something they know intimately, and feeling unsure about what contexts are relevant to their picture or item—but through reading and discussing an example of my own, as well as through practicing the skills in brief in-class conversations, they generally come to do strong work on both levels in their finished first stages. Exemplifying this stage's possibilities was the student who chose to focus on a teddy bear that had been passed down from her grandmother (who grew up in London during the Blitz) to her mother (who had immigrated to the United States for college) to herself: not only did the student's stage one help her begin to think about both continuities and changes across these three generations, but her close descriptions of the bear led her to an interest in material objects and culture that became both a focal point for her final project and an ongoing academic interest beyond the course.

That particular example notwithstanding, the work that the students do on the first stage is in some ways more practice than starting point for the final project; that is, it is not necessarily the case that the object or photograph will end up being featured in any explicit way in the project. The second stage, an interview with a family member, however, serves both roles, providing information that will certainly be relevant to the final project while also allowing the students to continue honing their research and reporting skills. Moreover, the interview stage is a particularly good one for which to introduce the analysis skill, primarily because it is important for this stage's own success that the students be able to pull out from the interview what is most appropriate for such broader analysis. I ask them to do so in two steps: providing me with a partial transcript, one that only includes those topics or themes on which they want to focus their analyses; and then writing a few analytical paragraphs, ones where they do not have to worry about reporting the information (that's what the transcript is for) and can instead focus entirely on what they want to say about it. While the analysis thus originates with evidence from within the interview, this is also a good moment for students to begin making the kinds of external connections—to ongoing class themes and questions, to specifics from one or another of the shared class texts, and so on—that can make their analyses specific and complex. And just as the responses to our paired readings often take the students in unexpected and impressive directions, so too do the links between their interviews and our discussions—I can still remember my surprise and excitement when one student, an evangelical Christian of German ancestry who had begun the semester criticizing African Americans during our Douglass/Wright discussions, linked his own strict and religious grandmother to Richard Wright's, analyzing the role that both women played in their families and realizing as a result that he and Wright had a great deal in common.

Having moved through these two stages and introduced all three skills, we can then turn our attention to drafts and revisions of the two pieces of the final project: the timeline, where the research and reporting skills remain paramount (although I do ask students to include eight relevant outside events—whether local, regional, national, or international—on their timeline, the choices of which are themselves analytical and provide starting points for the history's fuller analyses); and the history, where analysis (linking the evidence featured in that timeline to broader class contexts) is foregrounded. In my experience, the single most daunting aspect of both pieces is their length, a concern that is perhaps exacerbated when I give the students my own sample timeline and history (which are, me being who and what I am, the maximum required length of 3 and 7 pages respectively). And so working together to draft each piece, and having them both submit preliminary and partial drafts to me (on which of course I give feedback) and discuss them with their classmates in small groups, allows the students to break up that work, assemble their final project gradually, and alleviate that concern.

The project's history paper and then the final exam (in those literature courses that utilize an exam, anyway; although I think that even if it is optional it makes sense in this case for the reasons I'll detail) can work together very well to exemplify the project's connections across the student-material perspective gap. The history is not only the most extended (5–7 pages) and complex piece of individual work that the students will produce, but also their most explicit and best opportunity to connect the analyses of their own family and identity to the class's topics and questions. Interestingly, the moment where those connections become most significant is in the planning stage of the paper, when students decide how they want to structure their history. Almost all students will work within a chronological structure of one kind or another, whether beginning with the earliest covered generation and moving up to the present (their own), or reversing the chronology and working backwards from their generation to the earliest ones; in any case their thoughts about these chronological elements, and especially their decisions about how to transition between and across the paper's various generations and sections, greatly help in their analyses of multigenerational continuities and changes within their family's experiences. But I also stress to the class throughout the draft and revision phases that the history paper cannot be solely or even primarily structured chronologically, so as to avoid it becoming simply a report, rather than an analysis, of the details and experiences behind the timeline's material. Instead, the students need to incorporate the key elements of analytical writing at every stage of the paper: from an introduction that sets up their main analytical topics and ideas, to sections and paragraphs framed and guided by clear statements of their analytical topics, to analyses within every paragraph that connect the details and evidence to those broader topics (and that make use of class discussion points and, where appropriate and helpful, readings to contextualize and strengthen those analyses), to a conclusion that makes clear what the author has learned about both his or her family's multigenerational identity and experiences and the broader, shared topics. These components of analytical writing are, of course, ones that can be taught and strengthened in the communal setting, despite the deeply individual nature of the content of each student's paper;

it is for that reason that we bring the project into the classroom more fully at this point in the semester, through the paper's drafts and revisions, along with peer review conversations and the project samples that I produce (on both of which more shortly).

If the history paper thus exemplifies, both in its structure and writing and in the process of producing it, how the students are asked in the project to begin with their individual families and identities and ultimately connect them to the classroom conversations and topics, the final exam represents the semester's best opportunity to practice moving analyses in the opposite direction. That is, the exam is the one piece of individual work where I ask the students to foreground analyses of our shared readings, and then to link those more traditional academic analyses to what they've produced and analyzed in their project throughout the semester; for example, for the second of the exam's two mini-essay questions (the first being the aforementioned creation of their own pair of course texts, across any two of our existing pairings), I ask students to choose one individual character (real or fictional) from any of our class readings and connect him or her, whether through similarities, differences, or any other comparative analyses, to an individual from their family history. It was in response to this second question, more than in any other element of our class discussions or individual work, that I saw students finding ways to bridge the gap between their families and identities and those of our texts and authors, often in striking and impressive ways: a student connected his working class, Irish American father's Vietnam War experiences to those of Henry Lamartine in Erdrich's story "The Red Convertible"; another considered both similarities and differences between her grandmother's immigration from Finland to Wisconsin and the old and new world experiences of Tan's Linda Jong; and, in one of the most complex and compelling pieces of academic writing I have ever read, a third student grappled with the relationship between Richard Wright's struggles with his family over language and writing and his own ongoing battle with both a learning disability and his status as the first person in his family to attend University.

Just as was the case with the paired readings, so too does the timeline and history project bring its share of potential drawbacks, and that third student's exam answer highlights the most significant of them: the possible presence of uncomfortable or even deeply painful aspects of a family's or individual's experiences, aspects which can result in difficulties performing the research for or writing of the project's stages. Besides being entirely flexible about what information a student does or does not include—i.e., allowing a student to focus entirely on his mother's side of the family, because of his father's absence from his life—I believe it is also important to build into the project, and make clear and available to the students from the class's first meeting, alternate options for central subjects; a multigenerational timeline and history of Fitchburg State University, or a particular park or building, or the Boston Red Sox, requires the same skills of research, reporting, and analysis, and can yield the same kinds of analytical connections to our course topics and texts. Doing as much as possible to ensure that the students are comfortable as they work on the project is also vital because of the various ways in which I make sure that their individual work becomes part of our communal discussions, so as to avoid a second potential project drawback: the students' likely unfamiliarity with this kind of work, and so their significant uncertainty about their ability to produce satisfactory versions of each and every stage. It is to help ameliorate those worries and give them an evolving set of examples and models for the project's stages—and also to make clear my own implications in all of the class's questions and topics—that I produce and share with the class my own versions of each stage; but I also create space in the syllabus for the students to talk to each other about the project, not only in the draft and revision stages of the history paper, but also both earlier in the semester (as they plan and work on the shorter stages) and in its concluding weeks (when I ask each student to give a brief, informal presentation on the project, highlighting particularly interesting or significant details they have learned and analyses they have developed, including a visual aid of some kind to help share their work with their peers, etc.). It is also important to acknowledge a distinct, professorial kind of uncertainty that inevitably accompanies the project, particularly the first time one includes it on a syllabus: an unfamiliarity with how to grade the students' work on it. To be honest, I believe it is almost impossible to grade the first stage (with its entire focus on research and reporting), provided that students meet the basic length and content requirements; but the later stages, with the increased prominence of analysis, do become easier to grade, since my feedback and grade can focus entirely on those analytical skills and ideas, rather than on the content of the family history itself (which remains, I would argue, largely ungrade-able).

All of those drawbacks are real, and all merit explicit thought both at the planning and execution stages of a syllabus that includes this project. Each time I have taught this course—and I have now had the chance to do so three times in the years since that Fall 2007 starting point—I have worked to tweak and strengthen its elements, especially through more targeted use of the weekly emails and more overt and frequent in-class discussions of the project's stages, skills, and goals. I have also continued to consider and modify the readings, such as substituting an Irish American second unit (featuring

Mary Curran's *The Parish and the Hill* and Michael MacDonald's *All Souls*) and pairing Tan's novel with Erdrich's in the final unit. Whatever the specific choices and arrangement, I remain convinced that the paired readings are the right choice for this course—and I similarly believe that the benefits of including the timeline and history project, or at least of finding some parallel way to make the students' families and identities a significant part of the class's analytical subject, more than outweigh any difficulties. Besides all of the individual benefits I have highlighted, and the communal benefits that the class derives from hearing and discussing each other's projects, I have found an additional and particularly striking result: relatively early in the semester, usually around the time that the students are working on the project's first stage, many students—including some who might be very unlikely to share ideas about course readings in our discussions—begin to bring details and analyses from the project work into our conversations about the shared texts, so that it starts to feel as if we're discussing three texts at any given moment: the two shared ones, with all of the individual and comparative complexities I discussed above; and the specific one represented by each student's family narrative. And that trio of texts exemplifies the goal and ideal of both of these pedagogical strategies—giving the class a sense of analytical contexts for any one text and author, allowing us to triangulate with specifics (from these multiple, shared and individual, narratives) rather than simply jump from text to generalization. When it works, when these strategies combine in this ideal but certainly achievable way, the result are analytical conversations about ethnic American texts and identities that stay very much grounded in complex specifics but that are consistently informed by both a strong sense of the bigger pictures—including generational (historical), generic (literary), and cultural frames—and an equally strong recognition of and ability to analyze the biggest and most important picture of all: American identity, and how each American, from those whom we read to those who are doing the reading, is a complex, significant part of that picture.

Notes

1. The reported numbers vary somewhat, perhaps because of different ethnic subcategories, varying levels of response, or distinct moments of data collection: The *Princeton Review* University information website lists FSU's white non–Hispanic population at 91.3 percent; the U.S. University Search site calls it 95 percent. The awkward "white non–Hispanic" is how both sites, and others like them, delineate this category.

2. I wrote about that initial course, that new syllabus (which I had begun developing but had not yet put into practice), and the specific issues related to teaching ethnic American literature at Fitchburg State University in an earlier article that certainly com-

plements this one: "Discovering Other Voices: Teaching Ethnic American Literature at a Predominantly White State University," *Teaching American Literature: A Journal of Theory and Practice* 1.1 (Winter 2007): 34–43. http://teachingamericanlit.com.

3. Rudnick, Smith, and Rubin, eds., *Instructor's Guide to American Identities: An Introductory Textbook* (Malden, MA: Blackwell, 2006), 1–3. See also Rudnick, Smith, and Rubin, eds., *American Identities: An Introductory Textbook* (Malden, MA: Blackwell, 2006).

Works Cited

Cisneros, Sandra. *The House on Mango Street*. New York: Knopf, 1998.
Douglass, Frederick. *Narrative of the Life of Frederick Douglass, An American Slave, Written by Himself*. Boston: Bedford, 1993.
Erdrich, Louise. *Love Medicine: New and Revised Edition*. New York: Harper Perennial, 1993.
Espada, Martin. "Jorge the Church Janitor Finally Quits." From *Rebellion Is the Circle of a Lover's Hands*. 4 June 2009. http://www.martinespada.net/jorge.htm.
Far, Sui Sin. *Mrs. Spring Fragrance and Other Writings*. Urbana: University of Illinois Press, 1995.
Lahiri, Jhumpa. *The Namesake*. Boston: Houghton Mifflin, 2003.
Tan, Amy. *The Joy Luck Club*. New York: Penguin, 1989.
Wright, Richard. *Black Boy*. New York: Harper Perennial, 1993.

The Power of Visual Pedagogy in Teaching American Ethnic Literature

Danette DiMarco

The image text should hold an important place in any discussion of twenty-first century American ethnic literatures and pedagogy. Jeff Adams (2008) argues that "[t]he emergence of the image text (graphic novels, comic books, or illustrated novel) in the latter stages of the twentieth century has been accompanied by a pedagogic impulse, a desire to recount and relay traumatic incidents from the past for a contemporary audience" (35). Calling the image text a "visual pedagogy," Adams understands it as an avenue through which author-artists guide contemporary readers to deeper knowledge about the past. Frequently, this "documented" past is one of social crisis (36), a way "in which we [readers] come to experience, and to know, traumatic history" (37). For Adams, when events and experiences are nearly impossible to represent in words, image-text literature assists author-artists in conveying their personal feelings and encouraging affective response in readers.

Section one of this two-part essay argues that one form of image text—the graphic novel—is important to an evolving discussion of teaching American ethnic literature. The first portion of the essay examines the effectiveness of teaching a contemporary although lesser-known graphic novel, *Cuba My Revolution*, by Inverna Lockpez and Dean Haspiel (2010). A highly teachable work, *Revolution* is a memoir of Lockpez's traumatic experiences in Cuba during Fidel Castro's early days as its leader. Lockpez (aka Sonya), a doctor who is jailed and terrorized during the Bay of Pigs invasion because she is mistaken as a CIA agent, reveals to her readers her struggles with being faithful to Castro's ideals and her subsequent choice to leave her home for the United States (where she has lived and worked as an artist since the late 1960s). Instructors frequently include other popular autobiographical and/or memoir graphic novels in general or world literature courses, most familiarly Art Spiegelman's *Maus* and Marjane Satrapi's *Persepolis*. Including visual texts in American literature classes is also a sound instructional choice, especially given the now common acknowledgment of the value of designing pedagogy with multiple intelligences in mind. Frederick Luis Aldama (2010) further reasons that memoir's usefulness is in how it attempts to capture past experiences of family and community, doing so in a critical way; this is what *Revolution* seeks to accomplish as a memoir, even as it extends itself to serve as Adams' "visual pedagogy," using image text to document trauma.

In taking up a discussion of *Revolution* as "visual pedagogy," part one of this essay is not interested in critiquing from a "New Orientalist" or postcolonial perspective, although it certainly examines questions of ethnicity, race, and class.[1] I mention this because since *Revolution* is a fictional, albeit partially autobiographical, work about Fidel Castro's overthrow of Batista, and Castro's early years as a Communist leader, written by a Cuban exile living in the United States, it could appear to take on a "New Orientalist" position that places the United States as a "savior" against Cuban "devilry." This essay routes itself differently, instead examining how *Revolution*, as a Cuban emigrant/American immigrant story, contests binary reading through its "visual pedagogy." It will examine how Lockpez's traumatic and personal story unfolds through her illustrator's reversioning: his intertextual appropriations of personal and historical events as well as his decisions about color, vertical and horizontal framing, and the gutter.

Part two of the essay argues for the importance of pairing graphic novels like *Revolution* with scaffolded image-text student assignments. Using Susan Ambrose et al., and their arguments about scaffolding in *How Learning Works: 7 Research-Based Principles for Smart Teaching* (2010), I will discuss how instructors can make the pedagogic leap to pair image text readings with image text projects. Particularly, once students learn to work the interpretive "gutter" of an image text, they are more able to work autonomously in the creation of such texts. As well, use of new medial technologies like Voice Thread that focus on both visual and print literacy may be helpful to student interpretive experience, fostering engagement and self-expression.

Self-expression is about identity—questions of ethnicity, race, gender, class, and sexuality, not to mention a host of other subjects. Leonard Rifas (2010) recognizes in the image text the possibility for connecting the individual with his/her broader community. In his essay "Race and Comix" he writes:

In relation to the struggle to end racism, underground comix' [sic] most valuable legacy may have been their reinvention of comics as a medium of self-expression. Their example eventually evolved into the "graphic novel," a form through which an increasingly diverse group of creators has been able to add their stories to our common body of knowledge as America continues to wrestle with questions concerning racial inequality and the dream of a fair and free society [38].

Instructors including image text literature and assignments provide twenty-first-century college students further meaning for through difficult questions regarding trauma and/or about past inequities in order to better understand the importance of fighting for a more democratic future.

Thinking Out of the Box with the Box: Contesting the New Orientalist Paradigm

Fatemah Keshavarz (2007) influenced scholars interested in immigrant stories and postcolonial criticism when she assessed the disabling results of what she identified as "New Orientalist" approaches in popular literary works like Azar Nafisi's *Reading* Lolita *in Tehran*. Applications of Keshavarz's research consider how some literary works, whether conscious or not, reproduce political views central to the mainstream United States. Attentive to similar diasporic literatures as Keshavarz, El Habib Louai (2013) appropriates the "New Orientalist" paradigm for reading Nafisi, extends the discussion to Khaled Hosseini, and reveals both writers' "considerable distortions in […] official histories" in Iran and Afghanistan in their literary representations. For Louai, works like Nafisi's or Hosseini's *A Thousand Splendid Suns* perpetuate Keshavarz's "New Orientalism," and this "status derives from […] [the writers'] native or semi-native immigrant status."

It is important to face this critical way of reading when considering an immigrant memoir like Inverna Lockpez's *Cuba My Revolution*. Lockpez, the story's feminist and ecologically conscious artist, left Cuba in the late 1960s after studying both medicine and art at two separate Cuban educational institutions. Her emigrant status and the controversial Cuban–U.S. history, perhaps symbolized best in an insistent and ongoing U.S. trade embargo of Cuba since the early 1960s and repeated, extant rhetoric of vilifying Castro in the mainstream U.S., opens *Cuba My Revolution* to applications of Keshavarz's paradigm, even if the novel doesn't take up the "East" as its topic. This essay is less interested, however, in understanding Lockpez's work in the manner of Keshavarz. Rather, it considers how a "New Orientals," or new Othering, approach is contested, in part because of the work's generic classification as a graphic novel. It may be precisely because of its image text form that *Cuba My Revolution* is able to challenge monolithic and mainstream perspectives of Cuba. As it asserts such a challenge, it serves as a visual pedagogy for readers to understand the complexities of traumatic memory.

Dean Haspiel, the illustrator for Lockpez's tale, provides thought on why some people do not publicly tackle trauma through aesthetics. Haspiel's desire to bring Lockpez's story to life through his visual art was stymied for a period because of her leaving gaps in her life narrative. About Lockpez, his mother's dearest friend and his "second mother," Haspiel remembers that

> [o]ver the years, I kept a mental checklist of the various and mysterious anecdotes Inverna shared about her experience in Cuba and started to knit together a narrative tapestry. However, there were giant plot holes and I didn't understand some of things that happened to her. I needed to know how, what, and why ["Interview"].

However, once Lockpez agreed to collaborate with Haspiel, he more fully realized that "some of the things we experience in life are put in a box for a reason." While Haspiel alludes in the above quotation to trauma as something frequently hidden, his "box" imagery also invokes attention to the most appropriate or best medial approaches to storytelling. For Haspiel to successfully capture the effect or experience of Lockpez's traumatic and immigrant experience, he would need a "cold" medium, to use the now familiar phrasing of Marshall McLuhan (Bobbit). Although graphic forms have been gaining popularity and "heating up," this form continues to bring with it the opportunity for a different kind of active audience engagement than reading traditional print. Lockpez and Haspiel here use the comic "box" because it actively invites readers in with print *and* image. The strategic use of intertextual allusions (personal and historical), color, the simultaneous horizontal and vertical ways of reading, and the gutter engage readers in moving beyond any monolithic way of understanding Lockpez's personal story and Cuba's national one.

Strategies of the Image Text: Intertexts, Color, Vertical Reading and the Gutter

Haspiel identifies personal intertexts as critical in the creation of this story. Rachel Aydt questions him on the emotional difficulty of illustrating "the more nightmarish parts" of Lockpez's narrative, most likely referring to the character Sonya's brutal treatment in a Cuban jail because she is thought to be a CIA spy. Twelve full pages, in the dead center of a narrative that has no page numbers, are dedicated to Sonya's torture. The pages record the brutal interrogation of a stripped-naked Sonya who is incarcerated in a "dark [...] cell [that] smells of excrement and urine." She is repeatedly hosed with hot and cold water so she will reveal her informant. Haspiel's decision to devote multiple pages to Lockpez's traumatic and prolonged torture shows his awareness of the importance of that experience to the narrative as a whole. The purposeful slowing down of this painful time also deeply impacts Haspiel since his record is a kind of repeated torture of Lockpez, even as it is to bear witness. He recognizes the discomforting paradox of publicly acknowledging this physical trauma, and his part in recreating it as the illustrator. In order to capture this dilemma, he includes himself in one frame during the interrogation, cast in the role of a silent torturer, standing behind the primary guard. About this choice, Haspiel states to interviewer Rachel Aydt, "If you'll notice, I cast myself as one of the torturers of Sonya, because my being a torturer could protect her in a way if that makes any kind of weird sense." In other words, as he helps to recreate the traumatic moment of incarceration and abuse, he also stands by her as a witness to the "memories that she'd literally buried." In an interview, Lockpez reflects on what happened just before she was jailed and her affective response to help an injured man considered an "enemy": She recalls that she heard a wounded enemy "crying and crying the whole night and I couldn't take it." She continues, "A grenade had exploded on his shoulder" and "I gave him pain killer." When asked if Haspiel's depictions of her torture are real—"Is what we see on the page what happened to you?"—she answers, "[t]hat's really the tip of the iceberg" ("Cuba").

Lockpez's personal narrative is tied to historical exposition through Haspiel's invocation of iconic images. For instance, the story charts Sonya's decision to follow Fidel and support the Revolution by referencing directly a famous moment in Cuban history, Fidel's first speech at the Columbia military base after he and his guerrillas have successfully pushed Batista out of the country. This speech, given early in January of 1959 upon his march into Havana, is memorable in part because one of the white doves released to celebrate "democratization" of the nation lands on Fidel's shoulder. Sonya relays how the crowd is "electrified" by this, a sign that he is the "chosen one." She writes, "In the Afro-Cuban Santería religion, the white dove represents the god Obatala—a divine king who molds humans from clay in heaven." Sonya, too, is "drawn to Fidel's bold and dominating figure."

The Power of Visual Pedagogy (DiMarco)

Cuba My Revolution by Inverna Lockpez, Dean Haspiel (2010).

In the above sequence, the color red and the simultaneous reading of frames vertically and not just horizontally add critical interpretive meaning.

A first glance at *Revolution* reveals the novel's minimalist color scheme—red, pink, gray, and black. Haspiel recalls, "I elected to abandon my ink brush and only pencil the story while limiting the color palette. After much deliberation, we arrived at gray and red tones with the colorful mastery of Jose Villarrubia [...]," who ultimately won a 2011 Harvey award from DC Entertainment for his work as the novel's colorist. At times in the novel, red backgrounds emerge when Sonya contemplates her personal power and her role in the Cuban Revolution. In the Fidel-dove illustration, two of the four horizontal frames use such a background. In horizontal frames two and four, the tops of heads are cut off, or bleeding, into the above frames; the heads severed by gutter lines encourage additional vertical reading. In two instances, the top of Fidel's head is out of frame. Only Sonya's head is fully within the bottom frame. Lights, looking like stars, circle her head, seen fully in the last frame. This scene reveals Sonya's awakening. Had this framing been set up as a left to right sequence only, the emotional response that Sonya has might seem more rational or sequential. By using the long vertical frames, the linear sequence is replaced with an affective one that shows an idealistic young woman wanting to live "up" to her leader's dreams. In addition, the first frame attends to Fidel's monumental face. Shaped like a mountain, perhaps the one where he hid and from which he descended with his guerrilla army, the face is the direct subject of Sonya's devoted gaze. The addition of the red coloring in frames one and three also supports her emotional, not intellectual, response. To capture the emotional response to Fidel's first famous speech in Havana, Estela Bravo's footage of the iconic moment is useful supplementary material. In her documentary *Fidel: The Untold Story*, Bravo highlights the exact moment that the dove lands on Castro, including the crowd's response, which confirms the "truth" of Sonya's narrative.

The Fidel-dove scene also relates to a much later dream sequence where Sonya's faith in Fidel and the Revolution waivers. Near the end of Part Two, a full-page frame depicts a Roman arch with two bas-reliefs of Fidel in Roman dress, including garlands around his head. Additionally, the arch is littered with cracks, red flowers sprouting from them. Several smaller birds are tethered to the arch at its top, making it look like they are trying to lift or carry it. The entire frame uses a red sky and pink clouds as its canvas. Sonya recalls, "That night, I dream of a huge stone arch, like the ones in Paris and Rome built to commemorate historical battles. Fidel is carved in the stone like Caesar, and a multitude of flowers grow out from the tops of the arch."

Given the earlier message of the symbolic dove, the frame seems to revise the purpose of birds as a critique in the Revolution. The flowers shooting from the stone suggest organic matter underlying great human construction. Ultimately, no great leader is a match for time and death.

In this later frame, it is possible to see Sonya's attitudes change. Her Romanesque and monumental Fidel, who descended from the mountain, is

The Power of Visual Pedagogy (DiMarco) 271

Cuba My Revolution by **Inverna Lockpez, Dean Haspiel (2010).**

no longer marching of his own accord. He can barely be lifted by his people, his birds. His use of the people has begun to make them feel oppressed or captured. Once convinced of his ideological approach that would bring Cubans liberty, a sort of free flight, they are now limited to how they move, carrying the weight of the monumental construction with them. Sonya is associated with the tethered birds. Fidel helps her to fly at first, but the more she tries to help the Revolution, the more weighed down and "exhausted" she feels. This time, the red background suggests Sonya's disempowerment felt by the Revolution. The red Soviet flag positioned neatly under one of the carvings of Fidel, and identified by its hammer and sickle, reveals a point of departure from Fidel for Sonya; once Fidel's democratic ideals are "supported" by the Soviets, the mire of the Cuban Revolution becomes too difficult for too many.

In the last frame of the novel, the tethered birds turn into an airplane that Sonya takes to the United States. Again in a vertical framing, this page positions the airplane at the center, but over it is a headshot of Sonya wearing sunglasses and crying. The right sunglass lens is missing, although her closed eye is visible. Below the airplane is the outline of Cuba, the island, which in its free-floating form on the page looks like a cloud over which the ascending airplane soars. The bottom, middle, and upper-middle sections of the background are red, the top a light pink turning white until it reaches the crest of the page.

Certain references to the Fidel-dove scene, and the Roman arch and tethered bird frame, the novel's final visuals reveal that truly unfettered freedom may never be just that; freedom comes with all sorts of costs. A "New Orientalist" reading might understand the dark shade of Sonya's glasses as her feelings about Cuba, the bright side her attitudes about going to the States. This sort of "through a glass darkly" mentality, however, is only one way of thinking about the final message. Sonya's love for Cuba will not go away just because she leaves the country, not will her desire for democratic ideals. Sonya is unsure about what will happen to her in the United States. Whether the shaded lens or the missing one symbolizes her transport to the States, the outcome of her choice to leave is still far from clear. Even her eyes are full of tears, blurring her vision. In an interview about the book, Lockpez, who continued to have leftist leanings in her life in the U.S., recognizes how difficult it is to put democratic ideals into practice, "It's much easier to make a revolution that to build it" ("Cuba: My Revolution"). To undertake a revolution demands passion, but may also bring with it blood. The red background of this final image may infer this as well as the "red" allegiance that shifted the direction of Fidel's revolution.

The complexity undergirding Lockpez's experience speaks to how difficult it is to understand trauma. The novel, thus, utilizes a variety of approaches to meaning making for readers. While some of the frames in *Revolution* move more linearly and deductively, some utilize the gutter in a way that expects readers' to interpret mood. Scott McCloud, in his seminal work *Understanding Comics: The Invisible Art*, captures the heart of a visual medium like comics stating that "[i]f visual iconography is the vocabulary of comics, closure is its grammar. And since our definition of comics hinges

Cuba My Revolution by Inverna Lockpez, Dean Haspiel (2010).

on the arrangement of elements then […] comics is closure" (67). He continues, "Closure is about readerly participation. Participation is a powerful force in any medium" (69). The place where active participation and closure occur is in the gutter. According to McCloud, it is "in the limbo of the gutter" that "human imagination takes two separate images, and transforms them into a single idea" (McCloud 66). In effect, closure is interpretation and vice versa.

One important scene where "readerly participation" is important is when

Sonya wishes to buy her family visas and, in order to do so, exchanges sex for money with a lecherous and much older "family friend." In this troubling scene, Eduardo tells Sonya, "I have been wanting to sleep with you since you were a child. Anytime you need some cash, you know you can come see me ... but don't get greedy with your daddy." As Eduardo says this he has already mounted her. The next frame, finished in black and bright red, shows Sonya's bottom half as having transformed into a fish tale. This scene invokes the earlier traumatic experience in jail when Sonya imagines herself as a black panther, literally following that metamorphosis up by slinging her own "shit" at the guard. In both instances, she has decided to retreat from what is physically painful in order to psychically survive: a panther or a mermaid are one. This awareness of dehumanization is also prevalent in Lockpez's art that she smuggled out of Cuba, and that Haspiel redraws and uses at the start of each section of the three-part novel. It is an abstract art that, when isolated, makes less sense than when considered across the narrative. These images are products of Lockpez's (and by extension Sonya's) self-expression, and require readers to make it meaningful in terms of Sonya's broader experiences described in the novel.

Haspiel's appropriations of Lockpez's visual art are an unfamiliar allusion for most readers. If readers do not know Inverna Lockpez, they will not recognize some of the drawings as her art. More familiar allusions haunt the text though—for instance an image of Celia Sanchez or a famous poster advertising Operation Pedro Pan—so her art may take a back seat to more traditional historical exposition. The opening artwork to Part Three shows her abstract drawings of what appear to be people, one with an arm made out of a saw, another a hammer. The piece calls attention to a utilitarian theme where people are simultaneous used as tools but also able to rebuild themselves. Given that "Part Three" is about how Sonya begins to heal, this choice of artwork makes sense.

While some authors like Lockpez turn to the graphic novel as a particular form of image text to negotiate social crisis and trauma, others, like Jewish-American author Jonathan Safran Foer, work in the illustrated book form, as in his novel *Extremely Loud and Incredibly Close*. According to Ross Watkins, in his essay "Disaster Dialogues: Word, image and the effective/ethical spaces of illustrated books," illustrated books are

> narrative form[s] able to articulate the experience or witnessing of disaster via the creation of *spaces* (effective, ethical) between words and images. Such spaces are not only fundamental to the functionality of illustrated books, the "closure" required by the reader in the act of interpreting these spaces is central to representing the "unrepresentable" [11].

A pedagogic choice to pair graphic novel like *Cuba* with an illustrated book like *ELIC* also challenges students to see how generic variants of image text are simultaneously able to effectively represent the hard to represent with respect trauma, encouraging affective response in readers.

For instance, Foer's protagonist, the nine-year-old Oskar Schell, creates a "Things That Happened To Me" scrapbook as an externalization of experiencing the traumatic death of his father in the World Trade Center collapse. Watkins points out that Oskar collects multiple and what initially seem like disparate images: a picture of Stephen Hawking on a camcorder or a photo of the tennis champion Lleyton Hewitt celebrating a victory. A critical point to remind students of, however, is that Foer selects and organizes the fictional "Oskar's" images in a conscious manner, much like graphic novelists structure frames in a conscious way, and readers seek coherence and meaning within that order. It is only through such ordering of printed text and image that readers create "a space" where "readers are invited to construct their own interpretive meaning" about how trauma is mediated in text (Watkins 12). In this space, akin to McCloud's "gutter" where closure is ensconced (not unlike the gutter between Lockpez and Haspiel's frames in *Cuba*), readers interpret, or bring closure, to the multiple verbal and visual elements of the traumatic text.

The Power of Visual Pedagogy: Student Engagement and Image-Text Assignments

Students reading trauma through image-text literature should have the opportunity to study visuals and print in isolation through a traditional form of literary analysis before considering the image and print synergy. Doing so helps students to work closely with a text. When they expand their analysis to "hinge" the two, they may more easily begin to understand how interpretation, or closure, in such books necessarily turns on both image and print. It is helpful to design activities that ask students to select a scene from such works, having them write or discuss only what they think the print portion of the story offers. Then they may probe how their first answer changes based on the examination of the image. The order—print to image or image to print—is not as important as the process of them attempting isolated work and layering synthesis work on. Students may also consider what harmonies or tensions exist in reading this way. Following this type of activity, students should read the chapter from McCloud's work on the gutter. His work does an excellent job of explaining the interpretive process as image text, and students grasp the process of thinking and metacognition when considering his approach. As a first step in instructional scaffolding, these activities provide students with ways to lay the groundwork for greater autonomy in completing their own multimodal projects (which I will discuss later in the essay).

Ambrose et al. define scaffolding as "the process by which instructors provide students with cognitive supports early in their learning, and then gradually remove them as students develop greater mastery and sophistication" (215). The authors point out that students frequently "undervalue or omit" early stages in learning; thus, instructors including such stepped exercises while also providing feedback during earlier stages will most likely discover that students will find more success later when they "progress toward more complexity and integration" (215). In my own classes, this isolated analysis work comes in several forms. It may simulate the critical sort modeled in part one of this essay, and students may write individually or work collaboratively to study frames or sequences of frames or images, presenting their interpretations to the class. If students are assigned different parts of the novel to report back on for the collaborative and collective class discussion, then their reporting creates a layering effect where each time someone speaks new information is necessarily negotiated with prior knowledge.

Once students have experienced the interpretive "gutter" at work in image texts, they are ready for applying such analysis skills in a new medial form like Voice Thread (VT), which encourages both typed and spoken response and is visual-friendly. VT technology takes the best of academic discussion boards and social networking sites and allows students to post responses to visuals. Since exercises in VT depend on an uploaded Power Point, the instructor may wish to initially create the visuals to which students respond. During VT discussions, students are forced to comment on one slide at a time, and all comments for a given slide are presented in a sort of holistic or "aerial" view, unlike discussion boards where scrolling is necessary and time consuming. It is this latter quality that makes VT especially attractive in the classroom because multiple postings are visible on one slide, in one place. In addition to being able to type or speak comments, students may also draw or "doodle" on screen to highlight items, or post hyperlinks into responses. When instructors upload a PPT that they have designed to a VT, they can then post instructional questions for any or all slides prior to giving students the share link, which is easily embeddable in most course learning management systems. The posted questions or prompts fulfill Ambrose et al.'s notion of direct guidance that will prepare students for working independently. The screen shot that follows on the left is an example of my uploaded participant picture for VT (all participants upload a photo), and how a question appears in a bubble box; the adjacent slide is an example of a visual to which students might be directing their interpretation. Below that visual is the "comment" icon where students click. They are given a choice to type or speak their answers. All participants who post will find that their photos and bubble boxes will align on the left and right sides of the slide. One key for the instructor in creating PPTs in preparation for VT upload is using *any* visual that opens students to deepening their interpretation of the printed story.

My students considered the above slide (which was one of four) in the context of Rosario Ferré's short story "The Youngest Doll." One student, clearly working in the interpretive "gutter" space responded as follows regarding the print story and the visual representation. He writes:

> The nieces in the picture are located behind the maiden aunt. The nieces are both looking up to the aunt, which signifies their adoration for her. The fact that the girls are positioned behind her relates to their discreet curiosity of the aunt's leg, which we know from the quote that "they would sit around her and furtively lift the starched ruffle of her skirt so as to sniff the aroma of ripe sweetsop that oozed from her leg when it was at rest" (Ferré 1142). The doll in the yellow dress is positioned behind all three characters. The doll is bigger than the nieces. The size and location of the doll signifies the importance the dolls to this family. They record the age and look of the nieces growing up. And without the hard work and dedication of the aunt (as well as her pride in her nieces), these dolls would not have existed.

There is a blurring between Ferré's text and the student's image text so much so that a reader of this student response cannot fully separate visual from literary interpretation. Here, the "new" text in VT helps the student reader to create a space for interpreting Ferré's story and trauma (and the disorientating face of the embedded prawn in the aunt's leg)—seeing that which is unrepresentable as representable through reading print and image in tandem. If

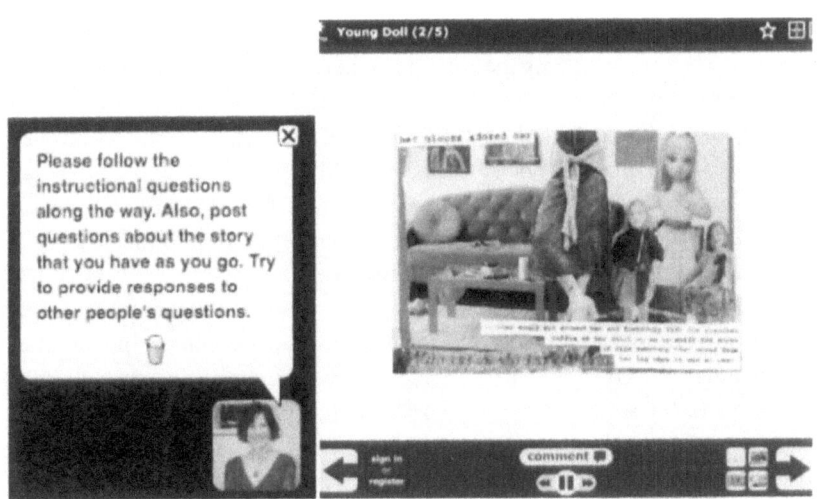

"The Youngest Doll," Voice Thread Slide created by a student.

assigned as part of out-of-class participation in a face-to-face class, and brought back during in-class discussion through projection onto a classroom screen, VT posts can be used to further deepen critical thinking and classroom discussion. This "return design" is necessary to help students connect the dots between in-class work and homework, consciously bringing home to school and vice versa (DiMarco and Danielson).

Clearly, in-class and VT discussions require more structure and instructor-led direction. How can we progress toward an image-text design that involves students more autonomously? In order to make this move, I offer students opportunities to create their own image text assignments. One assignment is offered as a culmination of a semester's worth of work. After reading a host of texts, students select one of the two options. They may create a multiple frame image text that adapts a scene from a piece of literature that we read during the term. Or they may include themselves into a framed sequence of events as a character participating in the reading and interpretive process, also for a text we read during the semester. They may do this alone or with a partner. The requirements include having to complete the frames on an 8½ × 11 sheet of paper that can be scanned and digitally uploaded to a drop box in our course shell. (Instructors not using a course management system can easily collect paper copies.) They are also required to write and upload an accompanying narrative (instructor's choice of word or page length) that explains what they tried to do and why. Otherwise students are free to draw, paint, collage, Photoshop, etc. in order to get the product that they think is deemed fit. Students do not need to be "great" artists to do this since collage or other methods like tracing can be similarly effective. Also, written text can be penned, penciled, or typed. I remind students that they have been seeing such student work all semester in the form of VT discussions. In fact, the VT for Ferré's story that I showed earlier is an example of student work from such a final assignment. Student work encourages another sort of positive modeling, and I have found that seeing and responding to such work engages the class. Students are also nicely surprised that the visuals they have been responding to in VT posts are peer designs and that those peers had once been enrolled in the very course.

Students bring a hard copy of their work to the final exam period where we post all the work (frames and narratives) and turn the room into an image text installation. Over the years I have received superior and well-thought-out projects for various literary works, including Edwidge Danticat's *The Farming of Bones*, Louise Erdrich's "The Red Convertible," and (more recently) *Cuba, My Revolution* (see visuals in this order on the following page).

During the final exam time I also ask any student who is willing to grant

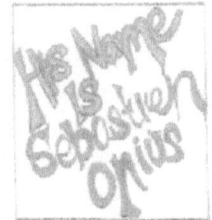

The Farming of Bones, "The Red Convertible" and *Cuba My Revolution*, Multiple Frame Image Texts created by students.

permission for their work to be used in future classes to fill out a form that I have brought to class. This offer is completely optional and up to the discretion of the student. Ultimately, I find that most students are very proud of their work and willing to share it with future students. They recognize that even after they have moved on, their voice stays on in a form of important interpretive meaning making. If students give permission for their work to be used, I use screen capture technology and take shots of each frame from their digital uploads, organizing them into PPT and uploading to VT where I can then add instructional questions and commentary.

For instance, although I briefly discussed my own argumentative claims about topics like the role of color or the symbolism of Sonya's sunglasses earlier in this essay in my critique of *Revolution*, I also ask my students what they think about these topics, juxtaposing such questions with a former student's visual interpretation. What follows is the final slide of her multi-frame work once it has been uploaded as a VT.

My prompt reads:

> The student interpreter uses the bathing suit as symbolic of a general discomfort with emigration: Sonya is in a full-piece; Mirta in a two-piece. Note that the student has retained Sonya's sunglasses, invoking the final image in the novel. First, discuss the symbolic value of the sunglasses and what they say about Sonya's feelings. What image might you use to represent Sonya's thoughts as she leaves Cuba? Why?

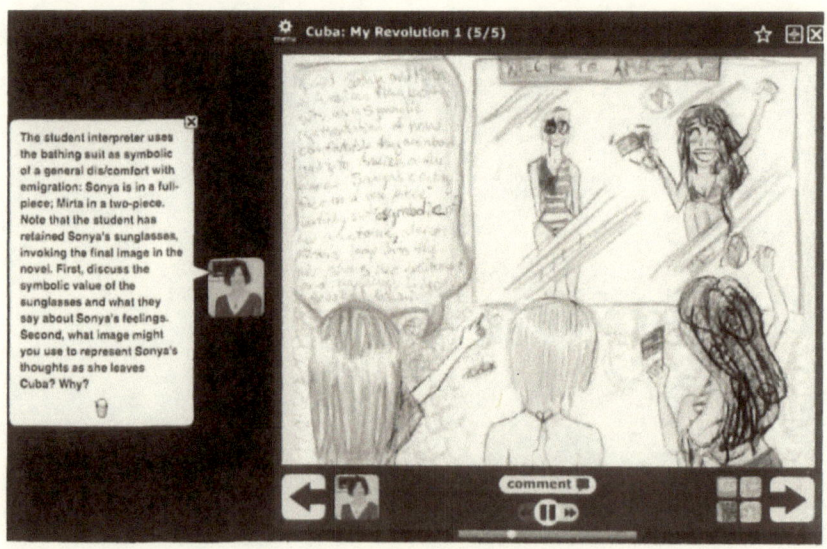

***Cuba My Revolution*, Voice Thread Slide created by a student.**

The first question asks students to consider both graphic novel and student visual, requiring analysis and synthesis. The second question guides them toward considering what sort of visual they might make. Regarding the first question, one student posted that

> Sonya's sunglasses relate to her own feelings about the Cuban Revolution. In a sense, she has one eye opened and one eye closed to the things occurring around her. Since she is a militant soldier, who originally supported Castro's cause, Sonya is hesitant to accept the feelings of rebellion and bitterness experienced by her mother, Carlos, and Mirta—real Cubans living with the revolution.

The same student adapts Haspiel's vision by making slight alterations to it:

> To effectively portray Sonya's feelings at the end of the novel, I would depict a frame of her sitting in the airplane with her sunglasses. I would use a frame to depict how she feels about coming to the United States. (This frame would be drawn within the shaded lens of her sunglasses.) I would also include a frame of her looking back upon her struggles in Cuba (This frame would be drawn within the open lens of her sunglasses. This would symbolize Sonya's "hindsight being 20/20." Her personal reflections of the past would become clear as she continues to look back.) This image would relate to Sonya's torn feelings of leaving Cuba and her uncertainty about her and her country's future.

The student's interpretation reveals his return to the graphic novel as well as engagement with his peer's visual representation. It also shows how seriously students will take their peers' work when it is shown in new medial forms.

Although I have been discussing how to use image text projects in subsequent semesters to join student voices across terms, instructors may have students create projects during the course of the term to be used as the basis for online VT discussions. If instructors do this, it may be helpful to consider how the student creating the image text may feel about peer interpretations of works. Instructors looking to add another layer to the complexity of interpretation may wish to share portions of the student artist's narrative so others may see some of their intention—and then have student posts focus on developments or turns in thought. The student who designed the *Cuba* visuals seen earlier developed her narrative in the form of a VT (although she had a choice to also construct it as an academic paper). It gives insight into her process, especially her decision to insert herself into the story as a reader, which most of her peers missed. Readers looking carefully at her drawings will see that she is in every frame, with text bubble over her head, providing interpretive comment to Sonya's experiences. Had at least a portion of her strategy been shared with her peers prior to them posting their responses to her work, there may have been less omission of this one important rhetorical choice. As she pointed out in her VT narrative about her process, it may have been helpful for her peers to know that "[e]very visual representation of *Cuba My Revolution* contains a cartoon version of myself explaining my reaction to Sonya's decisions and situations she faced throughout the novel." She even provides interpretive annotation: "In this particular picture, she is inspired to support Fidel when she sees him speaking on television." Revealing too much about the student-artist's interpretation may constrict others' thoughts; however, including important elements about purpose may help guide them to best understanding through context.

Other types of image text assignments may be included in courses that wish to turn to the power of visual pedagogy as well. For example, I referenced Foer's *ELIC* earlier in the essay, reminding how the images of the novel turn on Oskar's "Things That Happened To Me Scrapbook." When I teach this illuminated novel I ask students to identify several themes, finally selecting one that most interests them. Then I ask them to go back through the novel and collect quotations that address the theme, in a sort of commonplace book. In a next step I have them write an argumentative academic essay on the significance of the theme, integrating the quotations from their commonplace book into a coherent discussion. This portion of their experience has them working solely with printed text. Finally, after this essay is drafted, I have them make their own image text scrapbook where they use their "academic" interpretations (from the essay) to select images that reflect their ideas. They are required to include at least ten pages in their scrapbook. These pages must contain both academic text and other image text options. One suggestion that I give them is to cut up their essay into sections, gluing their work into their scrapbook to retain the integrity of their argument. From there, the image designs can more easily fall into place, and there is a sense of cohesion—even as they begin to see that they are working in the gutter, bridging academic and image narratives. Scrapbooks have included very real, tactile objects like cutout jeans pockets, birdseed, keys, spoons, paper clips, and a map of Central Park (all elements important to the development of Oskar as a character and his handling of the traumatic loss of his father in the towers collapse). I have also seen a creative pop-up of a Manhattan skyline and a pop "down" of a skyscraper elevator. Although this assignment does not expect students to be fully "autonomous" initially, it is scaffolded in such a way that the steps become models for student progression toward greater synthesis and evaluation of image text. This particular assignment has garnered amazing results, far exceeding my expectations.

Ultimately, reading graphic novels and illuminated books interests students. Certainly, new medial technologies and image text assignments can foster student engagement with this very literature, fostering deep critical thinking and moving students toward autonomy in their own work. Visual pedagogy can also tap into a student's personal self-expression, ensuring that such expression is connected with a wider academic community. And it can provide twenty-first-century college students written and visual forums for thinking through difficult questions about trauma as well as social inequity. Doing so is critical for them to personally and collectively realize the role of healing in times of trauma, and the urgency to fight complacency when it is clear we should be living to reap a more democratic future.

Note

1. For more reading on "New Orientalist" literature, see Fatemah Keshavarz, 2007, in *Jasmine and Stars: Reading More Than* Lolita *in Tehran*, a study of the potentially disabling results of Azar Nafisi's *Reading* Lolita *in Tehran*. And for a critique of "New Orientalist" discourse in the graphic novel see Lisa Botshon and Melinda Plastas "Homeland In/Security."

Works Cited

Adams, Jeff. 2008. "The Pedagogy of the Image text: Nakazawa, Sebald and Spiegelman Recount Social Traumas." *Discourse: Studies in the Politics of Cultural Education* 29.1 (March): 35–49. Print.
Aldama, Frederick Luis, ed. 2010. *Multicultural Comics Today: From* Zap *to* Blue Beetle. Austin: University of Texas Press. Print.
Ambrose, Susan, et. al. 2010. *How Learning Works: 7 Research-Based Principles for Smart Teaching*. Foreword by Richard E. Mayer. San Francisco: Jossey-Bass. Print.
Aydt, Rachel. 2010. "Graphic, Novel: *Cuba: My Revolution* Brings the Harsh Reality of Castro's Revolution to Comics." *Publishing Perspectives*. 26 October. Web.
Bobbit, David. 2011. "Teaching McLuhan: Understanding Media." *Enculturation: A Journal of Rhetoric, Writing and Culture*. 30 December. Web.
Botshon, Lisa, and Melinda Plastas. 2010. "Homeland In/Security: A Discussion and Workshop on Teaching Marjane Satrapi's *Persepolis*." *Feminist Teacher* 20.1: 1–15. Print.
"Cuba: My Revolution." PRI's The World: Global Perspectives for an American Audience. Web.
DiMarco, Danette, and Brian Danielson. 2012. "Return Design: Boosting Student Engagement by Applying Online Instructional Strategies to Face–2–Face Courses." Presentation. *Fusion*: Desire2Learn Users Conference. Boston, MA. July. Print.
"Estela Bravo." 2012. The Paley Center for Media Paley Center Screening Room. 9 May. Web.
"Interview with Dean Haspiel." Web.
Keshavarz, Fatemah. 2007. *Jasmine and Stars: Reading More than* Lolita *in Tehran*. Chapel Hill: University of North Carolina Press. Print.
Louai, El Habib. 2013. "Unveiling a New-Orientalist Discourse in Azar Nafisi's *Reading*

Lolita in Tehran and Khaled Hosseini's *A Thousand Splendid Suns*." *Xenophile: A Journal of Comparative Literature* Issue 1 (25 April). Web.
McCloud, Scott. 1994. *Understanding Comics: The Invisible Art*. New York: William Morrow. Print.
Rifas, Leonard. "Race and Comix." Aldama, 27–38. Print.
Watkins, Ross. 2012. "Disaster Dialogues: Word, Image and the Effective/Ethical Spaces of Illustrated Books." *Social Alternatives* 31.2: 11–14. Print.

About the Contributors

Helane Adams **Androne** is an associate professor of English at Miami University of Ohio, Middletown, and interim director of the Ohio Writing Project at the Oxford campus, where she is also an affiliate of Black World Studies, Latin American Studies, and Women's Studies. She is a member of the National Council for Teachers of English and sits on the editorial board for *Open Words: Journal of College English and Open Access*.

Shawnrece D. **Campbell** is an associate professor of English at Stetson University, where she served as the director of the Africana Studies Program for nine years. She specializes in twentieth-century African American literature and cultural heritage preservation. Her research addresses the transmission of African healing practices in the transatlantic new world.

Mary F. Dulworth **Gibson** lives and teaches in Cincinnati, Ohio. A graduate of the Ohio Writing Project at Miami University, she has taught in the Cincinnati Public School system since 1999.

Danette **DiMarco** is a professor of English at Slippery Rock University. She has served as the university's faculty coordinator for the Center for Teaching and Learning and has published in *Mosaic, Sagetrieb, Papers on Language and Literature, College English*, and *Teaching English in the Two-Year College*. She co-edited *Inhabited by Stories: Critical Essays on Tales Retold* with Nancy A. Barta-Smith and co-authored an essay in *Eloquent Images*.

Stefanie **Dunning** is an associate professor of English at Miami University of Ohio. She is a graduate of Spelman College and the University of California, Riverside. She is writing her second book, *The Anatomy of Damage*, which uses multiple modalities to explore personal, textual, and social trauma.

Monika **Giacoppe** is an associate professor of comparative world literature at Ramapo College, where she offers courses on African American women writers, European literature, fictional histories, and literature survey courses. Her interests include literatures of the Americas, international women's writing, francophone literature, and translation theory and practice.

Dulce María **Gray** is a faculty member of the English Department and Women's Studies Program at West Valley College in Silicon Valley, California. Her publications include two books on the construction of ethnic identity as it intersects with the acquisition of high literacy: *High Literacy and Ethnic Identity: Dominican American Schooling in Transition* and *Meanderings on the Making of a Diasporic Hybrid Identity*.

C. Winter **Han** is an assistant professor of sociology at Middlebury College, where he teaches courses on race, social psychology, and cinematic sociology. He is the author of numerous articles that have appeared in academic journals including *Critical Sociology, Symbolic Interaction, Social Identities,* and *The Archives of Sexual Behavior*.

David **Magill** is an associate professor of English and co-chair of Women's and Gender Studies at Longwood University, where he teaches courses in American literature, African American literature, and gender studies. He focuses on issues of identity and culture in literature, film, and media. He is working on manuscripts about modernist nostalgia and jazz age white manhood and on contemporary culture and the rise of ethical manhood.

Tawnya **Pettiford-Wates** is an associate professor at Virginia Commonwealth University, a visiting scholar at the University of KwaZulu Natal and the Artistic Director and Founder of The Conciliation Project (TCP), a social justice non-profit arts organization. She has been acting and directing for over 30 years, including with the New York Shakespeare Festival's Broadway production of *For Colored Girls Who Have Considered Suicide / When the rainbow is enuf, Life or Something Like It* with Angelina Jolie, David Lynch's *Twin Peaks*, and *Twice in a Life Time* with Gene Hackman.

Ben **Railton** is an associate professor of English studies and coordinator of American studies at Fitchburg State University in Massachusetts. His most recent book is *The Chinese Exclusion Act: What It Can Teach Us About America*; he has also published *Redefining American Identity: From Cabeza de Vaca to Barack Obama* and *Contesting the Past, Reconstructing the Nation: American Literature and Culture in the Gilded Age, 1876–1893*.

Jeff **Sommers** is an associate professor of English at West Chester University and emeritus professor of English at Miami University. He is editor of the National Council of Teachers of English journal *Teaching English in the Two-Year College* and continues to teach general education writing and literature courses and to write about pedagogical subjects.

Tereza M. **Szeghi** is an assistant professor of English teaching comparative literature and social justice at the University of Dayton in Ohio. Her research focuses on the historic and continued uses of literature by indigenous peoples throughout the Americas to articulate and achieve the realization of their rights.

Index

The Absolutely True Diary of a Part-Time Indian 74–99
Acadians 29, 32–37, 51
Acculturation 170
Action Cadienne 33–34
Adams, Gleason R. W. 42, 44
Adams, Jeff 264–265
African Americans 38, 40, 41, 42, 169, 205, 208, 212
African perspective 228
African ritual inheritance novels 206, 215, 217, 221
Afro-Creole 30–31
Alexie, Sherman 4, 72–82, 84–85, 87–88, 90–91, 93–95, 97–99, 170, 173, 174, 175, 179, 181
American Creole (film) 41
American Indians 169, 174, 175, 181; alcoholism 72, 74–75, 77–80, 85, 88, 90, 92; reservations 74–80, 82, 86–92, 97
Amish of Hillsboro, Ohio 134–137
Ancelet, Barry 35–6
Appalachia, Appalachian students 102, 104, 125
Applied Learning Project 106
Applied Theatre Practice 237
Arceneaux, Jean *see* Ancelet, Barry
Artifacts: use in projects 108, 110–112, 115, 121
Assimilation 75, 79, 85, 89–92, 94, 97, 170, 179, 180
Association for the Study of American Indian Literature 85
Atwood, Margaret 122
Aydt, Rachel 268

Bad Indians 94
"Bad NDNs" 94
Baldwin, James 226, 230
Barr, Robert 185
Bass, Randy 187, 202
Baxter-Magolda, Marcia B. 186, 189, 192
Beausoleil 34
Bell, Caryn Cossé 45, 48–49

Benoit, Michelle 41
Bernard, Shane K. 30, 35–6
Berry Brill de Ramírez, Susan 173
Bird, Gloria 78, 80–81, 84–85
Birkenstein, Jeff 171, 173
Bluest Eye 211
Bonilla-Silva, Eduardo 96
Brada-Williams, Noelle 176
Bravo, Estela 270
Brody, Jennifer DeVere 16
Bruce, Clint 36
Busch, Frederick 188, 196

Caesar, Judith 180
Cajuns 12, 29–33, 36–38, 52
Carrasquillo, Marci L. 2
Castille, Jeanne 36–37, 49–50
Catholicism 31, 43, 45, 50
Caulfield, Ruby Van Allen 39
Ceremony 92
Chaumette, Alexandre 46
Chekhov 223
Cheung, Floyd 43
Chicano/as 31
Cisneros, Sandra 181, 252–253
Citizenship, global 162
Clan 235
CODOFIL (Council for the Development of French in Louisiana) 37
Cognitive development, of students 74, 83, 88, 97n2, 97n7
The Colbert Report 84
Colonization 73, 77
Common Core State Standards 110, 129
Communitism 93
The Conciliation Project (TCP) 236
Content and form 234
Contextualizing 150
Continuum, cultural 224, 225
Coordinated Studies 236
Cosmopolitanism 179
Council for the Development of French in Louisiana (CODOFIL) 37

287

Index

Crenshaw, Kimberle 55
Creole of Color 39–41, 43, 45–47, 50
Creoles 12, 29, 30, 31, 32, 36, 38–43, 49–52; see also Cajuns
Cuba: Castro and revolution 264, 268; and the United States 265
Cuba My Revolution 264–271
Cultural studies 3, 4

Dabtara (also spelled debtara) 207, 212, 213, 214, 215, 216, 218, 219, 220
Daniels, Harvey 119; literature circle adaptation 120, 121
Davis, F. James 27
Davis, Ossie 223
de la Houssaye, Sidonie 50–52
Dennucio, Jerome 174
Desdunes, Jeremiah 46
Desdunes, Pierre-Aristide 45, 48–49
Desdunes, Rodolphe 31, 41–42, 45–47, 49
Dormon, James H. 39
Douglass, Frederick 250–251
Drama 227
Dubois, W. E. B. 169, 238–39

Education, general 184, 185, 187, 194
Edutainment 236–37
Eikstadt, Helen 79
El Habib Louai 266
Elie, Lolis Eric 40
Ellison, Ralph 15–28; *Invisible Man* 12; staging racial ambiguity 22–28
Eng, David: racial castration 60
Erdrich, Louise 176, 181, 253–254
Espada, Martin 252–253
Ethiopian healing scrolls 205, 206, 207, 208, 212, 213, 215, 216, 220
Ethnomedicine 217; criticism 213, 217, 220
Eurocentric Model 225
Evans, Stephen 80

Facilitator 233
Falk-Ross, Francine 79
Far, Sui Sin 251–252
Faubourg Tremé (film) 40–41
Ferre, Rosario 277
Fidel: The Untold Story 270
Flight 73
Foer, Jonathan Safran 125, 274
Fourth wall 227
Fugard, Atol 240

Garcilaso de la Vega 38
Goodspeed, Edgar J. 4

Graff, Gerald 185, 186, 202
Graphic novel 264–283
Greene, Graham 84
Grotowski 223

Haddox, Thomas 43, 45
Haiti 30, 46–47, 51–2
Haladay, Jane 85, 97
Haspiel, Dean 264, 267
Healing arts, writing as 206
Hendrix, Jimi 174, 175
Historically White Colleges and Universities (HWCUs) 96
Hommel, Christian 52
hooks, bell 55, 132
Hosseini, Khaled 266
House Made of Dawn 92
How Learning Works: 7 Research-Based Principles for Smart Teaching 265
Hurricane Katrina 30, 40–41
Hypodescent 27

Identity formation 170
Image text 264–283; strategies of 267–275; student engagement with 275–283
Immigration 170
Improvisation 233
India/Indians 173, 175, 177, 178, 179, 180
Intersectional Theory 65, 66
Intertextuality 191, 198
Isip, J.D. 1, 2

Jackson, Elizabeth 179
Jewish Americans: culture 188, 193, 195, 199; fiction 184, 185, 186, 188, 190, 191, 192, 193, 194, 195, 196, 199, 200, 202
Jolivétte, Andrew 40
Jones, Jerah 42
Joseph, Raina L. 18

Kennedy, J. Gerald 171, 172
Kerouac, Jack 35
Keshavarz, Fatemah 266
Kimball, Bruce 185
Kincaid, Jamaica 181
Kingston, Maxine Hong 176, 181
Koshy, Susan 179
Kress, Dana 46, 48

La Cour, Lair 41
Lahiri, Jhumpa 170, 175, 176, 177, 178, 179, 180, 181, 253–254
Landry, Lucille Augustine Gabrielle 38, 49–50

Index

Language acquisition 170
Lanusse, Armand 41, 43–45, 47
Latortue, Régine 42–45
Laveau, Marie 31
Learner-centered teaching 95
Learning: blended 142, 145–147, 152–153, 160, 161–163; connected 146; interdisciplinary 243–44; student outcome 147–148
Learning communities 236, 244
Lee, Spike 132
Leong, Russell 56
Lescher, Robert 170
Life/death/transformation cycle 227, 234, 241, 242
Lilly Conference on Teaching 10
Liotau, M. F. 44
Literature, use of in composition classes 73–98, 145–146
Location, physical and emotional 243
Lockpez, Inverna 264, 266
Logsdon, Dawn 40
Louisiana 29–46, 51–2
Louisiana Creole Heritage Center 41

M. Butterfly 60, 63
Madama Butterfly 62, 63
Magic "if" 235
Maitino, John R., and David R. Peck 7
Mardi Gras 38
Marsalis, Wynton 41
Marshall, Paule 208
Martin, Trayvon 137
Matrix of domination 56, 65
Maus 264
McCants, Sister Dorothea Olga 46
Mercier, Alfred 51
Mercier, Jacques 212, 213, 214, 215
Métis 34
Miller, Arthur 232
Miranda, Deborah 87–88, 90, 94, 98
"Model minority" 66, 68
Momaday, N. Scott 92
Morrison, Toni 211, 213
Myth of the Ecological Indian 75
Myth of the Vanishing Indian 74, 81

Nagel, James 170
National Writing Project 9, 10
Native American Literature Symposium 72
Native Appropriations 84
Navarro, Mary Ann 16
New Orientalism 264–267
"Novena to Bad Indians" 94

Obama, President Barack 138
Opposition, dichotomous 223
Over the Rhine (Cincinnati, Ohio) 133, 138
Owens, Louis 78, 98

Pacht, Michelle 176
Pedagogy 223; transformative 159
Persepolis 264
Pitre, Glen 41
Plessy, Homère 40
Plessy v. Ferguson 40, 48
Populus, Auguste 44
Praisesong for the Widow 208, 217, 220
Privilege 3, 6, 101
Problem-Based Learning (PBL) 184, 187, 189
Process, transformative 237

Reading Lolita in Tehran 266
Reflection, ritual 118
Reid-Pharr, Robert 17
Reservation Blues 78, 84–85
Retention/persistence/success 144, 160
Richard, Zachary 32–36
Riel, Louis 34
Rifas, Leonard 265
Rillieux, Victor Ernest 48–9
Rite of passage 13, 234, 239
Ritual 227, 229, 233
Ritual Poetic Drama Within the African Continuum (RPD-WAC) 224, 226, 227, 230, 233, 235, 237, 240, 244
Rodman, Bill 41
Rodriguez, Abraham 141, 151–152, 154–155, 160, 161

Said, Edward 59
Saint-Domingue 30, 52
St. Germain, Sheryl 29, 36
St. Pierre, Michel 44
Santería (Afro-Cuban) 268–269
Séjour, Victor 50–51
Shange, Ntozake 225, 240
Shapiro, Norman 42–44, 51
Short story cycle 169, 170, 171, 172
Silko, Leslie Marmon 92
Spidertown 141–146, 148, 150, 151–154, 156–163
Spirit of a Culture (film) 41
Spokane Indians 76–79, 81–82, 85–86, 88, 90, 92–93, 95
Stanislavsky, Constantin 223
Station, Elizabeth 4
Stereotypes 72, 77–80, 82–84, 95–96

Story 226, 238
Storytelling 173, 238–39, 240
Strange, Aralee 133
Sublette, Ned 31
Survivance 93

Tagg, John 185
Tan, Amy 251–252
Tantine *see* Landry, Lucille Augustine Gabrielle
Teacher-centered teaching 95
Teaching 185, 186, 187, 188, 202
Teaching American Ethnic Literatures: Nineteen Essays 7
Thierry, Camille 43
Thomas, Timothy 138; discussion of Cincinnati riots with students 139
Tompkins, Jane 186, 202
Tregle, Joseph, Jr. 38–9
Tremé (neighborhood) 40–41, 45
Trevigne, Irving 40
Trévigne, Paul 40, 46

Uncle Tom's Cabin 236
Understanding Comics: The Invisible Art 272–273
University of Chicago Magazine 4

Vappie, Don 41
Vautour, Jackie 35
Vizenor, Gerald 93
Voice Thread 265, 276–278, 280–282

Wahpeconiah, Tammy 73
Warbourg, Daniel 47
Warbourg, Eugène 47
Watson, Cedric 38
Weaver, Jace 93
Weiss, M. Lynn 51
"The well-made-play" 225, 227, 232
Wellness narrative 213
Wells, Ida B. 48
Western model, traditional 230–231
Whiteness 67
Williams, Tennessee 232
Winter, Morley 174
Witnesses 234, 235, 237
Wright, Richard 250–251
Writers, basic 143–144
Writing as a healing art 205, 207, 212

Yew, Chay 55–71
"The Youngest Doll" 277

Zydeco 30, 32

www.ingramcontent.com/pod-product-compliance
Lightning Source LLC
Chambersburg PA
CBHW051211300426
44116CB00006B/516